信仰与责任

——全球化时代的精神反思

Faith and Responsibility

张志刚 严 军◎主编

吴 飞 谷 雪◎副主编

北京论坛秘书处
北京大学宗教研究院 编

宗教文化出版社

图书在版编目（ＣＩＰ）数据

信仰与责任:全球化时代的精神反思/张志刚,严军主编.
－北京:宗教文化出版社,2011.9
ISBN 978 － 7 － 80254 － 422 － 2

I.①信... II.①张...②严... III. 宗教－文集 IV.①B91－53

中国版本图书馆 CIP 数据核字(2011)第 184873 号

信仰与责任

——全球化时代的精神反思

张志刚　严　军　主编

出版发行：	宗教文化出版社
地　　址：	北京市西城区后海北沿 44 号　（100009）
电　　话：	64095215（发行部）　64095234（编辑部）
责任编辑：	霍克功　刘洪宇
版式设计：	高秋兰
印　　刷：	北京人卫印刷厂

版权专有　不得翻印

版本记录：	787×1092 毫米　16 开本　27.25 印张　360 千字
	2011 年 9 月第 1 版　2011 年 9 月第 1 次印刷
书　　号：	ISBN 978 － 7 － 80254 － 422 － 2
定　　价：	50.00 元

作者简介

第一部分作者

王作安,中国国家宗教事务局党组书记、局长。

Tony Blair,英国前首相,中东问题四方小组特使,托尼·布莱尔信仰基金会创始人。

卓新平,中国社会科学院学部委员,世界宗教研究所所长、研究员,中国宗教学会会长。

Mustafa Cerić,波黑共和国大穆夫提。

Jüergen Moltmann,德国图宾根大学荣休教授。

杜维明,美国哈佛大学教授,北京大学高等人文研究院院长。

Alexander N. Chumakov,俄罗斯哲学学会第一副主席,俄罗斯科学院哲学研究所教授。

Thomas Banchoff,美国乔治敦大学伯克利宗教、和平与世界事务中心主任,教授。

张志刚,北京大学人文特聘教授、宗教文化研究院院长、外国哲学研究所研究员,中国宗教学会副会长。

第二部分作者

楼宇烈,北京大学宗教文化研究院名誉院长,北京大学哲学系、宗教学系教授。

王宗昱，北京大学哲学系、宗教学系教授。

王博，北京大学哲学系、宗教学系主任、教授。

Jaeyoon Song，加拿大麦克马斯特大学人文学部教授。

曾亦，复旦大学哲学学院副教授。

李四龙，北京大学哲学系、宗教学系副主任，宗教文化研究院副院长教授。

张桥贵，云南民族大学副校长、教授，中国宗教学会副会长。

（Sakurai Yoshihide）櫻井義秀，日本北海道大学大学院文学研究科教授。

Pier Cesare Bori，意大利博洛尼亚大学教授。

傅有德，山东大学犹太教与跨宗教研究中心主任，山东省"泰山学者"特聘教授，中国宗教学会副会长。

张旭，中国人民大学哲学院副教授。

孙向晨，复旦大学哲学学院院长、教授。

第三部分作者

赵敦华，北京大学人文特聘教授、外国哲学研究所研究员，中华外国哲学史学会理事长。

Miroslav Volf，美国耶鲁大学信仰与文化中心主任、教授。

Alberto Melloni，意大利约翰二十三世基金会主席，意大利博洛尼亚大学教授。

Arvind Sharma，加拿大麦吉尔大学比较宗教伯克斯教授。

（金在荣）Chae Young Kim，韩国宗教史学会副主席，西江大学教授。

Seyed Mohammad Marandi，伊朗德黑兰大学世界研究院北美研究室主任，副教授。

刘金光，中国国家宗教事务局政策法规司副司长。

Anantanand Rambachan，美国圣奥拉夫学院教授。

菅野博史（Hiroshi Kanno），日本创价大学文学系教授。

杨慧林，中国人民大学副校长、教授，中国宗教学会副会长。

序　言

　　本书所汇集的论文,主要精选自北京论坛(2010)的分论坛"信仰与责任——全球化时代的精神反思",同时收入英国前首相托尼·布莱尔(Tony Blair)在论坛闭幕式上的演讲稿,德国图宾根大学荣休教授于尔根·莫尔特曼(Jürgen Moltmann)所做的大会主旨报告,莫尔特曼教授访谈录,波黑共和国大穆夫提穆斯塔法·宰里奇(Mustafa Cerić)访谈录、杜维明教授与莫尔特曼教授对谈纪要等。

　　北京论坛是经中国教育部批准,在北京市政府的指导与支持下,由北京大学、北京市教育委员会和韩国高等教育财团联合主办的国际性学术论坛。该论坛创办于 2004 年,每年举办一次,总主题为"文明的和谐与共同繁荣"。为拓展这一总主题,北京论坛(2010)的研讨主题具体落实为"文明的和谐与共同繁荣——为了我们共同的家园:责任与行动",并专设下列七个分论坛:(一)信仰与责任——全球化时代的精神反思,(二)全球环境问题——政策与行动,(三)全球治理与中国作用,(四)构建和谐的世界城市,(五)全民健康——医学的良知与承诺,(六)全球失衡及其治理机制,(七)变革时代的教育改革与教育研究——责任与未来。就以上研讨专题而言,分论坛(一)所触及的内容可谓基础性或根

本性的理论课题,其学术立意主要如下:

众所周知,全球化趋势在推动人类文明进步的同时,也使人类面临着越来越多的严峻挑战,如全球生态危机、国际金融危机、政治和军事冲突、宗教或民族冲突、恐怖主义、贫富差距等等。我们认为,面对如此种种难题,国际理论界不仅需要从科技、经济和政治等方面来分析原因,共商对策,而且亟待从信仰、道德和价值观上来深入反思,探求出路,因为若不展开这种深层次或根本性的精神反思、思想交流与文明对话,我们便无法理解"彼此的生存信念",无法达成"基本的价值共识",更无法为了"我们共同的家园"而共担责任、共同行动。

正是基于上述立意,北京论坛(2010)的"信仰与责任——全球化时代的精神反思"分论坛广邀国内外著名专家学者,围绕如下三个议题进行了深入探讨:(1)现实的反思——全球化时代的道德与责任,即从价值观上来深刻反思全球化时代面临的诸多重大现实问题,以探讨全球化时代所呼唤的价值观与责任感,包括文明和谐理念、社会平等观念、生态伦理重建、经济伦理重建等;(2)经典的启示——东西方传统的当代诠释,即针对全球化时代所面临的诸多重大问题,发掘东西方哲学与宗教传统的丰厚思想资源,像儒家、道教、佛教、犹太教、基督教和伊斯兰教等,以阐释各大文明传统的精神启示和现代价值;(3)信仰的对话——走向求同存异的多元价值观,即本着"求大同、存小异"的理念,通过真诚的学术对话,交流与分享各大文化传统下所形成的信仰、道德和价值观,以继承发扬人类精神的共同遗产,从基础理论上阐发全球化时代所应持守的良知与责任。

本书包括的三部分内容——全球化时代的信仰理念,全球化时代的宗教传统,全球化时代的宗教对话,便是上述三个议题的研讨成果。尽管这些成果只是初步探索,远不够成熟,但论坛结束后,我们诚邀各位作者加以修改完善,并认真汇编成书,唯望把北京论坛(2010)上初显的"这一道理论风景线及其诸多亮点"传递给国内外读者,以引起大家共鸣,共同致力于"全球化时代的精神反思",携手思索"全球化时代的信仰与责任"。

北京大学人文特聘教授、宗教文化研究院院长 张志刚
2011 年初春记于北大燕园

目　录

第一部分

◎ 全球化时代的信仰理念

宗教和谐——全球化时代的新理念

王作安

摘要：应对全球化时代宗教多元化趋势带来的挑战，要树立和倡导宗教和谐新理念。在承认宗教多样性、差异性的基础上，各宗教通过对话增进彼此间的了解和理解，通过合作承担起维护和平与正义的共同责任，形成宗教内部、宗教与宗教之间、宗教与社会之间的和谐共生。促进宗教和谐，应当倡导和而不同理念，学会彼此尊重，共同担当社会责任，反对利用宗教达到不良目的，防范宗教极端主义。

随着全球化进程的加快，宗教的交流和碰撞日益增多，多元化趋势更加明显，宗教关系由此面临新的机遇与挑战。讲机遇，是因为随着宗教交流的增加和频繁，给各宗教提供了更多的相互学习和加强合作的机会。在人类历史上，尤其是在东方的一些国家和地区，人们已经积累了足够多的发展多元文化的经验和智慧。讲挑战，是因为宗教多元化趋势在有利于交流和合作的同时，宗教之间的矛盾甚至冲突也会随之增加，目前在一些国家和地区，由宗教多元化引起的宗教之间的不信任情绪在日益滋长，人们对发生新的宗教冲突的忧虑也在不断加深。

面对机遇和挑战，各国政府、各个宗教以及有关方面，都要承担起历史的责任，倡导宗教和谐理念，化解宗教纷争和冲突，促进社会和睦，维护世界和平。

所谓宗教和谐，就是在承认宗教多样性、差异性的基础上，各宗教通过对话增进彼此间的了解和理解,通过合作承担起维护和平与正义的共同责任,形成宗教内部、宗教与宗教之间、宗教与社会之间的和谐共生。在宗教内部,要以宽容的态度讨论信仰问题和教义思想,加强教派之间的协调与合作;在宗教与宗教之间,要彼此尊重,相互包容,通过对话增进理解,通过合作加深信任;在宗教组织与政府之间,共同致力于宗教信仰自由,按照政教分离原则各自履行职责,实现良性互动。在宗教与社会之间,要通过自身的不断调整以适应社会进步和时代发展,遵守世俗法律,尊重公序良俗,并通过自身优势和特点为社会服务,发挥积极作用。

宗教信仰自由是国际社会的普遍共识,也是实现宗教和谐的前提和基础。没有宗教信仰自由,就没有宗教和谐。同时,我们已经意识到,宗教信仰自由并不能有效防止宗教之间的仇恨和冲突,宗教和谐则在宗教信仰自由基础上提供了化解宗教矛盾和冲突的新愿景。

实现宗教和谐,有许多不同的方式和途径,其中宗教对话是重要的方式和途径之一。宗教对话只有以宗教和谐为最高的价值追求,才有明确方向和不竭动力,从我做起,从现在做起,从点滴做起,以百折不挠的精神不断推进。

促进宗教和谐,应当倡导和而不同理念。《礼记·中庸》中有句话,叫"万物并育而不相害,道并行而不相悖",准确表达了和而不同的理念。和而不同是和谐思想中的核心理念,也是一种很高的精神境界。中国多种宗教并存,几千年来能够共同生活在一个大家庭里,和睦相处,共生共长,最重要的原因就是共融于和谐文化之中,懂得一荣俱荣、一损俱损的道理,能够相互包容、彼此关照。和而不同强调一个"和"字,但"和"不是靠强迫一致来实现的,恰恰相反,它是以尊重文化、信仰的差异性和多样性达致的,如同烹饪需要各种味道调配才可口,音乐需要各种音符相和才悦耳。试图强求一律,或者试图用一种宗教文化改造另一种宗教文化,势必造成矛盾和冲突。诚如我国西周时期思想家史伯所言,"和实生物,同则不继"。只有承认各种宗教文化之间的差异,并且尊重宗教文化差异的合理性,才能形成各种宗教各得其所、各行其道、和衷共济、相得益彰的同生共荣局面。当今时代,多元文化的口号已经越来越流行,但推行起来又困难重重,希望能到崇尚和而不同的东方智慧中去汲取灵感。

促进宗教和谐,必须学会彼此尊重。世界上的各种宗教有大有小,历史有长有短,但不应有高低之别和优劣之分。种族问题上的种族主义已经不得人心,文化问题上的自我中心主义也越来越没有市场,宗教问题上唯我独尊现象似乎还很少有人敢于说点什么。事实上,宗教平等、互不歧视早已成为共识,只是现实生活中发生的许许多多事情还不那么让人乐观。既然基督教教堂可以建钟楼,那么伊斯兰教清真寺也应该可以建宣礼塔。要真正实现宗教平等,仅有法律、公约和文书是不够的,还需要各个宗教学会彼此尊重。正如人与人之间的关系一样,宗教与宗教相处,彼此间应有起码的尊重。当你扬言要烧掉另一个宗教的经书的时候,你所点燃的是仇恨和冲突的火焰。没有尊重,就难以对话和沟通,没有对话和沟通,就谈不上理解和合作。宗教对话遇到的一个死结,就是各个宗教都宣称拥有绝对真理,在我之外别无真理。实际上,真理是客观存在的,实践是检验真理的唯一标准,各个宗教都拥有追求真理的权利。通向真理的道路很多,条条大路通罗马,可以并行不悖。以自己独占真理自居而阻挠他人追求真理,其行为本身就是有悖于真理本质的。宗教和谐是一种宗教之间的友好相处,得饶人处且饶人,退一步海阔天空,不是非要事事比个高低,分出胜负。圣经上说,有人打你的右脸,连左脸也转过来由他打。要是大家真的能有这样的雅量,世界上的冲突肯定会大大减少。如果各宗教多一点包容心,少一点排他性,宗教之间会更容易相处,而宗教本来就应该是这样的。

促进宗教和谐,应当共同担当社会责任。宗教与人类文明相生相伴,是人类文明的重要组成部分。随着社会进步和时代发展,宗教的社会作用也在发生着改变。面对世界多极化、经济全球化进程,各宗教需要携起手来,同担责任,共谋善举,为促进世界和平、社会安宁、人类福祉发挥积极作用。我们面临许多全球性问题,如自然灾害、饥荒疾病、地区冲突、恐怖活动、社会动荡等等,各宗教都可以发挥积极作用。宗教存在的价值,是通过提升道德、净化心灵来实现的,也是通过担当社会责任来实现的。每个宗教都应当担当,但如果各个宗教共同担当,其影响和作用就会呈几何级数增长。中国古代著名思想家荀子指出:"和则一,一则多力,多力则强,强则胜物。"意思是说,各种力量只要能够和谐相处,就能取得一致、形成合力,无所不胜。这种共同担当责任、共同努力的过程,也将成为各个宗教彼此间积累信任、心生尊重的过程。

促进宗教和谐,应当反对利用宗教达到不良目的。宗教植根于现实社会,与政治、经济、文化、民族等领域的矛盾和问题相互交织,呈现出特殊的复杂性。无论是历史上还是现实中,总是有些个人或者组织利用宗教来达到不良目的。一个国家可利用宗教干涉别国内政,一个组织可以利用宗教从事破坏民族团结、分裂祖国的罪恶活动,一个个人也可以打着宗教旗号损害他人权益和危害社会稳定。这些行为不仅玷污了宗教信仰,而且危害了社会公共利益。各宗教都应维护宗教信仰的纯洁性,还宗教本来面貌,不给一切别有用心的个人和组织以可乘之机。当今世界因为政治意图和经济利益纷争不断,围绕领土、资源、民族等问题冲突频仍,宗教应当为促进和解、止息纷争提供帮助,而不能让信仰因素卷入其中,造成更为复杂的局面,使问题更难解决。利用宗教旗号为冲突提供神圣依据,应当受到抵制和谴责。

促进宗教和谐,必须防范宗教极端主义。各个宗教都追求和平、反对暴力、崇尚大爱、劝人向善。但若偏离正道正信,也容易走向偏执和狂热,陷入宗教极端主义。以宗教信仰的名义煽动仇恨,甚至进行暴力恐怖活动,危害尤甚,已经成为当今国际社会的重大威胁。宗教极端主义的产生有其深刻的时代背景和社会根源,国际社会应当共同致力于建立公正的国际政治新秩序,促进共同发展繁荣,消除滋生宗教极端主义的土壤。同时,各个宗教应当挖掘和弘扬教义中慈爱亲善、中道温和的思想,自觉抵制和防范各种极端主义倾向,维护宗教正常秩序,与暴力恐怖活动划清界限。要防止把暴力恐怖活动归咎于某个宗教,煽动新的仇恨。要防止在反对宗教极端主义、打击暴力恐怖活动问题上搞双重标准,这样做最终的结果只能是搬起石头砸自己的脚,既害人又害己。

世界多极化、经济全球化的深入发展,把人们带进了一个彼此相连、利益共在的"地球村"时代,可谓是"城上青山如屋里,东家流水入西邻"。以"文明的和谐与共同繁荣"为主题,是对全球化时代不同国家和地区、不同组织和个人社会责任的积极回应。宗教多元趋势并不可怕,宗教冲突并不是不可避免,关键是我们要有正确的态度,积极去应对。促进宗教关系和谐,倡导宗教和谐理念,对推动建设持久和平、共同繁荣的和谐世界具有积极意义。

全球化世界中的机遇与挑战

托尼·布莱尔

　　尊敬的周其凤校长，您好！非常荣幸，非常高兴能够来到北京大学，与大家见面，也非常荣幸能够参加北京论坛（2010）的闭幕式。首先我要向各位表示敬意，表示感谢，尤其要感谢北京大学周其凤校长，还有北京论坛严军秘书长，还有韩国高等教育财团金在烈总长，还要谢谢我们北京论坛的各个主办方，包括北京市教育委员会、韩国高等教育财团，以及北京大学的各位领导。

　　文明的宗旨是要创造条件，让人们能够生活在一个和谐的社会之中并人尽其能，促进世界范围内各个社会之间的和谐，我非常高兴看到各位朋友和各位同仁，包括墨西哥前任总统 Zedillo 先生，以及来自各个国家、各个文明的代表能够汇集一堂，参加这个重要的论坛。

　　全球化使世界越来越紧密地联系在一起，因此对宗教信仰的尊重成了非常简单明了的问题：那就是宗教信仰是否能成为文明力量，来塑造和推动造福于全人类全球化，还是起着反作用，阻碍全球化带来的各种变革，封闭世界，使得各个社会彼此分隔，相互对立？

　　我觉得21世纪，我们不会再去重蹈以前的覆辙，上个世纪我们是经历了非常激烈的意识形态之争的，这个覆辙我们要避免重蹈。时至今日，我们大家都意识到我们要充分发挥经济与政府的双重作用，但是在21世纪我们还是可能会发生问题，实际上我们已经看到在宗教信仰和文化意识形态方面,存在一些根本的对立。

我们都知道,宗教是有能力造福全人类的,举一个例子,在非洲最穷的那些人民,他们接受的医疗服务中40%都是由宗教人员提供的,但是我们也都知道,宗教也可能成为恐怖主义和各种邪恶罪行的源泉,当今世界的大部分冲突都会带有浓厚的宗教色彩。

但是我们也有其他的发现,在西方曾经有人预测,随着国民财富的增长,宗教信仰会日渐势微,最终消亡,事实证明这些预测完全是错误的。在当今世界,宗教的影响在不断的增强,比如穆斯林国家人口的快速增长,伊斯兰教也更加强大。另外我还了解到,在拉美地区福音天主教派也发展极快。在美国有70%的美国人认为宗教信仰是他们生活中的重要的、甚至是非常重要的一部分。同时我们不要忘记,在印度有数以亿计的虔诚的印度教徒,那里的锡克教和犹太教的影响也非常大。

而中国宗教信仰多元化也具有非常鲜明的特色。在中国穆斯林教徒的数量超出了欧洲所有穆斯林教徒的总和,中国的新教徒也超过了英国的新教徒,而信仰天主教的中国人也超过了意大利的天主教徒。另外,据估计,中国有一亿多人认为自己是佛教徒。

当然,在世界上还有一些方面也非常重要。我们知道大众传媒的影响以及现代通讯技术和交通的发展,使得这个世界变得越来越小了。21世纪的年轻人因此可以更多地与来自不同的背景、种族、肤色、国籍和宗教信仰的人接触,这种接触即使不是面对面的交流,也可以是通过电视和电影这样的媒体所进行的交流与互动,这种多元化的体验和人际互动,将会成为新世纪的常态。

我认为,在这个新的世界里,我们不能有对宗教的无知和无视,因为在当代世界,要做好任何一个国家、企业或者公民组织的领导人,必须要对宗教有深入的了解,必须了解宗教在不同社会里所发挥的重要作用。所以我感到非常欣慰,也感动非常激动,这一届的北京论坛把"文明的和谐"定为主题的一部分,而且其中一个分论坛的主题定为"信仰与责任——全球化时代的精神反思",我觉得这样一场讨论非常及时。我也想借此机会祝贺北京大学与托尼·布莱尔信仰基金会合作,开办了一个"信仰与全球化"的课程。为了这个课程的准备,我们都付出了很多努力,在此我也向北京大学表示敬意,感谢你们在促进信仰对话方面所做出的工作。这从另一个层面也显示出中国在不断开放,积极参与重要的国际事务,并且努力发挥其国际领导力。

从我的经验来看,要想理解一个国家,不能只看他的政治宣言,也不能只研究他的经济数据,测量他的产出,要想理解一个国家,最好的方法是去深入了解它的文化、它的传统、它的各种对其社会和国民产生影响的特性。因此,中国表现出良好的意愿参与到这个过程中来,将大大促进东西方关系的发展。我没记错的话,中国应该是有56个民族,其宗教信仰的多元化是显而易见的,因此中国建设和谐社会的历程,不仅对世界有重大意义,而且会产生很多供我们研究和学习的东西。同样,其他国家的宗教信仰如何促进社会的稳定和和谐的经验,也同样非常值得中国去研究和了解。

对于西方的我们,以及对于中东、远东和中国的人们而言,我们面临着同样的挑战,那就是如何确保宗教信仰只发挥造福于人类的作用?对于实现文明内部以及文明之间的和谐,我想提出以下七个方面的建议。

首先,我们必须承认宗教信仰的作用,鼓励宗教信仰更真实地表达其核心作用,因为宗教信仰最重要的作用是价值观的缔造,而不是要形成意识形态。宗教引导人们相互关爱、友好合作;通过友爱和同情,使社会更加有效地运转,实现更深的和谐。我们可以考察一下那些最伟大的宗教,你会发现他们对宗教的虔诚和对上帝的敬爱,通常体现在邻里之间的友爱上,比如他们会说:"爱邻如己"、"推己及人",或者"救人一命胜造七级浮屠"。所有这些情感上的共鸣,在大部分宗教都有共性的表达。孔子是一位哲学家而不是神学家,他曾经说过:"己所不欲,勿施于人"。从这个角度来看,我们发现宗教信仰和哲学之间的界限是模糊的。信仰体现价值观,可以牺牲小我,完成大我;宗教还激励强烈的慈悲心和勇气,这些才是宗教的本质所在。因此,宗教的本质并不是那些仪式、那些教义、那些抽象的神学理论,虽然这些也非常重要,但是说到底宗教的本质是人的感情。

第二点,我们要反对把宗教作为一种身份的象征,不要因为一种宗教信仰而去反对其他的宗教信仰。当然,一个基督教徒肯定会虔诚地信仰基督教的教义,而穆斯林也肯定会坚信《古兰经》里伊斯兰教的教规。每位信教的人自然会根据宗教信仰确定自己的身份,而且对自己的信仰笃信不移。虽然我自己是基督教徒，并认同这个身份，但是我并不会因其他宗教走的是不同的救赎道路，而看不起他们。我认为在上帝面前，我们要谦卑，不要自以为是。因为我们希望自己的信仰得到尊重，所以我们就一定要去尊重他人的信仰的自由和权利。

第三点，我们应当从我们自己的经典和传统中汲取智慧，这一点非常重要，因为通过这样的学习，我们可以了解我们的信仰和我们的文化是如何发展而来的，信仰并不是一个静态的东西，它在不断地演变，不断地发展，正是这种智慧和思想的传承，形成了我们现在的社会。有了这种认识，我们就不会流于自大，不会以为 21 世纪就代表人类的历史，认为人类的历史从 2000 年才开始。其实我们每一个社会都可以从我们自己的智慧、社会、哲学等方面的传承中汲取精华，这种传承都已经延续了数百年了。对过去的学习和认识，还会更好地引导我们走向未来，这是切切实实的历史，有时候甚至比伟大的历史事件和人物更加真实。比如说在中国，我们不仅要学习孔子的智慧，也要去了解道教和佛教的经典和传统。

第四点，当今全球化的世界使我们享有巨大的机遇来创造物质财富，这是前所未有的，我们也为此感到非常的庆幸；然而我们要清醒地记住，我们还需要树立价值观、原则观，以及超越物质财富基础之上的理念，这是迫在眉睫的事情，必须立即开展。当然宗教信仰并不是价值观的唯一源泉，很多人并没有宗教信仰，但是也会同样表现出强烈的悲天悯人的人道主义思想。一方面，我们面临着机遇，另一方面，机遇带来的经济和社会变革在改变着我们的社会，宗教信仰可以很好地平衡这两个方面，让我们时刻记住，我们在享有权利的同时，也承担义务；我们在关注自身利益的同事，也要对他人负责。

这方面最好的例子就是环境保护。我们都知道我们要对子孙后代负责，要保护环境，不要破坏环境。因此，宗教信仰可以让我们自律，激发我们的良知，让我们不沉迷于自我，学会宽恕，摆脱仇恨和绝望，学会悲悯，抵制诱惑。它也会帮助我们回答"生命的意义"这一根本性的问题，我们的生活会因此变得更加有意义，更加有清晰的目标，我们会更懂得我们生活在这个世界上，除了追求个人理想之外，我们还是社会的一分子，肩负着社会的责任。

第五，信仰在人与人之间和社会与社会的不断关注和讨论中，会获得其应有的地位，宗教领导人不应该发号施令，他们应该有能力发出自己的声音，提供自己的见解。

第六，我们不仅要实现社会内部的和谐，更要实现不同文明之间的和谐。那些拥有信仰的人应该接受这样一个事实，每个人都平等地享有参与的权利，这种权利的获得必须以尊重今天大部分的国家可能拥有多种宗教信仰和宗教传统为前提；任何一种的宗教信仰都不应该试图去控制，或者居高临下于其他的宗教信仰与传统。

第七，现在正是我们实现以上六个方面的良机；因此，鼓励与促进不同信仰间的和谐与理解至关重要。如果我们能拥有更多的知识，我们就会有更深刻的理解，而有了更深刻的理解，就更有希望实现不同信仰之间的和平共处。我们常常会对未知的一切感到恐惧，常常不愿去考虑我们难理解的事物，而常常又正是这些原因导致了冲突的产生，所以我们不仅要创造一种信仰之间的和谐交流的情绪，更重要的是拿出实实在在的行动，推动合作，实现共处。

托尼·布莱尔信仰基金在世界上很多国家开展了工作，我们的工作思路很清晰。一个是在学术方面，这包括与北京大学的合作，我们最初的合作始于耶鲁大学，现在我们已经与七所大学合作了，包括澳大利亚的西澳大学，新加坡国立大学，耶鲁大学、墨西哥的蒙特雷科技大学，还有北京大学。在未来我们会将中东和亚洲更多大学纳入其中，我们希望建立一个专业，其学术研究和论文、著作的发表都围绕着信仰和全球化这两个概念来开展。我们认为这种做法可以让宗教走出神学院而和整个社会的研究融合在一起。同时我们还有一些学校的项目，三天之前我们让旧金山的学校也参与进来，这些项目利用网络技术和精心设计的教材，使来自不同的信仰，不同文化的 15 个国家的高中生联系在一起，进行交流与沟通，这些国家包括巴基斯坦、英国、印尼和澳大利亚等。学生告诉我们，他们在打破隔阂方面的收获有时甚至可以说是非凡的。

同时我们还有一个实现联合国的千年发展目标的联合行动项目，这个项目是从预防疟疾活动开始的，在非洲，一些地方没有医院和诊所，但是他们有教堂，有清真寺，这些场所可以为当地居民传递公共卫生的信息，弥补政府公共卫生普及性不足的缺陷,通过宗教网络及其影响,对根除疟疾死亡产生了真正的影响,同时保证不同信仰的人受到公平待遇。

明年我们将会建一个新的网页,来展现当今世界信仰的生动画面,它包括信仰的变化、发展趋势,以及持有不同信仰的人们的观点。

中国作为合作伙伴参与到我们跨宗教研究项目中,对我们来说既是一种光荣又是一个机遇,这让我们认识到,要了解今天的世界,需要了解宗教的重要作用。宗教有的时候是扮演着负面的角色,但是如果能够让其适当表达,也会成为积极的力量,成为我们建设文明的全球化所需要的价值观的源泉。此外,尤其重要的是这会让我们相信和谐的社会以及不同文明之间的和谐,不是一个遥不可及的梦想,而是实实在在的可以实现的愿景,它激励我们担起自己的责任,来创造一个更加美好的世界,在这个美好的世界里,精神和物质一样繁荣。通过我们的共同努力,我相信这种愿景是可以实现的。

我环顾世界,我看到我自己的孩子也在逐渐的成长,我的小儿子只有十岁,他所在的学校也给他提供了学习中文的机会,所以在学习语言方面我们英国人也跟上了。在他学校的游乐场,我看到说着不同语言的很多孩子在一起嬉戏,参加他生日聚会的朋友,有一些是穆斯林的孩子,有一些是印度教的孩子,有一些是基督教的孩子。我是在英国东部长大的,我记得我小的时候,第一次遇到某一个人不是白人,或者遇到正统的宗教信仰不是基督教的白人时,我很惊讶。在那个时候不同宗教信仰的人在一起相处是非常奇怪的事,但是在今天,这对我们周围的年轻人来说却是很平常的事情。因此,如果不同信仰的人能够直接去沟通,或者借助网络去沟通的话,产生变化的力量是惊人的。在我们今天这种变化的力量就是全球化,它不是政府主导,是人民推动的。只有当全世界的人民获得了这样的能力,他们就会变得更加开放,这也是世界带给我们的一个良机。

正确的价值观和精神力量是实现世界的和平和繁荣的根本保障。我们知道,宗教有的时候会给我们带来错误的信息,从而导致冲突的出现;但是我们也知道,宗教也有其积极的方面,那就是无论任何形式的宗教,或者任何信仰,都在回应人类精神和所处环境的根本问题。而与宗教相辅相成的哲学,实际上诠释了这些价值观,它包括团结的价值观,相信别人的能力和自己能力的价值观。有了这些信仰和宗教价值，我们就能够建设和谐社会，促进不同文明之间的和谐。这些信仰帮助我们在担负责任的同时，行使好自己的权利。我坚信，理解宗教信仰在全球化进程中的力量和作用是至关重要的。

听到我这样的政治家从政治的角度去谈宗教信仰的问题，而不是宗教学家在谈这个问题，也许你会觉得奇怪。但是宗教信仰问题正是 21 世纪所出现的真实情况，今天的世界已经看到了这种情况的发生，中国也已经出现了这样的情况。中国正在推动社会主义的市场经济，各个领域都在推动平衡，这种大的政治上的冲突，是 21 世纪思想意识形态上的冲突，很大程度上取决于不同宗教、不同信仰的人们如何相处共存的问题。

我真诚地希望这次北京论坛能在一定程度上诠释中国的角色，实际上中国也一直在进行这方面的努力。中国有博大精深的文化和哲学，其影响源远流长。中国为全球寻找答案非常重要，可以帮助我们回答这个时代的其他问题。我非常荣幸今天能跟各位共聚一堂，相信北京论坛能为世界发挥重要的作用，在面临挑战时，我们人类能够共同应对，谢谢各位！

信仰包容——全球化时代的精神共存

卓新平

引　论

对于信仰,人们有着不同的理解。一般可将之分为两大类型的认识,一种认为信仰乃为宗教所独有,离开宗教则谈不上信仰,因为"信"是一种确定性或肯定性前瞻,而"仰"则有仰望、敬仰之意;如有人强调,"信仰,就其本义来说,是专用于神或崇拜对象的宗教术语。"中文的"信仰"一则为"信",即有相信者;二则为"仰",即要为信仰者,而且乃因其神圣和超越才崇拜敬仰也。只有被信仰的对象具有神圣性、精神性和超越性才值得"信"且"仰"。任何世俗理念、个人、物体、主义或理想都不具有这样的特征,因而并非正当的信仰对象。①"信"为认知的超前性,而"仰"则为行动的超越性,指一种往上的、超然的心态及其相应的实践行动。这种观点认为,只有终极实在或终极神圣才能让人由"信"而有仰慕、崇拜之举;而相信现实的或"次终极的"真理则只能称为"信念"而未达"信仰"之层次。显然,这种认识对信仰有着较专一的限定。

另一种则认为信仰不只是宗教信仰而有着更为宽泛的蕴涵,因为"宗

---

① 参见安伦:"化解信仰危机的积极对策",未刊稿。

教并不是信仰必然的和唯一的外化形式",实际上"信仰是比宗教更为根本的东西。"①也就是说,除了宗教信仰之外,还有其他(世俗)信仰。虽然西方社会更多强调信仰的宗教意义,却仍没有断言信仰只有宗教这种唯一的形式。《不列颠百科全书》中文版在解释 belief 时将之译为"信仰",其定义为"在无充分的理智认识足以保证一个命题为真实的情况下,就对它予以接受或同意的一种心理定势(或态度)。"这种解释认为"信仰显然是一种由内省产生的现象,……信仰因其肯定的程度不同而有所差别,如推测、主张或坚信。只有在对信仰者来说一个命题显然是真的时,信仰才能变成知识。"②可以说,信仰与信念、信赖、理想密切关联,甚至就包含有这些内容,其所指既可以是宗教的、也可以为世俗的。只是在谈到 faith 时,《不列颠百科全书》中文版才将之译为"信",并视之为专门的宗教术语,其解释说"信"(faith)乃"宗教名词,指人对于至高上帝和终极救恩的内心态度、信念或依赖。"③与之相似,中国的《辞海》在解释"信仰"时也持上述宽泛之态,认为"信仰"是"对某种宗教,或对某种主义极度信服和尊重,并以之为行动的准则。"④这里,宗教和"主义"可同为信仰的对象。

这样,按照第二种理解,信仰则是一种涵盖较广的概念,通常被人视为"是人对一种事物,一种理想,一种价值观、人性观,甚至是对一种虚幻的世界观的向往和追求,是一种源于现实的更高的心理追求和实践努力的方向。是与信念和理想紧密相关的一个概念。"⑤由此来看,信念可以包含在信仰之内,是支持信仰实践的相关基本观念。"信念,一般认为,乃是一种接受或同意某一主张的心理态度,是对还不能充分肯定的东西予以接受。信念中具有相信的成分,是建基于有限事实或者有限证据上的心理肯定。在证据不足或者说还不清楚所有背景知识和经验的情况下,人们之所以能够发现或者整体把握某一事物或知识,是由于存在着只可意会不可言传的

---

① 荆学民:《人类信仰论》,上海文化出版社,1992 年,第 14 页。
② 《不列颠百科全书》2,中国大百科全书出版社,1999 年,第 345 页。
③ 《不列颠百科全书》6,中国大百科全书出版社,1999 年,第 204 页。
④ 《辞海》缩印本,上海辞书出版社,1980 年,第 247 页。
⑤ 李铁华:"信仰与宗教信仰",高惠珠、王建平主编《科学·信仰与文化》,宁夏人民出版社,2007 年,第 321 页。

支援线索在支持着我们的认识活动。"①信念中虽暗含有未知的因素,具有猜测和神秘的因素,但其作为人们把握世界之独特方式的基本观念却被相关人群视为确信或坚定的理想。根据这种理解,信仰及其核心构成的信念应是指"未然"但被相关人群强调为"必然"的向往和追求目标。因此,信仰具有前瞻、远眺、希望、渴慕的因素,它虽无现实中的确定性,在相关人群中却有心理上、情感上的确定性。当然,以这种心理、情感之确定,也必须面对信仰实践中的未知性、冒险性、或然性,如此才有帕斯卡尔"信仰之赌"或基尔凯郭尔"信仰跳跃"之说。

基于上述分析,本文对"信仰"的理解将持一种开放态度、涵括神圣与世俗两大层面。而且,从对信仰的根本特点之理解出发,理应发现信仰之中及信仰之间都有着很大的商讨、探究的空间。确切地说,"信仰"即对"未知"、"未然"之信,尽管对这种"未知"或"未然"的了解、把握、领悟的程度不一,认知背景有别,也就是说,其掌握的可能成为"知识"的相关"证据"互不相同,然其前瞻性、预设性都是一致的。对于"未知"世界,尚不能用确定的"知识"来把握,人们的相关断言,预见因而只能靠信仰。应该说,信仰的空间在这种意义上要远大于知识和科学,这虽然看似匪夷所思,却乃人类认知的一大特点。

一、一种信仰还是多种信仰?

信仰是人类求知的产物,是对"未知"的一种具有模糊性、神秘性、整体性把握;显然,这其中也有对尚无法获得答复之问的"自答"、"自解"。为此,泰戈尔曾说,"信仰是个鸟儿,黎明还是黝黑时,就触着曙光而讴歌了"。人们在此意义上通常也将信仰视为"未来学"的范围,指出其认知特征即对"未知"、"未来"的前瞻、预设、断言、宣称。实际上,人的认识过程是极为复杂和漫长的,有着求知本性的人类与生俱来就在不断探索、询问,而其答案

---

① 谢伟:"科学与信念",高惠珠、王建平主编《科学·信仰与文化》,宁夏人民出版社,2007年,第344页。

在留给后人后也仍在不断调整、完善。有人曾比喻说,人的认识似一个圆圈,圈内是已获知识,即已经确证的真理;圈外为未知世界,人对之断言、宣称则为一种未定的信仰表述。而且,人的知识越多,其圆周就越长,所接触的外在未知边沿就越大,感到人的未知领域也越多。就目前科学界通过现有科学手段已能感知到的外在世界而论,科学家认为人类对之掌握的确凿知识仅为其应知全部知识比例的百分之四,探究空间可以说是无限之大。而用有限的认知去谈论无限的世界,用局部存在去把握整体,这就进入了信仰的领域。在此,信仰和科学乃在同一起跑线上,科学对之也只能是科学信仰的表述。也就是说,信仰即对未知、未来之整体加以把握的"最普通"、"最广泛的形式"。

既然如此,人类的信仰就不可能是单一的。尽管信仰有着最为典型鲜明的排他性,我们仍然坚持表明有着多种信仰而不是一种信仰这一事实。首先,信仰分有层次,不同层次的信仰可以和谐共处,甚至同时共信。此外,同一层面的信仰中也可分为多种,彼此同样可以从相互排斥经过对话、理解而走向共同存在、和平相处。

一般而论,信仰可以分为世俗信仰和宗教信仰这两大层面,其中世俗信仰从"此岸"、"今世"的角度关注人类相关领域的未来发展,对之表达一种追求、坚信和确认,因而其"神秘化"的因素不太明显,但不一定全无;与之相对立,其"神圣化"的表述则并不亚于宗教信仰。宗教信仰则设定一种终极神圣或终极实在的存在,认为一切、包括未来均在这一超然神圣存在的把握、掌控之中,而人们对其认知、信仰则多为神秘化的形式,但同样也并不排斥理性认知的可能性和必要性。这样,信仰的存在就有了各自不同的空间或领域,而不同信仰之间的对话或跨信仰沟通自然也大有可能、大有作为。

从世俗信仰或现实信仰来看,信仰在方法论上可以分为理性信仰、科学信仰、哲学信仰、法律信仰、从众信仰等方面,而从其涉及的领域及范围则可分为政治信仰、社会信仰、文化信仰、民族信仰、大众信仰、民俗信仰等层面。如我们在中国社会所常论及的共产主义信仰,其实质即一种政治信仰。在政治信仰中的不同,就形成了不同党派、不同"主义"、不同政治主张。就共产主义而言,其"实现"无疑是未来的发展,人们对之追求、向往、坚信,则只能从"信仰"意义上来理解。在以往社会主义国家、甚至在争取社会主义制度的社会中,其信奉者曾希望并相信共产主义会"早"实现,但苏东社会主义阵营发生的巨变和政治制度及观念上的回返,使人们认识到其路漫漫之"修远";中国人在认识到其"跑步前进"之不现实后也承认自己的社会主义尚处于"初级阶段"。正因为如此,对于"共产主义"乃以信仰为主,而对其具体的涵括则有可能语焉不详。其从"空想"到"科学"之转变,也只是从历史唯物主义角度来相对而言。不过,在政治领域,政治信仰的排他性是非常明显的;不同政治理念、不同政治信仰之间有着非此即彼的尖锐斗争,甚至往往不允许任何调和、妥协,其结果使整个人类历史基本上为政治斗争史。尽管如此,政治信仰中仍有对话的空间和实践。一种政治信仰并不是孤立形成的,而往往是综合、继承的结果。例如,共产主义信仰就绝非一家独成,其中包含有诸多欧洲文明的因素,而且对犹太教、基督教信仰也有深层次意义上的间接吸纳和借鉴。所以说,政治信仰尽管有较强的排他性,但对同一层面的信仰和其他层面的信仰仍有一定的开放性和吸纳性。

在中国语境中,信仰沟通的一大难题就是将政治信仰与宗教信仰放在同一个层面来理解,结果使许多人认为二者势必相互排斥、水火不容。就其排他性来看,若从不同层面来理解政治信仰与宗教信仰则不存在彼此之间的排斥和否定,不必面临非此即彼的生死抉择。"如果政治信仰与宗教信仰不在同一个层面,两者是平行关系而不是交叉关系,那么则有可能使两者并行不悖、和平共存。"①二者倘若在同一层面,其冲突、抵触或许会更为明显。但二者如果根本就不在同一层面,则可能避免了其看似必然的矛盾、冲突,也就不必要去设置信仰选择上不可调和的"底线"。其实,马克思主义经典作家已注意到共产主义信仰与宗教信仰的异层性和不可比性,故此避免了二者之间舍谁存谁的被动表态。例如,列宁就曾谈到宗教信仰者"加入"无产阶级政党、即成为共产主义信仰者的问题。在此,他并不认为这两种信仰在同一种人的信奉、实践上会产生矛盾或冲突,而是觉得可以

① 卓新平:《"全球化"的宗教与当代中国》,社会科学文献出版社,2008 年,北京,第 13 – 14 页。

做到兼顾尊重二者的共存。列宁为此指出,"我们不仅应当容许,而且应当特别注意吸收所有信仰上帝的工人加入社会民主党,我们当然反对任何侮辱他们宗教信念的行为,但是我们吸收他们是要用我们党纲的精神来教育他们,而不是要他们来积极反对党纲。"①在这种考虑中,显然已说明政治信仰和宗教信仰因不同层面而并无必然冲突,在政治层面让宗教信仰者同时具有政治信仰也是完全可能、甚至可以的。为此,"如果有一个司祭愿意到我们这里来共同进行政治工作,真心诚意地完成党的工作,不反对党纲,那我们就可以吸收他加入社会民主党。"②通过这种分析比较,则充分说明在信仰分层的情况下政治信仰并不一定要彻底排斥宗教信仰,相反,政治信仰与宗教信仰可以共存共在,达到和平共处。实际上,政治信仰、社会信仰、文化信仰和民族信仰也并不截然与宗教信仰分开,而是有着各种复杂关联。

在宗教信仰层面,多种宗教并立共在、各自发展也是铁的事实。所以,不可能以一种信仰来涵括整个人类的精神生活。从具体宗教信仰来看,并没有"放之四海而皆准"的"普世信仰"。由于宗教信仰层面的排他性,历史上不乏宗教纷争和战争的实例。在人类文明尤其是其精神思想的发展中,宗教信仰占有很大比重。宗教信仰作为人类文化的宝贵遗产和重要象征,已经影响到人类社会的方方面面。因此,如何协调不同宗教信仰之间的关系,在人类社会的稳定、不同文明之间的和谐中就起着举足轻重的作用。

二、信仰排斥还是信仰包容?

在众多信仰表述中,宗教信仰可能是最为典型、最为深刻反映出信仰内涵的表述。应该说,信仰是人类文明中最为普遍的现象,历史上各个民族都有其宗教信仰,任何社会或国家都不可能长久地彻底消除宗教信仰,这种信仰可以被新的信仰崇拜所取代,但人类本身的信仰并不能被完全消

---

① 列宁:"论工人政党对宗教的态度",《列宁专题文集 论无产阶级政党》,人民出版社,北京,2009 年,第 178 页。

② 同上,第 177 – 178 页。

灭。正是在信仰意义上,伊利亚德才称宗教为"人类学常数"。诚然,这一"常数"也只能相对而言,它取决于"人类"何时"形成"、"宗教"何时"诞生",以及二者发展和融合的过程。但宗教信仰作为人类社会的常态、人类文明的重要标志之一,则是不争的事实。

宗教信仰的产生已形成了不同的特色。对于宗教信仰,人们可将之分为三类,一为绝对一神论的宗教信仰,二为二神以上之多神论的宗教信仰,三为抽象、升华而似乎呈现为"无神"的宗教信仰。当然,从严格意义上讲,宗教信仰必以"神明"崇拜为内容,故而"无神"论的宗教信仰似为悖论。不过,从对"神"的理解中,人们则可以看到人类宗教信仰的不断升华和自我超越。

在产生人类宗教信仰的三大板块中,以西亚板块中形成的"绝对一神论"的宗教信仰影响最大,同样其带来的问题也最多。此即所谓"亚伯拉罕传统宗教"范畴的犹太教、基督教和伊斯兰教。这些持守"绝对一神论"的宗教信仰从人类认知深度和思维能力上表现出很高的水平,体现出其对未知探索上已达到了整体、普遍和统一性认知。然而,也正是因为这种"绝对一"的信仰观念而导致其对他者的"排斥",其结果使这三大宗教信仰虽有悠远的内在关联,却冲突最频,伤害最深,迄今仍有未能化解的深层次矛盾。而且,这种"绝对一神"的宗教信仰对外还有咄咄逼人、不容妥协的一面,从而深深卷入人类历史发展上的纷争。在一定程度上,这种"绝对一神论"的宗教信仰还影响到与之相关的文化、政治和民族信仰,并使之多少染上了"唯我独尊",贬低、排斥他者的特性,这在其政治理念、文化观念和民族意识上多有表现。政治上的斗争和文明上的冲突,可以从这种"绝对一"的宗教信仰中窥其根源、找出主因。

而在东亚、南亚两大板块中,其宗教信仰以"多神论"为特色。尽管不同宗教信仰在形而上意义上已经找到或表现出"绝对一体"、抽象整体的思考,但其存在形式仍以"多神论"、多元主义为基本特征。这充分说明宗教信仰即是一种精神追求、更是一种生活方式。既然在信仰上能够体会、承认"多神"并在、共存,那么其面世方式也多为神性兼容、相对多元,有着更大的宽容性和包容空间。在此,宗教信仰上更容易出现"转宗"、兼信和融合现象,其信仰底线并不十分明确。

　　值得注意的是,这三大宗教信仰的生成板块都在亚洲,而且自古延续至今的文明宗教基本上是这些源自亚洲、传到全球的宗教信仰体系。因此,亚洲的"宗教性"、亚洲人的"信仰"特性就值得我们高度重视。同理,主张、推崇信仰包容,促成信仰融合,作为亚洲文化核心地区的中国显然有着举足轻重的地位,也要担负义不容辞的责任。宗教信仰之间的排斥和纷争,在亚洲地区及亚洲宗教中格外突出,这也使化解冲突、和谐共存成为亚洲宗教信仰理应体现出的时代新兆、未来远景。

　　就信仰本身而论,大凡信仰乃说明了人的认识之有限性。而从宗教信仰来看,其"作为宇宙主宰的终极神圣是无形的,难以被人类的有限智慧完全认识,也不能被人类的有限语言完全表达。"①鉴于作为信仰者之人本身的有限性,其宗教信仰及其表述本身也应该是相对的、开放性的,并不存在彼此排斥的必然前提。如果各自平心静气,认真对话和交流沟通,则会发现"各宗教虽然教义不同、形式各异,但在信仰目标、信仰对象和道德伦理等基本面上却有相同的本质;看似完全不同的各宗教其实是大同小异"。②

　　这种求大同、存小异乃是宗教信仰宽容的有效之途。纵观历史发展,宗教信仰之间的宽容也已经有了相应的积淀和经验。仅从基督教这一世界最大的宗教信仰而论,其中世纪思想家库萨的尼古拉曾以"一种宗教的多种崇拜礼仪形式"来理解当时互不相同、各自鼎立的三大宗教。而近代欧洲启蒙思想家莱辛曾在《智者纳旦》中以"三个戒指"之形同来求犹太教、基督教和伊斯兰教信仰之同,而不涉及其"真伪"之意义问题,从而巧妙地化解了"排他性"难题。到了当代社会,英国宗教思想家希克也指明了求同存异的宗教信仰包容通途:他认为各大宗教信仰都有对唯一"终极实在"的信仰解释和实践,这一信仰精神是相同的,而其信仰语言、崇拜实践则各不相同,有其语言、文化、民族认知上的相对性和局限性,由此使对"终极实在"的表述在犹太教中为"上帝"、在基督教中为"上帝"、"神"或"天主",在伊斯兰教中为"安拉",在印度教中为"梵"或"梵天",在佛教中为"佛",在道教中为"道",等等。这些相对性的信仰术语可以在绝对性的信仰精神中

---

①　安伦:《理性信仰之道》,学林出版社,2009年,上海,第4页。
②　同上,第5页。

"万流归宗"、融合为一。通过漫长的信仰理解发展,应该说,今天的信仰尊重和包容之条件已经成熟,我们在此的努力或许可乘"水到渠成"之势。

结 语

信仰包容是全球化的时代精神及需求,这体现出人类的信仰如何承担文明共存的责任,有效完成其时代任务。对此,宗教信仰和其他任何层面的信仰并未达其完善或理想之境,但已看到沟通、和解和融汇的希望。所以,我们在全球化时代的精神反思中必须包括并积极推动人类信仰层面的深刻反思,并将这种反思转化为推动人类进步的重要力量。

Spiritual Revolution:
The Challenge of 21st Century

Raisu-l-ulama Mustafa Cerić

Allah is the Light of the Havens and of the Earth. The similitude of His Light is as it were a Niche wherein is a Lamp: the Lamp within a Glass: the Glass as it were a pearly Star. From a Tree right blessed is it lit, an Olive-tree neither of the East nor of the West, the Oil whereof were well-nigh luminous though Fire touched it not: Light upon Light! (Qur'an, 24:35)

But as for those who cover the Truth, their deeds are as it were massed Darkness upon some fathomless sea, the which is overwhelmed with billow topped by billow topped by cloud: Darkness on Darkness piled! So that when a man putteth forth his hand he well-night can see it not. Yea, the man for whom Allah doth not cause light, no light at all hath he! (Qur'an, 24:39)

There is an old saying that God Almighty has created three kinds of beings: angels with reason without passion; animals with passion without reason; and men with reason and with passion. If the passion prevails over the reason, then the animals are better than men, but if the reason prevails over the passion, then the men are better than angels.

The 21st Century will be spiritual or will not be. (André Malraux, The Voices of Silence 1963)

Nearly two centuries ago the German philosopher Immanuel Kant predicted that eventually world order would come about either through intellectual or moral insight or through the experience of chaos. We are still in the position to make that choice.

Why We Need Spiritual Revolution?

The word revolution designates "the action by a celestial body of going around in an orbit or elliptic course"; it is "a progressive motion of a body round an axis so that any line of the body parallel to the axis returns to its initial position while remaining parallel to the axis in transit and usually at a constant distance from it" (Webster's Dictionary).

Thus, "from antiquity through the early modern period, a revolution" invoked the idea of a periodically recurring cycle. In Copernicus's new astronomy of the mid-sixteenth century, for example, the planets completed their revolutions round the sun... The idea of revolution as a radical and irreversible reordering developed together with linear, unidirectional conceptions of time. In this newer conception revolution was not recurrence but its reverse, the bringing about of a new state of affairs that the world had never witnessed before and might never witness again.

Both of these two meanings of revolution may be applied to the idea of spiritual revolution, first, as of man's need to return to his origin, to his initial position, and, second, as of man's realization that there is an alternative to his way of life. What are the divine revelations of the Tawrat (the Torah), the Injīl (the Gospel), the

Zabūr (the Psalms), and the Qur'an but a progressive motion of a transcendental word round the axis of the divine so that any meaning of the transcendental word parallel to the divine returns to its origin, to its initial position. Hence, we need spiritual revolution in order to return to the initial position round the axis of divine spirit out of which we all have been made.

[For,] lo, thy Sustainer said unto the angels:-Behold, I am about to create a human being out of clay; and when I have formed him fully and breathed into him of my spirit, fall down before him in prostration! (Qur'an, 38:71 – 72).

While asking man to change his way of life of Jahiliyyah (of Ignorance or Negligence), the Qur'an is offering to him the alternative of Islam which is nothing more than the return or submission to the orbit of divine spirit, which man had ignored or neglected and thus had put himself in danger of falling out of a natural law, known as the Sunnat Allah. This natural law as the Sunnat Allah demands respect for freedom of religion as a fundamental principle, fallowed by respect of human life, human equality, human dignity, human community, human justice and human decency.

In fact, Islam means "revolution" in the sense of Muslim who is munīb, the returner, the one who comes back to the basics of human relationship with God and his fellow human being after it was broken due to man's ignorance or negligence. As a paradigm for a multiple spirituality, Ibrahīm, (a. s.), (Abraham) is described as " a compassionate, attentive and revolutionary (munīb) in the sense of returning to the initial position of humanity toward God[Qur'an, 11:75].

But for him to have been elevated to that God given honor, Ibrahim, (a. s.), had to go through different temptations which had led him to spiritual revolution, which had brought about a radical and irreversible reordering of human faith in One God as an everlasting alternative to human way of life. He first saw a star as his Lord, but when it disappeared, he was attracted by the moon to be his guide, but when it set too, he then saw the sun rising and said: "This is my Lord. This is the greatest of all". But when the sun disappeared as well, he said: "O my people, I am free from your falsehood. I am returning my face toward Him Who created the heavens and the earth and never shall I be attached to falsehood. " (Qur'an, 6:76 – 79)

Still, Ibrahim, (a. s.), was revolutionary by asking provocative questions: "My Lord! Show me how You give life to the dead" said Ibrahim. "Don't you believe?" God said: "Yes! But to satisfy my own heart or my own understanding"... (Qur'an, 2:260)

But the case of Ibrahim (a. s.) as an inspiration for the need for spiritual revolution has its most appealing sign in the fact of him being put to the fire: "Burn him and protect your gods, if you are to do anything at all!" But God said, "O Fire be cool and peace for Ibrahim! (Qur'an, 21:68 – 69)

I don't know whether Terry Jones had a slightest idea about the attempt of the burning of Abraham's body which obviously failed, but his attempt to burn the copies of the Qur'an sounds like that of Abraham, which obviously failed because it would be self-burning or spiritual suicide. So, in the attempt of the burning of the Qur'an I see, indeed, the great sign for the need of the spiritual revolution of the Abrahamic paradigm because it is revolutionizing our approach to the basics of our human relationship towards God and towards our common human heritage.

Perhaps, it would be too simplistic to relate recent floods in the world to the biblical and qur'anic stories of Noah's flood, but it would be, on the other hand, too arrogant not to see in them the sign of warning that we should start building the Noah's Ark.

The problem of climate change is not anymore the knowledge of an expert team. It is a reality of every one's life and fear of human collective mind.

The nuclear threat is not anymore a political game of cold war. It is the life threatening for the whole humanity.

The poverty that is spreading around the world is not anymore far away from us. It is reality in our neighborhood.

There are so many things that make me proud of my faith, but when I see the state of the Muslim Society I do not find a big difference from the rest of the world. I see in my fellow Muslims the same paradox as elsewhere: the higher degrees in education, the less degree of ethics; the more knowledge, the less wisdom; the more experts, the less solutions; the more wealth, the less moral values; the more houses, the less families; the faster communication, the less decent human relation; the more books about pollution, the less care about natural environment; the more conferences about peace, the more wars around the world; the more call for reason, the less rational behavior.

The way out of this paradox of our global civilization is the spiritual revolution that is different from scientific, intellectual, political or industrial revolutions. It is the revolution of spirit that should embrace all of the positive results of the previous revolutions in the sense of the return to the God's light (nūr)-a source of His light with which He enlightens human hearts and minds, which is light upon light, which expels darkness one over the other, and which chases away darkness from human mind, which removes hatred from human heart, which cleanses human soul from Satan's evil. Then, we should listen to what the Prophet had to say: "Verily, God created the creatures in darkness, and then He poured them some of His light."

It is this God's light that has enlightened the human spirit and mind to lead humanity from slavery to freedom, from might to right, from mythology to science, from hatred to love, from terror to security, from fear to hope, from war to peace, from corruption to ethics, from poverty to wellbeing, from falsehood to truth, from selfishness to compassion, from arrogance to humility, from harshness to gentleness, from greed to modesty, from discrimination to equality, from pornography to chastity, from pedophilia to morality, from drug-addiction to self-esteem, from godlessness to Godliness, from suicide to the purpose of life, from jahiliyya to spiritual enlightenment, and that is a revolution which takes place when human beings realize that there is an alternative to their way of life, when they realize that they are reduced to the lowest of the low.

Thus, we need such God's light that will enlighten, once again, human spirit and mind that will lead humanity to a spiritual revolution which is to be of greater significance than the revolutions that changed the world. For, although it took a long time, human beings eventually understood that they are born free and that freedom is like a virus for which there is no an anti-virus. Also, over time human beings learned that their rights to life, faith, freedom, property and dignity are fundamental God given human rights and thus no human might is authorized to deprive any human being from these God's gifts.

Therefore, the ultimate purpose of state and society is not to lord over people, or to disturb them and violate their human rights, but to set each man and woman free from fear of a witch-hunt to which they are subjected simply because of their appearance and the way of dress, and to defend their rights so that they may build mosques, churches and synagogues in peace, in order to live and work in full security and without harm to themselves and their neighbors.

On paper we have it all-freedom, right and science, but deep in our soul we sense that we are losing these values as some people would like to take us back to the dark age of slavery, might and mythology or jahiliyyah-Is it a judgment of the time of jahiliyya that they are seeking? Who is better than Allah to judge people who are certain in their right beliefs . (Qur'an, 5:50)

Of course, science cannot replace the need of the soul to hear beyond what the ear can hear and to see beyond what the eye can see, through enlightened intellect. But also, human intellect which produces knowledge cannot renounce scientific achievements that have made man's life on earth easier.

Call for return to faith must not mean return to the world of mythology in which the light of intellect and the power of reason are dimmed. Spiritual revolution does not imply an eraser of human sagacity and rationality. It presupposes precisely what the last Messenger of God, Muhammad (a. s.) did, when he showed the way out of the dark age of jahiliyyah towards spiritual, moral and scientific enlightenment.

At the start of the 7th century of Mīlād, Muhammad (a. s.) surely led the most significant spiritual revolution in the history of mankind. With divine inspiration (wahy), he carried out the most convincing and most efficient reformation of religious thought by abolishing the institution of mediation between God and man; by freeing man from the inherited sin; by establishing the principle of non-violence in religion; by repealing racial discrimination; by freeing women from slavery and fear; by taking into consideration human reason as an important yardstick in faith; by elevating human knowledge to the level of faith and morality; and by establishing equilibrium in relations between the individual and society.

Muhammad (a. s.) established Islamic worldview which defines the individual as self-confident and autonomous human being which should be respected with all his human rights. He defined community as jamà'at, i. e. as an integral ummah, which integrates that which protects rights of the individual with that which makes community stronger, that is to say, people and nation. In the Noble Qur'an we read:

Thus We have appointed you as an integrative middle nation, that you may be witnesses for mankind, and that the Messenger may be a witness for you.

The idea of being integrative and inclusive was not strange to the great Muslim jurist al-Shafi'i when he was brought to the Caliph Harun al-Rashid to speak about the Book of God, but he replied to the Caliph:-About which of the Books of God you want me to speak, O the Comander of Believers, for God has revealed many books? (Qur'an, 2:143)

Furthermore, the Qur'an asks us to be tolerant in communication with people of all faiths, nationalities and worldviews:

When you want the others to understand your faith, invite them with wisdom and fair exhortation, and reason with them in the best manner. Your Lord is Best Aware of him who strays from His way, and He is Best Aware of those who go aright.

Therefore, spiritual revolution demands return to wisdom, tolerance and dialogue, the notions that have become lost in the flood of arrogance, egoism, extremism, holocaust, genocide, terrorism and violence in the streets and in homes. We have reached a point when the very mention of the word "wisdom" usually makes one think of elderly people who are wise because they have grown old and can no longer be ruthless.

Yes, ruthlessness has become what "wisdom" used to be for those who think that "wisdom" of life is to be found in narcotics, the "wisdom" of modern age in alcohol, the "wisdom" of freedom of choice in the lack of shame, the "wisdom" of wit in theft, and the "wisdom" of courage in violence. Of course, when one subjects his worldview to knowledge and information without morality and ethics, without wisdom and meaning, without decency and honor, without tolerance and the culture of dialogue, then we face violence, intolerance and discrimination in society.

Beside knowledge and information which are more accessible today than at any other time in history, especially to our youth, we need to learn wisdom as an ability to distinguish useful from harmful knowledge, useful from harmful information. Human soul, being divine inspiration, possesses this capacity for wisdom as a spiritual power which increases with piety and shields man from ruthlessness towards his and the life of people around him.

The pollution of human soul with lies and immorality is no less than the pollution of nature with poisonous gases and garbage. Moreover, it is not possible to cleanse nature as long as human soul remains polluted with wickedness and irresponsibility towards life on earth.

Man must learn tolerance and culture of dialogue because there is no other way leading to his success in this world and his salvation in the hereafter. It is therefore important to know that if Islam requires that Tewhīd (Qur'an, 16:125).

The representatives of my umma will not enter paradise with much prayer and fasting only, but also with wholesome hearts, generous souls and compassion for all people who are Muslim peacefully.

It is because of the lack of human compassion for all forms of life on earth and because of the absence of true tolerance and culture of dialogue among people and nations that the 20th century will be remembered as the century of dark ideas of racism, fascism, xenophobia, anti-Semitism and Islamophobia-the ideas that have induced people to commit the most heinous crimes in history of mankind: holocaust and genocide.

Death camps, Gulags, the atomic bombs that fell on Hiroshima and Nagasaki killed millions of people, more than in any other century. But, the 20th century is not only notorious for the numbers of those killed, but also because of the conviction that out of those killings a new, better world would be born.

In the 20th century industries of killing organized by states against its own citizens, were launched with the conviction that those who survived would live in a better world than was ever existed.

In the 20th century man tried to replace divine spirit with a satanic evil spirit, daring to utter the words: " God is dead ", becoming conceited in thinking that he can live as if there were no God.

But, today those of us who have survived the "dark moments" of the 20th century can bear witness that God is al-Hayy . (Indeed, Muslim means a peaceful man).

We the survivors bear witness that we are aware of the divine spirit in us which beckons us to spiritual revolution that should change the way of life in this century. We hope that the first signs of spiritual revolution will appear in al-Quds, in Jerusalem, in the Holy Land of Ibrahim's sons, for whom we pray here and now so that God Almighty may soften their hearts in order that they may remember that holy peace-not holy war-is on their hearts. The same we wish to the people of Iraq, Afghanistan, Pakistan and other nations that suffer conflict and violence.

We in Bosnia are truly proud of the centuries of coexistence and tolerance, because, in spite of the experience of genocide, we have not forgotten to read the verses of the Holy Qur'an:The good and the evil are not the same. Repel the evil with what is better: then will he between whom and thee was hatred become as it were thy friend and intimate! But no one is granted such goodness except those who exercise patience and self-restraint-none but persons of the greatest good fortune.

Hence, we need spiritual revolution in the 21st century so that we may learn how to exercise patience and self-restraint and thus to become human beings of the greatest good fortune.

Indeed, we need a Muslim initiative in the 21st century with the same vigor as it was in the 8th century in Bagdad the Muslim initiative for an intellectual revolution and as it was in the 12th century in Cordoba the Muslim initiative for a scientific revolution that brought about an epochal and irreversible change because it was applied in a systematic way to events in science and only later to political events. "In just this sense, the first revolutions may have been scientific, and the 'American', 'French', and 'Russian Revolutins' are its progeny".

And in just this sense, the first revolution in the 21st century should be spiritual through moral insight so that humanity may be spared from an immanent chaos of the 20th century.

Let me end my presentation with the quotation of Musa Eric Waldbaum who said: This century presents accelerating challenges for becoming. In order for us to become full human beings, we face the need to study, reconcile, understand and embrace consciousness, spirituality, ethics, values, culture, the sciences, arts, law, politics, economies, knowledge, actions, technologies and innovation. Individually, each of these areas only touches on the richness of meaning. The task is to see beyond reductionism and to make emergent the very meaning of our lives. To act responsibly in a world where man cannot know everything-indeed where uncertainty may be at the very core-faith is essential. But that faith cannot be doctrinaire. Rather it must be all embracing, seeking knowledge even to China as the Prophet (pbuh) said.

(Qur'an, 41:34 – 35), the University of Chicago Press, 1996 (Living), that He is full of hearing (al-Samī'), full of sight (al-Basīr) and full of knowledge (al-'Ālim) who writes everything on the, eternally preserved disc"" (Lewh-i mahfūz). And the Messenger of Allah says: (Oneness of God) dominate human reason, then it also requires that the principle of compassion towards fellow human being and nature should govern human heart. This is why prayer (salāt) and fasting (sawm) have greater value if they awaken in man compassion for life on earth, as the very mercy of God, which, as God Almighty says, embraces everything that exists: -My mercy embraces all things (Qur'an, 7:156) . (Qur'an, 24:39)(Qur'an, 24:35), the University of Chicago Press, 1996.

波黑共和国大穆夫提
Mustafa Cerić访谈录

访谈时间:2010 年 11 月 6 日
受访人:波黑共和国大穆夫提 Mustafa Cerić
访谈人:吴冰冰①

吴冰冰:您认为,当今伊斯兰社会面临的最主要的挑战是什么？ 例如,经济发展、政治改革、教育、伊斯兰思想的重建,这些问题中,哪些是(对伊斯兰社会)最主要的挑战？

Mustafa Cerić:你刚才提到的问题都是整个世界当前面临的挑战,但你特别提到穆斯林世界,我认为,我们可以从一个大背景下来看待穆斯林世界当前的处境。在理解穆斯林世界的历史时,我想说,它可以被看作是一个奇迹,抑或是一个难题。

伊斯兰历史的奇迹在于,公元 7 世纪,先知穆罕默德出现在历史舞台上,他出身于尚未踏入文明社会的游牧部落,甚至据传他不能写和读。尽管如此,他接收到真主之光,即天启。凭借这一来自阿拉伯半岛的朴素思想,他把启示带给当时的两个先进文明——拜占庭和罗马文明。伊斯兰能够吸收这两大文明,并将其整合成一种新的东西,即伊斯兰文明。通过《古兰经》和先知穆罕默德的使命,我们可以看到,这一使命是人类历史上最引

---

① 吴冰冰,北京大学外国语学院阿拉伯语言文化系副主任、副教授。

人瞩目的宗教改革。我现在身处北京,身处伟大的中华文明之中,我是出于我对整个世界的评价而言,请原谅,我是从我所处的地中海地区的经验而言,或者说,是从欧洲的世界观来说,如果你愿意,也可以称之为欧洲中心的历史观。当我们谈到伊斯兰教时,中国离它并不远,伊斯兰教从公元7世纪就已经开始在中国存在了。

然而,我想说的是,我观察到先知穆罕默德带来了四种主要的宗教上的改革:一是所有人出生时都是没有原罪的;二是先知穆罕默德取消了神职人员制度;三是种族平等的观念,任何阿拉伯人不高于非阿拉伯人,任何非阿拉伯人也不高于阿拉伯人,他们只因是否虔诚而分高低,这与中国的哲学观念相似,即道德是基础;四是先知穆罕默德带来了宗教无强迫的观念,你不能强迫人们皈依。这一文明带着先知穆罕默德这一使命的精神,它为世界文明贡献了两样伟大的东西:一是巴格达的智慧宫(Bait al-Hikmah),穆斯林学者在此组织了对古希腊哲学的翻译;二是在穆斯林于公元12世纪在西班牙发展出的文明,把人文主义和文艺复兴带给了欧洲。

在拿破仑入侵之后这一伟大的文明被边缘化了,在最近两个世纪退出了历史的主流。要了解穆斯林世界的现状,就必须了解,穆斯林在最近两个世纪以来一直在努力回归历史的主流。在穆斯林世界有两种运动,一种是穆斯林世界的世俗化,或者说是穆斯林世界的西化;另一种运动是穆斯林世界的"再伊斯兰化"(re-Islamization)。现在,你知道这两种运动的结果,二者在穆斯林社会中彼此对立,哪种潮流将会取胜?我们知道土耳其就是例子,突尼斯、印度尼西亚乃至几乎所有国家都经历了世俗化进程,但土耳其是世俗化最激进的。你也知道巴基斯坦的毛拉纳·毛杜迪(Maududi),他奠定了以和平方式实现伊斯兰化的思想基础。伊斯兰化运动的另外一翼,相信这一进程不可能是和平的,而是要通过武装斗争的方式,其领袖是后来的赛义德·库特卜(Sayyid Qutb),他被纳赛尔处决。

这两种潮流在过去两个世纪的并存,结果是什么?如我们今天所见,我认为世俗化在穆斯林世界已经失败了,穆斯林世界"再伊斯兰化"的运动或者氛围在绝大多数穆斯林国家已经取而代之。所以我的问题,或者说我们穆斯林所面对的最大问题是,我们应该走哪一种伊斯兰化或"再伊斯兰化"的道路,是在世界的全球化中与世界整合呢,还是走向孤立。我们穆斯林面对的一个艰难抉择就是整合还是孤立。第三种潮流是同化。穆斯林向何处去，其中最大的挑战是经济，取决于穆斯林的经济状况，然后取决于政治局势，全球的政治局势。但我相信，穆斯林走出这一危机、摆脱这一局面的正确途径抑或说是唯一途径就是教育。教育！教育！教育！正如我们在开始所说的。如果我们要问，先知如何从贝都因游牧的背景下带来了文明，答案是凭借"读吧！"凭借先知的圣训："学问虽远在中国亦当求之。"

中国正在开放，我希望穆斯林世界可以在正确的背景和正确的语境中解读先知穆罕默德的这段圣训，来看看中国人正在如何克服他们困难，他们不久之前还有很多困难。他们如何转型，从一种世俗化、异化或教条化，转向开放并与国际事务整合，既不是孤立也不是同化。同化，孤立，第三条道路是与世界历史整合，穆斯林必须做出抉择。

吴冰冰：您谈到了教育，那么，你所说的"教育"的内涵是什么？

Mustafa Cerić：教育包含两层概念，它不仅仅指人获得信息，把信息装进脑子里。仅仅获得一定的信息是不够的，更为重要的是，如何分辨好的和坏的信息，也就是说，要运用智慧。智慧是教育的关键。但是，一方面你能学习智慧，但它同时也是真主的赏赐，智慧是体验生活的过程，年龄越大、越成熟，就会得到越多的智慧。但是为了获得智慧，必须要有耐心，必须要形成一种视角，引导你达成想要达到的某种目的；这种目标必须是善意的、积极的、生产性的，这样你就不仅仅是一个消费者，还是一个生产者。至于穆斯林，因为他们是发展中国家，所以他们更多的是消费产品，而不是为别人制造产品。从消费阶段转向生产阶段，你需要教育。教育意味着学生在礼仪、道德、谦逊、勤奋方面得到提升，并接受这样一种观念：不要总是期待别人来帮你，你应当准备好去帮助别人。帮助他人越多，对自己的帮助就越多，因为只有给予他人爱与尊重，才能使得爱与尊重越来越多。如果只爱自己、只尊重自己，那么爱与尊重就会死亡，因为它们这样是无法存在的。因此为了自身的进步，你必须帮助他人。所以教育并不仅仅是获取知识，也是为了变得成熟和睿智，并运用这一智慧使他人获益。

吴冰冰：当前，一些西方学者，甚至部分伊斯兰国家的学者也在谈论伊斯兰主义、政治伊斯兰，甚至是原教旨主义。在您看来，在伊斯兰国家政治与宗教是怎样的关系，伊斯兰教是如何看待政府的？

Mustafa Cerić：这是个非常重要、非常复杂的问题，很难在一次访谈中加以回答。我想说的是，当我们谈到所谓的"伊斯兰国家"（Islamic state）时，我相信，并不存在根据某些人构建起来的理论被称作"伊斯兰国家"的东西，《古兰经》没有提到过"伊斯兰国家"，圣训也没有提到过"伊斯兰国家"。但是存在着很多原则，在其基础上可以构建共同体，这样的共同体组成国家。根据我的理解，包括对伊斯兰教的精神、《古兰经》的精神以及先知穆罕默德的使命的理解，我相信先知穆罕默德的使命就是建立一个穆斯林共同体，这样的共同体可以通过价值观来识别。这个共同体可以建立国家，穆斯林和其他人都可以在公正、真理和相互合作的基础上生活于其中。这样你就能理解，伊斯兰教有三个基本的原则：信仰表白，也就是见证真主独一，穆罕默德是真主的使者；沙里亚，即穆斯林共同体的法律，而不是非穆斯林的法律；哈里发制度，即市民社会，或者叫做社会契约。

对于穆斯林来说，不论是现在还是过去，尤其是过去，从未听说过"伊斯兰国家"，那时只有"王朝"，穆斯林王朝，有伍麦叶王朝、阿拔斯王朝、奥斯曼王朝。当穆斯林在文化上缺乏安全感时，他们比以往更为频繁地使用"伊斯兰"这个形容词。例如，在古典时代，在古典著作中你很难发现"伊斯兰"这样的形容词，例如安萨里（al-Ghazzali），他的著作里找不到"伊斯兰"这个词，书名大多是《宗教学复兴》这样的表述。在过去的两个世纪，穆斯林开始处于危机之中，这么多的书在谈论穆斯林和伊斯兰，但是当你打开这些书，其中并没有多少东西真的是"伊斯兰的"，那些书都是护教性的、防卫性的，并没有给出什么是伊斯兰国家的答案。

所以我相信，当代学者在讨论"伊斯兰国家"时，他们只是在构建一个理想国的理论，是一种乌托邦。即使是柏拉图的《理想国》，也是一种精神上的乌托邦，法拉比（al-Farabi）所构建的"美德之城"（al-Madinah al-Fadilah）同样是乌托邦。我们过去所拥有的政治理论都是乌托邦，直到我们有了国家"合法性"的观念。所以我认为，现在穆斯林思想家在讨论政府与国家时，应该从关于"伊斯兰国家"的理论转到"穆斯林国家"（Muslim State）的合法性。国家的合法性建立在民主的基础上，必须对穆斯林共同体进行教育，使其能够通过民主进程建立和运行一个可以被称为"穆斯林国家"的国家，其基础是真理、正义、平等、所有人机会均等的原则，捍卫所有人作为社会成员的公民权。在这个国家里,穆斯林只是与其他群体共存的一个群体,大家根据社会契约生活在一个更大的社会中,或者说,每一个人都属于这个社会。实现这一目标的前提是,理性的人可以就如下原则达成共识:为了所有人的利益互助和合作。正如北京论坛,其主旨是"为了共同繁荣"。这就是我所说的"伊斯兰国家"的含义。

吴冰冰:这些原则不仅适用于穆斯林或伊斯兰国家,也适用于那些非伊斯兰国家中的穆斯林少数民族,对吗?

Mustafa Cerić:绝对正确。比如说,在印度有一亿穆斯林少数族群,可能比所有的土耳其穆斯林和阿拉伯穆斯林加起来还要多。但我相信,在大的社会环境中,穆斯林群体依据自己的原则而生存,并在社会契约原则的基础上为社会做出贡献。社会契约是构建社会的共同意愿或共同目标。

当所有人都一样的时候,族裔相同、国籍相同、宗教相同,构建社会可能更容易。但经常出现的情况是,在同一个宗教、族裔和国家群体中发生的冲突,有的时候比那些彼此不同的人之间更多。就历史而言,比起彼此不同的人,彼此相似的人之间更容易相互敌对。你知道,在欧洲天主教与新教之间的激烈战争,在穆斯林历史上也存在着逊尼派和什叶派之间的激烈战争。不只是在宗教中,在共产主义意识中,彼此之间也有激烈冲突,因为他们彼此不同,尽管他们都在谈论着统一和意识形态。因此可以看到,只要人们想要彼此冲突,并不必然需要出自不同宗教、不同国家、不同族裔,就算人们来自同一个国家、同一种宗教甚或是生活在不同的社会都可以发生冲突。

当我们看中国经验时,我们认识到,中国有 56 个不同的民族,宗教也是多元的,中国人的智慧和传统给我留下了深刻的印象。我希望你们能继续成为世界的榜样,尤其是成为我们波斯尼亚和黑塞哥维那的榜样,因为我们具有多种文化、多种民族,我们是多文化的社会、多民族的国家,不同的宗教、文化、民族是可以共存的。我希望你们不要失败,因为你们是一个大国,因此,如果你们失败了,那么失败也将是巨大的;我们波黑没有那么大,如果我们失败了,那也只是一个小失败。我希望你们不要失败,继续解决问题。

一个月前我拜访了新疆喀什和甘肃兰州,我们参观了清真寺、经学院、幼儿园,我们与当地人攀谈,我们参观了马哈穆德·喀什噶里的家乡和他的墓地、优素福·哈斯·哈吉甫的墓地,参观了北京的伊斯兰中心,会见了佛教、道教、基督教的代表,昨天我还在牛街清真寺做了聚礼,见到了伊玛目。我要跟我那些中国的穆斯林兄弟说,当我听到中国的回族穆斯林用中国特有的方式诵读《古兰经》时,我留下了深刻印象,我被深深打动了。这种诵读方式与其他国家不同,但那是我永生难忘的,在中国所读到的一切让我有一种游历寰宇的体验,这就是伊斯兰的普世性,它跨越了民族、跨越了国家、跨越了种族,对我而言中国提供了这样的证据。

我还要利用这个机会感谢接待我们的政府部门,感谢中国全国政协主席贾庆林,中国国家宗教事务局局长王作安,新疆维吾尔自治区政府主席努尔·白克力,甘肃省副省长泽巴足,我们还与中国伊斯兰教协会的陈广元会长会面并座谈,他向我们介绍了中国伊斯兰教协会,他们出版了《中国伊斯兰教》,还有《中国穆斯林》杂志,我们翻译了其中的一篇文章,并将在我们的报纸上发表。

因此,我想对中国说,要发扬回族穆斯林将伊斯兰与中国的爱国主义相结合的原则。包括回族、维吾尔族、柯尔克孜族、哈萨克族、萨拉族、塔塔尔族、乌孜别克族、保安族、塔吉克族、东乡族等在内的所有的中国各民族,都应该融入中国社会,抓住中国经济、政治、教育和文化不断发展的契机。我相信,这是中国穆斯林群体成为世界穆斯林典范的宝贵机会。我祝福他们。

吴冰冰:非常感谢。最后一个问题,请您简单介绍一下波黑的穆斯林状况,或者您有什么想向中国,尤其是北京大学学生介绍的关于波黑的情况。

Mustafa Cerić:我想许多中国人都听说过波黑,它是前南斯拉夫六个联邦单位之一。和基督教与犹太教一样,伊斯兰是传入欧洲的,欧洲没有诞生过先知或天启的经典,所有的先知都来自于东方。变成基督教徒、犹太教徒和穆斯林的欧洲人,他们不能声称自己因为地理的因素而具有优越性,因为我们所有的启示都是从东方获得的。

公元8世纪伊斯兰教传播到伊比利亚半岛和西班牙,15世纪传到巴尔干半岛,波黑就位于该半岛。可以说,波黑是巴尔干半岛伊斯兰教的中心,1463年波斯尼亚人接受了伊斯兰教,我们不久前刚刚庆祝了皈依伊斯兰教600周年,伊斯兰教在14世纪就传到了巴尔干半岛。波黑现在的人口在

400万左右,其中51%是穆斯林,31%是塞尔维亚人,17%是克罗地亚人和天主教徒,我们也有犹太人。这都是战争前的情况。如你所知,有一百万人被从波黑驱逐,非常不幸,波斯尼亚穆斯林遭到了种族清洗,1995年7月11日塞尔维亚军队对波黑的穆斯林进行了种族清洗,他们在斯雷布雷尼察杀害了大概8000名穆斯林,我们在全世界有很多难民。现在我们正努力走到一起。我知道中国在萨拉热窝有大使馆,波黑在北京也设有大使馆。我来中国不需要签证,因为我持有外交护照,这非常重要。这是我第二次中国之行,非常愉快,我很荣幸参加了北京论坛,并希望未来双方能够交换学生,我会鼓励波黑学生来中国,学中文。

不知道你们是否了解,世界各地的人都在谈论中国,许多人认为,中国将在未来引领世界经济发展。所以,我要告诉波斯尼亚人,要尽快学中文,否则就将被甩在后面。

吴冰冰:非常感谢。

(北京大学外国语学院阿拉伯语言文化系研究生王倩茹根据录音整理和翻译。)

全球危机中的生命文化

莫尔特曼

我想谈谈一段时间以来令我最关注的问题：

  ——生的文化
  强于死的恐惧
  ——热爱生命
  战胜现世种种破坏力

因为我深信：

"哪里有危险，哪里就有拯救"（弗里德里希·荷尔德林）。

第一部分我会谈及现今我们面临的威胁，第二部分论及宜居世界的诸方面和爱的生命力。

一、现今对覆灭的恐惧

如今人的生命处于危险之中。并不是因为人的生命是有限的，这本是亘古不变的，而是因为人们已经不再热爱、肯定和接受生命了。二战后，法国诗人阿尔波特·加缪曾写道，"令人费解的是：在欧洲，人们不再热爱生命。"但凡经历过惨绝人寰的战争的人都明白他所指何意。一旦人们不再热爱生命，将会产生毁灭性的后果，生命也会渐渐消殒。

如今,我们面临一种新的死亡宗教,我并非意指伊斯兰宗教,而是指恐怖主义意识形态,它在21世纪是如此典型:"你们的年轻人热爱生命",阿富汗塔利班领导人毛拉·奥马尔说,"我们的年轻人热爱死亡"。2004年3月11日马德里大屠杀之后,我们看到很多信里夹着这样的信息:"你们热爱生活,我们热爱死亡"。似乎这是自杀杀手的现代恐怖意识形态。大概60年前,我们欧洲就存在这种意识形态,西班牙内战中一个法西斯老将这么喊道:死亡万岁!你不能威慑自杀杀手,他对死亡没有丝毫畏惧,也不再热爱生命,只想和他的被害人同归于尽。

恐怖分子的外表下掩藏着更深重的危险:国与国之间签订的和平及不扩散条约都有自不待言的前提:生存的愿望,双方都有活下去的愿望。如果一方不想活下来,只情愿死去,如果以他的死能毁灭整个"罪恶的"或"邪恶的"世界,会是怎样的情形呢?如果拥有核武器的国家醉心于"死亡宗教",因被逼上绝路已放弃所有希望而成为世界其他人眼中的集体自杀杀手,那又会是怎样的情形呢?只有当所有相关方有生的愿望并想活下去,威慑才起作用。

这种被当作陈旧的、罪恶或邪恶的毁灭世界的想法给人的诱惑可能会演变成全世界人同归于尽的愿望。如果一个人能毁灭整个世界,他将不惜牺牲自己似乎毫无用处毫无意义的生命。预示世界末日的"死亡宗教"是泯灭生的愿望、令人无法热爱生命、肯定生命的真正元凶。

如今各国常规生活中的政治变革还有一个潜伏得更久的威胁:核威胁。1945年8月投到广岛的第一颗原子弹结束了第二次世界大战,随之全人类进入世界末期。末期指一个时代,在这个时代里人类社会有可能在任何一刻终结。大型核战争之后的"核冬天"无人能存活。长达四十多年的冷战期间,人类就处于这种严重核战争的边缘。确实,1990年"冷战"结束后,大型的原子战就不大可能了,我们处于相对和平中。然而大国包括一些较小的国家的弹药库里还储存着那么多原子弹和氢弹,可能导致人类的自歼自灭。"开枪的人,随即死亡"。四十多年来这是所谓的"肯定的共灭"。大多数人已经忘却了核威胁,直到去年奥巴马总统在布拉格重温旧梦——"没有原子弹的世界"并同俄罗斯展开新的裁军谈判。陡然间,我们中间的大多数人突然再次意识到笼罩着各国的乌云般的厄运。足以为奇的是,我们都觉得核威胁公然存在,正如美国心理学家所谓的"核麻木"。我们压抑住焦虑,努力不去想这威胁,生活着,仿佛危险并不存在,然而潜意识里危险正折磨着我们,摧残我们对生命的热爱。

与核威胁不同,气候变化不仅是一种威胁,并且已然成为四处可见的事实。这一点大家都能看到、感觉到,并且闻得到。

在我们当前全球经济体制下导致的环境破坏将无疑严重威胁 21 世纪人类的生存。除非我们能干预事物当今的发展模式,现代工业社会已经破坏了地球有机体的平衡并且正逐步导致全盘生态死亡。科学家已证明二氧化碳和甲烷的排放已经破坏了大气臭氧层,而由于化肥和各种灭虫剂的使用,土壤已经不再肥沃。种种迹象表明如今全球气候已经发生了变化,以至于我们正经历着越来越多的"自然"灾害,如干旱、洪灾,实际上这些灾害并非自然发生的,而是人为因素导致的。南北极的冰正在融化,科学家预测下一个世纪如汉堡这样的海滨城市、如孟加拉国的滨海地区以及很多南海岛屿即将被淹。地球上的一切生命都面临威胁。

生态危机首先是西方科学技术文明带来的危机。这是毫无疑问的。

但如果认为环境问题只是西方工业国家的问题,这是不对的。相反,生态灾难进一步加剧了第三世界现有的经济社会问题。英迪拉·甘地说得好,"贫穷意味着最严重的污染"。

我们明白这一切,但我们无所作为。我们知道要避免最坏的后果需要有所行动,而我们迟迟没采取行动。这样的无所作为可谓"生态麻木"。没有什么比无所作为更能加剧即将发生的灾难。

人类能否战胜自己主导的命运并存活下来,我们不得而知。如果能,也很好。因为如果我们知道我们不能存活下去,我们不会有什么作为;如果我们知道我们将存活下来,我们也不会有什么作为。只有当未来有两种开放的可能性,我们今天就会被迫为了未来的延续做必须要做的事情。因为我们不知道人类是否会延续,我们现今必须有所作为,似乎人类的未来就取决于我们的努力,同时我们怀有这样的信念:我们及我们的子孙后代会战胜困难并延续下去。

人类作为一种族群必须存在吗? 或者我们只是自然界的偶然现象?如今地球上已经有 60 亿人口,并且人口数量还将快速增长。地球也可能

没有人烟。人类出现的数百万年前,已经有了地球,也许人类消失后,地球还会存在数百万年。于是就有了最后一个最深层次的问题:

人类出现在地球纯属偶然,还是生命进化注定人类必然出现? 如果自然界显现出"强大的人择原理",我们在宇宙中也很自在(斯图亚特·考夫曼)。如果无法证实这一点,宇宙将无法为关于人类存在的问题给出答案。然而我们能怎样热爱生命并肯定人类? 如果人类不过是自然界的偶然现象,是如此多余,同宇宙没有任何关联,或许就是大自然的错误? 是否有如汉斯·约纳斯所谓的"活着的义务"吗? 有任何理由热爱生命并肯定人类吗? 如果我们找寻不到答案,每种生命文化没有确定的根本性东西,其基础是不牢靠的。

二、生命文化应是人类同自然界共生的文化

(一)我们能不顾原子弹的威胁照常生活吗? 我想我们的智慧会逐渐增长,但如何增长?

奥巴马总统梦想没有原子武器的世界,这是光荣的梦想,但只是梦想而已。现在人们已经能做的事情,未来人类不可能不会。但凡学过原子分裂方程式的人就绝不会忘记该方程式。自 1945 年广岛遭原子弹袭击以来,人类已经丧失了"原子无知"。

但原子终结期也是各国第一个共同时代,所有国家同舟共济。我们面临同样的威胁,每个人都有可能成为牺牲品。新形势下,人类必须把自己当做一起存活的主体。1946 年建立联合国算是迈出了第一步。国际安全伙伴关系将挽救和平,给予我们生的时间,或许某一天人类跨国组织联盟将能控制住核破坏。依凭科学我们掌握了控制自然的本领,利用智慧我们能驾驭自身的能力。公众与政治智慧的发展与科学的进步同等重要。

我们获得的第一个教训是:威慑不再能确保和平,只有公正才能维护国与国之间的和平。除了公正的行动及利益的和谐平衡之外,没有其他途径实现世界和平。和平并不意味着消除暴力,而是彰显公正。和平是一个

过程,而非财富。和平是在人类的社会和全球关系中减小暴力、构建公正的通常方法。

国家内部的和平实质是社会公正的问题。贫困的出路并非财富;贫困与财富的共同出路是共同体,而共同体的精神在于齐心协力、同舟共济。这正是世界所有宗教道德提倡的精髓所在。

(二)敬重生命

在人类社会和自然环境联系在一起的生命体系中,如果产生了自然衰竭的危机,那么整个生命体系的危机也将抬头。我们如今所谓的“生态危机”不只是我们的环境危机,也是我们整个生命体系的危机,处理这种危机,不能光靠技术手段,也要求我们生活方式有所改变,以及我们社会的主流价值观及信念有所变更。现代工业社会不像前现代的农耕社会那样,跟地球的周期和节奏已经不再和谐。现代社会已经嵌入人类各项目的进展扩张之中。我们将地球沦为“我们的环境”,破坏了其他生命的生活空间,导致每年都有成百上千的物种灭绝,没有比将自然界沦为人类环境更具破坏性的了。

我们不应继续现代社会对自然界的主宰,而应该“敬重生命”,如阿尔伯特·史威泽和《道德经》教导我们的那样。尊重每一种生命,敬重人类世界和自然界共同的生命,敬重所有生命的大团体。后现代的生物中心论将取代西方和现代的人类中心论。当然,我们不能回到宇宙导向的旧的前现代的农耕世界,但我们可以开始实施工业社会必要的生态转变。为此我认为我们必须改变时间观念:关于生产进展和垃圾处置的时间线性观念应让位于关于“可再生能源”及“循环经济”的时间循环观念。只有生命的轮回才能为我们进步的世界赋予稳定性。然而,循环经济依然只是穷人们的经济。

1992 联合国组织地球宪章指出了这一方向:

“人类是自然界的一部分

每种生命都是独一无二的,值得敬重

不论对人类而言有多大价值”

我们是“自然界”的一部分,只有保持自然界的完整,才能生存。

(三)危机中对生命的热爱

人不仅是自然界的馈赠,同时人也承担着做人的任务。恐惧时刻接受人性的任务需要强烈的生活勇气。必须昂然反抗恐惧和威胁肯定生命。简言之:必须活着,被热爱的生命、人类世界和自然界共同的生命相对于全球覆灭的威胁威力更大。我认为有三方面的因素筑成生的勇气:

其一,必须肯定人的生命,因为人们也可以否定生命。我们都知道,孩子只能在充满信任的氛围中成长。在拒斥的氛围中孩子在心灵上身体上都会萎靡不振。只有当孩子被他人接受时他才能接受自己。对孩子而言如此,对人一辈子而言也是这样:当我们被认可、被欣赏、被肯定时,我们才有生活的动力;而一旦我们处于遭轻蔑排斥的敌对世界时,我们缩进自身的世界,对人防不胜防。我们需要有强大的生命肯定感以应对对生命的否定。每一次对生命的肯定都要强于对生命的否定,因为肯定能创造出新东西,而否定却不能。

其二,人的一生是参与和分享的一生。我们想人所想,就变得有了生机,我们同他人分享生活,我们就一直充满生机。只要我们对生活抱有兴趣,我们就有活力。也很容易找到反例:漠视导致无情。完全无情就是过无味的生活,躯壳死去之前,灵魂已经枯萎了。

其三,人活在追求快乐的过程中。从一降生人就在奋斗中并从中获取活力。自从美国独立宣言颁布以来,追求快乐就是一项基本人权。追求幸福不只是私人权利,也是公共的人权。我们所说的"好生活"或"有意义的生活"指的是在公众看来在一个良好和谐的社会充分发挥最佳潜力的生活,正如孔子所教育我们的一样。

当我们认真看待"追求幸福"时,如果我们遇到不幸的贫苦大众,我们会对他们的不幸感同身受。因为同情,我们进入了他们的生活,这样的同情是幸福追求的另一面。我们越有能力追求幸福,我们就越能承受悲痛,越富有怜悯之心。这就是人类生活的辩证法。

"然而哪里有危险,哪里就有拯救。"那么拯救如何生成?我一直在努力寻找着答案,解释是非之间如何可以相互包容,通过爱生命如何能够战胜死亡,致命的对立如何转化成具有创造性的差异或升级成更高形式的生命与共同体；或者正如杜维明先生所说的："当和谐意识到冲突与对立时，它会致力于将具有破坏性的矛盾转化成具有创造性的矛盾，从而使紧张的关系获得能量，形成一个更高层面的综合体。"

我想起荷尔德林在图宾根大学念书时结识的及后来一直的朋友、德国哲学家弗里德里希·黑格尔的名言：在1807年所著的《精神现象》中，关于辩证思考他写的第一句话是："精神的生活不是那种害怕死亡或者对劫难无动于衷的生活，而是忍受死亡并在死亡中坚守阵地。"

真正热心用心的生活是战胜恐惧和威胁的矛盾。每一真正的宗教精神都反映了即便有种种不安全因素仍然对生命、地球及未来大为肯定的一面。这可被称作辩证法的统一及生命大和谐。

莫尔特曼教授访谈录

访谈时间:2010 年 11 月 4 日

受访人:于尔根·莫尔特曼

访谈人:杨华明、洪亮、李林①

访谈背景:

于尔根·莫尔特曼(Jürgen Moltmann,1926～)是当代著名宗教哲学家,西方新教神学最重要的代表人物之一。莫尔特曼于 1926 年出生于汉堡,二战期间成为战俘,由此开始接触基督教并研习新教神学。1952 年莫尔特曼于哥廷根大学取得神学博士学位。其后相继任教于伍泊塔尔教会神学院、波恩大学、图宾根大学福音神学系,现为图宾根大学的荣休教授。1964 年,莫尔特曼的成名作《盼望神学》出版,使他在神学界赢得了世界级声誉,并正式开始了他的神学生涯。莫尔特曼神学著述颇丰,涉猎面广,影响度大。其代表作除《盼望神学》外,还有《被钉十字架的上帝》、《三位一体与上帝国》、《创造中的上帝》、《来临中的上帝》以及今年刚刚出版的《盼望伦理学》等,其中大部分已被译为中文。

2010 年 11 月,莫尔特曼教授来到北京,以特邀嘉宾身份参加本年度"北京论坛",其大会主旨报告题为《论时代危机中的生命文化》。"北京论

---

① 杨华明,哲学博士,中国社会科学院世界宗教研究所助理研究员,研究领域为当代西方基督教神学,著有《十字架上的盼望——莫尔特曼神学的辩证解读》(2010)。洪亮,德国图宾根大学博士候选人,师从莫尔特曼教授。李林,哲学博士,中国社会科学院世界宗教研究所助理研究员,研究领域为宗教学、伊斯兰教研究。

坛"会议召开前夕,应北京大学宗教文化研究院"虚云讲座"之邀,莫尔特曼教授于11月4日在北京大学英杰交流中心新闻发布厅做了一场精彩的演讲,题为《一种共同的大地的宗教——生态视野下的世界宗教》。当天下午,受北京大学宗教文化研究院院长张志刚教授委托,访谈人对莫尔特曼教授进行了一次深度学术访谈。年逾八旬的莫尔特曼教授依然精神矍铄、思维活跃,对访谈者提出的《盼望伦理学》的基本主旨、三一论在其神学中的地位、神秘主义与安息日理论、神学与辩证法的关系以及未来的研究计划等问题都做出睿智而极具启发性的回答。现将访谈的基本内容整理出来以飨读者。

问:您今年最新出版的《盼望伦理学》,据我们所知,其写作计划由来已久,在您出版《盼望神学》以后就已有此打算,现在完成这一著作,您觉得它与《盼望神学》的关系如何? 它是您盼望神学思想在伦理学意义上的运用吗? 它在您的整个神学体系中占据什么样的地位?

答:通过《盼望伦理学》的创作与付梓,我完成了一个自1964年出版《盼望神学》以来的一个学术圆圈。我搜集整理了我思想中的伦理观,包括医学伦理、生态伦理以及政治伦理等方面的伦理资源,我将我在这些方面的观点整合在一起,并将其置于盼望神学的整体架构之下。事实上,在20世纪80年代末的时候,我就有写作、出版《盼望伦理学》之意,但是由于当时我有一些其他的神学思想不断涌出,所以就推迟了《盼望伦理学》的写作计划。现在,我到了生命的"终末"阶段,就重回到我的这一观点。在我的《盼望神学》中,基本的观点是上帝对世界未来的应许,书中认为,就上帝的神圣应许及其带给世界的盼望而言,未来已经来到当下;而在《盼望伦理学》中,对未来的"期盼"(anticipation)是其主旨所在,我们期盼在既有的可能性上,未来已经在当下,我们期望有一个充满正义与财富的崭新大地,我们期盼,在地上的正义是与当今呼声甚高的生态伦理相照应的正义。故而,在我的《盼望伦理学》中的关键词是"期盼",这种伦理学不是世俗意义上的"责任",而是要改变世界现有的状况。如此,我们便可以期盼我们一直以来所希望的那个未来得以实现。

问:感谢您关于《盼望伦理学》思想的介绍,我们可以得出这样的结论:《盼望伦理学》中的"期盼"概念是一个与您在半个世纪以前《盼望神学》中提出的核心概念"盼望"相平行、相对应的一个概念,前者更强调人的主体回应性与积极行动性,而后者更强调自上帝发出的神圣应许。在这里,我想接着这一点继续就《盼望伦理学》向您提出一个问题。我认为,在您的神学中,除了强调未来与盼望的终末论思想以外,还有一个最值得我们关注的思想,就是您极具辩证特色的"三一论"思想。您不仅强调传统上彰显三一上帝内在三位格相互认同(identity)的"内在三一"与彰显三一上帝参与世界、与世界相关联(relevance)的"经世三一",而且强调人的社会存在乃以上帝的三一存在为基本模型的"社会三一",一方面是上帝神圣位格的自我揭示,一方面是人对上帝启示的积极回应,这刚好分别体现在《盼望神学》中彰显上帝神圣应许之维的"盼望"概念与《盼望伦理学》中彰显人的积极回应主体之维的"期盼"概念。那么,您是如何将这种辩证的三一论思想融入您的《盼望伦理学》之中的呢?

答:我们在《旧约》中可以看到上帝与世界之间的分野,世界并非神圣的,而是上帝的造物。如果我们用三一论的语言来描述这一过程就是:上帝父通过逻各斯子,在圣灵的大能下创造着世界 ①,这是一个在圣灵之中绵绵不断的创造过程,因此,上帝在这里不仅是超越的上帝,亦同时是内在的上帝。上帝的内在性在于赐予生命之灵的在场。我们所说的"创造"这个词汇在理解上时有偏颇,因为在我们提到"创造"时,总是脱离了"创造"这一具体行为的一个抽象概念,是脱离了"这一"行为的行为,只是就行为所产生的结果而言来理解的"创造"概念,总会认为这是已经结束了的事情。但我们忘了,我们并非生活于一个已然完成了的世界,而不如这样说:我们乃生活于一个尚未完成的世界,这是一个持续不断的创造进程。如果我们从末尾而不是从开始去读《圣经》,我们就会看到,真正的创造尚未在我们当下,真正的创造乃在我们的未来,不是我们来自哪里,而是我们要去哪里,这对于一种盼望伦理学而言是至关重要的。我们生活于其中的这个创造团体,以及其他与我们共生的一切造物,都处于富有创造性、赐予生命的圣灵那永无止息的创造过程当中。

---

① 莫尔特曼教授在这里用了进行时态而非过去时态,向听者展示出一幅上帝创造世界生生不息的活泼画面。

问:在您的神学思想中,您除了强调神学应有的"实践意义"之外,还强调了"荣耀神学"的意义,譬如在您的《神学与喜乐》以及《游戏神学》等作品中所包含的人与上帝共契的思想以及安息日的理论,那么,这中间是不是具有神秘主义色彩呢?

答:是的,我也希望是这样。犹太教与基督教这两大宗教中的神秘主义,不单单讲灵魂的一种内在融合,而是对安息日的庆贺,为大地的缘故而庆贺安息年的到来。在安息日,我们同安息的上帝一道休息,这中间,我们不再为各种劳作的辛苦所牵制,而是作为上帝的造物,享受万物的美好,享受我们肉身的美妙,这就是犹太教与基督教两大神秘主义传统的重点所在。我们可以想一想托马斯·莫顿这类神秘主义思想家,他提到"七重山",说人的心灵从内部一重一重地向上升华,到了第七重就是人的灵魂与上帝之间那神秘的婚姻。为什么是"七"这个数字呢? 就是因为安息日是第七日,这一天是向另一个世界的转变。如果我们每个礼拜都庆贺安息日的到来,我们就很自然的过上了一种神秘主义的生活,我们并不需要某种刻意的冥想,而仅仅是停下手中的工作,休息下来,庆贺主的安息日,欣赏我们身边作为上帝造物的世界,欣赏世界的美妙。在犹太教神秘主义看来,在每一个安息日,犹太人家庭认为他们与圣灵之间会有一种神圣的婚姻。我很愿意返回到这种原初形态的神秘主义状态,进入这个神秘的日子,时间与永恒在此相遇。

问:您知道,汉语学界新近出版的《十字架上的盼望——莫尔特曼神学的辩证解读》①一书是从辩证法角度对您神学思想的一种理解,您对这种解读方式是怎么看的?

答:这有赖于你所理解的"辩证思维方式"究竟为何意。根据我们伟大的思想家黑格尔,他的辩证法思想是通过"正题-反题-合题"的三一模式展开的。比如"生命-死亡-克服死亡",这是耶稣生命个体所度过的基本历程,这和辩证法的原初涵义相符。在基督教神学领域内,耶稣的生命与十字架在他的复活中实现了统一,我很喜欢这种辩证思维的模式,因为世

---

① 《十字架上的盼望——莫尔特曼神学的辩证解读》,杨华明著,社会科学文献出版社 2010 年版。

界并非处于某种稳定平静的和谐当中,而是在一种变动不居的辩证过程中,就如同你们中国哲学中所说的"阴""阳",这和我们所说的"正－反－合"相契合。辩证思维将僵化死板的矛盾对立转变为具有创造性的、活生生的矛盾关系。矛盾不应是简单平面的僵化对立关系,而应是包含丰富的生命感与创造性的。

问:我想就《十字架上的盼望》一书中的辩证法问题向您求教。您在很多著作与演讲中都曾提到《道德经》及其包含的辩证法思想。《十字架上的盼望》一书第三章《神圣辩证法》刚好也借用了"道生一,一生二,二生三,三生万物"的语言概括了您神学思想中的内在辩证逻辑,具体来说,即以"道生一"表达您强调一神论的启示观,以"一生二"表达您强调"十字架与复活"、"父与子"、"神性与人性"等基督教神学思想各个层面的二元辩证张力,以"二生三"表达您在系列神学著作中都深刻包含的"三一论"思想,而"三生万物"则更是恰如其分地彰显了您那独具特色的"万有在神论"与生态神学思想。我认为,您神学体系中包含的内在辩证逻辑的确与老子的观点有异曲同工之妙。

答:是的。我在《易经》、《道德经》中都看到了这种关于"道"的论述,其中的辩证法思想和我们的辩证法确有相似之处,不过我要说明的是,两种文化中的辩证思想还是有很大不同的。"道"的思维模式是圆圈循环式的,是"阴"与"阳"之间的轮回转换,不过在这里面没有"终末"的思想,因此也就不会有新的质素产生,万物都已然存在,处于一种动态运行的和谐状态中。而基督教的辩证思维模式中强调"盼望"、"未来"、"新"、"潜力"等质素,这些在"道"的思想中好像没有体现。

问:谢谢您对这两种辩证思维方式的比较,能让我们对自己传统文化中的辩证资源做进一步的反思。还想提一个问题,您觉得在当代基督教神学领域,除您以外,还有哪些神学家和思想家需要我们汉语基督教研究学界给予更多的关注与研究?

答:太多了。比如图宾根的汉斯·昆,英国的理查德·鲍克哈姆、阿兰·托伦斯、麦格拉夫等等,美国的大卫·特雷西、哈维·考克斯,他们的思想都各具千秋,他们在神学领域中取得的成就也不分伯仲,都值得深入研究。

问:您觉得在神学研究在未来的发展中可以有哪些方面的突破?

答:我认为,我们应该在宇宙基督论的意义上发展基督论思想,应该认识到基督不仅是要和人类和解,而且要与世界中的破坏性力量达成和解,这些思想在《新约》中的《歌罗西书》与《以弗所书》①中都有体现,这些思想对于未来的研究应该是非常重要的。如果要我的夫人伊丽莎白 ②来回答,那她肯定会说:"发展出一种中国的女性主义神学才是当务之急。"(笑)

问:在您的诸多作品中,您自己最为心仪的是哪一部呢?

答:这个问题要我回答,通常我会说最后的就是最好的。不过非要我选择的话,应该算是我的《三位一体与上帝国》以及《创造中的上帝》,还有《盼望神学》,那是在一种热情洋溢的情绪下创作出来的,而《被钉十字架的上帝》则是我的倾情之作。

问:最后想问您一个问题,您在未来的研究计划是什么?

答:我想我到了该休息的年龄了,该享受我的安息日了(笑),休息,进入那种神秘主义状态,进入永恒与时间的统一之中。不过,我在《盼望伦理学》中遗留了一章内容没有完成,这就是我还在继续写作的"经济伦理学"的内容。由于我们关于经济有一种"线性"的理解模式:生产出更多的产品,消费更多的产品。然而,我们却往往遗忘了"第三方"的存在,高生产、高消费制造的垃圾废品的数量也相应在增长,这就要求我们发展出一种循环经济模式。这是因为石油、金属等资源是有限的,由这些资源制造出来的产品往往一旦用过就被人当作废品弃之一边。比如说你的手机,是不是

---

① 参阅《歌罗西书》1:20－22:"既然藉着他在十字架上所流的血成就了和平,便藉着他叫万有,无论是地上的、天上的,都与自己和好了。你们从前与神隔绝,因着恶行,心里与他为敌。但如今他藉着基督的肉身受死,叫你们与自己和好,都成了圣洁,没有瑕疵,无可责备,把你们引到自己面前。"《以弗所书》2:14－18:"因他使我们和睦(原文作'因他是我们的和睦'),将两下合而为一,拆毁了中间隔断的墙,而且以自己的身体废掉冤仇,就是那记在律法上的规条,为要将两下藉着自己造成一个新人,如此便成就了和睦。既在十字架上灭了冤仇,便藉这十字架使两下归为一体,与神和好了,并且来传和平的福音给你们远处的人,也给那近处的人。因为我们两下藉着他被一个圣灵所感,得以进到父面前。"

② 莫尔特曼教授的夫人伊丽莎白·温德尔·莫尔特曼(Elisabeth Wendel Moltmann)是当代著名女性主义神学家,其著作《耶稣身边的妇女们》(The Women Around Jesus),《那一片流着奶与蜜之地:女性主义神学景观》(A Land Flowing with Milk and Honey)以及《吾即吾肉身》(I am My Body)等,都是当代女性主义神学界代表性著作。

每年都会换一部新的,那怎么处理旧手机呢?是当垃圾扔掉,还是回收利用?在我看来,未来的经济一定是循环经济成为主流。但是,就目前看来,循环经济却仅成为穷人的专利,只有那些人从事垃圾回收的工作,这是不足够的。我想,循环经济在未来一定会成为主流的经济模式。还有一个就是"共享之物"的问题,光、水、空气、土地,甚至还有知识,是所有人赖以生存的基础,也必须是所有人都可以免费享有的资源。

(杨华明　整理)

天·人·地

——杜维明教授与莫尔特曼教授对谈纪要

时间:2010 年 11 月 6 日

地点:北京大学百周年纪念讲堂

　　世界文明之间存在差异,但差异与冲突并非同义词。如何适切理解并表述文明差异,而不是退缩进"文明秩序的冲突",这不仅对深刻影响了现代世界格局的欧美基督教文明而言无可回避,也构成了处于"传统"与"世界"之间的现代中国更加准确的自我定位的基础。在此意义上,"文明对话"是学习恰当表述文明差异的练习。2010 年 11 月 6 日,德国新教神学家于尔根·莫尔特曼与中国当代新儒家杜维明在北京论坛(2010)上,围绕"天"、"人"、"地"这三个概念进行了一次对谈,两位学者各自所代表的传统似乎决定了此次对谈只能成为双方"自我表述"的一次交锋,但杜维明在对谈中对宗教问题的一再强调、莫尔特曼对《道德经》与基督教旧约传统的频繁引述却表明:文明之间能够达致一种"差异中的理解",特定文明的"自我表述"与其对"他者"的表述,以及"他者"的"自我表述"相辅相成。

一、天:创造与记忆

　　"天"是什么?杜维明认为,基督教传统区分创造者与受造物、天国与尘世,这种二元论思维对于儒家而言是陌生的。儒家把天视为一种创生性与关系性的力量,但没有像基督教传统那样把这种力量人格化,并进而强调天的全能与无所不在;相反,天并非全能,它要通过人的作为才能得到展现。

莫尔特曼指出,天在犹太﹣基督教传统中也可以看作是一种关系性的创生力量,这表现于"在天上的父"对其受造物的持续回应之中,但差异在于,这种关系性最终要落实在一个指向未来的终末论语境之中,即"天国"要"行在地上"。传统创造论把《创世记》的"起初"误认为是历史意义上的过去,没有认识到圣经创世思想的将来向度:新天新地。真正的创造是上帝在将来的创造,人类和宇宙还处于通向这个全新创造的过程之中。进化论的意义在于,它表明了进化过程中的动植物与人处于同一个创造团契之中,对于达尔文而言,通过"物竞天择"来理解人并非意味着要剥夺其同情与怜悯的能力,因而"社会达尔文主义"对人类"生存竞争"的片面强调实质上是对达尔文的误解;进化论的缺陷在于,它的决定论思维难以充分容纳"新"(novum)这个范畴。

杜维明认为,在中国古代思想传统中,人并不只是宇宙的观察者,他也能够通过自己的活动来影响整个宇宙的运化。人类与宇宙的协和要以对宇宙的尊重为前提,大禹通过"疏导"而治水成功就是一个例子,人类的确具有应对处境的惊人力量,但对这种力量的盲目自信则会导致人类与宇宙关系的失衡,"愚公移山"之"愚"恰恰体现于此。莫尔特曼认为,天与地的差异在死亡现象中得到了最为清晰的体现,后代对死者的记忆以及由此而生发的代际连续性在东亚思想中异常重要,这实际上与基督教的旧约传统比较相似。杜维明指出,从"未知生,焉知死"这句话推论出儒家只关注"生",这是错误的;相反,儒家十分重视死亡以及对死者的记忆,这种记忆不仅塑造了代际之间的连续性,也使儒家传统对于"身体"的理解获得了生物学范畴之外的历史性以及宇宙性维度。莫尔特曼认为,基督教传统的特殊性在于,它既强调上帝对受造物的记忆,又强调受造物对上帝所应许的未来之拯救的记忆。

二、人权:平等抑或责任?

何者为"人"? 杜维明认为,儒家传统对人的理解包含两个侧面:一方面,人虽因其人伦道德而卓绝特出于世间万物,但又与世间万物共同仰赖"气"这一"生物性能量"。阿西西的圣方济各(François d' Assise)在《太阳兄弟颂》(Canticum Fratris Solis)中称太阳为兄弟,把整个受造自然当作是人的亲族,这与《张子正蒙·乾称篇》里的著名说法十分相似:"乾称父,坤成母;予兹藐焉,乃混然中处。故天地之塞,吾其体;天地之帅,吾其性。民,吾同胞;物,吾与也。"另一方面,儒家又强调"天命之谓性",即人的本性来源于"天"这一"创造性力量"对人的肯定。与日本神道教传统的理解相似,产生于上个世纪的盖亚假设(gaia hypothesis)也把地球视为一个活的生命体,人只是其中的一个组成部分。今天,对人尤其是人权问题的思考除了要面对世界的世俗化,还应顾及到人与地球这个生命体的互动,人的奥秘发源于此。

莫尔特曼认为,人权不应被还原为一个世俗化问题,"人"这个词汇在各大文明传统中出现的那一刻也就意味着人权的诞生,某些语系没有"人"这个普遍概念,而只有"我们"、"他们"、"朋友"以及"敌人"这些用来指称"人"的词汇,但这并不意味着人权在由它们所中介的交流中是缺席的。美国《独立宣言》开创了从人格尊严的角度来理解人权的传统,《联合国宪章》则强调了人类是自然的一个组成部分,"自然"的权利的确也应该被整合到人权概念之中,德国的《动物保护法》把动物界定为与人类平等的受造物(Mitgeschöpf)就体现了这个思想。不过,自然不应该被美化为天堂,自然中存在很多可能导致混乱与毁灭的力量,因此《新约》强调,要与上帝和解的绝不仅仅是人类,还有整个宇宙。

杜维明认为,联合国在 1948 年通过的《世界人权宣言》强调了人权的普遍性,其思想基础是人作为个体的尊严,但这一思想其实是世界"去魅"时代的产物;另一方面,人权概念还需要补充一个责任维度,权利与责任向来不可分割,因此仅仅尊重无家可归者流浪的权利是不够的,我们对他还负有扶助之责。"富则兼济天下"意味着,一个人能力越大就越负有造福大众的责任。问题的关键在于,人权概念所包含的人格尊严问题如何获得一个责任维度。

莫尔特曼认为,人权概念已然蕴含了责任维度,追问"富人"和"有能力者"的社会责任及与此相关的"人格尊严"问题不无意义,但人权这一观念的核心是平等,它首要关注的是平等在最基本的经济生活层面的落实:每一个人都有权利使用自然资源、享有安全、工作并获取报酬。杜维明回应道,与平等这一观念形成对照的是这个世界在事实上的不平等:欧美发达国家的失业者所领取的救济金已经远远高于其他一些国家非失业者的工资收入,按照欧美发达国家的标准去落实所谓的平等将会耗尽地球的资源,而其他发展中国家和穷国则根本无缘于这种"平等"。莫尔特曼认为,这个问题需要通过资源共享得到解决,失业和无家可归是社会的恶,社会主义的观念基础就是资源共享,中国不应丢弃这个观念。

杜维明认为,在儒家传统中,人被理解为一种关系性的存在,人最基本的经验是溪流般的联结与交流,而非孤岛式的封闭个体(individuality),在此意义上,人是其各种关系和经验的中心,他的人格及其尊严来源于这个中心的持续生成。"交互性"(mutuality)是儒家伦理的基础,它不仅体现为"己所不欲,勿施于人"恕道,还体现为"己欲立而立人,己欲达而达人"仁道。莫尔特曼认为,"己所不欲,勿施于人"是一种带有普遍性的"金规则",不为儒家所独有,以这种形态体现出的"交互性"包含着一种以平等为基础的关系循环:与友为友,与敌为敌,它可以支持个体间的相互尊重,但在仇恨充斥的环境里却难以发挥作用。与这个"金规则"相比,基督教伦理则更进一步:要爱你的仇敌,克服仇恨本身,因为人对其仇敌负有责任,这可以说是基督教意义上的"责任伦理"(ethics of responsibility),与此相关,基督教伦理强调以善胜恶,而非以恶抗恶。杜维明认为,"己所不欲,勿施于人"这个"金规则"还需要"己欲立而立人,己欲达而达人"这一"人性原则"(principal of humanity)的补充,儒家传统对个人行为的规范以"仁"为纲,但并不强求超克私己的"博爱",因此报德之"德"与报怨之"直"是有差异的。莫尔特曼认为,儒家传统中的"仁"不仅关涉个人,同样也包含政治维度。今天的世界政治仍旧被一种"敌友"思维所控制,通过反对共同的敌人来达致团结,这种早已过时的二元论思维损害了国际政治,我们需要以一种新的整体性思维来面对世界融合的问题,"仁道"值得深思。

杜维明认为,如何重新去理解"人",这是当前各大文明传统都无法回避的。如何有效地回应这个问题,这取决于我们在以下两个方面能否有所作为:首先,重新理解人与地球的关系;其次,各大文明传统之间要有更深入的交流。通过给出不同的语言/意义体系,宗教深刻塑造了各大文明传统。但是,人本身要先于他的宗派归属,成为某一宗教的信徒是人成为人之后的选择,我们需要以这个新的理解为基础,寻找到一种可以跨越文明与宗派差异的全球化时代的语言,为更加开放的文明交流提供基础。

三、危机中的大地

我们应该如何来理解"地"? 莫尔特曼认为,他对"大地"问题的兴趣来源于《道德经》的激发,当然,今天的生态问题也在迫使我们要重新认识"大地"。杜维明指出,儒家传统对"地"的理解和《道德经》差异很大,但两者所提供思想资源在今天的生态危机中都值得认真对待。与《道德经》的返璞思维相比,欧洲的启蒙运动在人与自然之间塑造了一种新关系:自然要成为人类控制的对象。《旧约》的创世观念为这种启蒙思维提供了基础,因为人作为"神的形象"(imago dei)要成为自然的统治者。

莫尔特曼指出,"神的形象"在古代近东,比如美索不达米亚地区只能用来指称统治者,而《创世记》第一个创世报道把"神的形象"运用于上帝所创造出的一切男人和女人身上,这是对古代近东"统治者"观念的颠覆,或者说"民主化"。单纯从自然的角度来看,启蒙运动造成了人对自然的控制,但从人的角度来看,启蒙的诉求还包括人从自然中的解放这一维度,人无法脱离一定的居住与医疗条件完全"自然地"生活,我们今天仍旧处于从自然中获得独立的过程之中,但遗憾的是,"神的形象"这一观念在欧洲的殖民统治中被滥用,不仅自然环境,甚至亚非拉各民族都成了欧洲人控制和剥夺的对象。"神的形象"不应该只属于人,而应该被扩展到上帝创造的一切"活物"身上,人和它们同属一个整体。阿西西的圣方济各体现的是对自然的倾听,人类应该学习这种倾听的耐心,以回报自然对我们的耐心。

莫尔特曼认为,盖亚假设不无道理,但关于这个理论的争议点在于,地球可以被视为生命体吗?生命的特征是不断生产出其自身,但地球却在不断生产出"他者",如动植物和人,在此意义上,地球似乎只能称为有机体,但她又不是简单的有机体。总之,地球的确是独一无二、无与伦比的,我们要尊重她。《道德经》第五十二章曰:"天下有始,以为天下母,既得其母,以知其子",其意义就在于:我们要在重新认识大地的过程中,重新认识我们自己。

(北京大学高等人文研究院　整理)

Theory and Practice of Global Governance: Topical Issues

Alexander N. Chumakov

The main contradiction of modernity is that under the influence of globalization processes the world community, in fact, becomes more and more, according to all the parameters of social life, a single holistic system. At the same time, there are no governance mechanisms adequate to this holism. Moreover, global governance, which cannot emerge spontaneously, is not being built intentionally and theoretical discussions about it are rather rare today, not being in the center of everyone's attention as they deserve to be. Besides, governance in general and global governance in particular, unlike regulation, cannot emerge spontaneously. This issue is to be discussed below; now I would like to make some points about why it happens.

First, we talk about a principally new, unprecedented situation related to governing an extremely complicated and huge socio-natural system, which human beings never encountered in their history. This situation is exacerbated by the fact that experience accumulated by the humankind and the certified approaches to resolving complex problems are not valid any more. At the same time, no new approaches have been worked out.

Second, the world community, in spite of the increasing interdependence of different countries and peoples, still remains fragmented, divided into autonomous and self-defining structures, which function in accordance to their own laws targeting, first of all, their private profits and interests. These are nation-states, multinational corporations, and confessional systems, such as Christianity, Islam, Buddhism, etc.

And third, globalization itself and its numerous consequences remain a subject of serious discussions. Such discussions often conceal the main thing: globalization is, first of all, an objective historical process and not a project specially designed by someone, or someone's insidious plan and intention.

This should be emphasized because if rethinking globalization processes and their circumstances we would focus on subjectivity and pay attention, first of all, to who benefits from it and who behaves in which way, than we would start searching perpetrators and discussing globalization scenarios. In this case one faces inability to distinguish between the objective, natural course of events of social development and the subjective human activity. The former, of course, is the basis of such a development but it is not sufficient to provide governing complex systems without adequate structures and mechanisms. Thinking globally, one can not help recognizing the state of affairs: there are no structures and mechanisms of government adequate to the holistic global world. That is why, in my opinion, it is not productive to look for perpetrators or those responsible for globalizations. Moreover, such approach engenders illusions and is dangerous because it complicates the business and distracts from real solutions for the topical problems.

In case of understanding globalization first of all as an objective historical process (this is my position), one should look for means of resolving globalization-engendered problems (including governing social systems) in the sphere of structural changes of world society. This approach is based on a proposition that complex systems, or, at least, biosystems (human being is a part of them) in their development are regulated naturally, basing on natural laws. Here one can talk about self-regulation of complex systems. Apart from that, social systems are also governed, because an active element plays an important role in their development. This active element is a human being who, limited by hisher capabilities, consciously influences various parameters of development. It is evident that planetary-scale social system, being formed now, should also be not just self-regulated but also governed.

It is important to distinguish between *regulation* and *government*, because they are not the same. Government is a higher type of regulation, as well as *development* is a higher form of *movement*. That is why there can be no development without movement while we can commonly see movement without development. Similarly, governance presupposes regulation, while regulation can take place (occur) without governance.

Thus, via *regulation* (as well as self-regulation) one can solve the task of the most optimal functioning of a system, creating the most favorable conditions for interaction of different components of this system. Regulation is aimed at concerted actions of various part of a whole and can be done consciously (when a human being plays the regulative role), or spontaneously (when we talk about self-regulating systems). For example, the biosphere as a whole is a self-regulating system, whose balanced development is supported by the law of struggle for survival.

Unlike regulation, *governance* is always done with purpose and presupposes achieving a concrete result. Thus, general governance and global governance in particular can not emerge spontaneously or naturally. It only can take place in a society and can only be built consciously, purposefully and following certain logic, which provides specific parameters of such a governance. Here, unlike in the case of regulation, one always can find an active source – *subject of governance*, setting some goals and providing their achievement.

In this context we can talk about historical dynamics of development of social relations. For example, primitive people in the period of savagery and, at the large extent, in the period of barbarity, relations were regulated by force and survival of the strongest. As for governing social relations in the full sense, it emerges later, together with settled way of life, labor division, formation of a state and, finally, formation of the first civilizations. Such governance is already based on realization of certain interests and purposefulness. It does not replace natural regulation, but rather is supplementary to it, making social development more predictable and less contentious. This is how all social systems evolves, of which nation-states have become the largest and the most well-built.

From the mid-20th century the situation has principally changed, because due to globalization process the whole of humankind becomes a holistic system. It more and more looks like a single holistic organism basing on the central parameters of social life (economic, political, informational, etc.), on its interaction with natural environment, on exploring world ocean, outer space, etc. In other words, the anarchy of international relations has been gradually put in order.

So, "during the last two centuries there has emerged increasing number of less or more implicit principles that regulate the establishment of nation-states and their behavior within the framework of the global state system. This very system has spread all over the land surface of the world. Even uninhabited Antarctica was provisionally parceled among seven nation-states. Moreover, the U. N. Convention on the Law and the Sea (1982) allows each coastal nation state to exercise full sovereignty over a territorial sea up to 12 nautical miles and limited jurisdiction in an exclusive economic zone up to 200 nautical miles. The development of the unclaimed sea bed is to be regulated by an international organization" [1].

From this viewpoint, it is evident that humankind has reached a frontline, behind which spontaneous regulation of social relations can not last any longer. It should be supplemented with conscious and purposeful building of systemic governance, because the world of global relations without effective global governance would encounter serious testing.

Nowadays our world is like a tallship, which has so far no steering wheel, but is already being brought by wind from a relatively safe haven to the open see. Its crew, stuck in conflicts and making no efforts to provide governing the ship, inevitably becomes hostage of circumstances and natural elements. The world community, having entered the era of global interdependence, should acknowledge the danger of uncontrolledness of the modern world and to start acting in concord and with purpose. If not, this state of affairs promises nothing good for it. Without effective governance, the world community will only slide more and more into the abyss of increasing conflicts and contradictions.

Thus, the modern humankind simply has no alternative to global governance, which should be built at any price and as soon as

---

① Kamusella T. Global State System // Global Studies Encyclopedia. Ed. by Alexander N. Chumakov, William C. Gay, Ivan I. Mazour. - Moscow: Raduga Publishers, 2003, p. 199.

possible. But to solve this task, it is needed to answer several principal questions:

-How global governance is generally possible and what is the logic of this governance?

-Which are the main tasks of global governance?

-Which prepositions for building global governance we already have?

-What kind of international organizations and bodies corresponds (or will be able to correspond after some degree of reform) with the essence and principles of global governance?

-Which obstacles can be found in the way towards building global governance?

-Which principal decisions and at which level should be made as the first and the next steps in achieving the goals set?

-Who can and should take responsibility for building global governance?

-Finally, what is the price and who should pay it?

So, *how global governance is generally possible*?

In the decision of this problem we already have the certain theoretical and practical results. Theoretically this problem was seriously investigated by I. Kant, V. Solovyov, N. Berdyaev, K. Jaspers and others [1].

If we shall address to practice we shall see, that the world community has accumulated, during its history, a significant experience of governing large social systems – states, empires, kingdoms, confederations, unions, blocs, etc. **State** has proven in

---

① Kant I. , *Zum ewigen Frieden: ein philosophischer Entwurf* [On eternal peace: a philosophical essay], p. 75, Königsberg, Nicolovius, 1795. ; Jaspers K. Vom Ursprung und Ziel der Geschichte. Zurich. 1949: Berdyaev N. *Towards a New Epoch* (1949); Solovyov V. *Lectures on Divine Humanity*, ed. by Boris Jakim, Lindisfarne Press, 1995. http://www. utm. edu/research/iep/s/solovyov. htm

practice to be the most wide-spread and vivid form for organizing social life. **Morality** and **law** are the central instruments of social governance, through which one can provide the strongest influence on social consciousness and human behavior. We should also emphasize *ideology*, *politics*, *economy*, *finance*, *culture*, etc., through which social systems are also directly or indirectly governed. But morality and law, with no doubt, dominate these factors, because they literally penetrate and fasten together all the other spheres of social life, being, by this or that way, subdued to moral and legal norms and laws. Today, when globalization makes the whole world community a holistic system, governing this system becomes a demand of the time and it should be built taking into consideration the whole experience accumulated by humankind in this sphere.

It is also evident that global governance should be based on the historically tested principle of separation of *legislative*, *executive and judiciary* powers.

In this regard one can and should talk about the *World Parliament*, *World Government and World Law*. To see them realized, as well as to build an effective planetary system of governance, we should create adequate conditions, of which the most important are:

Universally meaning moral foundations, i. e. we should form universal values and universal morality for the planet. They should not replace, but enforce and amplify morality and values of different peoples. It seems that the Universal declaration of human rights, equating all people in their right to life, freedom and property, should be the starting point for the formation of such a morality.

A single legal system is another necessary condition for global governance, together with a planetary system of adaptation and implementation of legal norms universal for all countries and peoples. We should emphasize, that we talk not about international law, being already well-developed at the level of interstate and regional relations, but about global law, which would be really universal. Such a law does not presuppose abolishment of legal systems of separate states or regional structures, of international legal acts and institutions. It is important, but, that the former should be brought with correspondence with the latter and should not contradict them.

Global governance also means *providing cooperative security* and uniting efforts in maintaining it through various forms of cooperation. First of all, we talk about *economic cooperation*, which already successfully evolves in the modern world in the form of multinational corporations, consortiums, joint ventures, etc. World trade has already made all peoples of the planet involved into the single market of labor, goods and services.

Planetary *political cooperation* is the next needful condition for global governance. It should provide resolution of conflicts and peaceful coexistence through compromising and resolving disputes taking into consideration the maximum of interests of different parts. Global political cooperation, unlike economic one, still is to be built, because in this sphere relations are built so far on absolute priority of national and corporative interests.

Military cooperation, existing nowadays at the regional level and meeting the defence tasks of separate countries and peoples (i. e., protecting them from external threats), should be replaced by police forces providing law and order, protection from criminal activities.

The last world financial crisis has shown once again that *coordinated planetary financial policy* is a necessary condition for global governance. It is evident, that it is hard and even impossible to implement coordinated financial policy without a single currency.

Religious tolerance is necessary as the most important condition for peaceful coexistence and constructive interaction of different people, independent on their religious beliefs or non-beliefs.

Scientific and technological cooperation, as well as cooperation in the sphere of health and education presuppose building conditions for a balanced cultural and social development of various continents and regions of the planet.

Common (world) language for international communication is needed to support conversation in various spheres of social life and to develop intercultural interaction. As known Korean philosopher Yersu Kim marks: "A culture can be compared, within limits, with a language. A culture, like a language, is a system of symbolic meanings that serve the common needs of its members" [1].

Of course, we have not listed all conditions needed for building a system of global governance. But these are the most important ones, without which the rest will have not sense.

Now let us talk about *the central tasks for global governance to resolve.* First of all, it should provide adaptation and implementation of universally coordinated decisions allowing to regulate social relations in the main spheres of social life purposefully and effectively. This means, of course, providing sustainable and balanced world socio-economic development and financial regulation, resolving the issues of health, education, environment and nature management, fighting international crime, preventing armed conflicts, etc.

Do we now have premises for the formation of global governance? It seems to me that we can definitely answer "yes". First of all, it is related to the sphere of social consciousness being globalized more and more.

---

[1] Yersu Kim. An Idea of University in an Age of Diversity and Transformation // Papers of the 2007 World Philosophy Day / Edited by Ioanna Kucuradi. Philosophical Society of Turkey, Ankara, 2009, p. 191.

In fact, we have to deal now with a world outlook, which was born in the Antique time and is called "cosmopolitanism". But there is a huge difference between the past and the present in this regard. In the ancient times, starting from cynics, who were the first ones to proclaimed themselves citizens of the world, and up to the middle of the 20th century, cosmopolitan ideas remained a domain of a very insignificant part of broad-minded people. Absolute majority of the population considered such ideas, at best, ironically. Now the global vision of the world and feeling of belonging to the whole humankind becomes more and more a mass phenomenon.

Here it is important to note, that global it is not necessary to oppose local. As the Japanese philosopher Naoshi Yamawaki has properly told: " The global and local viewpoints are seen as interdependent, and particularity and universality (or transversality) is regarded as inseparable ··· The cosmopolitan Self understands himself or herself as a member of the Earth, i. e. a cosmos in which all of humankind lives. Yet, it must be emphasized that this notion of cosmopolitan Self must be combined with other dimensions of understanding of the Self that are characterized by cultural-historical differences or particularities. Each individual who holds each multidimensional Self has the responsibility for his or her past and must make efforts to understand others who live in different cultures" [1].

We can, thus, talk about the emergence of global consciousness at the planetary scale, based on common values and behavioral norms. For example, all people, independently on their status and residence, nationality, confession or race, behave, in principle, in

---

[1] Naoshi Yamawaki. The Idea of Glocal Public Philosophy and Cosmopolitanism // XXII World Congress of Philosophy. Rethinking Philosophy Today. July 30-August 5, 2008 Seoul National University, Seoul, Korea, p. 31.

the same way and follow common ethics and logic of conduct at an international airport, or aboard a plane, at a railway station, or in a carriage, at supermarkets, during sport contests, at world resorts, international exhibitions, festivals, conferences, and so on. There are no significant discussions here on such issues as good and evil, justice and injustice, what is "good" and what is "bad", decent or non-decent. Common wellbeing, security and respect to human dignity are perceived in such situation as indisputable values because of their evidence.

The above-said is, of course, a necessary condition for building the system of global governance, but not a sufficient one. Among the existing premises to implementation of global governance one can stress also a well-developed at a planetary scale transportation network allowing to move along the Earth within hours. It is possible not only for political and business elite, but for a significant part of the active population of the planet. We should also mention a single information zone, which emerged on the basis of modern telecommunication technologies, along with space communication and monitoring systems, modern mass media allowing each inhabitant of the planet to be (on-line) virtually at every spot of the Earth. This provides a possibility to make decisions quickly and to control their implementation on-line independently on distances. Without this, global governance is not possible.

A single language of communication is also important for global governance. By nowadays, the English language has become such a one due to several reasons we have no possibility to dwell on.

Now let us talk about basic *obstacles being in the way of building global governance*.

Absolute majority of modern states is functioning on the basis of principles, which had been formed when humankind remained fragmented and demonstrated no holism. Ruling elites of various actors of international relations, which have become an organic part of the existing network, continue thinking fragmentarily even now, in spite of changes demanding a systemic, global vision of the world. From these positions they produce and sustain unfounded fears regarding the loss, as a result of globalization, of original cultures of different people, of national identity, etc. Devoted to the position of independence and national sovereignty, conducting active policy of patriotism and nationalism they are not ready to share even insignificant part of their authorities with supra-national structures. But we talk about relatively significant authorities, which will have to be handed over to World Government and the other global governance structures.

First of all, we mean *security issues*. This presupposes gradual reforming and diminishing national armed forces with final integration of them into a single system with common command. Police structures, remaining locally and regionally based, will also require common planetary coordination.

Global law is another necessary element of global governance system. It is not equal to international law and is to be constructed in the future. While international law related to bi-and multilateral relations between international actors functions for a long time and is relatively effective, global law, which would embrace the whole planet, we have not yet managed to build. Even offensive crimes of Somalian pirates, harmful for many countries involved into ocean trade, have not forced international community to create a legal barrier to this outrage. This state of affairs is mainly caused by the absence of adequate world structures and necessary procedures, which would provide working out, adaptation and unequivocal implementation of legal norms obligatory for all countries and peoples.

This task in principle can not be resolved outside global governance system. But global governance is also not possible without legal support. Thus, the processes of building global law and global governance should be conducted simultaneously.

Socio-economic backwardness of a significant part of world community and a huge gap between excessive wealth and poverty at the planetary scale is another important obstacle in the way of building global governance. This task also can not be solved without mechanisms of coordination of global socio-economic development and planetary system of financial regulation.

Introduction of a *single currency* has become the demand of the time. It has been demonstrated by the last world financial crisis. Now dollar in a way plays the role of the world money, but it can not resolve the problem in principle, because of its being a national currency depending on decisions of one state – the US. World currency as a universal purchasing unit should be equally independent from various actors of international relations, of which states are the most important ones. It is evident that such currency, as well as *world language* as the means of intercultural and international communication, should be indispensible conditions for building an effective global governance.

Now let us discuss the issue of which *international organizations and structures correspond (or could correspond after some reforming) the essence and principles of global governance.*

Since modern states are sustainable and effective enough social systems, while modern political elites last for self-sufficiency and independence, the humankind is to fulfill a complicated and not so short passage to organized and governed world community. Thus, a *confederation of nation-states* can be, in the foreseeable future, the most optimal form for organizing social life for the purpose of global governance. It would provide reasonable balancing between global and national interests. Complicated but generally positive experience of the European Union is a basis for sound optimism with regard to this issue.

The World Constitution should be based on the Universal Declaration of Human Rights. Although it is not perfect from the viewpoint of various cultures and traditions, it has fully proven its humanistic orientation, as well as effectiveness and vitality.

Basing on the principle of separation of powers, the UN can pretend to become the *legislative* power, or World parliament. But this organization should be seriously reformed to acquire the functions of the legislative power. Since it will adopt laws and legal norms mandatory for all countries and peoples, it is important to ensure their equal representation in this legislative body of global governance. Evidently, the formation of the World Parliament should be gradual: from representatives of separate countries to direct elections. First steps and evolution of, for example, the European Parliament, may serve a good example in resolving this issue.

The executive power is to be created virtually from a scratch. In some extent, G7, which, under the influence of the last financial and economic crisis started to evolve into G20, could become in the future a prototype of an executive power structure where all countries and nations are represented equally. But this prospect is too distant and hardly foreseeable, what makes resolution of this issue particularly topical against the background of increasing global problems. Evidently, serious contractions the humankind will inevitably fact in the near future, will open new opportunities for a radical decision in this regard.

Judiciary power, directly connected with the formation of global way, should be built up from a scratch. The world community has some experience in this regard and it can become the basis for the future world court, whose sources can be seen in the Nuremberg, Hague and European human rights courts.

Some words regarding *which principal decisions and at which level should be made initially and afterwards to achieve the goals set.*

Decisions regarding building the global system of governance should be made, of course, at the planetary level. A World Conference, roughly analogical to the World environmental conference in Rio-de-Janeiro (1992), could become the first step. It could also be a Word summit of heads of all states, which would work out principal approaches to global governance. In the future operative tactical and strategic decisions would become more and more the prerogative of the newly emerging structures.

Finally, *who can and should take responsibility for building global governance and what is the price and who should pay it?*

First of all, this responsibility lies on the world academic, political and business elites, i. e., on people having adequate worldview, possessing necessary knowledge, have the strongest authorities and material resources. On the other hand, the most developed countries (the USA, the EU, China, Russia, India, Brazil and others) should take initial basic responsibility for building the system of global governance. They also should carry the main burden of financial support of a reform of modern international relations. This does not mean, however, that there should be countries or nations at our planet, which would be free from their own reasonable contribution into common expenses.

Someone may say that it is all a utopia, and that global governance is impossible, while above-listed arguments in its support are insufficient. This viewpoint has its right to exist, because we can not so far provide a final proof of the truth of our statements. Someone can question correctness and sequence of the steps proposed and this person may also be right, because we discuss a topic having no analogies in human history. That is why it is so important to observe the possibility of global governance from different angles, including the position of philosophy, which, unlike science, is oriented not so much towards finding concrete, final solutions but towards broadening the scope of various approaches to resolution of a problem. Such philosophical analysis is especially valuable where exact scientific methods have not been worked out yet, but the situation needs immediate resolution. The problem of governing contemporary global world is such a case.

Faith and Responsibility in World Affairs: The Persistence of the National Frame

Thomas Banchoff

Both the emergence of global policy challenges and an awareness of their strong value dimension demand a reorientation of world politics. Today's most pressing problems, including financial and economic instability, poverty and social inequality, environmental degradation and climate change, terrorism and human rights violations, have a strong transnational dimension. Addressing them effectively will require a global frame of reference informed by shared values of peace, justice, equality, freedom, and dedication to the global common good – values anchored in the world's diverse religious and philosophical traditions.

Those who espouse these twin convictions – that world politics as usual cannot continue and that reliance on faith and values might help to inaugurate a new era of greater global responsibility – run up against the still dominant structural characteristic of the international system: the existence of sovereign nation states locked in economic and security competition.

The persistence of the state system is not only an institutional obstacle to a new global departure; it has a cultural basis as well.

Even in our global age, faith and values remain nationally grounded. National identity is a powerful emotional force that shapes and channels the practice of ethical and religious commitments. National values, narratives and interests mediate between those commitments and the policies that shape global economic, social, and political life.

Globalization, it is true, has challenged effective control over national economies. It has generated transnational problems beyond the reach of state institutions, from global warming to pandemics. And it has spawned greater global consciousness, world-spanning consumer culture, growing individualism, and more critical attitudes towards state power.

But globalization has not undermined the strong national identities of most of the world's citizens. The global wave of national fervor that began with the French Revolution and was later reinforced by two world wars and anti-colonial struggles continues to roll forward. Today's globalization has unfolded with and through it. National identity provides a source of solace and solidarity in the face of international competition, a wellspring of "we feeling" in the face of the foreign. The Olympic Games and the World Cup are obvious examples.

When it comes to questions of global responsibility, there exist some true cosmopolitans, whose allegiance is first to humanity and only second to their nations, local communities and families. But they are a politically insignificant minority everywhere. Similarly, when it comes to matters of faith, there are true saints, who put universal ethical and spiritual commitments ahead of particular national or subnational attachments. But they, too, are few and far between.

It does not follow universal ethical and religious commitments have no political significance. But they matter in world affairs primarily when refracted through national interests, identities and institutions. We may read the same scriptures, or pray to the same God, or revere the same philosophers. But when it comes to thinking through the policy implications of our spiritual and philosophical traditions, we are citizens of our nations, not of a global polity. We may aspire to a world with deeply embedded shared values and intercultural and interreligious commonalities. But it is not the world we inhabit today. With some exceptions our lived ethical and spiritual frames of reference – and our imaginations – remain nationally bounded. What the philosopher Hans Georg Gadamer called a "fusion of horizons" eludes us at the global level.

Recognition of the primacy of the national is not cause for despair. It is rather a starting point for an objective analysis of faith and responsibilities in the world today. Only a quest for greater international understanding and a meaningful global ethic that takes the real existing nation states and their relationship to universal values as a point of departure will succeed.

This paper will explore the tension between universal values and the national frame in the critical case of the United States and suggest its relevance to other cases, including China, as well.

Christianity and National Identity
in the United States

The majority faith tradition in the United States, Christianity, was the ideal type for what German sociologist Max Weber called an ethic of brotherly and world-denying love. Christians are, by their own self-understanding, children of a loving God and brothers and sisters to one another, whatever their particular local, regional, or national attachments. In a famous passage in the Letter to the

Galatians, St. Paul reminds the early Church: "There is neither Jew nor Greek, slave nor free, male nor female, for you are all one in Christ Jesus." (Galatians 3) Jesus' call to universal solidarity encompassing those *outside* a particular community is most clearly expressed in the parable of the Good Samaritan who takes in the abandoned stranger (Luke 16) and in the story of the Last Judgment (Matthew 25), where Christ rewards solidarity with the downtrodden: "For I was hungry and you gave me something to eat, I was thirsty and you gave me something to drink, I was a stranger and you invited me in, needed clothes and you clothed me, I was sick and you looked after me, I was in prison and you came to visit me."

In practice, of course, most Christians throughout the centuries have failed to live up to this ideal. They have put allegiances to self, family, tribe, and nation ahead of service to God and their fellow human beings. Or, to put it more charitably, they have struggled to combine a universal ethical and spiritual calling with attachments to particular lived communities.

In the British North American colonies, and later in the United States, many Americans have sought to finesse this tension by equating their political experiment with divine will. This equation was clearest among the Puritans fleeing political and religious persecution in Britain who saw in the New World a place where Christian values of freedom, love, peace, and justice, could flourish in practice. Political community and spiritual purpose were to be of a piece. The founder of the Massachusetts Bay Colony, John Winthrop, famously quoted Jesus' call to his disciples to be a "city on a hill and a light among nations" (Matthew 5).

The idea of the United States as a vehicle for Divine Providence would survive through almost four centuries of dramatic social, cultural, economic, and political change – through a revolution, civil war, the destruction of Native American communities, industrialization, depression, two world wars, and the country's emergence, after 1945, as a global superpower. In 2010 it remains axiomatic for the vast majority of Americans, whatever their race, gender or social class, that the United States is the greatest country in the world. For President Barack Obama, too, America is "the greatest nation on earth" and a "force of good in the world." [1]

The claim to American greatness is often justified through reference to secular criteria, such as past and present levels of military and economic power or support for democracy, human rights and other goods around the world. At the level of symbols and political culture – that is to say, at the level of emotion – it is sustained by a wide, if often unacknowledged religious sensibility nicely captured in Robert Bellah's idea of "American Civil Religion." [2]

Civil Religion and National Identity

The phenomenon Bellah described in 1967 had Christian roots but had developed over time in a general religious but not specifically Christian direction – a transformation evident at the level of both constitutional law and political culture.

Constitutional Law

The founding documents of the United States, the Declaration of Independence (1776) and the Constitution (1787) are secular in

---

① Transcript of October 4, 2008 presidential debate with John McCain. http://www.cbsnews. com/stories/2008/10/08/politics/2008debates/main4508405.shtml.

② Robert Bellah, "Civil Religion in America," *Journal of the American Academy of Arts and Sciences* 96 (1) 1967:1 – 21.

orientation. The Declaration moves quickly from an acknowledgement that all men "are endowed by their Creator with certain inalienable Rights" to a long list of economic and political grievances to justify the break with the British Empire. The Constitution, which sets out the political machinery of the new nation, includes no mention of God or Christianity. Its First Amendment emphasizes the differentiation of church and state, not their integration: "Congress shall make *no law* respecting an establishment of religion, or *prohibiting* the free *exercise* thereof."

This secular construction was not directed against religion; it was intended rather to create a safe space where religions could compete and coexist with one another without state persecution. The First Amendment did not build a "wall" of separation between Church and State. It did preclude the formation of a national church on the British model and insure religious freedom from state domination. But it has not historically proved incompatible with the official affirmation of God as a foundation for American politics and society. Every session of Congress from the beginning of the United States, for example, has opened with a prayer, established churches persisted in several states into the 1830s, and the teaching of the (Protestant) bible in many local public school systems continued into the 20th century.

Since the Civil War, Supreme Court jurisprudence has gradually pushed American civil religion in a less Christian and more non-denominational direction. The non-establishment clause of the First Amendment has been interpreted more strictly to preclude the teaching of religious doctrines or teacher-led prayer in public schools, for example, and the public display of religious symbols, such as the Christmas crèche and the Ten Commandments have been curtailed. A recent and ongoing judicial and political skirmish centers on the constitutionality of the phrase "One Nation under God" as part of the Pledge of Allegiance recited every day by schoolchildren across the United States.

Efforts to root out God from American public institutions are unlikely to meet with success. The Supreme Court has generally interpreted the symbolic invocation of the (non-denominational) deity in official context as the expression of culture and tradition, not the establishment of religion. We should not expect the motto " In God We Trust," emblazoned on US currency, or other symbolic and institutional instances of civil religion to disappear any time soon.

Political Culture

The emergence of a non-denominational civil religion has been reinforced by transformations of political culture. The United States still remains a Protestant majority nation, accounting for about three quarters of the 80 – 85% of Americans who self-identify as Christian. But the Catholic population has steadily increased from its insignificant levels during the colonial era to over 20% of the overall population, and there are significant Jewish, Muslims and smaller Buddhist, Hindu, and other minorities. Hostility between Protestants and Catholics, long a leitmotif of US history, began to drop sharply between the two world wars, as did widespread anti-Semitism. By the 1950s the idea of a " Judeo-Christian" identity informing a shared American citizenship took hold. With the growth of the Muslim population the question of whether a Judeo-Christian identity will eventually become Abrahamic is now on the political agenda. As the Manhattan Mosque controversy of summer 2010 illustrated, it remains sharply contested.

It would be wrong to overstate the movement away from a Christian to a non-denominational cast of civil religion. In a 2006 poll, 2/3 of Americans agreed with the characterization of the US as " a Christian nation. " [1] Another poll around the same time found that

---

[1]　http://pewforum. org/Politics-and-Elections/Many-Americans-Uneasy-with-Mix-of-Religion-and-Politics. aspx#1

half of Americans thought "to be a Christian" was "very important" for being "truly American. " [1] But political leaders, especially those running for national office, rarely make specifically Christian appeals, preferring instead to address "people of faith" or "family values" in the abstract. They certainly tend to describe themselves as religious or spiritual people, whatever their own personal convictions may be. Not to do so is to take a political risk. One of the most striking illustrations of the pervasiveness of civil religion in the US is the almost complete absence of avowed atheists in Congress. In 2009, only 1 out of 635 members fit the category.

Given the combination of constitutional and cultural support, it is hardly surprising that every US president has invoked elements of civil religion in public discourse. Barack Obama is no different. Two key passages from his January 2009 inaugural address construed America and its political system as an expression of universal, divinely-sanctioned values.

> *What is required of us now is a new era of responsibility-a recognition on the part of every American that we have duties to ourselves, our nation and the world; duties that we do not grudgingly accept, but rather seize gladly, firm in the knowledge that there is nothing so satisfying to the spirit, so defining of our character than giving our all to a difficult task. This is the price and the promise of citizenship. This is the source of our confidence - the knowledge that God calls*

---

[1] The question posed in the international survey was: "Some people say that the following things are important for being truly (American, British, etc). Others say they are not important. " To the follow-on question, "How important is it to be a Christian?" The percentage responding "very important" in the US went from 39% in 1995/96 to 50% in 2003/04. The corresponding figure for the UK, Germany, and France in 2003/04 were 18, 12, and 9 percent. See Matthew Wright and Jack Citrin, God and Country: Religion, Religiosity, and National Identity in American Public Opinion (2009). APSA 2009 Toronto Meeting Paper. Available at SSRN: http://ssrn. com/abstract = 1451321.

on us to shape an uncertain destiny.

And in closing:

> *With hope and virtue, let us brave once more the icy*
> *currents, and endure what storms may come. Let it be said by*
> *our children's children that when we were tested we refused to*
> *let this journey end, that we did not turn back nor did we*
> *falter; and with eyes fixed on the horizon and God's grace*
> *upon us, we carried forth that great gift of freedom and*
> *delivered it safely to future generations.* ①

Faith, Responsibility, and US Foreign Policy

The Obama inaugural, with its reference to "duties to ourselves,
our nation and the world" and to "knowledge that God calls us to
shape an uncertain destiny," also incorporated the foreign policy
dimension of American civil religion. The idea that America has
global responsibilities in line with Divine Providence can be traced
back to the concept of Manifest Destiny that accompanied the
country's westward expansion, and through Woodrow Wilson's
Fourteen Points (1918) and Franklin Delano Roosevelt's Four
Freedoms (1941), which outlined the universal values pursued by the
United States as a rising power. Over the postwar period and up to the
present, successive US Presidents have viewed divine will, the spread
of freedom around the world, and the national identity and interests of
the United States as one and the same historical movement. "We
Americans have faith in ourselves, but not in ourselves alone," Bush

---

① "President Barack Obama's Inaugural Address," January 21, 2009, http://www. whitehouse.
gov/blog/inaugural-address/.

stated in his 2003 State of the Union Address. "We do not claim to know all the ways of Providence, yet we can trust in them, placing our confidence in the loving god behind all of life and all of history. "

Obama, it is true, has introduced some new accents into this foreign policy discourse. He has abandoned the triumphalism and unilateralism of his predecessor and is more cosmopolitan in outlook. He has been critical of the projection of US power and of the gap between American ideals and the pursuit of its foreign policy. At the same time, however, he has continued to affirm universal values as coterminous with American values and held up American understandings of freedom and democracy both as historical inevitability and as an expression of divine will.

The most important single foreign policy address of Obama's first in office, in Cairo, Egypt in June 2009, demonstrated both change and continuity. Entitled "A New Beginning," the address was intended to improve relations between the US and the Muslim World. "America and Islam are not exclusive and need not be in competition," Obama told Al Azhar students and a worldwide audience. "Instead, they overlap and share common principles— principles of justice and progress; tolerance and the dignity of all human beings. " He did not identify terrorism as a specifically Muslim problem. "These extremists are not the first to kill in the name of God", he noted. "The cruelties of the Crusades are amply recorded. " Obama also reminded his listeners of his cosmopolitan credentials. "I'm a Christian, but my father came from a Kenyan family that includes generations of Muslims. " He went on to cite the

①　Address of January 28, 2003, http://www. washingtonpost. com/wp-srv/onpolitics/transcripts/bushtext_012803. html.

Qur'an, the Talmud, and the New Testament, and concluded: "The people of the world can live together in peace. We know that is God's vision. Now that must be our work here on Earth."

In a critical respect the speech was not a new departure. Amid the self-critical tones and assertions of universal spiritual and ethical values Obama also underlined the global calling of the United States as a progressive force in history. "Just as Muslims do not fit a crude stereotype," he told his audience, "America is not the crude stereotype of a self-interested empire. The United States has been one of the greatest sources of progress that the world has ever known." He continued:

> *We were born out of revolution against an empire. We were founded upon the ideal that all are created equal, and we have shed blood and struggled for centuries to give meaning to those words—within our borders, and around the world. We are shaped by every culture, drawn from every end of the Earth, and dedicated to a simple concept: E pluribus unum—"Out of many, one."*

A further passage underscored the ultimate identification between American and universal values on a transcendent foundation.

> *And I believe that America holds within her the truth that regardless of race, religion, or station in life, all of us share common aspirations—to live in peace and security; to get an education and to work with dignity; to love our families, our communities, and our God. These things we share. This is the hope of all humanity.* [1]

---

[1] "Remarks by the President on a New Beginning," June 4, 2009, http://www. whitehouse. gov/ the_press_office/Remarks-by-the-President-at-Cairo-University-6 – 04 – 09/.

Several months later, in his first address to the UN General Assembly, in September 2009, Obama continued his emphasis on multilateralism and intercultural and interreligious understanding. "It is my deeply held belief that in the year 2009 – more than at any point in human history—the interests of nations and peoples are shared," he insisted. "The religious convictions that we hold in our hearts can forge new bonds among people, or they can tear us apart." The emphasis was to be on peaceful interaction based on mutual recognition: "We must embrace a new era of engagement based on mutual interest and mutual respect, and our work must begin now." Obama distanced himself from the Bush administration's efforts to spread democracy through diplomacy and force of arms. "Democracy cannot be imposed on any nation from the outside," he insisted. "Each society must search for its own path, and no path is perfect. Each country will pursue a path rooted in the culture of its people and in its past traditions." ①

Only a year later before the General Assembly, however, Obama struck a very different tone. Perhaps recoiling from domestic criticisms that he had not placed enough of an emphasis on democracy and human rights, he used the occasion of his second major UN address in September 2010 to press their importance and to uphold the American model more explicitly. After citing the 1948 Universal Declaration of Human Rights, with its recognition of the inherent dignity and of the equal and inalienable rights of all members of the human family is the foundation of freedom, justice, and peace in the world, Obama elaborated: The idea is a simple one—that freedom, justice and peace for the world must begin with freedom, justice, and

① Remarks by the President to the United Nations General Assembly, September 23, 2009, http://www. whitehouse. gov/the_press_office/Remarks-by-the-President-to-the-United-Nations-General-Assembly/.

peace in the lives of individual human beings. " For the United States, he continued, this is a matter of moral and pragmatic necessity. As Robert Kennedy said, ' the individual man, the child of God, is the touchstone of value, and all society, groups, the state, exist for his benefit. ' "

With an astounding openness, Obama moved from this emphasis on individual freedom as God's gift to a pledge that the US would work around the world to advance human rights and democracy, including outside formal government channels. "Civil society is the conscience of our communities and America will always extend our engagement abroad with citizens beyond the halls of government," he said. "And we will call out those who suppress ideas and serve as a voice for those who are voiceless. " As if to pull back from the full implications of this statement, Obama again acknowledged the limits of American power. "Now, make no mistake," he persisted. "The ultimate success of democracy in the world won't come because the United States dictates it; it will come because individual citizens demand a say in how they are governed. " But even this turn of phrase suggested an alignment of interests between American ideals and the aspirations of citizens around the world.

In an unusual finish to the speech, Obama equated the building of a just and peaceful world directly with the American experience, and that of New York City in particular. "And though we will be met by dark forces that will test our resolve, Americans have always had cause to believe that we can choose a better history; that we need only to look outside the walls around us" – a reference to Manhattan beyond the UN Headquarters' walls. "For through the citizens of every conceivable ancestry who make this city their own, we see living proof that opportunity can be accessed by all, that what unites us as human beings is far greater than what divides us, and that people from every part of this world can live together in peace. " ①

In Obama's rhetoric during the first two years of his presidency we see the articulation of universal values in a national idiom. He asserted the ideals of the Universal Declaration of Human Rights as ethical and spiritual ideals and pointed out the world's diverse philosophical and religious traditions as foundations for a more just and peaceful world. But he also insisted that the United States was itself the best approximation of those ideals. The idea that US had a global mission to realize universal values, a mainstay of American civil religion, remained. In this key respect, continuity dominated over change in the articulation of US foreign policy.

American Exceptionalism?

Is the United States exceptional? Is it, on account of its specific history, particularly inclined to fuse universal faith and national identity in articulating its vision of global responsibility? Perhaps not. Other governments articulate their conceptions of universal values through national frames that are, like the American one, shaped by historical experience and religious and philosophical traditions. Each of the states within the European Union, for example, draws on Christian and secular ideas, in different mixtures, in espousing its approach to national identity, European integration, and global engagement. Today's state-sponsored Russian nationalism draws on Russian Orthodox understandings of the country's historical and universal mission. India's vibrant religious pluralism, and the existence of an outspoken Hindu Nationalist movement, shapes its

---

① Remarks by the President to the United Nations General Assembly, September 23, 2010, http://www. whitehouse. gov/the-press-office/2010/09/23/remarks-president-united-nations-general-assembly.

international relations. And of course the brand of Islam institutionalized in Iran and Saudi Arabia impacts those country's foreign policies.

China provides another interesting example of a national framing of universal values. The interrelated ideas of a Harmonious Society and a Harmonious World, first introduced by President Hu Jintao in 2005 – 06, draw on the national philosophical and spiritual tradition of Confucianism to craft a particular understanding universal values and their policy implications, domestically and internationally. The idea of harmony as ordered interaction in accordance with norms of sovereignty, equality, justice, and peace informs the official Chinese interpretation of the universal values enshrined in the UN Charter and the Declaration of Human Rights. Like the official US interpretation of those values, from which it differs in significant respects, the Chinese government's views are related back to national interests, institutions and identity.

Conclusion

It is perhaps hardly surprising that issues of faith, values, and responsibility in world affairs should be articulated in a national register. National leaders are embedded within domestic political contexts. When they address global issues they are also – and in many cases, primarily – speaking to national audiences. They are bound by what Weber called an "ethic of responsibility" – the idea that, given constraints of office, and their responsibilities to protect and defend their citizens, it would be irresponsible to put abstract universal values ahead of national interests.

What happens instead is the creative interpretation of universal values through a national frame and their articulation in an idiom that draws on national historical experience and religious and philosophical traditions. From this perspective, the primacy of the national is not hypocrisy, or opportunism, but a structural constraint imposed by the structure of the international system.

From a religious and philosophical perspective, however, there is a deeper problem. To the extent that universal values are grounded in religious, spiritual or philosophical resources that have humankind as a whole as their frame of reference, the resilience of the national frame is problematic. It leads almost inevitably to the instrumentalization of universal values for particular interests. Perhaps we can live with the primacy of group – in this case, national – allegiances, as we have for all of human history. But given the increasingly global and transnational nature of contemporary threats, including economic instability, violent extremism, and environmental crisis, we should try to nudge our national perspectives in a more universal direction. The global frame is too important to be left to philosophers and saints.

共建和谐世界的"中国经验"

——中国前辈学者探索成果评述

张志刚

一、引言：宗教对话与世界和平

近几十年来，"宗教对话"已成为国际宗教学界的一个热门话题、一个前沿领域。自上个世纪 80 年代末，《全球伦理宣言》起草者汉斯·昆（Hans Küng，又译孔汉思）就再三强调：没有宗教之间的和平，就没有民族、国家乃至文明之间的和平；没有宗教之间的对话，就没有宗教之间的和平；没有宗教研究，就没有宗教之间的对话。这三句话构成了"一个阐明宗教对话之重要性的三段式"。按照它的推断，宗教对话显然太重要了，不但事关宗教之间的和平相处，而且关乎民族、国家乃至文明之间有无和平可言。回到上个世纪 80 年代末，如果说那时还有很多人怀疑，这个"三段式"是否把宗教对话的重要意义"无限上纲"了，不过二十年，随着冷战后宗教现象及其问题的日渐突出，诸多民族性、国家间和文明间等形式的矛盾与冲突越来越受宗教因素或宗教背景的明显影响，这种关于宗教对话之重要性的判断，已成为全球政要、宗教领袖、尤其是宗教学家的共识了。

关于宗教对话的紧迫性，美国著名神学家尼特（Paul F. Knitter）尖锐地指出，在"后 9·11 世界"的地理－政治事态发展中，恐怖导致愤怒，愤怒导致暴力,这在一些民族和国家愈演愈烈。在许多人看来,亨廷顿(Samuel Huntington)的观点已被证实,"文明的冲突"越来越严重了。但更令人担忧,也更有威胁的是,文明的冲突似乎由于宗教的冲突而"火上浇油"了。恐怖主义分子和帝国主义者都巧借宗教信念来为各自的邪恶行为辩护,他们把对方称为"邪恶的",就是自视"善良的",这是一种"宗教宣称",意味着"上帝与我同在,让我惩罚你"。就此而言,宗教正在被用来助长文明的冲突,这也正是宗教成为一个全球性问题的部分原因。然而,宗教信仰不但可以、而且应当推动文明之间的对话与合作,因为世界上的各类宗教人士若能信守其创始人和经典里的教诲,都会赞同这样一个方针:宗教信仰必须有助于人类和平,而决不能沦为暴力冲突的思想资源。①

正是鉴于宗教对话的重要性和紧迫性,国内外学术界近十几年来越来越注重反思东西方宗教文化传统,以发掘有助于促进宗教对话、化解文明冲突、共建和谐世界的历史经验和思想资源。本文所要评论的是我国老一代著名学者所做的相关理论探索,主要包括三部分内容:一是,关于中国宗教文化历史特点的重新认识;二是,关于中国宗教文化优良传统的概括总结;三是,中国文化传统可为促进宗教对话、化解文明冲突、共建和谐世界提供的思想资源。

二、中国宗教文化的历史特点

若想阐发中国宗教文化传统可为促进宗教对话、化解文明冲突、共建和谐世界提供的历史经验和思想资源,就要首先认识中国宗教文化传统的历史特点。然而,自明末清初中西方文化相遇以来,如何认识中国宗教传统及其特点一直是个学术难题。

著名的比较宗教学家斯马特(Ninian Smart)是这样着笔介绍中国宗教的:"西方人经常会对中国的宗教感到困惑……从西方人的观点来看,中国

---

① 参见尼特:《宗教对话模式》,王志成译,中国人民大学出版社,2004 年,"作者致中国读者",第 2 - 3 页。

宗教实在是一个大杂烩。"①更有甚者如汉斯·昆所言:"西方学者曾经推测,中国古代社会实际上并没有宗教生活。"②为什么竟会如此呢? 我们可从杨庆堃(C. K. Yang)先生的《中国社会中的宗教》里找到耐人深思的线索。该书"导论"里有一节"有关中国社会宗教特征的某些观点",其中提到,那些来华传教士最早发现了一种与基督教迥异的情形:中国人的信仰是迷信,从那时起这种观点在西方已流行了一个多世纪。另一个重要原因是,儒家伦理观念在中国历史的大部分时间里支配着社会价值体系,这就取代了基督教在西方社会的宗教伦理功能,而没有出现强大的宗教组织,也没有发生长期的政教(国家与教会)之争。因此,西方汉学家一向认为,儒家思想传统在价值观上是世俗性的,在宗教观上则是不可知论的,这样一来便轻视了宗教在中国社会的地位及其影响。可以说,正是受上述西方观点的影响,现代中国学者发挥了"中国社会是非宗教的"这一论点。例如,梁启超怀疑,"能否写中国宗教史";胡适认为,"中国是个没有宗教的国家,中国人是个不迷信宗教的民族";陈端生指出,"中国人是非宗教的,中国没有伟大的宗教……"③笔者之所以提及以上学术背景,就是为了凸现下述研究进展的参考价值。

为了消除长期以来"西方观点"对于中国宗教研究的偏颇影响,楼宇烈先生近几年来在多次会议和讲演中阐明了中国宗教文化传统的如下 10 个特点。

(1)中国历史上从未出现过神权凌驾于王权的现象。自夏、商、周三代以来,"普天之下,莫非王土,率土之滨,莫非王臣"的观念一直占主导地位,所以神权总是从属王权的。而在西方长达千年的中世纪,神权是高于王权的。

(2)中国历史上从未出现过"一神信仰",而一向是"多神信仰"。虽然中国宗教中有多种名称的至上神,像"帝"、"上帝"、"天"和"太一"等,但它们并非绝对化的信仰观念。所以,在民间没有"只能信这个神而不能信那

———————

① 斯马特:《世界宗教》(第二版),高师宁等译,北京大学出版社,2004 年,第 113 页。

② 汉斯·昆:《世界宗教寻踪》,杨煦生等译,三联书店,2007 年,第 129 页。

③ 详见杨庆堃:《中国社会中的宗教——宗教的现代社会功能与其历史因素之研究》,范丽珠等译,上海人民出版社,2007 年,第 21 – 24 页。

个神"一说,老百姓往往是见庙就烧香,见神就磕头。这完全不同于西方基督教"只能拜上帝"的信仰观。

(3)祖先崇拜。中国的神常常是祖先,比如"帝"和"上帝"等在甲骨文里主要是指"部落祖先",即指对本部落有贡献的英雄人物,他们死后会保佑下方子孙。这可以说是一种英雄崇拜、圣贤崇拜。但到周代,即使这种想法也开始变化了,这些祖先神或圣贤神并非盲目地保佑其子孙,而是要看他们是否有德。例如,周代出现了"皇天无亲,为德是辅"的思想;春秋时进一步讲"天听自我民听,天视自我民视","民,神之主也"。因而,西周以后,逐渐形成了"以人为本、人文精神"的文化传统。

(4)在人神关系上,不唯神命为听,不相信神有绝对权力,而是如同处理人际关系。孔子说:"未能事人,焉能事鬼?"又说:"务民之义,敬鬼神而远之,可谓知矣。"梁启超指出,西方的宗教可称为"神道的宗教",中国的宗教则可称为"人道的宗教"。这就是说,在中国文化中,对人伦关系的关注远过于神人关系。

(5)中国人的宗教信仰具有很强的现世性和功利性,而缺乏神圣性。譬如,《坛经》里说:"佛法在世间,不离世间觉,离世觅菩提,恰如求兔角。"费孝通先生讲过,我们中国人对鬼神是非常实际的,供奉他们为的是风调雨顺,免灾逃祸;我们的祭祀很有点像请客、疏通、贿赂;鬼神对我们是权力,不是理想,是财源,不是公道。

(6)中国人的宗教信仰带有比较浓厚的理性色彩,而不是完全情感化的。近代以来,有人说中国佛教是宗教,有人说是哲学,有人说既是宗教也是哲学,还有人说既不是宗教也不是哲学,而是一种方法——佛法。人们之所以争论不休,就是因为佛教里有相当丰富的理性成分。从另一个角度来讲,佛教又是一种"无神的宗教",以其"缘起"、"业报"等理论而否定"神创造世界和生命"的说法,主张从事物内部找根本原因,讲"自作自受"。

(7)中国的宗教信仰强调"个人内在的自我超越"。以儒家思想为主导的中国文化,可以说是一种"修身的文化",即通过"修身"来提升自我,超越自我。在这样的文化氛围中,中国佛教最重要的一个宗派——禅宗,就充分张扬了佛教自我解脱的人文精神,强调自性自度、明心见性、见性成佛。这种注重伦理的心性修养是中国宗教的特色。道教以道家思想为主要依据,道家尊重自然,主张自然无为,归根结蒂,就是尊重人的主体性,要最大限度地发挥个体的能动性。

(8)中国的宗教缺乏强烈的传教精神。这跟中国传统文化有很大关系。儒家就是典型,《礼记》中说:"礼闻来学,未闻往教。"可谓姜太公钓鱼——愿者上钩。佛教、道教也是如此。佛教并不强求别人信,而是佛度有缘人。西方传教士哪有这种现象? 西方宗教的传教具有进攻性,而中国宗教则具有保守性。

(9)在中国历史上王权对于宗教是比较宽容的,允许不同宗教并存。由于王权在中国一直占主导地位,从整体上讲,王权采取了一种比较宽容、调和与利用的态度,让各种宗教互相竞争,以稳固政权。这便使中国诸种宗教在教义和仪式上频繁交流,形成了你中有我,我中有你的局面,但同时又你是你,我是我,保持了各自特色。

(10)中国是一个多民族国家,所以有大量的民族宗教问题。民族宗教与前述宗教有共同之处,也有很多差异。比如,同样是佛教,藏传佛教、南传佛教就跟汉地佛教不一样,前两者跟当地的民族文化相结合,甚至成为其民族文化的象征。①

国内同行知道,牟钟鉴先生长年潜心于中国宗教史的学科建设,他和张践教授合作完成了近百万字的《中国宗教通史》(上、下卷,2000 年)。在这部通史的最后一章,牟先生专用一节归纳了中国宗教的 5 个特点:(1)原生型宗教的连续存在和发展;(2)皇权始终支配教权;(3)多样性与包容性;(4)人文化和世俗化;(5)三重结构的衔接与脱节。若将牟先生关于这 5 个特点的具体解释与楼先生指出的 10 个特点相比,我们可得到下述几方面的理论启发。

第一,两位先生的看法具有一致性。这明显地表现为,牟先生讲的特点(2)就是楼先生首先强调的,"在中国历史上从未出现过神权凌驾于王权的现象",或者说"皇权始终支配教权"。但这里指的一致性,更多地反映在下一方面。

---

① 以上概述详见楼宇烈:"探求合乎本土文化传统的宗教学研究理论",《中国宗教》,2008 年第 11 期。

第二，牟先生所讲的特点（1）、（3）和（4）比楼先生的讲法更有概括性。譬如，牟先生就特点（1）指出，与中国历史上长期存在的宗法等级社会相适应，自然崇拜、鬼神崇拜、祖先崇拜等原生型宗教信仰，不但没有像希腊、埃及、波斯和印度等文明古国发生的情况那样，到中世纪便被创生型宗教取代了，反而被完整地保存下来，并得以发展和强化，以致天神崇拜、皇祖崇拜、社稷崇拜与皇权紧密结合，形成了宗法性国家宗教。这种解释既包含了楼先生所讲的第（2）、（3）两点意思，又能使我们理解其历史原因。又如，关于特点（3），即"多样性与包容性"，牟先生是着眼于中国传统文化的多元一体结构、儒家哲学"和而不同"的包容理念和中国社会的宗教宽容氛围来做出解释的，这就把楼先生所讲的第（2）、（9）和（10）几个特点统合起来了；再如，牟先生所讲的特点（4），即"人文化和世俗化"，不但包括了楼先生讲的第（4）、（5）和（6）等几重意思，而且解释要点大多一致，像中国宗教文化传统具有鲜明的伦理性、现世性、功利性、人性或理性等。

第三，两位先生的有些观点虽不相同，但各有见地，可使我们互为参照，更为全面地认识中国宗教文化传统的整体特征及其复杂性。譬如，楼先生所指出的特点（7）和（8），即"中国宗教信仰注重内在的超越性"和"中国宗教传统没有强烈的传教性"。又如，牟先生所阐述的特点（5），即中国人的信仰结构主要是由"官方信仰"、"学者信仰"和"民间信仰"形成的，这三大群体的信仰状态既彼此贯通，又相对独立，甚至有所脱节，所以不应用一个简单的判断来概括中国人的信仰特征。

汉斯·昆曾中肯地讲，"西方汉学家眼中的中国"与"中国人眼中的中国"是大相径庭的。① 从上述中国宗教史研究成果来看，我们可以说，中国宗教文化传统在"以前的中国学者眼中"与"现今的中国学者眼中"也是截然不同的。下面就让我们接着看看，前辈学者是如何基于晚近研究成果来总结中国宗教文化传统的优良传统的。

---

① 参见汉斯·昆：《世界宗教寻踪》，第129页。

三、中国宗教文化的优良传统

牟钟鉴先生根据其长期而系统的中国宗教史研究,将中国宗教文化的优良传统概括为如下五点。

(1)多样性与和谐性,即和而不同,多元一体,这是中国宗教文化的一个显著历史特点。

中国是一个多民族多信仰多宗教的大国,但这"三多"并没有使它困扰于对抗和分裂之中;相反,民族在差异之中走向和谐,信仰在交流中走向理性,多宗教在互动中走向丰富。①

首先,中国是一个多民族的国家,现有56个民族,但能共同组成中华民族。中华民族作为东方古老文明的共同体,在文化上有巨大的凝聚力,作为统一国家已有数千年历史,并正在复兴之中,这在世界上是绝无仅有的。

其次,中国是一个多信仰的国家,既有以人文理性为特征的儒家仁礼之学,也有以神道崇拜为特征的诸多宗教信仰。哲学与宗教、人学与神道交织互动,使得中国的哲学多少带有宗教的神圣性和神秘性,也使中国的宗教具有较强的人文理性。因此,中国历史上没出现强大的禁教思潮,也没出现浩荡的宗教狂热。

再次,中国是一个多宗教的国家,历史上有祭天祭祖祭社稷的国家民族宗教,有土生土长的道教,有诸多民间信仰和民族传统宗教,有外来的佛教、基督教和伊斯兰教,还传入过犹太教、摩尼教、琐罗亚士德教等。可以说,中国犹如一个"宗教百花苑",从原始宗教到世界宗教都能在这片大地上共同生存、和平相处。各教之间没有发生过大规模的武力流血冲突,更没有发生过西方宗教史上那样的残酷而长期的宗教战争。

(2)重视行善积德和道德教化,把去恶为善放在首位,作为宗教的主要

---

① 牟钟鉴:"继承和发扬中国宗教文化的优良传统",《探索宗教》,宗教文化出版社,2008年,第86-87页。

精神方向,这是中国宗教文化的又一个突出的历史特点。

例如,佛教讲慈悲,而且是"无缘大慈,同体大悲",怜悯一切有情众生。道教受老子"尊道贵德"和"报怨以德"的思想影响,十分重视道德善行在修道中的关键作用。南北朝时期有儒、佛、道三教之争,最后达成共识,便是三教虽异,同归于劝善。所谓"三教",实质是指三种道德教化之道。所以,中国传统宗教,其本质特征是道德宗教,所谓"神道设教",目的在于淳厚社会道德风气。这种道德宗教传统也影响到中国的伊斯兰教和基督教(包括新老教),使其教义中的道德内涵逐渐得到充实和凸现,从而强化了它们的社会道德教化功能。

在中国,各种宗教必须具有良好的道德形象,才能生存和发展;提倡仇杀和诱人为恶的教门被视为邪教,是无法在光天化日之下流行的。这种深厚的道德性传统使中国宗教不容易产生极端主义,而拥有较多的道义上的力量。①

(3)善于把爱教与爱国统一起来,这是中国宗教文化的另一个优良传统。

鸦片战争后,中国沦为西方列强的附庸,饱受殖民主义的压榨欺凌;日本帝国主义侵略中国,中国人面临亡国灭种的危险。在争取民族独立和解放的斗争中,我国各大宗教的人士,主流是爱国的,他们积极投身于抗外侮、救国家的社会运动。佛教有"利乐有情,庄严国土"的教义。抗日时期,弘一法师提出"念佛不忘救国"的号召,动员僧人奋起抵抗日寇侵略。道教大师陈撄宁提倡仙学,明确主张"信仰道教,即所以保身;弘扬道教,即所以救国"。中国伊斯兰教界成立了"中国回民救国协会",伊斯兰经学家虎嵩山提出了"国家兴亡,穆民有责"的口号,回族英雄马本斋组织了"回民支队",宣誓"为国为民,讨还血债"。

在中国,爱教必须与爱国相结合,不爱国的教徒无法立足。帮助帝国主义欺负中国的教徒不齿于人群……同时中国宗教界主流又不是狭隘的民族主义者,他们努力争取的是国家的复兴和民族的平等,反对的是以强凌弱,以暴欺善,他们愿意与世界上一切民族和宗教平等往来,友好相处,

---

① 牟钟鉴:《探索宗教》,第89页。

消解仇恨,反对战争,保卫世界和平与安宁。①

（4）中国宗教文化还有与时俱进、勇于改革的优良传统。

譬如,佛教传入中国后,在理论上不断创新,形成了中国特色的禅宗,近代又创建了"人间佛教"。又如,从"外丹道的肉体长生说"到"全真内丹学的性命双修说",从"新仙学"再到"生活道教",道教也是在不断创新中续写历史的。伊斯兰教与中国文化相结合,在教义教理和教法礼仪上都有所创造,特别是淡化"圣战"的理念,强化和平、仁慈的精神。天主教和基督教传入中国后,一直面临本土化问题。明末清初,耶稣会士采取尊礼俗融儒学的方针,得到中国人的好评;而多明我、方济各等差会欲用教皇神权限禁中国教民的宗教礼俗则遭驱逐。民国年间,发生"非基督教运动",基督教致力于"中国本色化教会",其宗旨为"一方面求使中国信徒担负责任,一方面发扬东方固有的文明,使基督教消除洋教的丑号"。20世纪50年代以来中国基督教的"三自"爱国运动,90年代以来的神学思想建设,也是不断改革创新的表现。

（5）注重自身人文素质的提高,为繁荣社会文化多做贡献,这也是中国宗教文化的一个优良传统。

以佛、道二教为例,它们各有博大丰厚的文化体系,对于中国的哲学、道德、文学、艺术、科技、民俗和中外文化交流等产生了广泛而深远的影响,成为中国优秀文化的重要组成部分。在哲学上,佛教的体悟智慧和道教的性命之学各有特色,对于中国哲学的宇宙论、本体论、心性论、人生论、认识论、修养论和辩证法的丰富发展,都起过重要推动作用。中国哲学史上有三个理论高峰:禅宗哲学,儒家道学和道教内丹学,佛、道有其二;而宋明儒学是融摄了佛、道二教的思想营养才得以创新的。在道德上,佛教的三报论、众生论、五戒十善论,道教的清静论、重生论、苦己利人论,都补充和丰富了儒家所弘扬的传统道德。②

牟先生的上述看法并非一家之言,而可以说是我国老一代专家学者的

---

① 牟钟鉴:《探索宗教》,第90页。

② 关于中国宗教对于中国文化和社会的历史贡献,牟先生在《中国宗教通史》(下)的总结部分有全面的论述,详见该书第十三章的"中国宗教的历史作用"一节。

共同见解。方立天先生在谈到宗教对于构建和谐社会的重要作用时,把中国宗教的优良传统概括为如下4点:

(1)宗教间互相包容的传统。中国宗教史表明,各宗教之间虽有对立的一面,但也有融合的一面,如佛教与道教就由冲突走向融合,道教与民间宗教也长期处于融合的状态。中国宗教并没有因为信仰价值的差异而导致长期冲突,更没有宗教之间的战争,相反是在长期的和睦共处中各得其所。

(2)爱人利他的传统。如佛教的平等慈悲,容忍布施的理念;道教的"齐同慈爱,异骨成亲"思想;基督教和伊斯兰教的爱人仁慈、慈善公益的主张,都有助于人与他人、人与社会的和谐。

(3)爱国爱教的传统。历史与现实都表明,中国宗教都主张把爱教与爱国统一起来,积极维护国家的主权、独立、荣誉和根本利益。如佛教提倡的"庄严国土,利乐有情";道教的"弘扬道教,即所以救国";伊斯兰教的"国家兴亡,穆民有责"等主张,都体现了中国宗教的爱国、护国的崇高精神。

(4)关爱自然的传统。宗教普遍认为,宇宙是一个整体,人与自然也是一个整体。如佛教的缘起共生论,认为人与自然万物都是由各种原因、条件而相待相成的;道教视天、地、人为一个统一的整体,都十分尊重自然,主张善待万物,提倡人与自然的和谐。①

比较牟先生和方先生所做的概括总结,可留下两方面的深刻印象:一方面,虽然两位先生各自把中国宗教的优良传统总结为5点或4点,但显而易见,他们关于前3点的概括与论证是基本一致的,综合他们的提法,我们可把这3点优良传统称为"提倡兼容并包"、"注重道德伦理"和"力主爱国爱教";另一方面,两位先生所讲的其他3点尽管有别,但它们因视角不同而有互补性,均有助于日后更完整地阐扬中国宗教文化的优良传统。关于此项研究的理论价值和现实意义,牟先生是这样解释的:

用跨文化的眼光和比较宗教学的视野来回顾和观察中国宗

---

① 以上4点概括,详见方立天:"和谐社会的构建与宗教的作用",《中国宗教》,2005年第7期。

教文化的历程,我们就会发现,中国宗教文化有着与西方宗教文化很不相同的轨迹和特点,它的传统在许多方面都是很可贵的。尤其是在当今国际上民族宗教冲突日益加剧,以基督教为背景的美国与以伊斯兰教为背景的阿拉伯国家之间的对抗日趋激烈的今天,中国宗教文化的优良传统更显示出它特有的价值和长处,既值得我们自豪,更需要我们认真去继承发扬,这对于推动中国社会的稳定和繁荣,对于促进世界的和平与发展,都是非常重要的。[1]

四、中国文化传统的思想资源

在前两节基础上,我们可把研讨思路再深化一步,即探讨一下前两节论述的"显著特点"和"优良传统"与中国文化传统思想资源的内在关系。为什么要探讨此种内在关系呢? 正如楼宇烈先生所言:"宗教是一种重要的社会文化现象。宗教作为文化的一个重要组成部分,也包含了它的价值观念、思维方式、生活样式以及信仰习俗等等,同时又都是跟整个文化的这些观念紧密联系在一起的。所以,我们研究一个民族、一个地区或者一个历史时期的宗教文化时,就不能脱离它所赖以存在的整体文化环境,否则将不可能准确揭示这一宗教文化的特点。"[2]关于中国宗教文化特点的研究是这样,对于中国宗教文化传统的认识也是如此。因而,将"中国宗教文化"置于"中国文化整体",通过探究它所赖以形成的思想资源,我们才能透彻理解中国宗教文化何以具有前述显著特点和优良传统。

中国文化传统主要包括儒、道、佛三大思想源流,这种看法已是我国学术界的共识。方立天先生对此有精练的表述:在中国特定的地理条件和历史背景下,中华传统文化主要是由儒、道、佛三大支柱构成的,儒、道、佛三家相近的文化旨趣都在于关注人文价值,但其内涵则有显著的差别,并呈

①　牟钟鉴:《探索宗教》,第86页。
②　楼宇烈:"探求合乎本土文化传统的宗教学研究理论",《中国宗教》,2008年第11期。

现为不同的文化传统分支。方先生认为,弘扬中华文化的优秀传统,最要紧的工作应是大力弘扬中华传统哲学——主要是儒、道、佛哲学的优秀传统。历史表明,三家哲学的优秀传统具有广泛、持久的影响力,长期以来熏陶、浸润着中华儿女的精神世界;三家哲学的优秀传统具有激励进步、鼓舞向前的积极作用,是促进社会和谐、推动历史发展的内在动力。① 这种注重弘扬中国哲学传统思想资源的主张,是契合中国文化、思想和学术背景的。冯友兰先生早就指出:"哲学在中国文明里所占据的地位,一向可跟宗教在其他诸多文明里的地位相比。"②所以,我们主要品评一下,前辈学者是如何抓住重大的理论与现实问题,阐发儒、道、佛的哲学思想资源的。

中国文化传统能否为"文明的共存"做出贡献呢? 这是汤一介先生为反驳文明冲突论而思考的问题。在"'文明的冲突'与'文明的共存'",一文里,汤先生着重探讨了儒、道两家的传统哲学观念所能提供的积极思想资源。这里择要如下。

1、儒家的"仁学"所能提供的积极思想资源

《郭店竹简》中说:"道始于情"。这里的"道"是指"人道",即人际关系或社会关系的原则。人与人的关系是从感情建立开始的,这正是孔子"仁学"的出发点。按孔子的说法,"仁"就是"爱人"。这种"爱人"思想从何而有呢? 孔子说:"仁者,人也,亲亲为大。""仁爱"精神是人所具有的,而爱自己的亲人最为根本。但"仁爱"精神并不止此,孔子的"仁学"是要由"亲亲"扩大到"仁民",也就是说,要"推己及人"。

做到"推己及人"并不容易,须以"忠恕之道"作为"仁"的准则,即"己所不欲,勿施于人","己欲立而立于人,己欲达而达人"。而将"仁"推广于社会,就是孔子说的"克己复礼曰仁"。按朱熹的解释:"克,胜也。己,谓身之私欲也。复,反也。礼者,天理之节文也"。这就是说,要克服私欲,以合乎礼仪。费孝通指出:"克己才能复礼,复礼是取得进入社会、成为一个

---

① 参见方立天:"弘扬中华文化的优秀传统",《人民日报》,2005 年 2 月 4 日,第 15 版。

② Fung Yu-Lan, *A Short History of Chinese Philosophy*, Edited by Derk Bodde, New York, NY: The Free Press, 1976, p. 1.

社会人的必要条件。扬己与克己也许正是东西方文化的差别的一个关键。"

"仁"是人的内在品德,"礼"指规范人们行为的礼仪制度。"礼之用,和为贵",人们遵守礼仪制度,必须是自觉的,出乎"爱人"之心,所以孔子说:"为仁由己,其由人乎?"有了追求"仁"的自觉要求,并把"仁爱之心"按照礼仪予以实现,整个社会就和谐安宁了,"一日克己复礼,天下归仁焉"。

孔子和儒家的这套思想,对于一个国家的治国者,对于现在世界上的那些发达国家(特别是美国)的统治集团不能说是没有意义的。"治国、平天下"应该行"仁政",行"王道",不应该行"霸道"。行"仁政"、"王道"可以使不同文化得以共同存在和发展;行"霸道"将引起文明的冲突,而使文化走向单一化,形成文化霸权主义。如果把孔子的"仁学"理论用于处理不同文明之间的关系,那么在不同文明之间就不会引起冲突以至于战争,而实现"文明的共存"。①

2、道家的"道论"所能提供的积极思想资源

老子《道德经》里,"道"是基本概念,而"自然无为"是"道"的基本特性。如王充《论衡》里讲:"自然无为,天之道也。"

老子提倡"自然无为",我们可以理解为:不要做(无为)违背人们愿望的事,这样社会才会安宁,天下才会太平。老子引用古代圣人的说法:"我无为而民自化,我好静而民自正,我无事而民自富,我无欲而民自朴。"这就是说,掌握权力的统治者不应对老百姓过多干涉(无为),不要扰乱老百姓的正常生活(好静),不要做违背老百姓意愿的事(无事),不要贪得无厌地盘剥老百姓(无欲),这样老百姓就会自己教化自己(自化),自己走上正轨(自正),自己富足起来(自富),自己生活朴素(自朴)。

如果我们对这一段话给以现代诠释,那就不仅可以使一个国家内部安宁,而且对消除不同文明之间的冲突无疑有重要意义。对这段话我们可以作如下诠释:在国与国之间对别国干涉越多,世界就越加混乱。大国强国

① 汤一介:"'文明的冲突'与'文明的共存'",《学术的风采——北京大学学报创刊五十周年论文选粹》(人文科学卷),程郁缀、龙协涛主编,北京大学出版社,2005年,第581页。

动不动用武力或武力相威胁,世界越是动荡不安和无序。大国强国以帮助弱国小国为名而行掠夺之实,弱国小国越加贫穷。发达国家以越来越大的欲望争夺世界财富和统治权,世界就会成为一个无道德的恐怖世界。据此,我认为"无为"也许对新帝国的领导者是一付治病良方,如果他们能接受,将会使世界得以和平和安宁。①

3、中国佛教哲学理念所能提供的积极思想资源

中国佛教哲学在当代社会,在世界现代化进程中,还有没有价值? 如果有的话,又有什么样的现代价值? 这是方立天先生在厚重的《中国佛教哲学要义》的"结语"部分所要回答的问题。为此,方先生先是考察了"21世纪人类社会的基本特点与基本矛盾";又着眼 21 世纪的发展趋势来诠释了"中国佛教哲学的基本理念",像"缘起"、"因果"、"平等"、"慈悲"、"中道"和"圆融"等;然后,针对当代人类社会的三组基本矛盾——人与自我的矛盾、人与人的矛盾和人与自然的矛盾,逐一阐发了中国佛教哲学的现代意义。其中,尤以第二部分内容,即"协调人与人的矛盾,维护世界和平",与我们的话题密切相关。

方先生指出,人与人的关系,包括人与他人、人与社会、人与民族、人与国家等多重关系。由此来看,当今世界的主要问题有二:一是,由于民族、宗教、领土、资源、利益冲突等因素引发的局部动乱冲突,某些地区的人民正在遭受战争的苦难;与此同时,恐怖主义等各种非传统安全问题又日趋严峻。二是,南北贫富差距更加扩大,世界上还有相当一部分人生活贫困。中国佛教哲学的一些基本理念,对于化解这些问题,是有理论启示和现实意义的。

上述两个问题中,和平共处是最大的难题。20 世纪的两次世界大战,残杀生灵数以千万计,如果 21 世纪重演世界大战,人类有可能同归于尽。要避免战争,就要消除战争的根源,其根源之一即在于:不懂得人类共依共存,自利利他的缘起之理,不重视沟通和解,不尊重他人生命。佛教的平等

---

① 汤一介:"'文明的冲突'与'文明的共存'",《学术的风采——北京大学学报创刊五十周年论文选粹》(人文科学卷),程郁缀、龙协涛主编,北京大学出版社,2005 年,第 583 - 584 页。

理念强调，人人本性的平等、人格的平等、尊严的平等。平等意味着尊重，意味着和平；和平来自对人我平等的深切体认，基于平等的和平，才是真正而持久的和平。所以，佛教的人我互相尊重的思想，有助于人类和平共处，追求共同理想，建设人间净土。此外，佛教所讲的"慈悲济世"、"五戒"和"十善"等理论，均以"不杀生"为首，突出地表现了佛教尊重生命、尊重他人的崇高品格；而慈悲思想则体现了对他人的同情和关爱，也是远离战争，呵护和平的。自太虚法师倡导人间佛教以来，中国佛教一直关注世界和平，渴望世界和平，呼吁世界和平。可以说，维护世界和平已成为当代佛教弘法的重要内容之一，佛教对于推动世界和平已发挥了独特的、不可替代的重要作用。

南北贫富悬殊问题，一部分人的生活贫困问题，不仅直接关系到弱势群体和劳苦大众的生存，还会构成动乱的根源，并直接威胁地区乃至世界和平。佛教的平等慈悲观念，为化解这些问题提供了指针。佛教一贯重视慈悲济世，助人解除痛苦，给人以快乐。佛教的布施是重要的修持法门，以慈悲心而施福利于人，施与他人以财物、体力和智慧，为他人造福成智。当前，两岸佛教着力发扬菩萨"不为自身求安乐，但愿众生得离苦"的大慈大悲精神，充分发挥慈善救济的功能，扶贫济困，施医送药，赞助"希望工程"，教化失足者和罪犯等，使受救济者既得到物质的援助，也得到精神的提升。

中国佛教哲学的现代意义在于，其重要原理日益得到充分阐发，并经创造性诠释后其作用开始彰显；把佛教哲学思想运用于缓解人类社会的基本矛盾，必将有助于提升人类的精神素质，减少人类的现实痛苦，满足人类的新需要，进而促进人类社会的和平共处和共同发展。[①]

4、中国文化传统的基本哲学精神

前面分头叙述了儒、道、佛哲学思想资源的重要现实意义。这三大思想源流交融而成的中国文化传统，显然是一个有机的整体。那么，整个中国文化传统的基本哲学精神何在呢？此种哲学精神又可为推动宗教对话、化解文明冲突、构建和谐世界提供何等重要的思想资源呢？这两个问题可

---

① 方立天:《中国佛教哲学要义》，下卷，中国人民大学出版社 2002 年，第 1218 – 1219 页。

以说是我国学者自改革开放以来、尤其是近十几年来一直探索的前沿课题。现有大量学术成果中,还是要数学贯中西的老一代学者所做的理论探讨最值得重视、最有参考价值。

季羡林先生在上个世纪 90 年代初就一言蔽之:中国传统文化的精髓就是"天人合一",就是"和谐"。现在我国学者论及中国文化传统的基本哲学精神时,也大多强调"和谐"观念,并主要用孔子的"和而不同"思想来予以解释说明。虽然这可使我们了解和谐思想的主要来源,但仅此思路是不够的,还应将其提升为中国哲学传统的一个基本范畴,以揭示它所蕴含的中国哲学智慧。让我们来看冯友兰和张岱年两位中国哲学史学科开创者就此范畴所做的理解和阐释。

对待不唯相冲突,更常有与冲突相对待之现象,是谓和谐。和谐非同一,相和谐者不必相类;和谐亦非统一,相和谐者虽相联结而为一体,然和谐乃指一体外之另一种关系。和谐包括四方面:一相异,即非绝对同一;二不相毁灭,即不相否定;三相成而相济,即相互维持;四相互之间有一种均衡。①

这是张岱年先生对于"和谐"的界说,他是将此范畴上升至哲学思维层次,作为辩证法的一个基本概念来理解的。冯友兰先生的探求思路也是如此。冯先生以 95 岁高龄写就的《中国哲学史新编》(七册),是以传扬"太和"观念的历史启示来收笔的。他指出:中国宋代哲学家张载曾把辩证法的规律归纳为四句话:"有象斯有对,对必反其为;有反斯有仇,仇必和而解。"(《正蒙·太和篇》)"和"是张载哲学体系中的一个重要范畴,《正蒙》开头就说:"太和所谓道,中涵浮沉、升降、动静、相感之性,是生絪缊、相荡、胜负、屈伸之始。"所谓"和",是充满矛盾斗争的,而并非相反。所谓"浮沉、升降、动静、相感之性",就是矛盾;所谓"絪缊、相荡、胜负、屈伸",就是斗争。因而,张载认为,一个社会的正常状态就是"和",宇宙的正常状态也是"和"。这个"和",称为"太和"。冯先生接着深有体会地做出如下总结:

　　在中国古典哲学中,"和"与"同"不一样。"同"不能容"异";

---

① 张岱年:《哲学思维论——天人五论之一》,《张岱年全集》,第三卷,河北人民出版社,1996年,第 35 页。

"和"不但能容"异",而且必须有"异",才能称其为"和"。

"仇必和而解"是客观的辩证法。不管人们的意愿如何,现代的社会,特别是国际社会,是照着这个客观辩证法发展的。

现代历史是向着"仇必和而解"这个方向发展的,但历史发展的过程是曲折的,所需要的时间,必须以世纪计算……人是最聪明、最有理性的动物,不会永远走"仇必仇到底"那样的道路。这就是中国哲学的传统和世界哲学的未来。①

两位先生的以上见解,并不仅仅代表中国学者对于本文化传统的基本哲学精神的价值认同,国外饱学之士也有同感,也认此理。譬如,宗教对话和全球伦理的倡导者汉斯·昆,向西方电视观众介绍中国宗教文化传统时便讲解道:在整个中国哲学传统中,一以贯之的就是寻求天地间的和谐一致;时至今日,中国人依然寻求天地间的和谐:人与自然、天与人间的和谐,社会以及人自身的和谐。他把此种中国哲学传统称为"大和谐精神",并相信此种精神不但对中国的未来有重要意义,而且对构建世界伦理有重大贡献。②

关于人类社会和世界文化的发展前景,费孝通先生有句名言:"各美其美,美人之美,美美与共,天下大同"。如此饱满"和谐精神"的美言美意,是否可为促进宗教对话、化解文明冲突、共建和谐世界提供"富有古老智慧的中国经验"呢? 笔者信以为然。

---

① 以上概述和引文详见冯友兰:《中国哲学史新编》,第七册,第八十一章;也可见于冯友兰:《中国现代哲学史》,广东人民出版社,1999 年,第 251 – 254 页。

② 参见汉斯·昆:《世界宗教寻踪》,第 180 页。

第二部分

◎ 全球化时代的宗教传统

佛教的现代价值

楼宇烈

佛教的现代价值问题，其实本不是一个问题。佛教在今天能够存在，当然是有其现代价值的。但是长期以来，由于我们对佛教这样一种文化现象有各种各样的误解，甚至于曲解，所以我们对于这个问题才会产生怀疑。因此，我在这里首先就要讲一讲，为什么我们现在要来讨论这么一个不成问题的问题。

这其中原因有很多，但是我想主要从三个方面来讲一讲：

第一个方面是我们现在思想中经常会有的问题，那就是佛教作为一种宗教，而我们现在是处于一个科学的时代。那么，科学与宗教是不是相互冲突、矛盾的？我们在这样一个科学的时代是不是不应该再信仰宗教？这个问题并不是现在才有，上世纪初新文化运动时期就提出要高举两面大旗，一面是德先生，一面是赛先生。所谓德先生就是民主，所谓赛先生就是科学，新文化运动就是要提倡民主与科学，因此对于我们的传统文化进行了极力的批判。这其中，对于儒家的批判，主要在于认为它是维护封建专制主义的，与民主思想是对立的，当然要打倒，也就是所谓的"打倒孔家店"。而另一方面，新文化运动认为我们提倡科学就不应该再去信仰迷信的宗教。在当时看来，宗教就是一种迷信。所谓迷信，就是对神的盲目崇拜和绝对服从。所以当时一些先进的中国人都是提倡科学，反对宗教，并且成立了"反宗教大同盟"，我们一些著名的科学家、学者都参加了这个同盟，比如说著名的北大校长蔡元培先生、胡适先生、陈独秀和李大钊先生。因为他们认为宗教是迷信，而现在是倡导科学的时代，宗教当然就没有它存在的价值了。马克思主义传入中国后，人们对宗教也是抱一个批判的态度，认为宗教是被统治阶级利用以麻痹人民的鸦片，所以在科学时代我们不能再提倡宗教。很多人在对马克思主义宗教观的解释过程中指出，根据马克思主义的分析，宗教有其产生、发展和消亡这样一个历史过程。宗教之所以产生是由于人们在科学知识低下的情况下，对自然和社会的许多现象无法做主，无法控制它。因此就要抬出一个神灵来加以祈求，希望他们帮助我们解决这些问题；其次，是历代的统治阶级，为了要更好的统治人民，借助于宗教这样一种文化来麻痹和毒害人民。这就是所谓宗教产生的认识论根源和社会根源。而且据此就预言，等到有一天我们人类有能力来掌控自然，掌控自己的命运，推翻阶级社会的阶级压迫，社会成了没有阶级压迫的社会，那么宗教就失去了它存在的根基，就会自然消亡。这种说法在我们的头脑中可以说是根深蒂固的，所以我们觉得现在科学发达了，进入了社会主义，消灭了阶级压迫，那么宗教肯定早晚会消灭，因为它不符合时代的要求，不符合科学的要求。可事实上我们看到，宗教的产生不是那么简单的，仅仅有认识的根源和社会的阶级根源，我们只要仔细想一想，宗教之所以产生，在很大程度上，还有人们一种对神圣的向往，一种心理慰藉的需要。人们总是向往着要比现实中的人更加纯洁一点、完善一点、美好一点，我想每个人都会有这种追求，每个人都不会满足于现实中的这样一种状态。此外，人类的心里还有其他各种各样的需要。即使我们从认识根源和社会根源来讲，也并不是那么简单。不是说我们能够认识我们的生存环境的各种事物的规律，就可以完全把握我们所生存的天地之间的万物。因为从哲学上讲，从马克思主义哲学来讲，有一个矛盾是永远不能解决的，那就是人的认识的局限性和世界的无限性之间的矛盾。这就告诉我们，人是不可能完全认识我们生存的这样一个世界的，也就是我们对于世界的认识其实是很有局限性的，我们只能认识世界的一部分。而且从科学认识的角度来讲，人们也会发现，当我们对客观存在世界认识越多的时候，我们就会发现没有被我们认识的方面也会越来越多。其实不要说我们对世界的认识，就拿我们每个人读书的经历来讲，当你读了几本书后，就觉得自己已经知道很多了，什么话都敢说。但是当你读书越来越多的时候，你就会发现我不知道的东西也越来越多，话也就越来越不敢说，这是非常正常的事情。所以说人的认识是非常有限的，而这个世界是无限的。中国古代庄子就说过一句话"吾生也有涯，而知也无涯。以有涯随无涯，殆已！"我的生命是有限的，最多几十年或者上百年，而我要认识的世界是无限的，没有尽头的。我要想用有限的生命去把握无限的认识对象，那是非常危险的，不可能做到。所以我们从这些方面来讲，不是简单的有一天我们认识了世界的规律是怎样，我们就可以完全掌控世界了。人类科学发展到今天，许多的自然现象和自然灾害，我们仍旧无法去把握和控制它，这就说明我们人不管是知识也好，能力也好，都是非常有限的，这也可以说是宗教产生的一个基础。也正因为这样，我们的科学越发展，宗教也在同步的发展，可以说比过去还要兴盛。现在在西方，宗教的发展，五花八门，比传统宗教要复杂得多，全世界的新兴宗教也有上万个。所以，并不是像我们原来所想象的，科学发展了，宗教就不需要了，就会自动消亡，不是那么简单的。科学的时代并不意味着宗教就没有生存的基础和原因了。

同时，宗教跟科学是不是就是对立的呢？我想也不是，它们基本上是属于两个角度的文化和知识。科学是侧重于对外在世界物理现象的探求，而宗教，包括哲学、历史、艺术、文学等，更侧重对人的内心世界的探求。所以我们常讲有人文的知识，有科学的知识，人文知识不能代替科学知识，反之亦然。这并不是说两者是对立的，而是人文知识可以从科学知识中吸取很多的营养来丰富发展自己，反过来科学也可以从人文知识中学习到许多思维的方式。世界这近几百年的历史充分证明了这一点：当科学发展起来以后，许多人文学科就借用、吸取了科学研究的方法和成果来对人文的许多问题提进行深入的分析、定性。反过来，当科学的发展遇到了许多问题的时候，就借鉴人文的思维方式来进一步推动自身的发展。其实在我们许多人的观念里，科学的概念基本上还停留在西方18世纪以来实证科学的框架里。而从20世纪以来，科学已经突破了实证科学的理念，我们称之为现代科学。现代科学界和哲学界，把实证科学称之为简单性科学，把20世纪以来的科学称之为复杂性科学，这两个概念实际上有很大的变化。实证科学是强调普遍适用,如果没有普遍意义,就认为是不科学的。实证科学的思维方式是直线性的因果关系,强调的是定量、定性的分析。可是现代科学早就突破了这些,现代科学强调的是整体性、系统性、随机性,非线性,不一定具有普遍适用性。这样的变化就是它从人文学科学习到的,因为人文学科研究人的历史,研究人心灵的变化,它有很多测不准的东西,是变动不拘的,那么现代科学就吸收这些东西来发展。大家都知道,中医是整体性的、系统的、模糊的、随机的,而且相当个性化的医疗方式,同样一个病在不同的人身上,其药方是不断进行修改的,不可能说一个药方在所有人身上都适用。所以从上个世纪开始一直到这个世纪,人们一直都在讨论中医科学不科学。前几年还提出中医是不科学的,应当从医疗体系中除名,引起了全国性的讨论。我们的钱学森先生就发表了一个看法,他说中医讲究的是系统性和整体性,这恰恰是现代科学最核心、最重视的一个理论,怎么能说中医不科学呢?它只是不符合原来的实证科学的观点。因此现在有人就用复杂性科学来诠释中医。我们现在之所以对宗教提出这些问题,其中一个很重要的原因就在于,把它跟科学对立起来,事实上它们并不是对立的,而是属于不同的知识体系。因为时间关系,我这里只能比较简单的来讲。

第二个问题,就是所谓无神和有神,唯心和唯物的问题,这也是我们非常大的一个思想障碍。宗教毕竟是唯心的,有神的,而我们现在强调的是唯物主义,强调无神论,这就产生了对立。我们讲唯物主义无神论,就要批判唯心主义有神论,而宗教是唯心主义有神论的。其实这样的认识是有问题的。因为从上个世纪以来,我们接受的宗教概念是从西方传来的,它基本上是欧洲在从中世纪走向近代的过程中间,近代的启蒙思想家、哲学家,对西方中世纪基督宗教的一些特征的概括。因此到现在为止,在我们很多人头脑中对于宗教概念的理解,还是它至少要具有四个特征:第一,它是有神信仰的,尤其是一神信仰。例如基督宗教的上帝就是唯一的,绝对的。第二,它追求彼岸世界,它的关注点不是现实世界,而是彼岸世界,比如要追求上天堂,到上帝身边去。第三,它提倡对于神的盲目崇拜,反对人的自由理性。不允许人自由思考,只能听上帝的,是独断的。我们看到,在欧洲中世纪许多人因为自由思考,提出了对世界不一样的解释,就马上遭到宗教法庭的审判,或者绞死,或者烧死,许多科学家都是这样死的。因而在欧洲启蒙运动思想家眼中,宗教就是绝对地服从,是独断论的。第四,宗教跟科学是对立的。因为科学是人的自由理性的产物,人摆脱了神的束缚,自由地去观察、探讨世界,然后才创造了近代科学。由以上四条,上个世纪就产生了关于中国传统文化中间有没有宗教这样一个问题的讨论。

如果拿这四个标准来衡量,中国传统文化中第一条就找不到。因为在中国传统文化中间没有一神的信仰。神是有很多很多的,哪里都有神,山有山神,河有河神,门有门神,灶有灶神。但是这些神又都不具有绝对的权威,因为他们都是福善祸淫的。什么是福善祸淫呢?就是福是给善人的,祸是做坏事的人的。这句话说明神是按照人来分配福祸的,最终决定的是人自己。这就是中国文化的根本特点,也是跟西方宗教文化的不同点。中国的儒家思想根据的是西周一代的文化,我们在《尚书》里面可以看到这么一句话,可以说是中国文化根本特征的凝聚:"皇天无亲,唯德是辅",皇天上帝是不讲亲的,而是看你有没有德。你有德我就帮助你,你没有德我就不辅助你。在《春秋左传》里面有也有这样一句话,"神聪明正直,依人而行",神是非常聪明正直的,耳聪目明,而且是非常正直的,但是他这个聪明正直是按照人来行使的。所以中国文化是把人的主体性放在第一位的,而不是神,这是很大的一个差异。中国人强调道德的自觉和自律,所以上世纪的人们一检查中国文化的特征,不符合上述西方宗教的标准,就说中国人没有宗教信仰。西方人也是这么看,说中国人没有对于神的神圣性的敬仰。刚改革开放的时候,我们许多人出国到了欧洲需要填一张表,表里有一项是"有没有宗教信仰?"一般的中国人都会填无,这在欧洲人看来,就非常可怕,没有宗教信仰,那不就是想怎样就怎样,没有人可以管束他。这就是他们不理解在中国的文化中强调人的自觉自律,靠自我来约束。所以从上个世纪一直到本世纪都还在讨论儒家是宗教还是不是宗教,这是学术问题,我们不去说它。然而这也就说明,人们认为中国文化中是没有宗教的。我们不会提出"佛教是不是宗教?道教是不是宗教?"这样的问题,我们习惯了认为它们属于宗教。

可是我们不知道历史上儒家也是宗教,"儒释道三教"是传统的称呼,把儒释道看成是同等的。同时这也说明中国佛教和道教的特性并不同西方的宗教概念是一样的。如果我们承认佛教是宗教,那么我可以告诉大家,佛教是无神论的,大家可能觉得这很奇怪,宗教怎么会是无神论的,可事实就是如此。上个世纪初,康有为提出来要把儒教变成国教,遭到人们的批判。当时正好是打倒孔家店,批判儒家的时候,你还提出把儒教变成国教,这不是复辟、保皇么?所以康有为被看做是保皇复辟。可是这时候人们也看到,西方的强大不只是物质的,还有它制度上的先进,我们要学习他们的制度,就进行了戊戌变法、辛亥革命,可是都没有成功。于是人们就想到还有精神和思想观念的问题,所以搞新文化运动。而在思想观念问题里面,人们看到西方有宗教作为人们一个共同的精神家园,所以说中国要强大,也要有一个共同的精神家园,康有为是在这个基础上提出来以儒教为国教。可是他不合时宜,因为当时儒教是主要的攻击对象,所以大家都不能接受。于是有另外一位重要的思想家,辛亥革命中的重要人物——章太炎,他就提出要以佛教为国教。他当时提出的理由就是,佛教是一个无神的宗教,是合乎时代精神的。为什么说佛教是一个无神的宗教呢?他说因为佛教强调的是自力解脱。佛教是要讲了脱生死,解脱我们生命的烦恼和痛苦,它的办法就是靠自力,而不是靠他力,自力就是自己的力量。所以佛教不是叫你去求神来帮你解脱,而是来启发你的智慧,让你自己去觉悟,解脱,了脱生死。

这个问题从佛教的诞生来看也是如此。释迦牟尼当年在古印度创立佛教的时候,他所针对的对象是当时印度的婆罗门教,也就是现在的印度教前身。婆罗门教强调世界由神创造的,人的命运也是由神来决定的,其中最主要的一个神就是梵天,由他来决定世界和人的命运。佛教的兴起就是要破除掉这样一种说法,要破除这样一种因果关系。我们每个人都在这样一种生命状态下,也就是处于一种结果中。我们知道印度把人分为四等,第一等是神职人员,婆罗门;第二等是武士,那些部落的领袖;第三等人是那些商人,自由的手工业者;第四等人,奴隶。认为这四种人一辈子也不要想改变命运,因为这是由神决定了的,不可能改变,你的这个结果是由神来决定的,也就是神是因,你是果。佛教认为这种因果是错误的,所以称它为邪因论。佛教就要提出一个正确的因果观,认为你今天之所以受这样的果报,是由你自己以往的行为造成的,也就是你以往所造的业,所以佛教是讲"自作自受",那么当然解脱也要靠你自己。所以佛教从根本上反对由神来决定世界,决定人的命运。然而佛教在长期的发展过程中,开始受到印度其他宗教的影响,逐渐产生了一些神灵的信仰,最初佛就是一个——释迦牟尼,佛就是觉悟者,菩萨也是指觉悟的有情众生,所以它是没有神的。到了公元一世纪前后,也就是佛灭后五百年左右,佛教开始滋长了一种神灵的信仰,佛开始有了十方世界十方佛,有了三世佛,有了过去七佛,菩萨也有了各种各样的菩萨。在民众的信仰中间,就开始把它神明化。可是在根本教义上它并不是如此。佛教的经文里面,尤其是很多后期发展起来的经典里面,很多经文反复强调,佛、菩萨只是一种表法的东西。所谓表法,就是它表达了佛教的一种精神。譬如说,观音表达了佛教的慈悲精神,所以礼拜观音,就是要去学习观音的这种慈悲精神,用这种慈悲的精神来做人做事。所以佛教是这样一种特征的宗教,我们可以称之为无神的宗教。因此有神和无神并不是宗教和非宗教的一个根本的分野的特征。

中国的儒家能不能称为宗教?我觉得在某种意义上可以,因为宗教可以从不同的角度去定义:我们可以从它的起源、发生发展去定义它,也可以从它跟其他文化的不同特点去定义它,更重要的,我们还可以从它的社会功能去定义它。宗教作为一种文化,总要发挥一定的社会影响,总有一种社会的功能,也就是我们今天要探讨的"价值"。其实不管是什么宗教,什么文化,它对于社会的功能就是一种教化的功能,都是灌输一种价值观念和思维方式,一种生活习惯,一种信仰的习俗。当然宗教还会有一些其他的特征,比如说要有组织,教职人员等等。从另一个角度讲,宗教可能更多的是在人的生活当中发挥它的功能,比如说人生要生老病死,婚丧嫁娶,宗教都要把这些东西管起来。我们说西方的宗教基督教,在电影和书里我们都可以看到,人一生下来就要到教堂中受洗礼,受完洗礼实际也就给他登记上一个户口;结婚的时候要到教堂里面去行礼;死了以后教堂要给他超度,中国人叫超度,他们叫在墓地里安息。我们中国的儒教照样发挥了这样的作用,人生下来了要过满月、百岁、周岁;结婚要拜天地,拜祖先;死了以后要搞祭礼。儒家经典《礼记》里面讲得非常清楚,"礼始于冠,本于昏,重于丧祭"。"礼始于冠",从冠礼开始,也就是成年礼,标志一个人成年了,有了他的责任和义务。"本于昏,"立足点落实到婚礼上,婚礼是生命延续的重要关节。"重于丧祭",丧礼祭礼都是非常重要的,丧礼就是亲人去世,要有隆重严肃的丧礼,回报父母的养育之恩。祭礼,就是祭祖、祭天地,这也是不忘本,因为没有祖先哪有父母,哪有你呢? 这在《论语》里面就叫做"慎终追远",丧礼就是慎终,慎重的对待人们的死亡;追远就是祭礼,祭祖先祭天地,你的生命是祖先那来的,祖先的生命是天地那来的,天地是万物生命之根本,祖先是你这个族类生命之根本,不能忘本。这些礼仪其实就是进行一种道德教化,希望你信上帝也是一种道德教化。所以《论语》里面讲:"慎终追远,民德归厚矣。"慎终追远,民风就非常淳朴了。我们现代社会在一定意义上讲就是缺乏了慎终追远,不知道感恩,经常地忘本。所以儒教也一样起到了宗教的功能,照样也可以说它是一种宗教。

但是我们必须看到,中国的宗教跟西方的宗教有很大的区别。刚才提到的康有为给出了一个明确的说明。他讲:中国是有宗教的,但是中国的宗教和西方的宗教是有根本的区别的,西方的宗教是一种神造的宗教,中国的宗教是一种人造的宗教。所谓神造,就是以神为本;所谓人造;就是以人为本。所以宗教我们不要简单地用有神或者无神来区分,现在有些人主张儒教是宗教,有些人主张儒教不是宗教,都是用有神或者无神来区分。主张它不是宗教就是因为它无神,主张它是宗教就拼命去论证儒家是信神的,拜上帝的,跟基督宗教一样的。这样一种思维方式,根源都在于拿有神、无神来区分宗教,拿唯物、唯心来区分宗教,所以导致了我们很多的模糊和犹豫不定。所以我们讲到佛教的现代意义或者价值,这个问题也是一个很大的心理障碍。

第三个我们思想中间的障碍就是传统和现代。我们常常把传统和现代对立起来。好像走向现代就要抛弃传统,就要否定传统,就要跟传统断绝关系。应该说,这一百年来在这个问题上我们是很需要反思的。我们社会的进步、科技的发达、物质的富裕,并没有能够完全解决人类面临的种种矛盾、冲突、烦恼、痛苦、困惑等等,有的时候我们甚至会感到这些矛盾、冲突反而是增多了,加重了,究其根源,就在于这个社会对于精神文明倡导的不力,人文教育的滞后、传统道德观念和宗教信仰的淡化,而其中一个非常重要的原因就是传统的断裂。所以现在我们面临着一个前进的方向问题,我们社会发展到今天这样的程度以后,再怎么继续前进。是继续的背离传统,完全跟随在西方文化的后面发展呢？还是,我们要思考把现代化重新根植到我们传统文化的主张上去,这是现在摆在我们面前的一个非常尖锐而迫切的问题。我们如果不把现代化根植到传统文化的土壤上面,我们就会失去自我,就谈不上什么建设有中国特色的社会主义。因为社会的特色主要就体现在文化上,而文化是人类精神财富的凝聚,是民族精神的体现,你没了这个,就体现不出民族精神的特点。所以我们一定要在传统的基础之上,来推进我们的现代化。这个社会的发展,历史的发展,总是一步一步地,总是在前人的基础上一点一点积累起来的,所以我们今天一定要认真地去反思传统的文化。

其实传统并不是像我们想象的那样,是不可改变的,传统一定要适应时代的变化做出自我的调整,否则就会被淘汰。那么这种转化就要靠现代人去做,所以我们现在首先要从观念上面认同传统与现代是不能割裂的,我们必须要在传统的基础之上发展我们的现代,那么我们就会主动积极地去做转化传统的工作,来使得我们现代的文化更加丰富。我们现在正面临着非常多的传统文化流逝的危机。我们常常讲要进行爱国主义教育,这是没错的。但进行爱国主义教育,核心就在于让人们能够认同我们的历史,如果根本不认同我们的历史,谈什么爱国呢？而这个历史不是空的,历史就凝聚在我们的文化之中,文化是历史的载体,不认同文化,不认同我们的文化传统,那就不可能认同我们的历史。不认同历史而去讲爱国,那不是笑话么？你看台湾前几年要搞"台独",其中重要的措施就是把中国史改成外国史,本国史只讲台湾史。中国近代有位著名的思想家叫龚自珍,他讲过一句非常深刻的话,他说:"欲灭人之国,必先灭其史。"你要想灭掉一个人的国家,首先就要灭掉它的历史。人们忘掉了自己的历史,他怎么爱他过去的国家呢？所以我们要让人爱国,首先就要让他爱我们的历史,爱我们的历史就要落实到爱我们的文化,认同我们的文化,这是非常重要的一点。再进一步讲,文化又是靠什么东西来传承的呢？就是我们的文字语言,所以文字语言又是我们文化的载体。当然,还有其他的很多实物,比方说古代的建筑,我们现在也不太重视了,以前要改造就马上把旧的东西给拆了,其实建筑也是一个载体,我们很多其他的文物都是载体,但其中我想最重要的还是文字语言,尤其是文字。中国之所以文化能够得以传承不断,中国的文字是起到了决定的作用。尽管你说话别人不一定听得懂,但是写出来他就都懂了。中国的文字在文化的统一和传承上面起到了非常重要的作用。可是我们并没有注意到这一点,然而外国人都注意到了。《参考消息》前些日子发表了一篇文章,就讲到中国的汉字面临的危机:现在85%的中年以下的青年人都是提笔忘字,因为我们现代都用电脑打字了,字怎么写都不知道了。所以写字现在变成书法,书法又变成了艺术,而忘掉了书法根本的含义,书法就是书写之法度也,你把它变成艺术,那就变成画字了。我们常讲现在的孩子,不是在写字而是在画字。我的孙子,今年读小学四年级,他从一年级开始我就看他写字,怎么都是画出来的,不讲笔顺。他说老师都不教他们笔顺,也不去纠正他们笔顺的错误,所以他就画呗,画出来反正都是一样的。还有现在的许多的词都用英文字母的缩写,那慢慢的中国的文字就会大量的萎缩,文字所存储的文化气息也就会大量的流失。语言,混杂着外来的语言,这问题就是很大的。欧洲在二十年以前就要来抵制语言的混乱,要保持它语言的纯洁,这就是文化的保卫战。所以我们的传统和现代也要很好的结合。

我想,要讨论今天这样一个话题,其他原因可能还有很多,我这里只讲这三个方面:宗教与科学,有神和无神,传统与现代。这些方面就给我们带来很多问题,使我们想不清楚。只要我们想清楚了,宗教在我们现代的价值就不需要怀疑和讨论,它的存在本身就说明了它的价值和意义。当然,都有一些什么样的意义和价值,是我们可以谈,也需要谈的。下面我就结合佛教来谈一下。

去年在无锡举行的第二届世界佛教论坛中,我提供了一个稿子,题目叫做《科学时代下的佛教定位》,就跟我们今天的题目很有关系。在科学时代这样的环境下,我们找不到自己究竟是什么样的一个身份,确定不了自己该做什么,该怎么样定位。所以很多佛教学者就一直在探讨这个问题。我想,这个问题其实跟传统文化还是可以密切结合的。中国的传统就对佛教有一个定位。我刚才讲,中国是儒释道三教,而这三教在中国传统中是有一个定位的,这个定位是相对的,三者分工合作。怎么分工合作呢?中国从唐代以来就有这样的说法,"以儒治国,以道治身,以佛治心"。佛教的定位是治心的,儒家的定位是治国的,道教的定位是治身的,讲养生。当然这个定位是相对的,不是讲儒家只能治国,不能用到别的地方。我们儒家的很多思想就在讲修身养性,比如"仁者寿"、"德者寿"等等。但是这三教还是有一个相对的定位,由此三者相互配合来治国、治身、治心。佛教在今天,我们依然可以把它定义为治心,这也是跟佛教的教理密切相关的。

在现实生活中间,有人有大烦恼、大痛苦,有人有小烦恼、小痛苦,我不相信一个人一点烦恼痛苦都没有,只有大小的区别。佛教里面讲,一个生命有八个苦——生老病死,爱别离、怨憎会、求不得、五蕴炽盛。所谓五蕴炽盛,就是"我执"的顽固。我们为什么有这样的烦恼痛苦呢?佛教就是因为你造了很多的业。什么业?身口意三业。所谓身口意,身就是行动,口就是说话,意就是想问题,身有三业——杀、盗、淫,即杀生、偷盗、淫乱。口有四业,妄语,说假话、绮语,漂亮话,恶语,骂人的话,两舌、搬弄是非。意也有三业,就是贪、瞋、痴。所以生命,通过身口意三个方面在造十个业,如果是杀盗淫等等,是造的恶业,若不杀,不盗、不淫,是造的善业。不管是善业还是恶业,都会给你的生命带来种种快乐、痛苦,其实在佛教看来,快乐和痛苦是相对的。在某种程度上来讲,快乐也可能是一种痛苦。所以一个人活着总是要说话、做事、想问题,那么这三业就会导致这样那样的烦恼。那么,什么在支配这身口意三业?就是心,心在支配你。这里就回到刚才讲的唯物还是唯心的问题。再唯心的人也不会认为,人不吃饭就能活着,不会认为这个事物是我头脑想出来的,不会认为身体都没有了,还会有这样那样的想法。所以佛教也分析得很清楚,一个生命体是五蕴生,所谓五蕴就是色受想行识,色就是指的色身,就是你的肉体,受想行识就是指你的精神。所以任何一个生命都是物质生命和精神生命的结合,而且物质生命是基础,没有物质生命就不可能有精神生命。问题是,当这两者结合在一起以后,谁在起支配作用,当然是精神生命,所以说是你的心在起主导作用。所谓身心,身是基础,心是支配这个身的。你的言论也好,行动也好,都是这个心在支配的。中国人有一个成语描写的非常逼真,就是一个人如果失去了他的心,没有了灵魂,那么这个人就叫"行尸走肉",也就根本谈不上生命意义了。所以一个人的生命要有意义,是他的精神生命在起主导作用。中国儒家的荀子也讲过,心是君,眼耳鼻舌都是臣。既然如此,为了改变你的行为,消除你的烦恼,那当然必须从自心入手。

那么有哪些心呢？佛教讲得很清楚：贪瞋痴三心。贪就是你的贪欲，佛教并不否定人的欲望，七情六欲是正常的，刚才讲了如果没有心，人就不算一个完整的生命，而只是一个行尸走肉。所以一个真正完整的生命一定是有七情六欲的。但是如果过分的去求这个欲，那就是贪。尤其对人来讲，贪名贪利，贪食贪色，他的贪欲只要开发出来就是无穷尽的，中国人称为欲壑难填。也正因为有这样一种贪心，所以人就会做许多不该做的事情，损害了别人也损害了自己。瞋，指怨瞋、怨恨。就是老是要跟别人去比较，嫉妒比自己强的人，看不起不如自己的人。这种人的我痴、我慢是非常的严重，碰到事情从来不去反省自己，老是怨天怨地，怨人怨事。这样就只会越来越增加自己的烦恼。反过来如果人有一种感恩心的话，就不会有这么多烦恼。总是心存感激，知道自己的一切都是别人成就的，所以做什么事都是心情愉快的去做，而不是因为没办法才去做的。痴，就是愚痴。所谓的愚痴就是佛教讲的无明，是相对于明来讲的。明就是能够看得一清二楚，不仅看到现象，还看到本质。可是一般人往往只能看到表面的现象，看不到里面的本质。把表面的现象看成是事情的本来面貌，并据此来思考，就形成一种颠倒，颠倒就产生许多的妄想，所以我们常讲"颠倒妄想"。而人要破除无明，这不是一件容易的事情。因为我们不仅对外界现象看不清楚，我们对自己也看不清楚，也就是没有自知之明。我们经常强调人贵有自知之明，可是要达到自知之明其实是最难的。所以老子才有这样的话，"知人者智，自知者明"，你能够看清别人，说明你的确是很有智慧；可是只有你能够看清自己，那才是明。老子接着讲："胜人者有力，自胜者强。"你能够战胜别人只不过说明你有力气，你能够战胜自己，才能算是强者。所以强人并不是去战胜别人，而是战胜自己。明人不是去对付别人，是去对付自己。我们不仅要把现象世界看得明白，对自己更要看得明白。可是我们常常看不明白，所以叫愚、痴、无明。佛教认为我们的一切烦恼就在这三个心上面，真正要获得解脱就要消除这三心，佛教所有的修行可以说都是针对这三个心的。佛教最初创立，佛陀提出八正道、四念处以及其他的许多法门，归纳起来叫做三十七道品，也就是三十七种方法，其中最核心的是八正道和四念处。后来大乘佛教就提出了六度、四摄。这些复杂的概念归纳起来就是戒定慧三学。戒是戒律，定是禅定，慧是智慧，就是般若。戒、定、慧三学是——针对贪、瞋、痴三心的。戒是基础，是对治贪的。定就是禅定，禅修，通过禅修来使人们的心能够宁静下来，是对治瞋（怨恨）的。慧，是用来对治愚痴的，也就是无明。所以总体来讲，佛教强调"勤修戒定慧，熄灭贪瞋痴"，通过勤修戒定慧三学来熄灭贪瞋痴三心，这就是治心，这也可以说是佛教的核心，我想今天也还是如此，我们的烦恼就是因为我们人类整体和每个个体有太多的贪、瞋、痴，这个问题不解决，个人是永远在烦恼苦海中沉沦，整个的人类也会在五浊世界里面遭殃。所以佛教在今天的社会是有它的意义的。

我常讲我们今天如果考察世界文化的发展，有两个趋势：一个是向传统的回归。我们去考察世界的文化，无一例外都在反思，我们现代化发展到今天这样的程度给人类究竟是带来了幸福还是痛苦？这样一种发展物质文明、科学技术的道路，给人类造成了一个什么样的结果。所以讲要回归传统，最典型的就是我们现代的医学。西医应该说已经遇到了极大的问题，已经不止是医学上的问题了，医学已经被医疗器械的生产，新药的开发牵着鼻子走了。所以现代西方医生的培训，也不是医学院医理上的培训，而是医疗仪器公司、新药开发公司的培训，告诉医生怎么用这些新的医疗机械和新药。所以世界卫生组织在前几年就提出来，传统医学有它存在的合理性，过去认为现代医学是否定和超越传统医学的，现在不一样了。大家知道我们现在全国有多少同意中医的人？不少于三十万。全世界有多少同意中医的人？五十万。所以就整个西方文化来讲，都在反思在现代化的背景下，传统的思维模式、传统的文化都有其合理性。尤其在科学界，现在西方提出来一个口号，以往我们要掌握自然、改造自然，现在我们要重新回归，去顺应自然、尊重自然，这就是向传统的回归。

另一个世界文化发展的趋势，就是向东方接近，或者说向东方靠拢，认识到东方文化的合理性。中国儒释道三教的思想现在在西方其实受到了相当的重视。两次世界佛教论坛，吸引了大量的佛教徒和文化、宗教、思想的研究者。大前年在西安召开的世界道德经论坛，也吸引了大量西方的学者。可是世界上研究老子《道德经》的中心有三个，一个在德国，一个在美国，一个在日本，没有中国，这是个大问题。现在西方信仰佛教的人也是越来越多，禅宗对世界的影响也是越来越大，在欧洲、美洲，都有许多规模极其之大的禅修中心。甚至于影响了基督教，所以现在有一个新名词叫"基督禅"，还有许多蓝眼睛、黄头发的和尚、尼姑，甚至还有道士、道姑。美国万佛城的方丈——恒实法师，就是位地地道道的美国和尚。汉传佛教在西方的影响很大，藏传佛教在西方的影响也是到处可见。还有南传佛教，尤其是南传的禅修方法——内观法，在西方已经形成了产业。而且他们学的这些东西又返销回中国，我参加过很多大企业所开办的一些班，比如华为的星云治疗班，它的内容就是中国的禅宗这些东西。禅宗也已经被西方心理治疗大量的吸收。心理治疗也是治心的一部分，在西方，心理治疗越来越受到重视，因为人们看到人类的疾病绝大部分不是肉体的，或者被传染的，绝大部分是心理问题造成的。所以现在西方的心理治疗比身体的治疗受到更多的重视，而禅也是心理治疗非常重要的方法和内容。我亲身就经历过一位美国的心理治疗师，他是一位神父，来到中国研究禅在心理治疗作用上的作用和意义。所以从治心这个角度，我认为佛教在今天社会中是大有可为的。所以在科学时代，佛教还是要定位在治心上面，因为现代人心里的渴求和问题实在是太多了，而佛教在这方面是大有可作为的。

在这些方面我们不妨吸取其他宗教的一些特点，我们的寺庙是不是也可以像基督教那样，我们的法师是不是也可以像神父一样？为什么这样讲呢？基督教就是人有了问题，有了心里的苦恼，就到教堂里面找神父去倾诉、忏悔。神父就给他一定的启示，许多的心理问题就由此得到了缓解，我觉得这种形式是可以的。你也可以找法师去忏悔，法师也给你一定的启发。也可以搞一个场地，让大家对着佛像，或者自己静坐，自我反思。这是我在马来西亚、新加坡、港台地区的佛教活动场所里见过的，如此我们对社会就可以做出更多的贡献了，就可以更直接地为我们社会的老百姓服务。我们也可以组织禅修活动，禅修活动不要仅仅把它看做是宗教的活动，禅修在印度本来也并不是佛教才有的，其他的宗教都可以参与，它只是一种静坐静虑，获得心境安宁的方法。这种方法引导以佛教的教理，那就是佛教的禅修；引导以婆罗门教的教义，那就是婆罗门教的禅修；引导以我们平常人心理上的想法，那就是普通的禅修。这种禅修的方式在西方有很多，它不一定要带有浓厚的宗教色彩，甚至可以没有宗教色彩，因为禅修本身对于我们自身心灵的安宁就是非常有益的。例如说我们的天台智顗法师的止观法门，就是禅修里面非常重要的一种方法，是从数息观里面演化出来的方式。数息观里面最核心的就是调身、调息、调心。通过调身，坐姿也好站姿也好，首先要把身体调整放松，然后调息，调呼吸，由浅入深，由粗变细，由短变长，这样一点一点地调息。通过调身调息，然后再调心，把心里杂乱的念头，从多念尽量能够慢慢变成一念，由一念再把它变成无念。我们可以提供多方面的方法，我们可以给一些企业家、国家公务员、教师提供一日禅修，也不一定一直坐在那儿，可以上午喝喝茶，下午坐坐禅，有一个交流。人的很多心理问题都是自我封闭造成的。如果能够心扉开放，投入到人群中间去，让它有一个相互交流的过程，那么很多心理问题就可以解决了。所以我想这种治心的功能，是佛教的一个特长，我们要把它充分发挥起来。

下面我讲讲具体的佛教精神和观念，看看这些精神和观念如何让大家可以更好的改变人生，净化社会。第一就是佛教的慈悲精神。慈悲精神可以说从佛陀创教开始，包括随后所有的发展阶段，一直到现在，都是佛教的核心的精神和价值观念。慈悲分开来讲，慈就是给人以快乐，悲是帮助人脱离痛苦。慈悲就是去苦予乐，去除人的痛苦，给人以快乐，这是一个根本的精神。佛经里面反复地讲，佛以慈悲水灌溉一切众生。慈悲的精神是一种奉献的精神，人的价值只有在奉献中间才能实现。我经常跟我的一些年轻的学生讲，你们不要整天说自己多了不起，多有本事，多有价值，认为别人都看不到你的价值。价值不是你自己来吹嘘的，要让别人认同你的价值，这是不简单的，你一定要为别人做出贡献，这样才能让别人承认你，这是非常简单的一个道理。所以慈悲就是一种奉献。你只有奉献了才能体现出你的价值来。十几年以前，净慧法师，就是现在佛教协会的副会长，他在河北赵县的柏林寺创立了生活禅夏令营。在这个生活禅夏令营里面，他提出了这么一个口号，叫做"觉悟人生，奉献人生"。他提出这个口号实际是根据大乘佛教的根本精神，因为我们从经典和历史中间可以看到，大乘佛教始终强调是悲智双运。所谓悲智双运，就是慈悲和智慧两种精神要同时发扬。智慧就是自觉，就是自我的觉悟。所以大乘佛教讲自觉觉他，自渡渡他。大乘佛教强调的就是普度众生，就是慈悲和智慧两个精神的贯彻落实，我觉得这个解释非常的贴切。

　　智慧就是觉悟人生,慈悲就是奉献人生,这是现代的诠释方法。我们也可以用传统的方法来讲这两个精神,我经常给人讲这两句话,叫做"慈悲做人,智慧做事"。台湾的圣严法师,去年去世了。他就讲:"慈悲无敌人,智慧无烦恼",智慧可以化解一切的问题,智慧就是能够看清自我和现实的现象世界,就不会执着,就可以舍得放下,就自在而有烦恼。佛教用最简单的话讲,就是你能不能够舍得,能不能够放下,能够舍得、放下你就自在了。可是我们一般都舍不得也放不下,我们一天到晚执着于各种名相,一天到晚只看到、想到自己,执我为本。执其名相,舍不得,执我为本,放不下,所以你当然不能够得自在。这也就是慈悲,我们奉献了自己,就把自己放下了,所以慈悲精神我觉得在我们今天非常需要。我们现在的教育所有都围绕着智商的开发,最缺失的就是情商的开发。结果让我们的孩子们只懂得怎么样比别人强,对别人没有情感,这是很严重的问题。所以我说教育第一是开发情商,让孩子懂得怎么样去爱别人,同时也感受到别人的爱。慈悲就是个情商的问题,只有拥有丰富情商的人才可以有慈悲的精神。我认为慈悲这个理念也不仅仅是佛教的,有一次有一位漂亮的女士跟我讲,她最近看了一些佛教的书,接触了一些佛教的师父,觉得佛教很有道理,很多东西确实值得我们今天来学习实践,但是她不敢跟同事们说,因为怕他们认为,女孩子年纪轻轻的,长那么漂亮怎么会去信这些东西呢? 那是老太太、老头子信的。我说你可以跟人家说我送你两句话,说希望你慈悲做人,智慧做事。没有人听了会不喜欢,会说我不想慈悲做人,不想智慧做事。等他接受了,就可以慢慢跟他说,这两句话就是佛教的根本精神。这就是善巧方便。你不要板起脸说信佛就应该讲慈悲、智慧,这是可以变通的。所以佛教的慈悲精神是非常根本的,也可以说就是一种大公无私的精神,《华严经》里面讲:"不为自身求安乐,但愿众生得离苦。"

　　就像我刚才讲的,佛教里面还有一个根本精神就是智慧,佛教不是提倡迷信,浙江鄞县天童寺的现任方丈诚信法师,有一次在会上讲,佛法不怕不信,就怕迷信。你不信没有关系,不信可以有疑。禅宗里面反复讲,有疑才有悟,大疑大悟,小疑小悟,不疑不悟,是让你动脑筋的而不是盲从。所以佛教是开发理性,甚至是超越理性的信仰,而不是迷信。迷信就是自己不思考,它怎么讲就怎么样,而佛教是讲智慧性,通过你对人生的体悟,明白人生是怎么回事,看透现象世界,才能够破除我执、法执,从而获得解脱。所以智慧是佛教所提倡的,佛教的信仰是智慧的信仰,靠自己来明白事实和人生,来了脱生死,不是盲从等待的。而且不光讲智慧,更讲自信、自力解脱。所以如果说佛教是迷信,那就是对佛教没有真正正确的认识,佛教恰恰是反对迷信的。

台湾的圣严法师写过一本小册子,已经不知道在台湾印了多少版了,名字就叫做《正信的佛教》。正信的关键就是正信因果,因果也就是因缘。佛教认为我们人和万物都是因缘而生,因缘而起,都是因缘聚会才会有这个人、事、物。可是这个因缘怎么聚会,是哪些因缘聚会,这就有很多解释,佛教就是要给你一个正确的因果因缘的解释。所以智慧就是让你正信因果以后,悟到人的本质。人来到这个世界上,受到各种的影响,慢慢迷失了自己的本性。说得简单一点,佛教讲人的本性是清净自性,本来没有那么多的贪嗔痴,没有那么多的胡思乱想,来到这个世界上以后,受到污染,慢慢本性就没有了,被现象牵着鼻子走了,回归不了自我。中国的禅宗就是来发扬佛教的这个精神,就是让你回归自我。所以禅宗里面很多的公案、语录反复地问:"什么是你的本来面目?"拿中国传统的话来讲,我们每个人都是"赤条条的来,赤条条的去",光着来光着走,你什么也没有,你今天所有的贪嗔痴都是因为你没有认识到你是光着来、光着走的,所以产生了贪欲、嗔恨和愚痴。所以佛教的智慧是让我们认识自己的本来面貌,认识万物的本来面貌。万物本来也是一样的。我今天来的路上还在想,一块宝石和一块普通的石头,它们自己能够有分别说:我是宝石价值连城,你是一块破石头没有什么用处。会有分别吗?不会有吧,去区分它的都是我们人!都是人在分别,物本身不会有分别。所以佛教这一点看得很清楚,讲"相由心生"。都是由你的"识"产生了分别,识就是我们认识的功能,眼有眼识,耳有耳识,眼睛有辨别颜色形状的功能,耳朵有分辨声音的功能,就叫做眼识、耳识。"识"的基本功能就是分别,有了眼耳鼻舌的分别,到了心里就更有了分别,觉得这个宝石我要得到它,这个破石头我不要它,分别心、执着心就生起了,烦恼也就来了。得不到就难受,丢不掉也难受。所以我们要认识到,事物本身是没有分别的,用现在的科学一分析更没劲了,石头和宝石都是一种硅化物,就更没有分别了。佛教不是用化学的方法,是用原始的方法,你是色受想行识五蕴而生,我也是,没有什么差别。佛教为什么讲众生平等,因为从根本上来讲是没有分别的,是人自己用"识"来把它分别了,然后有各种的追求,于是烦恼痛苦都来了。大乘佛教核心的价值理念,第一就是"破相显性",中观学、唯识学两大学派里,中观学的核心理念就是"破相显性",破除外在名相的执着,认识到根本上的平等,无差别。唯识学的核心理念是"转识成智",要超越我们是非万物的分别,达到佛教所讲的智慧,就是般若,我们要增长的就是这种消除分别的智慧。有了这种慈悲精神和智慧精神,我想佛教就会给予我们很大的启发。

我在这里还可以告诉大家,所有的宗教都是让我们回到原来的自我中去。就中国来讲,儒释道也是这样。《老子》里面讲"复归婴儿",婴儿是无欲无求的、淳朴的,儒家让我们保住我们的赤子之心,佛教叫我们回归本来的自我。这都说明我们人类到了社会上以后,受到了染污,失去了本来的自我,所以现在只有把它找回来。现实中我们一切的痛苦、烦恼都是来源于自我的失落,我们做不了自己的主人,被物或者神牵着鼻子走了,这样自然就有烦恼。儒释道在净化心灵方面,都是让我们回归自我。这是中国的智慧,中国的文化,西方的基督宗教文化里面,是让你去跟上帝合二为一,回归到上帝身边去,这是西方文化。所以我们要了解文化的不同,这里我们并不是要做一个好坏评判,西方的方法也是一种解脱,只是心灵的净化和解脱有不同的方法,一个是以神为本的方法,一个是以人为本的方法,不能去评判它的是非高下,只能说方法不同,而目的是一个。

下面我想讲两个理论,一个是佛教的"缘起"理论,也可以说是因果理论,因为佛教认为一切事物都是有因必有果,有果必有因。因要结出果还要有缘,所以我们讲因缘聚会。这个不仅仅是佛教讲,因果是宇宙普遍的规律,但是佛教把它更多地强调出来,是为了告诉我们世界上一切的东西都是相互关联的,没有什么是绝对孤立的,独自的。这个世界就是一个共生共存的世界。现代科学的发展也已经认识到,世界万物本无绝对的分别,更无所谓的对立。世界万物都是相对的,都是统一整体的部分,不仅不可分裂,更是你中有我,我中有你。上世纪末,美国的一位心理学家肯恩·威尔伯(Ken Wilber),写了一本书,书名叫事事本无碍,这个题目就是来源于佛教,中国的华严宗讲事事无碍法界,也就是法界中的事事都是无碍的。

在这本书中他讲到："愈来愈多的科学家开始同意物理学家卡普拉的看法：'现代物理的两个基本论点，反映出东方人的世界观。量子学理论推翻了视一切为独立个体的观点，开始提倡参与融入的心态，取代旁观的心态。他已逐渐看出宇宙原是一个互通生息的联络网，我们只能透过部分与整体内的关系来界定每一部分。'简言之，现代物理学与东方哲学都一致公认，现实世界原非一堆界限及独立个体而已；它是不可分割的形态，有如一个巨大的原子，一件无间无隙的天衣，无二的世界。"他又引用《华严经》里的说法。"大乘佛教将宇宙形容为一堆光色映照的宝珠，所有的珠宝都反映在一颗宝珠上，同时每一颗宝珠也都映照在所有宝珠内。佛教徒称之：一切即一，一即一切。"既然是共生共存的世界，那么不能因为我而去灭掉你、灭掉他，对于万物众生都要同等的给予慈悲的关怀。所以佛教讲"无缘大慈，同体大悲"，这就是建立在我们是生存在一个缘起的世界，一个因缘相关联的世界，我们要相互的关怀。这个思想非常重要，对于我们今天建设生态文明是非常有意义的。

佛教始终强调人要相互尊重，在僧团里面提出"六和敬"，所谓"和"就是相互尊重、相互理解，相互关怀。佛教也指出对于周边的环境也要讲"和"，因为如果你把周边的环境破坏了，你自身也会受到连累，你们是共生的关系。所以我们常讲天下名山僧占多，因为僧占的地方，周边的自然环境就会保护的比较好，这与缘起的理念是有关系的。我常常讲生态文明可能应该是人类文明中的最高阶段，这应该是一个最理想的阶段，因为说实在的，我们过去的文明都有欠缺，我们对环境大肆的破坏，我们对其他秉持不同价值观念的人大肆的杀戮、战争，比野蛮还野蛮，比愚昧还愚昧。生态文明，应该是与一切人一切环境和平共处、和谐共处的这样一个文明。要建立这样一个文明首先要有一个生态的伦理观念，所谓生态的伦理观念就是应该相互的尊重。中国人讲伦理的核心就是敬，有了这样一种相互敬重的伦理观念，那么我们才能够恰当的共存，和谐的共存。所以只有先建立生态伦理，才有可能建立起生态文明。而佛教的缘起是我们建立生态伦理的一个重要理论依据。而这个缘起也并不是只能从佛教的角度讲，而是不管从哪个角度来讲，比如科学的角度，应该都能得到共识，所以我觉得这个理论应该大肆的发扬。

　　第二个理论是佛教讲业报的理论,业报理论与因果理论也是有关系的。所谓业报理论就是业是因,报是果,我造了很多业,就种下这个因,最后说的报就是果。佛教讲因果报应,你造什么业,就会受什么样的果。这并不是命定论。这种说法常常会被看成是命定论,当然可以从这个角度去理解,以前造什么业,现在就受什么果,所以是命定的,但是这里面也包含了命是可以由自己来改变的。既然你造这样的业有这样的果,那么也可以造那样的业得到那样的果,总体来讲命是由你自己决定的,命由己定,命由己造。业报论是告诉我们,你种业是一定会有报的,俗话说善有善报,恶有恶报,不是不报,时候未到,时候一到,一切皆报。因果关系也并不是那么简单,由因转化成果,它还需要许多的条件,就是需要许多的缘。我们作为个人来讲,你一造出这个因必然就会有许多缘来与你相合,马上就会结出果来。佛教是讲个人的因果关系,在中国传统的儒家观念里面,同样讲因果报应,但这个因果报应不是发生在个体身上,而是发生在生命的链条上。什么是生命链条呢?中国人的生命观念就是生命是一个链条,每个生命里面有一段一段的个体,这个个体结束,下个个体接着,说白了就是父母和子女。每个个体生命都有一个结束的时候,所以中国人相对来讲对生死看得很透,有生就必然有死,佛教是这样讲,中国传统文化也是这样讲的。就像一根木头一样,火总有一天要把这个木头燃尽,但是这个木头燃尽没有关系,另外一根木头接着烧,这就是“火尽薪传”,所以中国人讲“传薪”。生命既然是后一个生命接着前一个生命,子女的生命接着父母的生命,那么父母所造的因,子女就会受到报应。所以《周易》中有:“积善之家,必有余庆,积不善之家,必有余殃”。中国人强调的是前人栽树,后人乘凉,中国本土传统的因果报应是父母子女之间的因果报应,佛教的因果报应着重的是个人前后的因果报应。在中国这两者的因果报应是结合在一起的,并行不悖。

　　所以,我常常讲中国人的负担是特别重的,又要接受个人的因果报应,又要接受父母子女间的因果报应。中国儒家的因果报应观,我觉得是大的生命观念所决定的,中国人总讲你要为子女积德,所以中国人做什么事情都要为子女想一想,要为子孙后代想一想,这样你就绝对不会像现在这样不管后代子孙无穷无尽的开发,我们还得想想子孙后代怎么活下去啊,所以不要忽视这个因果报应。因果报应也体现在人和自然的关系上面,我们对自然的任何一个改造迟早都会受到自然的报复,这就是因果。这不是我在这讲,一百多年以前恩格斯就讲了,恩格斯在他的《自然辩证法》这本书里面讲得非常清楚,人对自然的任何改变迟早都会受到自然的报复,他当时举的例子就是英国人开发澳洲所受到的报应,所以因果是普遍存在的规律。你自己没有得到报应,你子女可能要得到报应,这个家里面没有得到报应,佛教讲还有共业,就是所有的人都要遭到报应。所以我觉得因果报应思想也值得让大家了解一下,那么做事情时就会慎重一点。它可以辅助中国儒家思想里面强调的"慎独",我们现在很多人缺乏自觉自律,那么你拿因果观念来想一想,我想也可以让大家达到一种自觉自律。他得考虑我这样做会对我以后有什么影响,对我子女以后会有什么影响,对整个的人类会不会有影响,对自己的行为就会有一种自我的约束。不是通过这个让大家去信宿命,恰恰是要让大家感觉到命运掌握在自己手里。大家如果有机会到庙里面去的话,可以去请一本《了凡四训》来看一看,《了凡四训》的第一篇讲的就是这个问题,佛教的因果报应告诉我们命是由自己造的,命是由自己决定的。我想"命由己定",是我们现代人最喜欢的,最愿意听的。我们自己来掌握命运,但究竟怎么样来掌握,那就是个问题了。佛教的因果报应绝对不是一种迷信,也不是一种命定论,而是一种积极的人生观,一种自觉的人生观,一种自律的人生观。

佛教的精神和基本的理念,还有很多,包括今天我讲的,从自心的角度提出的四个方面:慈悲的精神,智慧的精神,缘起的理论,业报的理论。如果我们能够从正面去传播这样一些理念和精神,我想可能对我们现实会有一定的意义。

道教信仰与当代中国社会

王宗昱

　　道教是中国的本土宗教,也是二十世纪受到最严重打击的宗教。进入二十一世纪以来,随着中国政治、经济和社会的发展,宗教活动日益活跃。中国宗教的复兴和中国最近三十年以来在政治和经济方面的变化是紧密联系的。然而,道教信仰是否能够以传统的形式继续生存下去?中国新一代的公民会以什么样的方式享用祖先的文化遗产?本文提出一些初步的想法,仅供参考。

一、道教复兴的一些特点

　　二十世纪初期的新文化运动提出打倒孔家店的口号,开始了对传统宗教的打击。这个打击到了六十年代的"文化大革命"达到极端。八十年代初期,中国政府的宗教政策开始落实,宗教活动也逐渐恢复。不过这是从上而下的恢复,而且只是局限于教团组织的恢复建设,还没有普遍地在民众里展开。随着中国政治经济的发展,到了二十世纪末期,中国真正有了来自社会而不是政府提供的宗教复兴环境。杨凤岗教授的中国宗教市场论已经讨论到这个环境。所谓三色市场说明宗教的复兴来自不同的社会阶层和表现形式。这也就是我要说的特点。

1. 和民俗相联系的道教复兴。这是最基层的民众对于道教文化的需求。这些需要并没有一致的特征。它主要和基层民众的传统习惯结合在一起。美国社会学家杨美惠以及中外的汉学家们都已经对浙江的民间道教的恢复做了多年的观察①。以赵世瑜为代表的对华北民间民俗复兴的研究都可以给我们提供民间社会道教复兴的信息②。刘仲宇教授的研究特别对上海都市道教的复兴做了深入考察③。这些民俗有节日喜庆民俗、生育丧葬民俗,还有命相风水等方术民俗。这些民俗活动有些是团体行为,也有些是弥散性的个别行为。它们基本上都属于民众的主动行为,不是发自道士教团的行为。和民俗相联系的道教活动是最朴素也是最传统的信仰和消费方式。他们是道教生存的最基层的土壤,也是最耐久的基础。这些民众可能并不自称为道教。他们崇拜的法师也很难被政府或道教协会承认为道士。但是,我仍然把他们看作最基本的道教现象。这些恢复以后的信仰活动和历史上有哪些区别,有哪些有新时代生长出来的外部特征,我们还需要认真研究。

2. 发自教团的复兴。道教教团的复兴和其他宗教一样从八十年代各地道教协会的恢复建立开始。进入二十一世纪以后,道教教团的复兴进入全新的阶段。首先是道教宫观的重建和新建。由于政治环境的宽松,道观已经成为宣传道教的最有效的工具,也是民众参与道教活动的最方便的场所。道观的建设也涉及了多方面的群体及其利益,形成了和政府、企业乃至其他宗教的合作或者竞争的关系。2000年以后,教团主办或者联合政府以及经济实体共同举办了许多大型道教活动。最著名的是2007年的"国际道德经论坛"。山东半岛的县市政府参与主办了全真教圣地的重建和学术讨论会④。四川地方政府和道教协会以及四川大学联合举办的道教文化节有着非常重要的历史意义。类似的活动最近几年日益频繁。大陆的道教团体和港台道教的联系日益密切。政府的世界华人联谊政策也为这种

---

① 比较著名的有法国远东学院等研究单位出版的《客家传统社会丛书》、中国台湾学者王秋桂领衔在大陆广泛实施的仪式与戏剧研究,以及浙江学者徐宏图等人的田野考察。
② 赵世瑜:《狂欢与日常——明清以来的庙会与民间社会》,三联书店,2002年。
③ 刘仲宇:《正逢时运》,上海辞书出版社,2005年。
④ 最重要的是2007年栖霞县主办的丘处机创建的太虚观的重建开光活动。

活动创造了良好的条件。因此,中国大陆的道教复兴推动了世界华人文化认同的潮流。几年来,教团和学术研究教学单位联合举办的学术讨论会逐渐密集起来,不少学者参与了教团旨在宣教的活动①。教团的行为既有宣传教门的目的,也有经济利益的追求。教团的这些行为和政府有互利或竞争关系。总之,道教教团在今天可以名正言顺地参与社会活动了。学者的参与有失客观,但是毕竟推动了道教的复兴。政府的行为则极大地强化了道教对社会大众的影响。需要指出的进入二十一世纪以后的这类活动中道教教团居于主导地位的比重逐渐增大。这个现象也说明道教教团开始寻求道路融入主流文化。这是有利于道教的现代化的。

二、道教形象一百年以来的演变

二十世纪是中国宗教衰落的世纪。这个衰落是由世界历史的发展特别是工业文明的出现造成的。欧洲的宗教衰落早就开始了,但不是那么剧烈和迅速。由于中国宗教的衰落成为了中国现代化的条件,所以它的衰落表现得非常剧烈。道教在不同时期的社会形象也是不同的。

1.作为封建余孽的道教。欧洲的工业革命和宗教革命是人类社会的里程碑式的变迁。这个变迁对传统宗教的生存方式产生了颠覆性的影响。我们看到国家和政府、经济实体和个人从不同角度也在不同程度上分解了传统教会的权威。如果我们把这个历史放得长一些考察,那么可以看到人类最近几百年的历史是瓦解或者废除人类花费上千年时间建筑和巩固的宗教契约。这个瓦解过程在历史的不同阶段和世界的不同地区是以不同的方式表现出来的。中国二十世纪初兴起的共和革命以及新文化运动是对旧政治和旧文化的批判。到了1928年末的《神祠存废标准》就表现出对以道教为代表的传统宗教的彻底打击②。它前面有一段绪论:

---

① 比较有代表性的活动是2009年重阳祖师灵骨安葬仪式。

② 1928年10月,江苏盐城当地官员和学生拆毁了城隍庙的神像,试图把庙宇改建成公共娱乐场地。村民不满,于是破坏政府机关和学校,一名学生被杀害。这次事件引发了中央政府内政部颁布了《神祠存废标准》,公布在11月26日的《申报》上。

查迷信为进化之障碍,神权乃愚民之政策。我国民族自有书契以来,四千余年,开化之早,为世界之先。乃以教育未能普及之,故人民文野程度相差悬殊,以致迷信之毒,深中人心。神权之说,相沿未改。无论山野乡曲之间,仍有牛鬼蛇神之俗,即城市都会所在,亦多淫邪不经之祀。际此文化日新,科学昌明之世,此等陋俗若不亟予改革,不唯足以锢蔽民智,实足腾笑列邦。且吾国鬼神之说本极浅薄,稍明事理,即可勘透,所以流传至今牢不可破者,一由于枭雄之辈假神权以资号召,一由于无聊文人托符异以贡谄媚。史册具载,可以覆按。先总理以旷代英哲,周览世界政俗,于讲述民权主义时述民权进化之经过。以民权以前为君权时代,君权时代以前为神权时代。现在不唯神权早成历史上之名词,即君权亦为世界所不容。我国以党治国,努力革命,所有足为民族民权发展之障碍者均应一举廓清,不使稍留余烬。以故国内之军阀官僚土豪劣绅,务必次第铲除,务绝根株。若对于盘踞人心为害最烈之淫邪神祠,不谋扫除之方,口倡反对君权,而心实严惮神权,欲谋民权之发展,真所谓南辕而北辙。本部有鉴于此,对于神祠问题力谋彻底解决之方,因参考中国经史及各种宗教典籍,详加研究,将神祠之起(原)[源],淫(词)[祠]之盛行,以及我国先贤破除迷信之事迹,神祠应行存废之标准,祀神礼节应行改良之必要等项,分别考订,列举事实理由,以释群疑。计应行保存神祠之标准有二:一曰先哲类。凡有功民族国家社会,发明学术,利溥人群,及忠烈孝义,足为人类矜式者属之。一曰宗教类。凡以神道设教,宗旨纯正,受一般民众之信仰者属之。应废除之神祠标准亦有二:一曰古神类。即古代科学未明,在历史是相沿崇奉之神,至今觉其毫无意义者属之。一曰淫祠类。附会宗教,借神敛钱,或依草附木,或沿袭齐东野语者皆属之。每类之中均举例证明,以资遵守①。

---

①　经周学农帮助抽印自《中华民国法规汇编》,中华书局,1934年,第807页。

所谓淫祀是古代官府对不合官方政治需要和意识形态的民间信仰的蔑称。从前面绪论看出中华民国政府制裁淫祀的理由已经和古代不同了，有了现代社会转变的背景。所谓神权、君权和民权的三段论就是断定了旧宗教从本质上不合新时代的需要。所谓"严惮神权"就是指旧宗教给人民带来的心理上的障碍。所谓"以党治国"就是指的新宗教，或新的价值标准。在存留的神祠章节内政府也补充了许多要禁止的项目，使得存留成为空名。例如道教部分的文字就说："道教为中国固有之宗教，唯以无人昌明，致为方士所混淆。其善者则从事于服饵修炼，其不善者则以符箓禁咒惑世。后世之白莲教、义和团、大刀会、小刀会，及最近之硬肚社、红枪会等皆其流毒也。应即根本纠正。凡信仰道教者，应服膺老子《道德经》，其以服饵修炼，或符箓禁咒蛊世惑人者，应一律禁止，以免趋入邪途。至世俗于人死后延请羽士唪经，一如延请僧人之唪经，尤为无稽。[1]"条例在道教目下列了老子、元始天尊、三官、天师和吕祖五个神明。老子条下云："道教中尊之为太上老君。姓李名耳，字伯阳。生为周柱下史，著《道德经》五千言，义理精奥，研究中国哲学者极重视之。奉道教者应以此书为圣经，发挥而广大之。"在元始天尊和三官条下都说"实无此人"。文件对天师作了大段说明，开首就说张道陵"以符水禁咒之法愚民"。这样的解释实际上不能说明为什么要存留这个祭祀。

这个条例公布以后在实施的过程中的情况目前还没有足够多的资料做研究 [2]。这个条例的精神在 1949 年以后被共产党的政府做了彻底的发扬，在"文化大革命"当中达到极端。"文化大革命"以后，尽管三十年来的拨乱反正宣布了传统宗教的合法地位，但是它们在主流文化中的声誉已经受到极大的破坏。2010 年的道士李一事件就是典型的例证。从欧洲殖民扩张以来至今，全世界五百年的历史里一直有一个潮流，就是认识和承认非官方非主流文化的存在，这是从外面来的力量。还有一个力量就是非主流非官方的文化要求被认识被承认的潮流，是从内部向外，希望被别人承

---

[1] 《中华民国法规汇编》，中华书局，1934 年，第 812 页。
[2] 已经有的研究可见《宗教与广东近代社会》，宗教文化出版社，2008 年，第 385 页。黎志添《民国时期广州市喃呒道馆的历史考察》，《近代史研究所集刊》第 37 期，2002 年。

认。这两者之间的关系从军事的宗教的冲突慢慢转变为经济的政治的和平。但是和平的代价就是大量非官方非主流文化被丢弃。这是社会发展的结果。全世界都在改变着生活方式。生活方式的改变就是我们的许多生活不再由旧时代的教会来安排了。这个过程在西方被称为去魅的过程或理性化过程,在中国表现为政治和文化的革命过程。

2. 教会道教和民众道教。当1978年中国结束了1911年以来对传统宗教的政治批判以后,我们会看到传统道教被分解为两个部分。一个部分是道士教团,另一部分是信奉道教的民众。这种分化在中国北方可能从金元时代就逐渐开始了。农村社会中的宗教结社成为民众宗教生活的决定者,而僧人或者道士只是社团雇佣的法师。道士可能是本土出身的,也许是从外来的。这些道士可能有一个跨地区的乃至以北京白云观为中心的全国的的网络,也许只是零散的没有门派的乡村道士。这在早期全真道士的事迹里可以看到很多例子,在明清时代的庙宇碑刻里也可以看到①。这些事例也使我们从中国找到了例子证明即使没有工业革命教会的权威也会受到削弱。因此,在那时候北方的道教就分割成教会道教和民众道教两个范畴。在南方这个分割不明显,直至现在道教还残存着古往的一些痕迹,还有生存在民间的道士。我说的分割是对总趋势的描述。大陆各地道士的宗教身份成为他们参与政治生活的资格。但是,道士教团以外的人没有这个资格。这样说来,大陆的道教目前是由教会道教代表的。对比香港和台湾,那里的道教信仰是民众性的,不是仅仅由道士代表的。民众还可以带着自己的传统的宗教信仰参与政治。在香港,道教可以建立自己的学校和医院,建立公益事业例如公园、坟场。在台湾,拜庙成为政治选举的重要节目,反映出宗教信仰在政治生活中的支配性影响非常巨大。在大陆,尽管仅仅在道士身上才能看出这个变化,但是这说明道教的社会形象和1978年以前不同了。目前大陆有道教协会的地方都有道士参加地方政协。这在国民党统治大陆时期是没有的事情。不过,既然道教被分割成两部分,道士这部分还不能完全代表实际存在的道教。

另一部分道教的形象则是由民众在崇拜和消费中表现出来的。我在

---

① 见王宗昱《全真教和地方宗教之关系》、《清代汉中地区的全真道》。

前一节的第一小段指出了和民俗相联系的道教复兴。不过这部分道教很受到主流意识的歧视。道教的形象既然和民众的崇拜和消费有密切关系，那么中国社会的宗教消费形式和崇拜形式的变化也会改变道教的形象。如果我们细致观察就会发现目前的民众道教有非常强的不确定性。值得注意的是民众道教在现代社会里新的表现形式，或者说是民众对传统道教的新的消费形式。道教也因此表现出新的存在形式和社会形象。而这个形象和现代的学校教育有密切的关系。

3. 作为知识体系的道教。这个形象是由当代的学校教育塑造的。这也是古代中国没有的事。在古代，道教的社会形象是由道士、庙宇和信徒塑造的。在当代社会，道士的社会影响急剧减低，而学校的影响逐渐加剧。学校教育培养了新一代的道教信众，影响了他们信仰道教的方式。这个学校教育是建立在所谓客观的学术研究基础上的，这和古代的宗教教育有本质的不同。

朱越利和陈敏两位教授在《道教学》[①]一书里已经对二十世纪中国道教研究的发展做了比较详尽的描述和总结。《道教学》把中国道教研究的历史分为三个阶段。第一个阶段是 1900 年到 1949 年，第二个阶段是 1950 年到 1976 年，第三个阶段是 1976 年到二十世纪末。该书作者认为前两个阶段的研究者多为非道教学专业，属于兼职研究。因此，道教学是在二十世纪的最后二十年才形成的。《道教学》也列举了一些数字说明道教研究的发展。第一阶段的研究者有 160 名，专著十多部，论文两百多篇。第二阶段时期大陆成果很少，论文只有五十多篇，港台地区成果丰富，有专著十多部，论文百篇以上。第三阶段的发展迅速，到世纪末已经有研究者一百多人，出版各种著作和读物两百多种，论文一千篇左右。

我目前尚不能对最近二十年的道教研究大发展的原因做出合理的说明。从《道教学》一书列举的数字可以看到道教在出版物方面表现出的巨大差别。作者对前两个阶段的统计是针对学术界的，而对第三个阶段的专著的统计则包括了非学术性的读物。尽管统计者可能忽视了前两个阶段大众读物的道教内容，不过我们都会感到最近以来社会舆论对道教的有意

---

① 该书 2000 年由当代世界出版社出版。

注意,而道教出版物的增多就是证明。我们会看到进入二十世纪以来学术界和道教教会的联系日益紧密。我们也会看到某些学术研究有失客观。但是,我认为更重要的是学术研究的发展和教会道教以及民众中传统的道教信仰方式有着根本的不同,也有着更强势的发展前景。道教史不可能建立起一个自我满足的知识系统,因为材料不够,并且道教可能也没有一个完整的历史。但是,如果我们运用宗教学的各种方法,我们会建立一个关于道教的知识系统。这个知识系统主要是帮助读者或学生通过道教去理解宗教。道教可能离听众很远,但是我们通过道教分析的宗教现象离听众很近。这才是听众能使用的知识。这个知识系统不是为了让听众了解道教的特殊性,而首先是要了解道教作为宗教和其他宗教之间的共同性。最终的目的是他们能够在以后的生活中举一反三,理解和自己不同的宗教习俗。从这个角度出发我们会对道教历史上的问题会有新的解释方式,或者是发现新的问题。例如道教为什么不讲究丧礼?是卫生的原因还是教义的原因?它的医学和它的教义是否有关系?他们为什么不给神吃东西?所以,这个关于道教的知识系统仅仅凭借道教历史材料还不足以建立,它要靠综合学科的力量。因此,我们通过学校教育认识到的道教已经不以能否描述道教为标准。这样的知识系统呈现出来的道教形象肯定和传统的道教形象不同甚至相去甚远。

三、道教在现代社会的生存环境

上述这种知识系统造就了新一代的道教信徒或者说道教消费者。这个新的群体的信仰方式要追溯到马丁·路德。他废除了教会横亘在教徒和上帝之间的中保角色。掌握在教会手里的那些行政的和经济的功能马上就被政府和经济体取代了。代表信徒个人和上帝沟通的这个功能被废除以后,通神就必须成为每个人要具备的宗教资格和能力。这个能力是逐渐表现出来的。牧师的通神和萨满教的神附体在本质上是相同的。人类的精神文明一定要由萨满的癫狂形式获得吗?但是,马丁·路德以前的宗教历史告诉我们教会不但倚仗萨满的癫狂垄断了真理的解释权,而且垄断了据说是根据精神文明产生出来的政治和经济权力。或许,芸芸众生并不愿意陷入癫狂,所以才转让了这些权利。他们有自己的通神方式,那就是劳动和群体性的狂欢。劳动当然能够产生精神文明,而且是安全的、理智的。萨满的脱离劳动的通神是危险的,因而也是神秘的,所以受到敬而远之的待遇。学校教育也是这种通神类型,不过基本上还是理智的。我们看到由于劳动生产率的提高,人类在过去一个世纪里从体力劳动获得了极大的解放。这也意味着人类要告别劳动通神的方式。他们原来由劳动获得的知识要改由学校的书本学习获得。二十世纪教育的普及给刚刚从体力劳动中解放出来的人类提供了一个相对安全的学习方式。在中国,新式的学校教育是由基督教教会学校传来的,但是1952年以后不再有教会学校。中国古代的私塾和书院是宣传儒家的教育。其他以庙宇为中心的教育也是宗教教育的性质。但是在1949年以后的中国,学校教育不再掌握在教会手里。虽然官方意识形态的灌输也是一种新类型的宗教教育,然而1949年以后由中国政府推广的普及教育顺应了世界历史的变迁。这样的教育培养出来的新一代公民和他们的生活方式是决定道教生存状态的重要因素。

1. 我们会看到1966年的时候中国的学校教育已经积累了相当数量的新公民。无论如何评价文化大革命中的知识青年下乡运动,我们都要注意这个新的公民阶层和传统宗教的信徒是根本不同的。我们也会从他们的回忆录里看到他们和村民们的价值观的矛盾。1978年以后至今,中国的学校教育培养出了更多的新公民。这些新公民目前集中在城镇就业,他们和同样来城镇就业但没有受过系统学校教育的民工群体有着截然不同的文化背景,也就是宗教背景。那些民工属于传统的宗教信众,而大多数有着高等学校毕业文凭的青年则不以宗教信徒的面目出现。后者决定着道教生存的客观条件。首先,这些学生不是从教会学校毕业的,他们没有传统的对于道教的宗教感情。其次,他们受到的教育决定了他们欣赏道教的新的方式。过去的磕头上香变成了读书看展览、看演出、或者举办学术讨论会。过去威严的神像变成了雕塑艺术品。从这个角度上说,北京东岳庙民俗博物馆提供的文化产品比传统道士提供的服务更顺应现代社会的大趋势。过去来庙的人通过拜神来尊重肯定自己,今天的青年一代不必通过拜神,他们也没有那种感情了,直接尊重自己就可以了。宗教生活变成了赤裸裸的商品消费、文化消费和文化娱乐。他们之所以敢于以迥异乎传统的方式对待神明,因为他们不是属于某个宗教教会的。

2. 既然学校教育成为人类愈来愈主要的学习方式,道教的以往居于主要地位的要素可能逐渐退居次要地位。我们知道早期在汉中地区的五斗米道主要以符箓行道,而东晋以后兴起了以存思静修、药物养生的新法门。宋代又兴起了内丹。这些都是知识分子的道教。尽管今天在台湾地区还盛行着符箓道教,但是我们应该看到以静修为主的道教将成为将来的主流。这不仅由于静修的道术相对脱离体力劳动,更由于这样的静修更表现出个人性的特征。生产率的提高创造了人类摆脱体力劳动的机会,创造了精神通神的可能。这当然是一条危险的道路。我在这里仅仅指出由于我们的生活方式变化了,导致道教的某些元素变得比以往重要了。养生文化在社会上的流行以及道士李一的众多信徒反映了这个趋势。目前电视上的养生课堂以及二十多年来气功热的几次爆发都表现出修道的个人性特征日益突出。

3. 我们还要看到科学技术的发展对道教生存形态的影响。我已经指出最近一百年人类学习方式的变化。科技的新发明促进了教育的普及。科学技术的影响是双重的。首先它帮助人类摆脱体力劳动的束缚,其次它也使人类的个体性凸显出来。人类体力劳动的缺乏,居住条件的提高造成的人际隔绝,这些都增加了癫狂的频率。但是,科学技术的发展提供了一些其他的设备或许可以缓解这些副作用。无线电的联络或许可以把人类重新结合在一起,把体力劳动和仪式场景里的传统联系重新建立起来①。但是,这些科学技术首先是为道教的传播形式创造了新的条件,决定了道教在新时代生存的形式。第一次道德经大会在西安香港两地举行,一些节目显示了现代科技带来的新手段和新形式。由道教举办的祭祀黄帝陵墓和赈灾祈福仪式的典礼通过电视广播造成了二十年以前不能想象的效果。二十年以前有道士强调:道不言道,道不外传。在科技发达的今天这个戒条可能会被打破。目前在意大利和英国出现了洋道士,2006 年由德国医学

① 我的老师施舟人教授在 2009 年秋天特别和我谈到这一点,表现出他对宗教发展的趋势有非常敏感和前瞻性的见解。

会主办的道教国际会议由许多爱好道教文化的欧洲人参加。作为中国本土宗教的道教开始跨越欧亚的文化界限向全世界传播。中国的政治革命造成了传统宗教的衰落,但是这个革命带来的新事物也必将给道教的复兴提供新的契机。

混沌与宽容

——道家思想的现代意义

王 博

　　当通过"名"表现出来的各种价值和规范不断地增强着它们对于世界的控制时,我们越来越发现自己处在一种无奈的被描述和被命名的困境之中,而这种描述和命名与真实的世界和生命之间并不符合,甚至存在着非常遥远的距离。更无奈的是,渺小的生命根本无法去对抗这种与之疏离的"名"的力量,从而彻底成为"名"的囚徒和牺牲品。因此,对"名"保持着足够清醒的反思态度绝对是必要的,这是对真实生命和世界的尊重,也是对"名者,圣人之所以真物也,名之为言真也"①宗旨的回归。我们发现,尽管这个世界在很多领域发生了翻天覆地的变化,但在另外一些方面,一切似乎都没有改变。现代社会的问题不过是古老世界中产生之问题的延续或者再现,在这种理解之下,重温一下古代的解决方案也许对今天的人们来说仍然是有益的。这正是阅读经典的意义所在。就上述的问题而言,以老子和庄子为代表的道家学派有着非常深刻的思考。通过混沌的观念,道家引导人们思考名之世界的有限性,并以此为基础发展出对于生命和世界的宽容态度。本文的讨论即在此问题意识下展开。

---

① 董仲舒:《春秋繁露·深察名号》。

一、无　名

如果我们回到两千多年前的春秋时代,会发现自己进入了一个礼乐的世界,或者也可以称之为礼坏乐崩的世界。作为三代文明的最主要象征和遗产,礼乐秩序是那个时代最大的背景,也是那个时代政治家和思想家们的核心关注。此秩序的核心,乃是通过一系列的"名"把各种各样的存在纳入到某种地位和关系之中。① 以西周的封建制度为例,各诸侯国分别对应着公、侯、伯、子、男五等爵的某一个等级,并根据此等级拥有其权利,并承担其相应的责任和义务。因此,对于秩序而言,名是最本质的和不可或缺的因素。"名位不同,礼亦异数"②的说法,意味着不同的名就决定了某物在此秩序中的不同角色和处境,因此也就以不同的方式被安顿。从这个意义上讲,名甚至是比某个真实而具体的存在更重要之物。因此,随着世界的剧烈变化,如果名和实之间的错位变得越来越严重,那么秩序的崩溃就成为必然,这正是礼坏乐崩的真相。

古代中国两位最伟大的哲人——孔子和老子——正诞生和活跃在礼坏乐崩之际,面对着类似的情形,他们给出的思考和解决方向是不同的。孔子的思考可以称之为正名说,希望通过名和实之间的再度统一来恢复礼乐的秩序。《论语·颜渊》记载:"齐景公问政于孔子,孔子对曰:君君,臣臣,父父,子子。"重复出现的这同一个字眼,分别具有名和实的意义,并要求着它们之间的一致。这个回答得到了景公的肯定,以为是维护政治权威和秩序的保证。《阳货》篇则借着回答子路的提问,明确提出了正名之论:

> 子路曰:卫君待子而为政,子将奚先? 子曰:必也正名乎! 名不正则言不顺,言不顺则事不成,事不成则礼乐不兴,礼乐不兴则刑罚不中,刑罚不中则民无所措手足。

这一系列的句子最足以表现名对于维系和规范此世界的意义,正是在

---

① 《左传·桓公二年》:"名以制义,义以出礼,礼以体政,政以正民。"
② 《左传·庄公十八年》。

名之中,世界上的每一个存在才能够意识到自己的角色和位置,由此做出恰当的选择,否则"民无所措手足"。这是一个名分的世界,一切都笼罩在名的网络之内,秩序和价值就在此中体现。正名说的实质,乃是根据着每一个存在之名来规范此世界,从而使秩序得以恢复。

《春秋》的意义在这个视野中可以得到最大的呈现。该书是孔子根据鲁史而创作,据说在笔削的过程中完全拒绝了弟子的参与,[①]因此也可以说是孔子最私人化的作品。孟子曾经如此交代孔子作《春秋》的背景和心迹:

> 世衰道微,邪说暴行有作,臣弑其君者有之,子弑其父者有之。孔子惧,作《春秋》。《春秋》,天子之事也。是故孔子曰:知我者其惟《春秋》乎! 罪我者其惟《春秋》乎![②]

《春秋》之作,正是由于君不君臣不臣父不父子不子的严峻现实,"孔子成《春秋》而乱臣贼子惧",其批判和重建的意义不言而喻。如《庄子·天下》篇"《春秋》以道名分"之说所概括的,该书的实质乃是通过对于名分的强调,以实现正名的努力。《春秋》之所以为天子之事,是由于正名的主体、制礼作乐的主体应该是天子,如《中庸》所说:"非天子,不议礼,不制度,不考文"。但时无天子,孔子乃不得已而代行其事,故有知我罪我之论。

与孔子以正名之说试图恢复礼乐秩序的努力方向完全不同,老子提出的则是无名说。《老子》三十八章"夫礼者,忠信之薄而乱之首也"的说法,表现出老子对立足于名的礼乐秩序之根本否定。从名的角度来看老子的有关论述,其洞见是石破天惊的:

> 道可道也,非恒道也;名可名也,非恒名也。无名,万物之始也;有名,万物之母也。

这是对名之世界的根本反省,并在此反省中回到万物之始的无名状态。目睹着曾经稳固的名的秩序的土崩瓦解,万物之名在世界变动中的灰飞烟灭,老子意识到可道与可名者皆非永恒。要达到这种认识并非困难之事,真正困难的是无名作为万物之始的发现。长期浸淫在名的世界之中,

---

① 《史记·孔子世家》:"至于为《春秋》,笔则笔,削则削,子夏之徒不能赞一辞。"
② 《孟子·滕文公下》。

我们已经习惯了存在与名的关联,甚至误以为名便是存在的本质。但名真的是存在的本质,存在之家吗?"无名,万物之始也"之说的意义,在于穿越名的迷雾,把无名确立为存在之家,确立为万物的本原。这也就同时确立了无名相对于名而言的优先性,或者存在本身之于名的优先性。只有在这个前提之下,《老子》四十四章"名与身孰亲"问题的提出才是合乎逻辑的,并且不会有歧义的答案。

万物之始的无名注定了会和作为万物本原的道联系在一起,并成为其核心的内容。《老子》中两次出现了"道恒无名"的提法,分别见于三十二章和三十七章。前者云:

> 道恒无名,朴,虽小,天下莫敢臣。侯王若能守之,万物将自宾。天地相合,以降甘露,民莫之令而自均。始制有名,名亦既有,夫亦将知止。知止所以不殆。

由"道恒无名"引申出来的是侯王以无名为基础建立起来的治道,侯王若持守此无名之道,百姓将自宾。此治道显然不同于以名及正名为基础的礼乐政治,在礼乐政治中,百姓不是自宾,而是被迫进入到某种外在的被强加的秩序之内。所谓"上礼为之而莫之应,则攘臂而扔之",即是对此情景的叙述。值得注意的是,老子的思考并不完全排斥名的位置,"始制有名"的提法明确地表现出其对名之必要性的承认。但此名的成立,一是必须要建立在无名的基础之上,二是必须具有"知止"的态度。王弼在注释此段时说:"始制,谓朴散始为官长之时也。始制官长,不可不立名分以定尊卑,故始制有名也。过此以往,将争锥刀之末,故曰:名亦既有,夫亦将知止也。遂任名以号物,则失治之母也,故知止所以不殆也。"[①]始制有名绝非任名,名并非这个世界的绝对之物,它必须意识到自身的有限性,意识到无名作为存在之家的事实,才能够发展出知止的态度。我们再看看三十七章的说法:

> 道恒无名。侯王若能守,万物将自化。化而欲作,吾将镇之以无名之朴。夫亦将不欲,不欲以静,天下将自正。

---

① 瓦格纳:《王弼〈老子注〉研究》,江苏人民出版社,2008 年,第 529 页。

侯王若能以无名治国,不以名化物,百姓将自化。而自化过程中可能出现的问题,亦可以无名之朴镇之。拨乱反正不是靠以正名对抗倚名,而是以无名来取代有名。

老子始终拒绝把名作为根本的治国手段,其深层的根据在于名根本无法把握和描述这个真正的世界。最初的存在(本原)是无名的也是不可名的,"窈兮冥兮"、"恍兮惚兮"以及"渊兮""湛兮"等都在呈现着道的晦暗不清,而"绳绳兮不可名"更直接地指出了这一点。按照老子自己的说法,"道"不过是我们勉强给予的"字",①"大"、"玄"等也须作如是观。应该注意的是,无名并不仅仅只和本原相关,通过本原,它关联着这个世界上所有的事物,因此也构成了万物的本质。在这个意义上,不仅最初的存在不可名,万物在本质上也都是不可名的。任何给予事物的命名都不过是权宜之计,不可执以为恒常。在这样的理解之下,那个曾经稳固的名的世界便彻底松动了,而建立在此名的世界之上的价值和秩序更是失去了其坚实的根基。

这种无名的态度延续到庄子,并随着主要问题的转移,而发展为一种"圣人无名"的生命姿态。庄子很明确地指出"道不当名",《知北游》谓:"道不可闻,闻而非也;道不可见,见而非也;道不可言,言而非也。知形形之不形乎!道不当名"。道是无法用名言来描述的,的确,以无作为其主要规定性的道,又怎么可能适用于名呢?《齐物论》"大道不称"的说法与此一致,更进一步的是,庄子在这篇文字中向读者呈现了物之名的相对性。名并非这个世界固有之物,它是属人的存在。"道行之而成,物谓之而然",某物之具有某名完全取决于是谁命名了它。物是彼还是是,依赖的是命名者的角度。物无非彼,物无非是,但自彼则不见,自是则知之。于是有"方生方死,方死方生。方可方不可,方不可方可"的情形出现。庄子以此揭示着物以及描述物之名的相对性,愚昧者执此物的分别执此相对之名以为常,但达者可以"知通为一":

> 物固有所然,物固有所可。无物不然,无物不可。故为是举

---

① 《老子》二十五章:"有物混成,先天地生……吾不知其名,强字之曰道,强为之名曰大。"

莛与楹,厉与西施,恢诡谲怪,道通为一。其分也,成也;其成也,
毁也。凡物无成与毁,复通为一。

在这种观照之下,名以及由命名而带来的很多分别究其实乃是被赋予
的。换一个角度来看,价值和秩序同时就是枷锁和桎梏,譬如仁义和礼乐。
庄子毫不掩饰他对于仁义礼乐等的拒绝,并认为只有忘记它们,才可以同
于大通,达到坐忘之境。因此,回到一个无名的世界就成为合乎逻辑的选
择。

二、混　沌

但无名就是混沌,我们就这样随着无名进入了混沌的世界。众所周
知,混沌观念最初可以在具有神话性质的材料中发现。《山海经·中山经》
曾经提到过名为帝江的天山之神,"其状如黄囊,赤如丹火。六足四翼,混
沌无面目,是识歌舞,实为帝江。"这应该就是庄子"中央之帝曰混沌"之说
的所本。①《左传·文公十八年》记载被舜所流放的四凶之一便有帝鸿氏之
不才子,"掩义隐贼,好行凶德,丑类恶物,顽嚚不友,是与比周,天下之民谓
之混敦。"②它与穷奇、梼杌和饕餮一起被赋予价值和秩序对立物的形象,
因此很自然地就被人伦世界的缔造者舜所排斥和放逐。但是这个被放逐
之物却在稍后出现的道家传统中得到了再生,并且占据了思想中心的地
位。

虽然老子没有直接使用"混沌"一词,但这个观念在他的哲学中却是无
所不在的,并且成为被积极肯定的东西。一方面是《老子》中混、浑、沌、敦
等字眼的大量出现,另一方面则是和混沌相关的各种意象。就后者而言,

---

① 这里并不讨论《山海经》的具体成书年代以及其与《庄子》的文本先后问题。无论如何,
《山海经》的记载体现着理性化之前的古老世界和传统。在这个意义上讲,其中呈现的一定是先于
庄子的观念。

② 混敦即混沌,根据朱起凤《词通》所列,与此意义和声音类似的字眼尚有浑沦、昆仑、崑崙、
混沦、浑沦、倱伅、昏沉、浑蛋、囫囵等。帝鸿即帝江,《说文》:"鸿,从鸟,江声",杜预等皆持此说。
参见庞朴:《黄帝与混沌》。

作为天地根或者万物之奥的道,就被规定为"混成"之物,①《老子》十四章有如下的文字:

> 视之不见名曰夷,听之不闻名曰希,抟之不得名曰微。此三者不可致诘,故混而为一。一者,其上不徼,其下不昧,绳绳兮不可名,复归于无物。是谓无状之状,无物之象,是谓惚恍。

混沌的最大特点就是未分化的无形的存在,它也因此成为不可名者。就如同这里提到的"混而为一",以及"不可名"和"惚恍"。由此,善行道者也就具有混一之象,如十五章所说:

> 古之善为士者,微妙玄通,深不可识。夫唯不可识,故强为之容。豫兮若冬涉川;犹兮若畏四邻;俨兮其若客;涣兮若冰之将释;敦兮其若朴;旷兮其若谷;混兮其若浊;澹兮其若海;飂兮若无止。孰能浊以静之徐清。孰能安以动之徐生。保此道者不欲盈。夫唯不盈,故能蔽而新成。

混、敦的字眼是明显可见的,而"微妙玄通,深不可识"也显示出其无法命名的特点,所以任何的形容都只能是勉强的。即便在这些勉强的形容中,我们也不能忽视在每个句子中都不可或缺的"若"字。这个字增加了内容的弹性,因此提醒我们不能太凿实。二十章则进一步描述了行道者的混一之心:

> 绝学无忧,唯之与阿,相去几何? 善之与恶,相去若何? 人之所畏,不可不畏。荒兮其未央哉! 众人熙熙,如享太牢、如春登台。我独泊兮其未兆,如婴儿之未孩;累累兮若无所归。众人皆有余,而我独若遗。我愚人之心也哉! 沌沌兮。俗人昭昭,我独昏昏;俗人察察,我独闷闷。众人皆有以,而我独顽且鄙。我独异于人,而贵食母。

沌沌的愚人之心,昏昏闷闷的字眼,都呈现着混沌的意象。在这种意象中,唯与阿、善与恶的区别淡化甚至消失了。与之相对的是看起来清清

---

① 《老子》25 章:"有物混成,先天地生"。

楚楚的昭昭和察察,人们在分辨着这个世界的同时也分裂着自己。在老子这里,从混一之道到体道者的混一之象与混一之心,混沌观念是一以贯之的。其实不限于此,我们还可以看到混沌的君主、混沌的百姓与混沌的政治。如五十八章所说:"其政闷闷,其民淳淳。其政察察,其民缺缺。"

比较而言,混沌的主题在庄子那里得到了更清楚地呈现。首先是《庄子·应帝王》中的寓言:

> 南海之帝为儵,北海之帝为忽,中央之帝为混沌。儵与忽时相与遇于混沌之地,混沌待之甚善。儵与忽谋报混沌之德,曰:人皆有七窍,以视听食息,此独无有,尝试凿之。日凿一窍,七日而混沌死。

混沌在这里被描述为没有七窍的中央之帝,具有待人甚善的品质,并在人为的谋凿中死去。出现在内七篇结尾处的这个寓言具有着多方面的意义,[①]在本文的视野之下,最重要的意义或许是通过怀念混沌,表达出对这个过于清楚的人为世界之反思。而《天地》篇的寓言,在描述了子贡和汉阴丈人的对话后,借孔子之口提出了所谓"修混沌氏之术者":

> (子贡)反于鲁,以告孔子。孔子曰:彼假修浑沌氏之术者也;识其一,不知其二;治其内,而不治其外。夫明白入素,无为复朴,体性抱神,以游世俗之间者,汝将固惊邪?且浑沌氏之术,予与汝何足以识之哉!

虽然是在寓言之中,但"孔子"的言论却很像是真的孔子。儒家显然和混沌无关,并且视混沌为需要凿破之境。而庄子确实是"修混沌氏之术者",老子亦然。

我们需要对混沌进行一些澄清,虽然这看起来有些吊诡。无论是无面目或者无七窍的描述,还是混成、混而为一的说法,都显示出混沌是一个未分化的存在。在这个意义上,混沌便是一。《天地》篇说"修混沌氏之术者"是"识其一不识其二,识其内不识其外",无疑是恰当的。从老子到庄子,与对混沌的积极肯定并存的,是对于"一"的强调。除了前引十四章中"混而

---

① 参见王博《庄子哲学》,北京大学出版社,2004 年,第 140 – 141 页;第 147 页。

为一"的"一者"外,三十九章特别突出了一对于天地万物以及侯王的意义:

> 昔之得一者,天得一以清,地得一以宁,神得一以灵,谷得一
> 以盈,侯王得一以为天下正。

一乃是这个杂多世界的维系者,正如它是此杂多世界之生成者。根据四十二章"道生一,一生二,二生三,三生万物"之说,杂多的万物皆从混沌中产生。混沌并不停留在一那个地方,它内在地具有化生的能力,①从而变化出二、三以至于万物。虽然是万物,在其都源自于一的意义上说,不过就是一。因此,杂多不过是一的另外一种存在方式。但一显然不是多,正如"少则得,多则惑,是以圣人抱一为天下式"所显示的,一而不是多才是圣人之所执者。

在把这个世界理解为一的方面,庄子要比老子彻底的多。从《逍遥游》的"将磅礴万物以为一"、《齐物论》的"天地与我并生,而万物与我为一"以及"道通为一"等说法,就可以看出庄子看待世界的态度。万物之间的差别在庄子的混沌和一中被融化了,"天下莫大于秋毫之末,而泰山为小;莫寿于殇子,而彭祖为夭",原本固定的界限突然之间不再存在,一切都在大化流行中融通为一。在庄子那里,一切都在流转中成为一体。包括庄周与蝴蝶,或者鱼和鸟。因此,杂多以及杂多的相对性不过是道通为一的证明。

三、宽　容

从无名和混沌出发,世界就不再可能是一个割裂的泾渭分明之物,一切的名以及它所代表的区别都松动甚至融化了,于是包容而不是分辨成为核心的价值。②在老子看来,这根本是一个无法分辨清楚的世界,对立的事物纠缠在一起,难解难分。《老子》第二章说道:

> 天下皆知美之为美,斯恶矣;皆知善之为善,斯不善矣。故有

---

① 杨儒宾:《混沌与太极》。
② 《庄子·天下》概括属于黄老学派的彭蒙、田骈和慎到的主张,提到"齐万物以为首……大道能包之而不能辨之"等。另《齐物论》"圣人怀之,众人辨之,以相示也",与此义同。

无相生,难易相成,高下相倾,长短相形,音声相和,前后相随,恒也。是以圣人处无为之事,行不言之教。

当我们试图告诉天下以美的时候,带来的却是恶;试图让天下知道什么是善的时候,不善也如影随形般地出现。以"有无相生"为代表,对立物的纠缠使得任何试图用清楚的名言分辨世界的努力落空。任何的分辨只能是粗暴的割裂,与真实的世界无关。在这个时候,除了包容之外,我们还能做什么智慧的事情呢?《老子》十六章有云:

致虚极也,守静笃也。万物并作,吾以观复。夫物芸芸,各复归其根。归根曰静,静曰复命,复命曰常,知常曰明。不知常,妄作,凶。知常容,容乃公,公乃王,王乃天,天乃道,道乃久,没身不殆。

老子强调知常的重要,所谓常即是归根复命、即是回到存在的根源处,依前所述,就是回到无名和混沌的状态。在此无分别心的状态中,没有了善恶美丑人我的分别,容与公乃是自然之事。因此,二十七章所谓"是以圣人常善救人,故无弃人。常善救物,故无弃物"之说也就不显得突兀。善救无弃,这正是宽容,道家哲学最核心的精神之一。我们应记住,宽容一词第一次正是用来描述老子思想的,《庄子·天下》云:

老聃曰:知其雄,守其雌,为天下谿;知其白,守其辱,为天下谷。人皆取先,己独取后,曰受天下之垢;人皆取实,己独取虚,无藏也故有余,岿然而有余。其行身也,徐而不费,无为也而笑巧,人皆求福,己独曲全,曰苟免于咎。以深为根,以约为纪,曰坚则毁矣,锐则挫矣。常宽容于物,不削于人。可谓至极。

"常宽容于物,不削于人"之句处于总结性评语的位置上,显得非常有分量。作为老子思想的发扬光大者,庄子及其学派对他的理解是相当深刻的。在老子那里,宽容是道的精神,也应该是君主和圣人的精神。道对于万物是宽容的,这从其"生而不有,为而不恃,长而不宰"的玄德中便可看出。此"莫之命而常自然"的宽容精神让"万物莫不尊道而贵德"。君主和圣人之于百姓也该如此,我想重点讨论一下四十九章:

圣人恒无心,以百姓心为心。善者吾善之,不善者吾亦善之,德善;信者吾信之,不信者吾亦信之,德信。圣人在天下,歙歙焉为天下浑其心。百姓皆注其耳目,圣人皆孩之。

宽容是承认和接纳与自己不同的想法及存在,《老子》中的圣人显然可以做到此点。与现实的君主经常把一己之心强加给这个世界,从而以己心为百姓心不同,圣人在永恒的无心中接纳百姓之心成为自己之心,使他者的生命得以呈现。在此前提之下,建立在己心基础上的善与不善、信与不信等区别都消失了,当然更没有什么所谓善者和不善者、信者和不信者。"善者吾善之,不善者吾亦善之"的说法并不能完全从字面上来理解,这不是对不善者的善待,而是对善和不善区分的拒绝。在究竟的意义上,善与不善以及信与不信不过是我们基于某种立场强加给世界的东西,与世界本身无关。真正的事物并无所谓善和不善、信与不信,它们是无名的混沌。很显然,老子并不希望君主按照自己的意志来规范或者塑造世界,当然更不希望以己见撕裂这个世界。所以他拒绝任何根据自我的标准来分裂混沌的做法,无论这个自我是多么伟大、想法是如何崇高。如果"伟大"和"崇高"对于这个世界而言是外在的,那么它就是不属于这个世界的。

不是从自我出发,而是从他者和世界出发,这就是宽容的精髓。政治意义上的宽容表现为君主的莫之命而常自然,或者辅万物之自然而不敢为。万物和百姓在没有外在压力和干涉的背景中呈现着自我,并以自我的方式存在于世界之中。在老子那里,我们可以看到一系列以"自"开头的字眼,除了"自然"之外,还有"自化"、"自正"、"自朴"、"自富"等,它们的主语都是万物或者百姓。"自"的前提正是君主和圣人的宽容。值得指出的是,宽容并不是和秩序对立之物,因此也不就意味着秩序的缺乏。其核心在于这是一个什么样的秩序:自生的因此也是内在的,或者强加的因此也是外在的。"自"要求的是一个属于这个世界本身的内在的秩序,而不是一个外来之物。老子之后的黄老学以"物自正也,名自命也"①的方式力图开展出的正是奠基于混沌基础之上的内在形名和秩序。

———————————
① 帛书《经法·论》。

如果说老子的宽容主要集中在政治的向度,最终表现为道法自然的态度,那么庄子的宽容则呈现为对不同生活方式的辩护。在《齐物论》中,庄子取消了一切普遍的东西,拒绝了任何特殊之物僭越为普遍之物的可能性,从而为每个存在的特殊性提供了存在的理由。没有物之所同是,意味着每个事物都可以各是其所是,因此善恶之名也就失去了着落。在《养生主》中,"为善无近名,为恶无近刑"的提法是读者熟悉的。与老子"善者吾善之,不善者吾亦善之"句相同,这句话的意义也绝对不能从字面去理解。这仍然是对善恶之别的否定和超越。更难理解因此也更具挑战性的是见于《大宗师》的如下说法:

> 与其誉尧而非桀也,不如两忘而化其道。

在一个分辨的确定性的价值世界中,尧和桀已经分别成为圣王和暴君的代名词。但在由道所确立的混沌和无名的世界中,他们不过是两个被如此描述和被如此命名的生命。也许在另一个价值体系中,成为暴君的会是尧,而桀则被描述为圣王。其实,尧就是尧、桀就是桀,他们与暴君和圣王无关。

Integration v. Co-existence: A Classic Confucian Discourse on World-order in the Medieval Chinese Empire

Jaeyoon Song

Power and Legitimacy

In the history of political thought in general, classical antiquity has served as an important point of reference, regardless of Western and Eastern traditions. Based on the large corpus of Confucian classics traditional Chinese political thinkers envisioned the ideal world of antiquity where the sage kings realized the long-lasting order of grand unity. Especially when the so-called Neo-Confucians refined the fundamental doctrines of Confucianism during 11th and 13th century China, they claimed to have restored the lost transmission of the Way through a direct interpretation with the intent of the sages without relying on the intermediate exegetical tradition. Likewise, ad fontes, meaning "back to the origins", was the motto of the European Renaissance movement (ca. 14th-17th centuries), and the American founding fathers frequently invoked the ancient models of Greece and Rome to draft a new constitution. We may say that antiquity has provided an intellectual forum for political thinkers throughout history to debate over the fundamental problems of good government and the good life. ①

Given this universal appeal of antiquity to a broad array of political thinkers, we might ask why antiquity matters. Antiquity matters in two distinctive ways. First of all, antiquity mattered because of the classics shared by political thinkers. The authority of classics as the shared texts of an intellectual community provided an intellectual fulcrum for political thinkers to address diverse issues of government. By commentating on the classics, political thinkers could articulate their views of good government with "classical authority." In this way, antiquity differs from legends or mythology. To sum up, antiquity matters while classics still hold authority. Second, as we saw in the example of the Renaissance, antiquity served as a point of reference for those who wanted to promote something new. Those who were critical of cumulative traditions looked back to the ideals of high antiquity to argue how things had gone awry once the perfect past went downhill. Ironically, political reformers who aimed to express discontents with the status quo aimed to find a new way in the ancient ways of life. In other words, antiquity matters because it trumps "traditions and customs" that might get in the way of innovative thinking.

Reform and Constitutional Agenda

We can ascertain these two points in the history of Chinese

---

① This is not to say that all the political thinkers are interested in revealing the ideals of antiquity; there have always been so-called "modernists" who denied the ancient modes of thinking as antiquarian or reactionary. When Kant defined Enlightenment as "man's release from his self-incurred immaturity," he recognized the human ability to think for oneself, freeing mankind from the thralls of traditions. Nevertheless, no less a modernist than J. S. Mill was a "Greek-infatuated man." J. G. A. Pocock, who brought to life the long-standing European heritage of republicanism in the *Machiavellian Moment*, writes that "the idea of direct conversation with antiquity is a key concept in all forms of humanism."

political thought. Chinese political thinkers had a shared tradition in the large corpus of classics. To those thinkers of the past, these classics were a reservoir of cumulative wisdoms; the sacred records of lived experiences of the ancient times. The so-called Confucian classics or canons, the body of the thirteen texts handed down from antiquity, formed an integral part of intellectual life in traditional China. Because the presence of classics in the minds of indigenous Chinese thinkers was so enormous, we tend to view them as merely passive preservers of antiquity, incapable of formulating ground-breaking political agenda.

For this reason, a majority of scholars have focused on the internal moral/ethical dimensions of Confucianism, especially since the rise of Neo-Confucianism in Southern Song. Indigenous Chinese political thinkers used classics to articulate their views of good government. Classics provided them with a rich political language, and they used this language voluntarily not only to interpret tradition but to articulate their views of government. They did not serve classics; quite the contrary, classics served their purposes.

I'd like to spell out this point by focusing on one of the largest state reforms, the New Policies (1068 – 1127) in Northern Song China. The New Polices was a full-scale state activist reform that lasted for almost half a century until the fall of the Northern Song in 1127. It was one of the most dramatic moments in Chinese history, and, consequently, drawn much scholarly attention.

During the 11th century, the Northern Song was surrounded by strong nomadic empires to the north and the northwest. In military tension with these empires, Northern Song raised an oversized standing army of 1.4 million, which constantly caused fiscal crises. The period is also marked by a swiftly growing private commercial economy, which threatened to outstrip the state's administrative capacities. At this time a group of tough-minded bureaucrats from the south enacted a set of interventionist reforms. During this time, the state tried to take the entire management of commerce, industry, and agriculture into its own hands.

The reform councilor Wang Anshi (1021 – 1086), the architect of the 11th century state-activist reforms called the New Policies (1068 – 1120s), called for active intervention in the private economy. He wanted to "strengthen the military and enrich the state." For this reason, he produced a large army of "entreprenurial bureaucrats", who would compete with big merchants and landlords in order to increase tax revenues. The government intervened in the private commercial economy by casting nearly six billion coins, the highest recorded level in China's imperial history. Furthermore, the government reasserted control over the peasantry by providing agricultural subsidies and by organizing local villages into a nested hierarchy of local administration. Accordingly, the bureaucracy expanded. The number of qualified officials jumped forty one percent in thirteen years. (from 24,000 in 1067 to 34,000 in 1080). Wang Anshi tried to increase the state income as well. Wang Anshi wanted to remove the powers of the local elite, and tried to build an absolutist state by taking direct control over the people.

Not surprisingly, Wang Anshi had his political enemies. His sweeping reforms were instantly met with a strong resistance from the leading conservative statesmen. In opposition to the New Party led by Wang Anshi, those conservative statesmen formed the Old Party. The tension between the two parties created an unforeseen factional struggle. The anti-reformists criticized Wang Anshi's policies as deviating from the long-standing dynastic laws set up by the founding emperors, and called for abolition of the New Policies. The rivalry between the so-called Old and New Parties soon grew into a full-scale constitutional discourse. I call it a constitutional discourse because their debates focused on the legitimacy of these reforms. Wang Anshi was hard-pressed. Wang Anshi hoisted the banner of "unifying morality and homogenizing customs" to attack his political rivals. However, he had to legitimate the New Policies in a more justifiable way.

As an excellent classicist, Wang Anshi chose to invoke the ancient Confucian Classics to secure the "constitutionality" of the New Policies. Wang Anshi's commentary on one of the ancient Confucian texts, especially the Rituals of Zhou, became the de facto constitution of the New Policies government. By reading "the intent of the sages (shengren zhi yi)," Wang Anshi legitimated the New Policies. According to his interpretation, the Duke of Zhou, the law-giver of the ancient Zhou dynasty, was an activist ruler who wanted to expand state control over the whole realms of society. Taking his cue from the Duke of Zhou, Wang Anshi argued that good government consists in ensuring the material welfare of the people as well as edifying them as public-minded individuals. Wang Anshi's commentary on the Rituals of Zhou (Zhouli 周禮) remained to be influential until the end of the Northern Song. It became the standard text for the civil service examinations; till the end of the New Policies, at least, two generations of literati were indoctrinated with this text.

Against this background I would like to point out just two most interesting aspects of political thought in historical context. First of all, in order to legitimate his political reforms, Wang Anshi invoked the ancient model of good government by interpreting one of the Confucian classics, namely, the Rituals of Zhou. According to his interpretation, the Duke of Zhou, one of the ancient sages who systematized the ideal form of government during the founding era of the ancient Zhou dynasty, was an activist ruler who tried to expand state control over the whole realms of society. Taking his cue from the Duke of Zhou, Wang Anshi argued that good government consists in securing the material welfare of the people as well as edifying them as public-minded individuals. Wang Anshi was hard pressed by his opponents to give up the reforms he set out to implement once he rose to power with full support from the emperor.

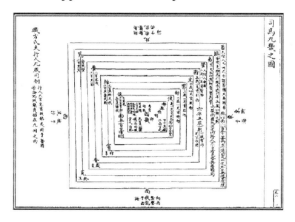

< The Diagram of the Nine Provinces in the *Rituals of Zhou* > [1]

Redefining Good Government:
The Decentralization Model

The New Policies, influenced the course of Chinese history afterwards in two great respects. First of all, Wang Anshi's New Policies represented the peak of state expansionism in medieval China. These reforms took place at the peak of the great socio-

---

[1]　The square area in the center represents the realm of the Central Government vis-à-vis regional states.

economic changes that began from mid-8th century through 12th century China. This long-term transition has been called in various ways: from an economic point of view it was called the medieval economic revolution, compared to the 12th to 13th century European medieval revolution. In pace with these changes, the imperial government during the New Policies responded to these changes to reassert control of the private commercial economy. By state expansionism I mean that the will to expand the actual size of the state in terms of the number of bureaucrats and the government's share in overall economic resources. During the New Policies the state expanded dramatically by producing a larger army of bureaucrats and increasing revenues by acting upon the private commercial economy.

Second, the New Policies influenced the course of Chinese history by setting up the negative example of state expansionism. The New Policies continued for half a century till the end of Northern Song. It was stopped quite abruptly because Northern Song was conquered by the Jurchens, the formidable nomadic tribal empire which, having conquered the northern half of China, established the Jin dynasty. Because these sweeping reformed failed due to sudden conquest by an exterior force, traditionally considered to be nomadic barbarians, those who opposed the reforms could criticize the New Policies. In their critique they not only demonized Wang Anshi and his reform colleagues but they also articulated their visions of politics. In retrospect we can reconstruct their debates on the New Policies into a systematic constitutional discourse on good government.

The discourse took place after the reforms. We can see many such examples in history. For example, the 1789 French Revolution gave rise to a disputed legacy, an on-going debate on its historical consequences. Interpreters of the French Revolution show a wide array of political spectrum. In the same way, we can talk about the historical consequences of Wang Anshi's New Policies. In the aftermath of the fall of the Northern Song, a large number of political thinkers discussed the historical consequences of the New Policies, which formed into a full-scale discourse on government. They wanted to redefine the roles and responsibilities of the government. Historians have somewhat neglected the significance of political discourses during this period. Political thinkers of this period have been overshadowed by Neo-Confucians who have been regarded as moral philosophers immersed in the problems of moral self-cultivation and ethics.

The New Policies resulted in dynastic fall, losing one half of the territory to the Jurchens, one of the nomadic peoples to the north. For this reason, in the aftermath of dynastic fall, Southern Song literati began to question what went wrong: they began to reflect on the consequences of the New Policies. It started out as one of those typical after-reform debates; however, with time it grew into a more systematic constitutional discourse on good government. This discourse, I have argued, lasted over one hundred fifty years until the imperial government finally decided to remove Wang Anshi's altar from the national Confucian Temple in 1241.

I have tried to show that this discourse formed a strong intellectual movement. It had three dimensions: The first dimension was the history debate, that is, how to judge the legacy of the New Policies. During Southern Song, a large number of historians became increasingly interested in the political history of the recent past, focusing on the New Policies as the central theme of their historical survey. They wrote and published private histories of Northern Song, in which they generally judged the New Policies as a total failure.

In Chinese history, the official history of a certain dynasty was compiled by the succeeding dynasty based on court records and diaries systematically produced by the imperial court. During the Southern

Song, a large group of historians gained access to these court materials and produced private histories on Northern Song; not surprisingly, the New Policies became the most contested theme among Southern Song historians. During the Yuan Dynasty, when the Official Song History was compiled under Mongol Rule, these private histories became the so-called "Foundation Sources".

To make a long story short, Southern Song historians produced a large body of private histories on the recent past, and these private histories would later form the Official History under the Mongol Empire. As a result, the standard history of the Song Dynasty would eventually villify Wang Anshi and his comrade reformers. Wang Anshi would not be rehabilitated until the late 19th century; Interestingly, during the Cultural Revolution in the 1960s, many historians re-interpreted Wang Anshi's New Policies as the first socialist revolution in human history.

The second dimension concerns Classical antiquity. A large number of Southern Song literati re-interpreted the ancient classics, especially, the Rituals of Zhou, which, as mentioned above, became the de facto constitution of the New Policies. The sheer number of Southern Song commentaries on the Rituals of Zhou should strike us. I have identified close to one hundred commentaries that had been written and published by individual scholars throughout Southern Song. I surveyed the authors and found that most of them were government officials, that is, they passed the jinshi examinations and served in the bureaucracy. Some of them were high officials including a few prime ministers. Many others were influential masters. Some others were local hermits and visionaries, etc. They commonly opposed Wang Anshi's interpretation of the classics. They redefined the underlying theory of government in the Rituals of Zhou.

Like Deng Xiaoping (1904 – 1997) after Chairman Mao (1893

– 1976）, Southern Song political thinkers struggled with the ghost of Wang Anshi. Like Deng after nineteen seventy eight, they shifted the direction of government afterwards. They forgo the autocratic ambitions of systematic control and articulated the ideal of a smaller government that relied on self-generating forces of local society. They generally opposed the intensification of state control through enactment of detailed rules and regulations. However, it would be misleading to view them simply as anti-reformists. They had in mind another type of reform, i. e. , an incremental or gradual process of restructuring. One Southern Song historian criticized the rash reforms of Wang Anshi by providing two different types of reform：

> *In general, a good reformer does not necessarily change the laws of preceding generations thoroughly. He has only to change the grand purposes, and the details will automatically follow. A bad reformer always changes the laws of ancient people; he often prescribes minute details while being too sketchy about the great* [*purposes*]. [1]

To paraphrase, a good reformer esteems traditions and institutions because he knows that the existing institutions and tools of society embody generations of cumulative experience. He would not prescribe specific rules and regulations according to an ideal scheme of his own; he would rather remain at an abstract level of improving the general constitutional framework of government. Traditions represent the epitome of institutions and experiments that have survived the test of time. [2] Therefore, a good reformer relies on them.

---

[1]　Ibid. 1. 7b – 8. a.

[2]　This idea is fully developed in Friedrich A. Hyek in his theory of liberty in the British evolutionary tradition. See his *The Constitution of Liberty* (Chicago: The University of Chicago Press, 1960), Chapter 4.

Quite the opposite, a bad reformer arbitrarily replaces the existing laws with an ideal plan of his own design. He does not see how the seemingly all-too-general laws contain in themselves the collective wisdom of past generations. In his view, existing practices, rules, and regulations form barriers to social welfare, and should thereby be replaced by more systematic plans. Instead of abolishing Qin legacies, the Han took advantage of the existing institutions and tools of government. Their laws might seem to have remained general, but they built upon previous generations. Tang laws were specifically prescribed but could not endure the test of time.

The Case of Ye Shi (1150 – 1223): Constitutional Plans of Southern Song Political Thinkers

With a new blueprint of incremental reform, Southern Song political thinkers articulated new constitutional arrangements for limited government. When a political theorist imposes legitimate constraint upon public power, we may call it ' constitutional. '[1] In this light, we can talk of the indigenous development of ' constitutional' thought in Chinese tradition. For lack of space, let me focus on Ye Shi 葉適 (1150 – 1223) one of the most systematic political thinkers from 12th to 13th century Southern Song.

As practical strategist and administrator, Ye Shi articulated his

---

[1] Some legal and political theorists have recently tried to illuminate the indigenous heritage of East Asian constitutionalism with a culture-sensitive approach. See Chaihark Hahm, " Confucian Constitutionalism" (S. J. D. , Harvard Law School, 2000) and Daniel A. Bell, et al, *Confucianism for the modern world* (Cambridge U. K. : Cambridge University Press, 2003).

plans for reform in four distinct aspects. [1] First, the scale of Southern Song state finance had become too large and should, therefore, be curtailed. Second, the number of the Southern Song military had grown too large and become weak for this reason, and should, therefore, be cut back. Third, the institutions and laws had become too detailed and dense to the extent of destroying customs, and should, therefore, be simplified. Fourth, the structural principle of the state had become over-centralized to the extent of undermining the authority of the state.

Therefore, the authority of the central government should be distributed among the bureaucrats through proper division and delegation of power. [2] Furthermore, Ye Shi argues, social and economic resources should reside not in the central state, but in the people who produced them. By reducing its size, the government could reduce the cost of administration and defense, and the economic resources seized by the government could be returned to the people. When the people take control of their economic resources, the economy should grow to the benefit of both rich and poor. In short, Ye Shi proposes a new constitutional plan for a small and effective government.

Ye Shi's constitutional plan is combined with his skeptical attitude toward the New Policies (1068 – 1120s) led by the reformer councilor Wang Anshi. Gaining the full support of the emperor, Wang Anshi attempted at the fundamental reformation; however, his plans to intensify government control ironically resulted in the weakening of

---

① This essay is from a series of memorials Ye Shi wrote in the 1180s. During the Xiaozong's reign, Ye Shi wrote two comprehensive sets of memorials, "the Presented Scrolls (1184)" and "Exterior Manuscripts (1185)." The former is a set of memorials Ye Shi submitted for the decree examination, and the latter picks up the proposed problems in more detail. These memorials address diverse matters of the state such as government structure, bureaucratic organization, fiscal policy, military organization, and social policies in a systematic way.

② *Ye Shiji*, pp. 767 – 769.《叶适集》Collected Works of Ye Shi

the state. Wang Anshi's reforms were prescriptive (dirigiste) as the government expanded without restructuring its unhealthy structure. Ye Shi proposes another way of strengthening the state by elimination of unnecessary rules and regulations. Instead, Ye Shi has in mind an idea of a permissive (laissez faire) reform, i. e., an effective retrenchment of government activities. This idea is encapsulated in his two grand statements concerning fiscal policy and military organization:

> "*The Military will be stronger by becoming smaller, and the fisc will be richer by taking less.*"[1]

In terms of fiscal policy, Ye Shi proposes the decrease of financial demands through a fundamental restructuring of the government apparatus. In terms of the military, Ye Shi also proposes a radical downsizing after the model of Taizu's Imperial Troops, which numbered only two hundred thousand.[2] The idea of a laissez faire reform guides Ye Shi's critique of Wang Anshi's activist reforms, and underlies his constitutional plans for Southern Song.

Regarding the importance of the military, Ye Shi says: "The reason why [national] wealth has become such an important matter is because the military is a matter of great importance."[3] In other words, Ye Shi believes that the rising military expense has incurred fiscal crises. The military expense occupied the three quarters of the national income around the mid-11th century when the number of military forces amounted to one point four million. According to Ye Shi, the fiscal activism of the New Policies was intensified during the Huizong's reign

---

① *Ye Shiji*, p. 784.

② Chen Fuliang also emphasizes this fact in his history of military. So did Lü Zhong who lectured on Northern Song political history a generation later (chapter 2).

③ *Ye Shiji*, p. 779.

and continued to grow harsher during 12th century Southern Song. [1] The number of the military, including the Four Frontier Armies, the Palace Guards, and provincial and local troops, exceeded one million in his time. In order to break out of this vicious cycle, Ye Shi thought it was necessary to reduce the size of the military.

Ye Shi's plans for finance calls for the lessening of government intervention: [2]

> *" The management of wealth and the exaction of taxes are two different things. What people call the management of wealth today is no more than the exaction of taxes. This is not only true for today. Since the Zhou declined, the management of wealth has long since lost it original meaning. People began to think that the management of wealth meant collecting revenues from the people for the use of the higher authorities. He who manages wealth well takes [revenue] so skillfully that people would not even notice. The higher authorities would have a sufficient amount while the lower people would not be agonized. Only this could be called the management of wealth. "* [3]

The ancient sages were without exception good managers of wealth, Ye Shi writes. Their method was not to concentrate wealth in the central government, but to diffuse wealth across all-under-heaven. The legitimate ground of state intervention in the economy is to ameliorate the flow of goods and redress imbalances between people across regions. For this reason, "King Yu and the Duke of Zhou

---

① See Winston Lo, *Ye Shih*, pp. 60 – 61.

② Ye Shi uttered this phrase even before they acquired the *jinshi* degree. Therefore, it is more likely that they adopted this idea from Ye Shi than vice versa.

③ *Ye Shiji*, "Fiscal Plans," pp. 657 – 658.

managed the wealth of all-under-heaven together with [the people in] all-under-heaven. " In other words, the ideal management of wealth should be for the enrichment of the people only. Wealth should reside in the people, not in the government.

Ye Shi also argues that economic inequalities have become the reality of life. To try to eradicate social and economic inequalities according to an ideal model of antiquity or a moral plan of an individual would be irresponsible, as seen in the example of the New Policies. The government should recognize the economic realities of society. Instead of competing with merchants and land-engrossers, the government should rely on them. They have become the active partakers of "governance" in multiple centers of all-under-heaven. For this reason, Ye Shi defends the rich as the bases of local governments and as the mediators between the imperial government and the commoners. [1] Ye Shi was trying to provide a systematic theory of government that considers the rise of commerce and a burgeoning private economy as the tractor of economic growth.

Ye Shi's plan for the welfare of the people in general fits nicely with his proposal for fiscal and military reforms. In Ye Shi's view, the role of the emperor as parent of the people no longer obtained in the realities of Southern Song. Therefore, the emperor should rely on the existing order of society instead of trying to reform it to an ideal model of the past. For this reason the government should try to alleviate the tax burdens of the rich. To relieve fiscal pressure, the only solution Ye Shi could find was to decrease the size of the military, which according to his calculation, occupied more than eight percent of the overall state income.

Of course, Ye Shi was not as powerful as Deng Xiaoping. His

---

[1] *Ye Shiji*, p. 657, "富人者，州县之本，上下之所赖也."

new visions of reform did not "revolutionize" the Southern Song government in the way Deng's political decision did the PRC after Mao. Rather Ye Shi simply represented Southern Song political thinkers' conception of good government. However, Southern Song constitutional discourse on good government would have long-term consequences in Chinese history. For one thing, never again in the history of later imperial China, the Wang Anshi type prescriptive reforms reappeared until the end of the Qing dynasty. When similar reformers of state-activism held sway, they consciously denounced Wang Anshi and his New Policies. For another, many scholars have noted that over the long swath of time (from the 8th to 19th century) the size of government in late imperial China did not keep pace with the population increase (from 50 million to 400 million), but remained more or less at the same level. Therefore, the actual size of administration retrenched over time. This long-term administrative retrenchment in Chinese history needs an explanation. [1] Since during the New Policies, the size of the state expanded dramatically, Southern Song was the moment when state and society relations were renegotiated. In this view, Southern Song constitutional discourses influenced the further course of Chinese history tremendously.

Southern Song classicists redefined good government through a fundamental re-interpretation of the ancient Three Dynasties. They changed the constitutional schemes in the received classics of antiquity, and formulated concrete plans for reorganizing state society

---

[1] According to the anthropologist Quentin Skinner's calculation, from 750s to 1100s the population doubled reaching 100 million. By 1600 the population was no more than 200 million; by 1850 it rose to 450 million. Over the long term, the population increased by five times. During that time the number of administrative units managed by the central government were more or less constant: 18 – 20 provinces, 300 prefectures, 1,200 counties with the number of officials that are in the civil service hovering from 20,000 to 40,000. When we think of the size of government, we generally consider the number of bureaucrats and its share in overall economic resources. In this view, the government decreased actually, but somehow remained unified.

relations for later imperial China. I have argued that Southern Song literati generally praised the ancient feudal system as the basis of good government. The discourse on the enfeoffment system represents an interesting aspect of Southern Song society; when local literati recognized the ancient feudal system as the model of good government, they could represent themselves as the active participants of governance. They are promoting the idea of "monarchical feudalism" to a certain extent.

Southern Song literati did actually attempt a fundamental revisionist reinterpretation and their views were recognized by the state as the standard theory of government afterwards. I have argued that with the fall of the Northern Song many literati began to criticize Wang Anshi's interpretation of the Rituals of Zhou. Over the course of one hundred fifty years in Southern Song, literati thinkers re-interpreted this classic as a completely different text.

Whereas Wang Anshi emphasized the centripetal aspects of the Rituals of Zhou and defined it as the constitution for the highly centralized absolutist government, Southern Song literati redefined the same classic with non-interventionist and decentralized visions of government, giving more leeway to local society and communities, with a conciliatory approach to the military, with a slimmer model of bureaucracy, etc. All these generally fit well with the framework of later imperial China.

In history, it is not strange at all that the same text could serve different political purposes, even those of binary opposition, according to the given contexts. We know that the American Constitution was redefined during the New Deal, and once again during the Regan Era in the 1980s (according to Bruce Ackerman's We the People). We can argue that indigenous Chinese political thinkers shifted the underlying paradigm of government through a fundamental re-interpretation of classics.

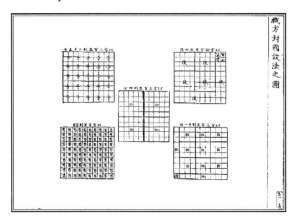

< The Diagram of the Enfeoffment System in the Rituals of Zhou >

Conclusion

" The legitimacy of power" is one of the most questions in political theory. Like many other political thinkers, indigenous Chinese political thinkers invoked the authority of the ancient classics to articulate their political visions. In the Northern Song, the rising military tension with the nomadic empires to the north and northwest gave rise to the unprecedented state-activist reforms called the New Policies. The architect of the New Policies Wang Anshi used the Rituals of Zhou to authorize the New Policies. According to his political theory, good government should ensure administrative centralization and the increased nationalization of economic resources.

Southern Song political thinkers redefined good government through a fundamental re-interpretation of the ancient classics. They changed the constitutional schemes in the Rituals of Zhou and formulated concrete plans for reorganizing state society relations for later imperial China.

I have tried to do justice to them as political, or even constitutional, thinkers. Consequently, we can see more clearly how Southern Song literati negotiated with the imperial court to discontinue with the state-activism of the New Policies government, to limit the expansion of the state at a moderate level, and to give more leeway to self-generating forces of local society in general. Therefore, my research provides an alternative explanation regarding the long-term stability of later Chinese empires. Through political debates and the working-out, Southern Song literati put a stop to the expansion of the state. As a result, the expansionist centralization project undertaken during the New Policies was put to a halt in Southern Song. Local society began to emerge and flourish while the imperial government adopted the new paradigm of government predicated upon self-government and decentralization.

孔教与康有为对儒学之重建

曾　亦

　　辛亥共和,数千年君主制一旦而崩溃,儒学亦颇受牵连,康有为、陈焕章等借鉴了基督教等宗教的某些仪式,而将孔子建立为一种宗教,并且,为了恢复儒家的传统地位与影响,进一步推动孔教的国教化。本文试图对康有为建立孔教的诸多原因进行分析,并由此探讨儒家在现代社会的命运及可能发展方向

一、康有为建立孔教之意图

　　"孔教"一名,当始于康有为。1895 年,康有为上疏朝廷,要求给予治经者以鼓励,且遍设孔庙,又建议派遣儒生到外国传播孔子之道,既扬国声,亦察夷情。[1]1898 年,康有为又上疏建议以孔教为国教,自京师城野省府县乡,遍立孔庙,尊孔子为教主,以孔子纪年,并在全国遍建孔教会 [2]。1912年,民国建立,康有为重提此议。[3]然而,种种主张未得到民国政府的充分响应,至于清政府,亦未稍加留意焉。

---

　　① 参见康有为:《上清帝第二书》(亦即《公车上书》),《康有为全集》(以下简称《全集》)第二,北京:人民大学出版社,2007 年,第 43 页。
　　② 康有为:《请尊孔圣为国立教部教会以孔子纪年而废淫祀折》,《全集》第四,第 98 页。
　　③ 参见康有为:《孔教会章程》,1912 年 10 月,《全集》第九,第 349 页。

然而,儒学素不为宗教,至少与西方意义上的宗教无涉。对此,章太炎说道:

> 盖中土素无国教,孔子亦本无教名,表章六经,所以传历史;自著《孝经》、《论语》,所以开儒术。或言名教,或言教育,此皆与宗教不相及也。①

章氏此说,代表了当时儒家士大夫以及今日治儒学者的普遍态度,实不容回避。因此,对康氏而言,必须在理论上阐明儒学之为儒教,实涵有宗教之意义,甚至超越西方宗教。

此外,康有为在建立孔教的过程中,充分借鉴了其他宗教的某些做法,譬如,以孔子为教主,定曲阜孔林为圣地,以孔子生日为圣诞,且有类似基督教的赞美诗,名为"昌教诗歌",等等。显然,这些做法非传统儒家所有,也恰恰证实了反对者的理由,即儒之为教,实非宗教,尤非西方意义上的宗教。

但是,这些理论上的问题还不是本文关注的重点,此处我们感兴趣的是康有为建立孔教的政治意图,或者说,康氏将儒学宗教化的意图到底何在?

戊戌间,支持康有为的湖南巡抚陈宝箴曾上疏说道:

> 逮康有为当海禁大开之时,见欧洲各国尊崇教皇,执持国政,以为外国强盛之效,实由于此。而中国自周秦以来,政教分途。虽以贤于尧舜、生民未有之孔子,而道不行于当时,泽不被于后世,君相尊而师儒贱,威力盛而道教衰。是以国异政,家殊俗,士懦民愚,虽以嬴政、杨广之暴戾,可以无道行之。而孔子之教散漫无纪,以视欧洲教皇之权力,其徒所至,皆足以持其国权者,不可同语。是以愤懑郁积,援素王之号,执以元统天之说,推崇孔子以为教主,欲与天主耶稣,比权量力,以开民智,行其政教。②

陈氏认为,康有为欲尊孔子,遂有孔教之主张,甚至以为欧洲之盛强,实因政教合一,教皇得以执持国政故也。康氏此种用心,其弟子梁启超亦

---

① 章太炎:《示国学会诸生》,载汤志钧编:《章太炎政论集》下册,第694页。
② 陈宝箴:《奏厘正学术造就人才折》,载翦伯赞等编:《戊戌变法》册二,上海:上海人民出版社、上海书店出版社,2000年,第358页。

言之,谓乃师"误认欧洲之尊景教为治强之本,故恒欲侪孔子于基督,乃杂引谶纬之言以实之"。①

康有为建立孔教的另一个理由,则是出于道德的考虑。1912 年 10 月 7 日,时为孔子诞辰日,陈焕章、沈曾植、梁鼎芬、陈三立、麦孟华等在上海成立孔教总会,举康氏为总会会长,"以挽救人心,维持国运,大昌孔子之教,聿昭中国之光"②。可见,孔教会之宗旨颇以振起道德而自任焉。

康氏甚至以孔教乃中国文明之所系。其《孔教会序》云:

> 耗矣哀哉,灭绝无余者,墨西哥也,为班所灭,并其古文字图画而灭之。今墨人面目,虽为墨之遗黎耶,而所述之圣哲豪杰、往训遗徽,皆班人之圣哲豪杰也,则是全灭也。故灭国不足计,若灭教,则举其国数千年之圣哲豪杰、遗训往行尽灭之,所祖述者,皆谓他人父也,是与灭种同其惨祸焉!何其今之人不自爱国,乃并数千年之文明教化,与其无量数圣哲之心肝、豪杰之骨血而先灭之欤?彼以孔教为可弃,岂知中国一切文明,皆与孔教相系相因。若孔教可弃,则一切文明随之而尽也,即一切种族随之而灭也。③

康有为将教与文明等同起来,是以孔教之灭,犹弃绝中国一切文明。至于墨西哥,人种虽存,而教则灭绝无余,正犹顾炎武"亡天下"之说也。

此外,梁启超在其《南海康先生传》中提及另外两种缘由:

其一,"先生幼受孔学,及屏居西樵,潜心佛藏,大彻大悟,出游后,又读耶氏之书,故宗教思想特盛,常持三圣一体、诸教平等之论"④,则康氏之宗教兴趣,与其对佛、耶二教经典之阅读有关。

其二,康氏"以为生于中国,当先救中国;欲救中国,不可不因中国人之历史习惯而利导之。又以为中国人公德缺乏,团体散涣,将不可以立于大地;欲从而统一之,非择一举国人所同戴而诚服者,则不足以结合其感情,

---

① 梁启超:《清代学术概论》,载《梁启超论清学史二种》,上海:复旦大学出版社,1985 年,第 65 页。

② 陈焕章:《孔教会序》,《孔教会杂志》第 1 卷第 1 号,1913 年 2 月。

③ 《全集》第十,第 345 页。

④ 梁启超:《康氏先生传》,《全集》第十二,附录一,第 427 页。

而光大其本性。于是乎孔教复原为第一著手"。①至于康氏不取佛、耶、回诸教，而独主孔教者，梁启超以为，"先生之布教于中国也，专以孔教，不以佛、耶，非有所吐弃，实民俗、历史之关系，不得不然也"，又谓康氏以为佛教苦行绝俗，耶教杀身流血，可谓极苦，皆不崇尚此间之乐，不过天国、涅槃之乐而已，至于孔教，"言大同，言太平，为人间世有形之乐"，孔子乃为"人道之教"也，故能切合于今世。②可见，康有为主张孔教，一则因孔教合乎中国之国情，一则因孔教乃人道教，最合于现代社会。

此外，康氏尚有现实政治的考虑，即应付当时频发之教案。盖西人以武力传教，所在教士、教民与百姓之冲突屡有发生，而政府常不知所措，"若是者于今五十年，而仰天束手，卒无一策以善其后者"。因此，康氏主张，"莫若直与其教会交，吾亦设一教会以当之，与为交涉，与定和约，与定教律"。③如此，以后若再发生教案，亦不过两国宗教之间的冲突，而不必牵连到政府，"凡有教案，归教会中按照议定之教律商办，国家不与闻"。④

康氏成立孔教会，尚有一种隐谋，即假孔教之名以行政党之实。民国初年，党派迭兴，康氏亦欲成立政党，且命名为"国民党"，然迁延未果，康氏自谓"愧恶欲死，真无以见人"。⑤寻即谋成立孔教会，虽憾于当时废孔之议，然其别有所图亦不容讳焉。不过，陈焕章本人似无意于此，而宣称"本会非政团"。⑥故有学者认为，陈焕章在政治上并不主张君主制度，"讳言君臣"，故在袁氏帝制与张勋复辟中，皆采取远离政治的立场，与康氏之积极主动不同。⑦

综上所述，康有为建立孔教，主要不是基于一种个人的宗教兴趣或理论追求，而是出乎一个儒者对民族与国家命运之关切而采取的政治实践活动，则孔教之为宗教，并不是一个理论问题，而是一个实践的问题。梁启超

---

① 梁启超：《康氏先生传》，《全集》第十二，附录一，第427页。

② 梁启超：《康氏先生传》，《全集》第十二，附录一，第429、430页。

③ 康有为：《请商定教案法律厘正科举文体听天下乡邑增设文庙谨写〈孔子改制考〉进呈御览以尊圣师而保大教折》，《全集》第四，第92、93页。

④ 康有为：《自编年谱》，《全集》第五，第94页。

⑤ 康有为：《与梁启超书》，《全集》第九，第335页。

⑥ 陈焕章：《孔教会杂志序例》，《孔教会杂志》第1卷第1号，1913年2月。

⑦ 参见韩华：《民初孔教会与国教运动研究》，北京：北京图书馆出版社，2007年，第267－271页。

尝论康氏之孔教事业曰:

> 吾中国非宗教之国,故数千年来,无一宗教家。先生幼受孔
> 学,及屏居西樵,潜心佛藏,大彻大悟。出游后,又读耶氏之书,故
> 宗教思想特盛。常毅然以绍述诸圣、普度众生为己任……常持三
> 圣(孔、佛、耶)一体、诸教平等之论。然以为生于中国,当先救中
> 国。欲救中国,不可不因中国人之历史、习惯而利导之。①

可见,康有为"欲救中国",遂汲汲以建立孔教为念。此种忧国之心,实
为康氏建立孔教最根本的动因。正是基于此,梁启超甚至称康氏为"孔教
之马丁·路得"。②

二、孔教之为国教与信教自由问题

康有为将儒学宗教化,此种努力得到了民国政府的承认,不过,他还试
图将孔教上升为国教,从而全面恢复儒家在古代的地位。这个做法就受到
了当时社会各界、尤其是基督教的抵制,从而最终失败。

《中华民国临时约法》规定"人民有信教之自由",此项条款虽不过肤引
外国法律,却对儒家地位产生了莫大冲击。其后,围绕国教之诸多纷争,莫
不因此条以启之。其后,袁世凯废除《临时约法》,不过,新颁布的《中华民
国约法》仍然有"人民于法律范围内,有信教自由"之条文。吴虞对"信教自
由"条款曾有过这样的评论:

> 我们中国约法的信教自由一条,本是随便抄袭来的。欧洲各
> 国,因为经过宗教战争,人民不愿意政府来强制人民信奉某教,或
> 强制人民不信奉某教,所以拿来规定在宪法里面,免得政府来干
> 涉人民的信教自由。③

---

① 梁启超:《康氏康先生传》,《全集》第十二,附录一,第427页。
② 梁启超:《康氏康先生传》,《全集》第十二,附录一,第427页。
③ 吴虞:《"信教自由"是什么》,载罗章龙编:《非宗教论》,成都:巴蜀书社,1989年,第125页。

在吴虞看来,中国本无宗教战争之历史,却简单引进此类宪法观念,不独无济于时用,且危害颇深。

宪法之"信教自由"规定对孔教造成了极大的破坏,种种毁庙罢祀、没收学田的行为皆藉此为据,至于外来之基督教,实为最大之受益者。其时即有人认为:

> 推原孔教之废,实由于信教自由一条有以致之。信教自由一条,粗观之非不粲然成文,及细按其实,则所谓教者,孔教乎? 耶教乎? 回佛道乎? ……今日有谓孔教非宗教者,则孔教不能享自由矣。①

是以康氏欲使孔教成立为宗教,不独出于学理之考虑,亦有其现实的逼迫。盖孔教若不成立为宗教,则孔教不能享受"信教自由"之保护,至于原来类似宗教仪式的祭孔亦将受到限制,至少不得行于学校教育中。可见,康氏建立儒学为宗教,既能收保全儒学之功,亦欲因以遏止基督教之势力焉。

进而,康氏藉袁氏政府制订新宪法之机,欲尊孔教为国教。1913 年 8 月 15 日,陈焕章、夏曾佑、梁启超等上书参众两院,请于宪法上明定孔教为国教。陈焕章等在请愿书中说道:

> 惟立国之本,在乎道德;道德之准,定于宗教。我国自羲炎以来,以天为宗,以祖为法,以伦纪为纲常,以宗孝为彝训,而规本于民。……一切典章制度、政治法律,皆以孔子之经义为根据,一切义理、学术、礼俗、习惯,皆以孔子之教化为依归,此孔子为国教教主之由来也。……今日国本共和,以民为主,更不能违反民意,而为专制帝王所不敢为。且共和以道德为精神,而中国之道德源本孔教,尤不能有拔本塞源之事,故中国当奉孔教为国教有必然者。②

陈氏以孔教为道德之根源,至于中国一切典章制度、政治法律皆以孔子经义为根据,一切义理、学术、礼俗、习惯皆以孔子教化为依归,故当奉孔

---

① 张尔田:《张尔田对于李佳白教师演说之意见》,《宗圣学报》第 17 号 18 期增刊,1916 年 11 月。

② 陈焕章等:《请定孔教为国教》,《孔教会杂志》第 1 卷第 1 号,1913 年 2 月。

教为国教。

请愿书后来在《时报》上公开发表,引起了强烈的反响,且得到社会各界的广泛支持,其中包括各省督军、省长,甚至海外华侨以及部分洋人、传教士的支持,此外,部分佛教、道教组织亦公开支持。社会各界赞同孔教为国教的主要理由,即以孔教乃道德人心之维系所在。不过,反对者亦甚众,致使未能载入宪法,仅仅在《天坛宪法草案》第 19 条第 2 项规定"国民教育,以孔子之道为修身之本"。

现代宗教乃政教分离以后之产物,不独无预世俗教化之权,且遵奉信教自由,与诸教并列,实未有高出其他宗教之特殊地位。若古之宗教则不然,政教本不分离,西方中世纪如此,至于儒家,不独修己,亦能安百姓,格致诚正修与齐治平乃是自内而外,一以贯之,此政教之所以合一也。然而,康氏试图建立孔教为宗教,而与政治相分离,担当文化载体的功能,"各国皆妙用政教之分离,双轮并驰,以相救助,俾言教者极其迂阔之论以养人心,言政者权其时势之宜以争国利,两不相碍,而两不相失焉"①,"今莫若令治教分途,则实政无碍而人心有补焉"②。此举实有保护儒家之动机,使之不致因君主专制之倾覆而受到牵连。不过,若仅止于此,康氏之孔教主张,不免降低了孔子及其学说的地位,此绝非康氏之本愿。是以康氏实欲进一步使孔教上升为国教,发挥政治教化及世俗教育之权,并且,又谓孔教为人道教,不重神权,最宜于今之世俗社会。儒学经此一番收造,不独未失其旧有地位,又能切合当今之现实也。

康氏又不欲与现实政治相牴牾,乃极论孔子之为国教,与"信教自由"原则两不相妨。换言之,康有为利用宪法中的"信教自由"条款了保护孔教,而当他试图将孔教上升为国教时,却又要在理论上证明国教与世俗社会的"信教自由"原则是不相矛盾的。

盖"国教"之名虽起于西方,然观乎儒家在古代之作用,实与"国教"无二。儒学作为"国教",不仅仅是一种帝王假以治世、或者只是缘饰吏术的政治学说而已,同时又是一种民间信仰,至于精英阶层的自我教育,亦假儒

---

① 康有为:《中华救国论》,《全集》第九,第 327 页。
② 康有为:《请尊孔圣为国教立教部教会以孔子纪年而废淫祀折》,《全集》第四,第 98 页。

学为途辙。至于西方曾经取得国教地位的基督教，其影响力亦不及儒学，更遑论后来失去此种地位的自由宗教了。

虽然，孔教绝未阻碍信教之自由，此儒、道、佛三教所以能长期共存也。盖自孔教视之，宗教既劝人为善，又不欲挑战君臣、父子之伦常，则宗教于王者之治世亦有补焉，且佛、老二氏，以出世为高，雅不欲干涉世俗之伦理。政府素不干涉个人之超越信仰，即便汲汲于儒术之士大夫，亦常以佛、道而自处。儒者有出有处，有进有退，圆通无碍，"达则兼济天下，穷则独善其身"，盖谓此也，而国教与信教自由之不相妨，正以此焉。

康氏又胪列亚、欧、美洲各国情事，既立国教之尊，又许人民信教自由。① 梁启超亦谓康氏素主信教自由，"先生之言宗教也，主信仰自由，不专崇一家排斥外道，常持三圣一体，诸教平等之论。"②

其时，陈焕章等在《孔教会请愿书》中亦论国教与信教自由两不相妨，他认为孔教自古皆为国教，盖自魏文侯受经于子夏，尤自汉武尊儒，孔教之国教地位历两千年而巍巍不动矣。且中国自古许人民信教自由，或佛或道，政府未见干预，即便三教之间纷争，不过形诸笔墨文字而已，与西方常因宗教差异而导致战争之残酷绝不同，是以今日明定孔教为国教，绝不致有排斥他教之虞也。西方因宗教战争之祸，故主信教自由，而中国素无此祸，故实无提倡信教自由之必要。若强服此药，犹无病而自病，因服食西人药方而致病矣，可谓大愚。③

虽然，康、陈不仅在理论上证成孔教素为国教，且与宪法中的"信教自由"不相抵触，其用心则是使孔教成为儒家之制度基础。这一运动最终失败，然其影响则颇为深远，稍后的新文化运动，不仅仅满足于辛亥革命在制度上摧毁儒家的制度基础，而其把矛头进一步指向儒家的观念层面，欲从文化上彻底消除传统儒家之影响。新中国成立以后，不断有文化革命，然皆承新文化运动之余绪而已，所谓"灵魂深处闹革命"，实欲彻底清除日常生活中的传统价值观念。然而，文化之革命终未成功，随着邓小平的改革

---

① 参见康有为：《以孔教为国教配天议》，《全集》第十，第93、94页。
② 梁启超：《康氏康先生传》，《全集》第十二，附录一，第427页。
③ 参见陈焕章：《明定原有之国教为国教并不碍于信教自由之新名词》，《民国经世文编》册八，第5054－5058页。

开放,而以儒家为主导的传统文化乃悄然复兴,先是传统观念之复兴,他日必将及于制度领域矣。近年来,大陆新儒家开始形成,颇有学者主张儒教乃至国教说,而其主旨则承康、陈之余绪,试图恢复传统儒家在制度领域中的影响力。

三、儒学与君主制度之关联与剥离

儒学在传统中国,不仅有着观念的基础,而且还有着坚实的制度基础。盖政府之各项政治、法律制度,以及依据儒家经典的科考取士,甚至包括民间的种种社会组织,莫不为儒学之坚实的制度保障。儒家之地位所以能够历两千年而不坠,始终在中国传统社会发挥着主导作用,其缘由正在于此。然而,辛亥革命推翻了君主制度,摧毁了儒学最主要的制度基础。而康有为谋求建立孔教为宗教,甚至为国教,则是试图在道德、信仰领域重建儒家的制度基础。那么,下面我们主要分析儒学与君主制度之关系,考察康有为是如何通过把两者关系脱钩而寻求给儒学奠立一种新的制度基础,从而最终导致了康氏建立孔教的努力。

康有为大概是晚清最早全面否定君主专制制度的。戊戌前后,康氏推演公羊三世之说,欲变中国数千年据乱世之法,乃极论君主政治之非,欲使中国预入升平、太平世也。[①] 其后,革命派承其绪余,丑诋君主制度至百无一是,遂祸及孔子及其学说。不论康氏早先之变法,抑或后来孙、黄之革命,皆以政治变革为急务,遂一意倾覆古代之君主专制,而代以西方之民主或君宪政治,然儒学之根基亦随之摇动矣。

在中国古代,君主制度与儒学实有着密切的关系。康氏既攻君主制度,而大张民权、立宪之说,然亦深知此种做法的危险性,故又希望通过剥离儒学与君主制度之关系,以保全儒学,此实为康氏建立孔教更深层次的动因。《不忍》杂志附页有康氏所撰《礼运注》广告曰:

---

① 参见曾亦:《共和与君主——康有为晚期政治思想研究》,上海:上海人民出版社,2010 年,第 213–228 页。

遍考遗经,大书特书发明大同之道者,惟《礼运》一篇。若此篇不存,孔道仅有小康,则君臣之义被攻,而孔教几倒。中国礼文,皆与孔为缘,随之同尽,则中国为墨西哥矣。

"君臣之义被攻,而孔教几倒",可见康氏非虑不及此者。而且,康有为还希望宣扬《礼运》中的大同、小康思想,使孔教能够超越与君主制度的狭隘关系,甚至以孔教高蹈于西学之上。若然,孔教犹能光被于当代也。

因此,康氏建立孔教之努力,就是把儒学与现实的政治分离开来,即通过使儒学成为宗教而实现政教之分离,而不至因君主制度的覆灭而受到牵连。并且,揆诸康氏之内心,甚至相信儒学对于现代社会具有积极意义。具体来说,就是把君主、君宪与共和三种制度对应于据乱、升平与太平这三个历史时期,一方面,中国要走向升平、太平,必须采用西方的君宪乃至共和制度,另一方面,儒家不仅仅包括据乱时代的学说,而且也颇言升平、太平之制,因此,即便君主专制被推翻,儒学依然能超然其上,并且,因为其包含的三世学说而对今天社会提供普遍的指导意义。①

惜乎世事难料,清朝在对外冲突中屡遭败衄,同时亦使君主制度走到了尽头。种种政治风潮孰非康氏能料,至君主制度一旦而崩溃,"孔家店"亦随之打倒矣。设若康有为初时稍能肯定君主制度之合理性,则孔子及儒学不致倾覆若是之速也。是以数千年中国传统之中绝,康氏当尸其咎焉。覆楚兴楚,皆康氏一人为之耳。

萧公权谓康氏"试图将儒学与专制政体分离,以求儒学的复苏"②,可谓深知康氏之苦心者也。可以说,康氏欲保全儒学的用心还是很明显的,绝非仅仅藉儒学之名以变法而已。康氏尝制订保国会章程,其中第二条规定"保全国土、国民、国教",第九条规定"讲求保国、保种、保教之事"。③ 显然,康氏亦以保全儒学为目标,不过,儒学必须要重新阐释。

其后,北洋政府欲尊孔,亦极力洗刷其与君主专制之关系。袁世凯尝颁布《复学校祀孔命令》,其中有云:

---

① 参见曾亦:《共和与君主——康有为晚期政治思想研究》,第 172 – 181 页。
② 萧公权引述 H. G. Creel《儒学与中国道路》,参见《康有为思想研究》,第 29 页。
③ 参见叶德辉:《与南学会皮鹿门孝廉书》,载《翼教丛编》卷 4。

顾孔学博大,与世推移,以正君臣为小康,以天下公为大同,其后历代人主,专取其小康学派,巩固君权,传疏诸家,变本加厉,而专制之威,能使举世学者,不敢出其范围。近自国体改革,缔造共和,或谓孔子立制,大一统而辨等威,疑其说与今之平等自由不合,浅妄者流,至悍然倡为废孔之说,此不独无以识孔学之精微,即于平等自由之真相,亦未有当也。孔子生贵族专制时代,悯大道之不行,哀斯民之昏垫,乃退而祖述尧舜,删修六经。《春秋》据乱之后,为升平、太平之世;《礼》于小康之上,进以大同。共和之义,此其道源。远如颜、曾、思、孟,近如顾、黄、王诸儒,多能发明宗旨,择精语详,大义微言,久而益著,酝酿郁积,遂有今日民主之局。天生孔子为万世师表,既结皇煌帝谛之终,亦开选贤与能之始,所谓反之人心而安,放之四海而准者。①

此中观点实据康氏三世说而来,颇能见康氏保全儒学之内在理路。盖袁氏既欲尊孔,又不愿站在民主共和的对立面,乃谓孔学博大,孔子为万世师表,不独发明小康君权之说,亦能通乎大同民主之法也。

然而,康有为在民国以来对君主制之坚持,以及积极参与张勋的复辟,却给反对者以确凿的证据,认为儒学与帝制、复辟有着千丝万缕之牵连。康有为虽然一直在理论上将儒学与君主制度剥离开来,但是他的政治活动又让人更紧密地看到了儒学与君主制度之关联,因此,后来"打倒孔家店"的风潮,很大程度上是与康有为民国以来的种种活动联系在一起的。对此,陈独秀说道:

孔教和共和乃绝对两不相容之物,存其一必废其一,此义愚屡言之。张、康亦知之,故其提倡孔教必排共和,亦犹愚之信仰共和必排孔教。盖以孔子之道治国家,非立君不足以言治。……盖主张尊孔,势必立君;主张立君,势必复辟,理之自然,无足怪者。故曰:张、康复辟,其事虽极悖逆,亦自有其一贯之理由也。②

---

① 《民国经世文编》第八册,第5119页。
② 陈独秀:《复辟与尊孔》,《独秀文存》卷1,第112–115页。

孔子之道与君主制度固有内在之关系,陈氏之说是也。其欲"打倒孔家店",亦据此逻辑而来。可见,在陈氏看来,康氏之复辟,以及陈氏之废孔,皆基于共同之一贯理由,即孔教与君主制之内在关系。

其实,不论康氏早期之攻君主,还是晚期之批评共和制,真正始终一贯者,就是他尊孔的立场。陈独秀之批评,代表了流俗一般的意见,对康氏之思想多有误解。盖康氏毕竟以民主共和为高,晚年虽以虚君共和适合国情,亦未必遽以复辟为惟一途辙,实民初废孔举措有以激成之也。是以康氏谓民国教育部废丁祭,收孔庙祭田,"则是直欲废黜孔子",种种变革,"非革满洲之命也,实革中国数千年周公、孔子之命云尔"①,"革一朝之命可也,奈之何举中国数千年之命而亦革之乎?"②盖戊戌间,康氏有"保中国而不保大清"之意;庚子之后,列强息其瓜分之谋,中国已无保国之虞矣,康氏乃汲汲以保教为事。且顾炎武以"亡天下"为重,以"亡国"为轻,则保教之责诚高于保国也。儒者之普遍主义立场,正在于此。康氏建立孔教,不过欲保教而已;其所以保教,不过以数千年中华文明泰半系于孔子之教而已。

四、结　语

可以说,戊戌变法前后,康氏试图通过将儒学与君主制度的脱钩,而与现代民主制度结合起来,欲藉此来挽救儒学。民国以后,虽然他并未放弃对共和民主的想望,但是,已认识到西方的制度未必适合中国的国情,对此,他一方面尝试了恢复帝制的努力,另一方面,则重新宣扬其孔教的主张。这种儒学宗教化的努力,既可以看做将其与政治脱钩,从而挽救儒学,同时,也可以看做在面对民初现实时,试图将儒学当做拯救世道人心的良药。殆康氏自革命而维新,自维新而保皇,其间固千变万端,然毕竟有一不变者,即尊孔也。

不过,康氏对君主专制的批评,对于儒学尚有着非常积极的意义。据

---

① 参见康有为:《覆教育部书》,《全集》第十,第115－118页。
② 康有为:《〈中国学会报〉题词》,《全集》第十,第17页。

康氏之三世学说,据乱世适合君主专制,而升平世则适合君主立宪,太平世适合民主共和,因此,康氏对君主专制的批判,并非消极地抽掉了儒学的根基,而是因为康氏看到民主共和已成世界大势,遂试图通过发挥孔子思想中升平、太平世的内涵,重新阐释儒学,从而使儒学具有现代意义。可以说,康氏对专制政治的批评与其对儒学的改造是联系在一起的,这与孔子"损周文益殷质"的改制有着同样的抱负。

就此言之,康氏试图通过修正儒学而保存儒学,甚至使之以一种崭新的面貌步入现代社会。然而,这种努力完全没有被当时保守的士大夫阶层意识到,或者说,士大夫们依然沉浸在传统儒学的优越性甚至是普世性之中,根本没有意识到儒学随后遇到的危机,而拒绝对儒学作出任何修正。

康有为的整个思想是以公羊三世说为依据的,这使得他对具体政治制度的选择具有相当的灵活性。康氏既认同民主共和为大同理想,然而,当他回到现实的中国社会,却主张小康时代的君主立宪是最合适的,而且,愈益强烈的现实感使其坚信君主立宪才是真正切合中国实际的政治抉择。晚年,康氏不仅放弃了大同时代的社会理想,包括其在婚姻、家庭方面的激进主张,至于在政治理想方面,亦放弃了民主共和的理想。其时康氏以为中国犹处据乱世,当用君主制度,且汲汲以保存国粹为急务,何暇遽及大同哉!

然而,观乎现代中国的历史进程,却是一浪高过一浪的革命。康氏不过以君主立宪取代君主专制而已,孙氏则以民主共和之大同理想为鹄的,至于共产党人,犹以孙氏理想为未足,先是以新民主取代旧民主,继则以共产主义取代民主道路。1970年代末,邓小平实施改革,其意义虽未到盖棺论定之时,然而,事实上我们不难确定,孙中山开辟的现代中国革命道路停滞了,甚至是终结了,而让位于一种改良渐进的道路。藉此改革的因缘,从来作为革命对象的传统文化亦开始得到复兴。迄至八十年代末,革命浪潮始渐趋回落,于是共产主义推至遥远的将来,大同理想乃为小康目标所取代。然而,政治领域中的民主呼声依然此起彼伏,这对小康目标之实施将是莫大的祸患,可不慎哉!

华人佛教与中国宗教的特色

——关于"世俗化"、"神圣性"的思考

李四龙

在全球化的时代,以汉人为信仰主体的中国汉传佛教,现在传播到世界各地,在弘法方式上已经有别于传统的中国佛教。本文把这种新形态的汉传佛教统称为"华人佛教",主要包括:中国大陆及港台佛教、以美国为主体的欧美佛教。当前的华人佛教改变了晚清民初衰败没落的佛教形象,表现出前所未有的一种生机与活力。与此同时,这个发展中的佛教遭到人们的质疑,教内外的批评声音时有耳闻。

一、人间性与世俗化

当前的大陆佛教与台湾佛教,直接受益于当年太虚大师提出的"人间佛教"思想。

中国佛教协会的宗旨,强调"庄严国土、利乐有情",佛教要为现实社会服务,要与社会主义社会相适应。台湾的佛光山、法鼓山、慈济功德会、中台山等著名的佛教团体,都有各具特色的接引社会大众的善巧方便,譬如佛光山的工作信条是"给人信心、给人欢喜、给人希望、给人方便",主张"以文化弘扬佛法、以教育培养人才、以慈善福利社会、以共修净化人心"。

美国的华人佛教,真正崛起于1960年代,以宣化上人创办的万佛城

（法界佛教总会）、佛光山星云大师创办的西来寺、著名佛教居士沈家桢先生创办的庄严寺最有代表性。万佛城坚持"日中一食"的僧团旧制，以"弘法、译经、教育"为三大志业；庄严寺重视佛学研究，依旧强调明清以来传统的禅净双修，并让那些受到高等教育的白领也来接受这种传统的修法；西来寺是西半球最大的佛教寺庙，贯彻佛光山以文教为主、慈善为辅的一贯理念，与西来大学相辅相成。我们从中不难发现，美国的华人佛教普遍重视教育，要在美国这样的以基督教—犹太教为主体的社会里弘扬佛法，事实上并不可能完全依照"人间佛教"的规划，有时还得借用明清佛教的思想资源，禅净双修或诵经拜忏。

人间佛教的理念，缘起于晚清、民国时期的佛教改革运动。明清以来的中国佛教，可以概括为以下的三个要点：禅净双修、念佛拜忏、三教同归。这是就精英层面而说，若论普通佛教徒的信仰生活，明清佛教常被贬为"经忏佛教"，甚至是"称名念佛"亦不地道，往往只是花钱请和尚代办佛事，以求功德。明清以来的佛教，因此忙于超度亡灵，成了"死人的佛教"。成天忙于赶经忏而不务参禅实悟，佛教之衰败已不言而喻。民国时期，太虚大师缘此打出"人生佛教"或"人间佛教"的旗帜，力挽狂澜于既倒。1949年以后海峡两岸的佛教、1965年以后的美国华人佛教，大多秉承佛教要为现实人生服务的宗旨。正如现代佛教泰斗印顺导师所说："我们必须立定'佛在人间'的本教，才不会变质而成为重死亡的鬼教，或重长生的神教。"他说："我们是人！需要的是人的佛教。"①星云在全球范围内积极推行人间佛教的理念，他说，人间佛教是"佛说的、人要的、净化的、美善的"。他的说法简洁明了，生动形象。"华人佛教"，就是这种接着明清佛教而来的现代中国佛教，处在全球化的语境里，努力使佛教重新回到中国人的精神世界，让全球华人的日常生活多一份超脱，少一丝烦恼。

当前华人佛教的成功与生机，来自于现代佛教的"人间性"，彰显现实的人文关怀，注重儒家的伦理规范。譬如，宣化在美国创办的各式学校，都以孝、悌、忠、信、礼、义、廉、耻的儒教八德当作做人基础，他办的小学提倡"孝道"，中学提倡"忠贞爱国"，大学提倡"忠孝仁义"。在当前的中国大

---

① 印顺：《佛在人间》，收于《妙云集》下编之一。

陆,不少寺庙在大学里设奖学金,支持学术研究,有的寺庙还设立专门的基金,推广弘扬儒释道三家的经典,提倡"大国学"的概念。现在,佛教寺院参与赈灾、医疗救助、心理治疗、慈善救济等具体事务,早已司空见惯,相当普遍。在近现代的中国,主要是基督教团体从事这方面的社会工作。但现在的华人佛教颇有后来居上之势,像台湾的慈济功德会,成立不过 40 余年,其影响力竟已跻身于红十字会、食物银行(Food Bank)等世界慈善界的"百年老店"之列。

然而,华人佛教的成功,佛教的"人间化",常被解读为佛教的"世俗化"。有人对佛教徒参与社会事务表示不解,网络上经常有人质疑当前大陆佛教的商业化色彩,动辄上纲上线,大扣帽子。佛教的根本是破除无明、智慧解脱,能够体悟人生与世界"性空"的真相,从而摆脱烦恼的束缚,消除死亡的恐惧,实现生命的永恒。华人佛教积极入世的努力,似乎有悖于佛教的根本,实际上恰好表现了大乘佛教的基本特色。

世俗化,是西方宗教在现代化过程里的处境。启蒙运动、工业化,以及自然科学的发展,促使天主教会掌管的领域逐渐萎缩,宗教的价值让位于世俗的知识体系。现在的宗教学研究,直接以"世俗化"讨论中国的宗教现象,在很多时候并不恰当。明清佛教被说成是世俗化的宗教,其实,这里所说的"世俗化"不过是指佛教的"民间化"、"生活化"。换言之,明清社会精英阶层的佛教信仰并不占据主体地位,反倒是庶民百姓的佛教生活成了当时的佛教主流。"民间化"只是社会阶层的变化,信仰佛教的主体从社会精英变为庶民百姓,其中并没有削弱佛教的思想价值,甚至是强化了佛教在社会上的信仰力量。因此,"世俗化"的说法,并不适用于中国佛教史的叙述,也同样不适用于解读华人佛教的"人间化"。

二、华人佛教的"神圣性"

在当前全球化的浪潮里,佛教对全球华人的精神生活还能保持多大的影响力?这是一个严肃的话题。前面说到把华人佛教的"人间化"看作"世俗化",这还只是概念上的误用。但在现实生活里,华人佛教的领地并没有明显的增加,甚至有些岌岌可危。

现在大陆某些地区,传统的佛教县市逐渐变为基督教地下教会或家庭教会的重镇;在全美约 350 万华人中间,佛教徒仅占 20%,基督教占 20%,天主教占 3%;在台湾,佛教徒人数虽然庞大,但其总数稍逊于民间宗教的信徒。而在全球范围内,佛教徒仅占世界总人口的 6%,远远低于基督教或伊斯兰教的比例。凡此种种,确实表明了华人佛教当前所处的严重危机。这些现象的成因相当复杂,有的是因为佛教对信众的现实关怀不够,也就是说,并没有充分体现"人间佛教"的理念。但无论如何,有一个重要的深层原因是,信众嫌弃佛教"神圣性"的缺失,认为和尚尼姑讲来世说因果,故弄玄虚,经常耽于事务,没有真才实学,不会讲空说禅,说不透当代人内在的心灵需求。现实关怀问题,属于人间佛教的实践层面;"神圣性"的缺失,则是属于深层次的理念问题,需要在此略作说明和解释。

何谓"神圣性"(holiness)?奥托在他的名著《论神圣》里讲到,"神圣"(the Holy)虽然在道德领域或法律领域被广泛使用,但这些用法都是派生性的,本源性的"神圣"观念乃是宗教领域的特有范畴。在西方宗教学里,神圣与世俗的两分,是基本的信条。例如,涂尔干说,宗教现象的真实特征是把"已知的和可知的整个宇宙一分为二,分为无所不包、相互排斥的两大类别",神圣事物和凡俗事物。他说,"神圣事物不仅受到了禁忌的保护,同时也被禁忌隔离开来;凡俗事物则是实施这些禁忌的对象,它们必须对神圣事物敬而远之。"因此,宗教信仰不仅表达了神圣事物的性质,也表达了神圣事物之间的关系以及神圣事物与凡俗事物之间的关系。[①]在西方的宗教传统里,人与神之间存在着不可弥合的鸿沟。世俗化的过程,被宗教徒看做是人的堕落、历史的恐怖。为此,伊利亚德想在一个世俗化的世界里寻找神圣的意义,现代人的出路是要恢复宗教的神圣感。在他的理论框架里,保留了"神圣的存在",与之相对是作为历史性存在的"世俗的人"。伊利亚德认为,"宗教的人"(homo religious)生活在一个开放的宇宙里,时刻能与"神圣的存在"积极交流,生活本身就是一种宗教活动;世俗的人则已忘记自己是宗教的产物,并把自己当做历史的唯一主体。

---

① 　涂尔干:《宗教生活的基本形式》,渠东、汲喆译,上海:上海人民出版社,1999 年,第 47 页。

在对"神圣性"的追问当中,"世俗化"的内涵被不断开显:人性的释放,即是宗教神圣感的缺席;"神圣"则是超越历史的永恒存在,与人世间(世俗)完全异质,人与神可以和好,却不能合一,更不能转换。伊利亚德对人的历史情境的描述,与佛教关于"正法、像法与末法"的历史观有异曲同工之妙。佛陀逝世以后的五百年间,众生能有机缘学佛,并能修成正果,是谓"正法"时期;随后的五百年或一千年,众生的学佛多少有些变味,最终未必能够成佛,是谓"像法";最后则有一万年,众生能有机会听闻佛法,已属侥幸,听了过后能否正信、能否实修,更无多大的机会可言,谓之"末法"。照此说法,当前属于佛教所说的末法时期,人的内心充斥了各种各样先入为主的成见,自以为是,顽固不化,甚至自命不凡,佯装神圣。

然而,佛陀关于"末法"的说法,并未设定迥异于人世间的神圣存在。佛教常被看作是一种"出世"的宗教,而且,"出世间"常被理解成对"世间法"(世俗社会或世俗的知识体系)的出离。因此,佛教在众人的心目里,成为一种消极遁世的代名词;"空门"成了无所事事的栖身之所。这实际上是对佛教流俗的误解,也是大乘佛教兴起之后主要批驳的邪见。所谓"出世间",是指对世间的超越,而真正的超越是"世、出世间不二"的境界。也就是说,主张"出世间"的佛法,在终极的意义上,是与"世间法"并无二致,同体共生。正是在这个意义上,六祖慧能说,"佛法在世间,不离世间觉。离世觅菩提,恰如觅兔角"。觉悟成佛的境界,并不是脱离日常生活的另类存在,一切众生皆有佛性,都有觉悟成佛的机会。佛教在戒律上反对所谓"神通"的显现,对那些在常人看来不切实际的神奇表现,大乘佛教表示明确的拒斥,认为菩提心(觉悟)的开显,奠基于慈悲心的实践。许多学佛的人很好奇成佛以后还能做些什么?佛教的回答:慈悲为怀,悟后起修。觉悟者最终的归趣,是对日常生活的回归。佛教的觉悟者,应有一颗真正的慈悲心,随缘应对是非善恶,关爱社会,助人为乐,才是佛门的真修行。所谓"空门",是指随缘应对,不着私心。这是一个刹那生灭、却又空灵清静的世界,佛法就在出入之间、大俗大雅之间。

当前华人佛教的"人间化",其最深层的理念是要实践大乘佛教的慈悲心,达到世出世间的无分别境界,也就是世俗与神圣没有差异的存在状态。那么,华人佛教当前遭遇的质疑与危机,意味着什么?首先这是世人对大乘佛教的误读,把一种西方式的"神圣性"强加到中国的宗教传统里,进而发出"神圣性"流失的感叹;其次,华人佛教在具体的实践过程中,经常未能表现出觉悟者的慈悲心,而是强调佛教自身的优越感,无法超越自我的局限去随缘应对,甚至还弄不清自己当前所处的机缘或环境。

在西方宗教学的视野里,华人佛教亦有许多令人称道的神圣性,诸如各种各样的佛教仪式(日课、忏仪等)、诵经、念佛、打坐参禅,等等。但在佛教内部看来,这都不是最主要的内容。像在禅宗的公案故事里,马祖道一曾因"磨砖不能成镜"而开悟。如果一定要表现佛教的"神圣性",那它就是内心的觉悟以及缘此而起的慈悲。这在中国佛教的传统里,即是"悲智双运"。恰好是在这一点上,我们看到了佛教对"世俗化"的深层理解,悲智双运是一种圆满的人格。太虚大师在讲人间佛教时说,"仰止唯佛陀,完成在人格,人成即佛成"。恰好是在这一点上,我们看到了佛教与基督教之间对"人性"的不同理解,佛教把人性的释放看作是一个觉悟的过程,基督教却视之为堕落的历史。基督教里的人是有原罪的,而在佛教里,与生俱来的"业"在根本上是无善无恶的。

在澄清了西方式的误读之后,当前的人间佛教,实际上要求佛教徒表现觉悟者的慈悲心,觉悟人生,奉献人生。苟能如此,华人佛教既没有世俗化,也没有神圣性,只有悲智双运,随缘应对,落实到刹那生灭的日常的生活世界。

小结:中国宗教的特色

在考察了华人佛教当前的成功与面临的危机之后,本文认为,源自西方宗教学的"世俗"与"神圣"的两元对立,并不适用于以佛教为代表的东方宗教。中国宗教有其自身的特色,并不主张"人—神"的两元关系,认为"凡圣不二",强调彼此的一致性。华人佛教对世俗社会表现出高度的认同感,提倡"出世的入世"。

奥托在讨论宗教的神圣感时,重点分析其中的非理性因素,以numinous 表示宗教崇拜时所呈现的神秘心态,即所谓"神秘感"。在他的笔下,个体在某个至高无上的绝对者面前所体验到的"神秘感",是"畏惧感"和"向往感"的二元组合。换言之,面对一个完全相异的神圣存在,个体会沉浸在敬畏感之中。这种心态,与东方宗教所要追求的境界完全不同。禅宗最经典的表述是,"平常心是道";道家强调"和光同尘"。平常心与敬畏感,表现了中国宗教与西方宗教关于"神圣性"的不同理解。

华人佛教把人间的"平常心"、"慈悲心"当做宗教信仰的内核,最终的解脱方式也是迥异于西方宗教:在基督教里,个人的被拯救,完全取决于上帝的恩典;但在佛教里,个人的解脱依赖于自身的修行力量,犹如禅宗的说法,"自性自度"。

因此,以华人佛教的"人间性"为例,中国宗教主张凡圣不二、平常心是道、自性自度,具有鲜明的人文特色,完全有别于西方宗教所主张的凡圣二分、敬畏感与他力拯救。

宗教旅游开发的思路、原则和措施

——以云南为例

张桥贵

一、宗教旅游开发的总体思路

宗教与旅游的天然密切联系是客观存在的。即使我们不从理论上进行研究,它们照样自然联姻。由于宗教本身存在的局限性,再加上旅游的市场化运作、商业化经营,放任自流可能会导致一系列问题。这就要求我们从理论上高度重视,对宗教旅游的本质、特征、规律、类型等进行认真研究,制定切实可行的开发思路,发挥其优势,改造其弊端,积极引导宗教旅游沿着与社会主义社会相适应、相协调、相和谐的正确轨道健康发展。我们提出的宗教文化旅游开发思路对云南省乃至全国都有一定的借鉴意义。

(一) 引导优秀宗教文化与健康旅游活动良性互动

宗教与旅游自古就有密切联系,大多数学者都赞同宗教朝圣是人类最古老的旅游形式之一,是现代各种旅游活动的雏形。对于古代社会大多数虔诚的宗教信徒来说,宗教旅游是他们唯一可能的旅游形式。随着生产力的发展,宗教世俗化的深入,越来越多的非宗教徒也加入了宗教旅游的行列。从宗教与旅游互动这一角度出发,我们认为宗教旅游经历了从"旅而不游"到旅、游并重的历史变迁,宗教旅游必将走上从"游而不教"到游、教并重的现代发展之路。而积极引导优秀宗教文化与健康旅游活动良性充分互动并且有机结合,是发展现代宗教旅游的根本保证。

所谓"旅而不游"是指旅游者在强烈的宗教目的支配下,对旅途中的风光全然无动于衷,"虽有荣观,燕处超然",全身心沉浸在宗教氛围中。这种极其虔诚的宗教朝圣旅游在世界各大宗教中并不罕见,比如佛教就不乏一步一叩首到圣地朝觐的信徒。

宗教观光旅游是"游而不教"的典型,游客在宗教圣地参观,看是看了塔寺碑林,听是听了梵呗道乐,拜是拜了佛祖菩萨,可是他们并没有深入领悟宗教的人生观、世界观、价值观。"教"是指宗教的伦理和道德教化,这是宗教的传统强势功能。我们在开发宗教旅游中注意发挥宗教的道德教化作用,不是让游客去信教,而是让游客通过对宗教文化和历史的了解,通过对宗教仪式的观看和感受,得到警示或启发,从而加强自我修养,完善自身建设,提高精神境界。宗教休闲旅游、生态旅游、体验旅游就是寓"教"于游,"游教并重"的优秀宗教旅游项目,代表了宗教旅游的精华,符合宗教旅游发展的方向。

(二)促进旅游、宗教文化和人的全面协调发展

宗教目的是旅游的动力之一,宗教推动了旅游的步伐,旅游进一步推动宗教文化的交流和发展。必须大力提升宗教自身的人文素质和文化素质,很多地方寺院修建得金碧辉煌,但是却没有高水平僧人入住,对于烧香拜佛的游客来说,确实"硬件有余",是一个好地方;但是对于发展高品味宗教旅游来说,显然"软件不足",使人空留遗憾。一些地方出现了"空有其寺,而无其僧"甚至"金玉其表,败絮其中"的现象。在社会中,并不是越奢华就越能体现自己的地位和价值,受到人们的拥护与尊敬。有些社会角色恰恰是因为清贫朴素而受到人们的信任和爱戴。宗教徒就是这样的角色。越是甘于寂寞,枯守清贫,就越具有高僧风范。因此,寺院金碧辉煌带给人们艳羡的同时,更多的是一种反感。佛教自身的特点决定了不能以世俗法则来证明其成功。发展宗教旅游,寺院建设是基础工作,僧团和道风建设才是关键。正如一所大学,并不是因为它盖有大楼而是因为拥有大师才能

培养出真正的好学生;一个寺院,也不是因为它建有多少高塔大殿而是因为它拥有高僧大德才能真正声名远扬。只有高水平、高素质的僧团才能推动佛教文化中的精华与现代社会的发展相结合,并将佛法精华深入浅出地讲解给大众。发展新型现代宗教旅游,离不开高水平、高素质的僧团。我们应该以发展文明、健康、和谐的宗教文化旅游为契机,推动宗教自身的改革,尤其是推动宗教培养一支真正高水平的僧才队伍,切实革除宗教内部存在的一些影响自身发展、影响宗教与社会主义社会相适应的不良因素。从而更好地开展包括旅游在内的各项活动、服务于社会主义和谐社会的建设。

我们应该以对人的心灵有所启迪、健康有所促进、社会有所助益、生态有所保护的原则,积极倡导和发展健康、文明、和谐的新型现代宗教旅游活动,使宗教旅游在不断提升自身文化品位和文化内涵的同时,促进旅游、宗教文化和人的全面协调发展,为社会主义和谐社会贡献应有的力量。

(三)实现社会效益、经济效益、生态效益三方共赢

宗教旅游过度商业化炒作,产业化经营,会丧失宗教文化的本色,致使宗教在信徒心目中的神圣形象大打折扣,不利于宗教道德教化、心理调节、社会控制等功能的发挥。宗教旅游的收益很大一部分来自游客的功德捐助,这些款项除了用于修缮和保护宗教文物古迹、支付相关部门和人员日常用度外,还应拿出一部分来开展社会慈善活动,这也是人们对以慈悲为怀、济世度人为宗旨的宗教的普遍期望。宗教自身过量拥有金钱,一方面与宗教自身的清规戒律相违背,另一方面极易导致宗教的腐化和堕落,这些已经为古今中外无数事例所证实。所谓"十方来,十方去,共成十方事",财富从社会的四面八方汇聚到寺院里,又以悲天悯人的宗教情怀投入到回报社会的活动中。有去无来,宗教"神圣资本"的再生产将难以为继;有来无去,宗教则沦为敛财工具,损害宗教自身的"神圣资本",最终被社会遗弃。对于宗教界来说,开展宗教旅游的第一目的不是经济效益而是社会效益。经济效益的提升只是增强了宗教发展自身、服务社会的能力。反过来,通过发挥宗教旅游独特的社会效益,必将带来更大的经济效益和生态效益,形成社会效益、经济效益、生态效益互利互赢、共同发展的良性循环

局面。

宗教除了拥有大量风景优美的自然风光外,还蕴涵着丰富的生态思想和伦理思想,宗教徒在长期的熏陶修行中大都能自觉地保护环境。一些原本人迹罕至的荒山秃岭经过一代代宗教徒筚路蓝缕、以启山林的艰辛开发,凿池引水、修寺建塔的辛勤建设,植树造林、禁牧禁伐的精心保护,逐渐变为庄严肃穆的人间净土,在这种意义上,佛教将祖师尊为"开山祖师"是再恰当不过了。我国寺庙宫观的一个显著特点就是具有很强的世俗性和开放性,总是欢迎人们前去参观游览、烧香朝拜。在出行不便的古代社会,寺观甚至还兼具旅店的功能。游客越多,香火越旺,功德越多,寺庙就越兴盛。有些并不具有自然资源优势的寺观往往会在周围开挖水池,堆叠假山,养花艺竹,一方面为自己修持学法创造一个幽雅的环境,另一方面也是为了吸引更多的游客。游客在游览观光时,于不知不觉中受到蕴涵在宗教文化古迹内的宗教思想、伦理道德、社会价值、人生哲学等的熏陶。宗教思想中的精华如止恶扬善、去贪禁杀、知足常乐、诚恳待人等至今仍有很强的社会影响力。我们应该使这些优良传统充分融入宗教旅游开发的新实践,大力挖掘宗教文化中蕴藏的思想精华,吸引更多的游客前来参观、感悟、体验,实现促进旅游和经济发展,促进人类自身和社会发展,促进环境和生态保护的三重目的。

（四）营造文明、健康、和谐的宗教旅游氛围

文明、健康、和谐的宗教旅游氛围有利于促进旅游、宗教和人的全面协调发展,实现经济效益、社会效益、生态效益三方共赢。

我们应该通过开展有中国特色的宗教旅游活动把这些精神发扬出去,补救科技文明的缺失,将"单相度"之人重新塑造丰满。此外我们还要发扬东方宗教圆融和谐的精神,倡导在旅游中人与人、人与自然和谐相处。构建社会主义和谐社会,为宗教旅游提出了新要求、新希望;健康、文明、和谐的宗教旅游活动获得了更为广阔的发展空间,低级、浅俗、落后的宗教旅游活动必将为时代所淘汰。以新型现代性为指导,以宗教文化精华为依托,以积极引导宗教与社会主义社会相适应为方向,有选择、有步骤、有重点的引导宗教旅游的现代转型,推动宗教旅游的良性运行、健康发展,将宗教旅

游的整体开发统一为新型现代宗教旅游的开发,努力打造社会主义的宗教旅游文化乃至社会主义的宗教旅游文明,使宗教旅游与社会主义社会健康、协调、和谐发展。这是宗教旅游在我国现阶段的最主要任务。

二、宗教旅游开发的具体原则

在引导优质宗教文化与健康旅游活动充分互动、有机结合的总体思路指导下,云南宗教文化旅游应该遵循文化性、生态性、特色性、保护性、参与性、合理性等原则进行有计划的开发,力戒"建设性的破坏"和"破坏性的建设",使宗教文化旅游健康发展。

(一)文化性原则

宗教文化不仅具有物质性的一面,如亭台楼阁、寺观塔院、雕塑绘画、音乐舞蹈;更有精神性的一面,如哲学伦理、价值理想、戒律清规;尤其在遭受发展困境的现代社会,宗教精神文化中蕴含的大量关于协调人与人关系、人与自然关系的价值理念具有重大的指导性意义。然而现有的宗教文化旅游并没有彰显宗教的优秀精神文化内涵,过于注重对有形物质文化的观光,停留在"看庙观塔"的低水平阶段。甚至个别地区利用宗教文化中神秘、庸俗甚至封建迷信的东西吸引游客。如果不能充分挖掘宗教精神文化中符合现代社会发展的优秀内涵,宗教文化旅游将不成其为文化旅游,也由此失去了可持续发展的基础。可以说,文化是宗教旅游的灵魂所在,是其与社会主义社会相适应,进而发挥经济效益、社会效益、生态效益的基本前提。

(二)生态性原则

宗教文化旅游必须走生态旅游的发展道路。宗教文化中蕴含着大量生态保护的思想资源,如道法自然、草木有情、禁杀护生等。通过长期的生态保护,以佛教、道教为代表的中国宗教具有保护生态的优良传统,既作为一种思想资源融入教理教义,又作为一种行动体现在日常修行,还作为一种环境烘托出寺院宫观的神圣氛围。

（三）特色性原则

宗教文化旅游既要有区别于一般旅游的特色，又要在不同宗教之内体现出自身的文化特色。然而，当前宗教文化旅游却呈现趋同化的发展态势，许多寺庙宫观建筑千篇一律，旅游项目高度重复。旅游部门有必要聘请有关专家学者参与宗教文化旅游开发利用研究，把握其最具特色的旅游资源，并通过健康合理的方式将其展现出来。

（四）保护性原则

由于宗教文化的敏感性、神圣性等特点，在旅游开发利用过程中极易受到市场化、世俗化等的冲击而遭受损害。同时大量游客的到来，难免对宗教旅游地的生态环境造成破坏。因此，在宗教旅游中处理好开发与保护的关系十分必要。旅游开发是破坏还是保护，问题的关键在于开发是否合理、科学、恰当。如果在旅游开发的规划阶段就注意着眼于对宗教文化的保护，则开发未必就会造成破坏，反而会对宗教文化起到保护、宣传的作用。宗教文化旅游，是在保护宗教文化的前提下发展旅游，而不应该是在保护旅游的基础上发展宗教。对于宗教与旅游的关系、保护与开发的关系，我们必须有清醒的认识。

宗教文化旅游开发是一项系统工程，在开发之前，必须进行可行性论证，对旅游地资源做详细地调查，特别是对资源的类别、数量、质量、规模、经济价值等诸方面进行评估，还要对开发规模、旅游服务设施规模和客源市场等各方面进行综合评估，在此基础上对可开发性进行详细论证，以避免盲目地开发。旅游资源开发还应对可进入性进行充分论证，旅游地资源距客源地和客源市场的远近、可进入状况和需要的投资、周期等等，都必须要有详细的开发规划。对于具有特殊文物价值的宗教旅游景区，我们也可以设立核心保护区，合理控制游客数量，拆除违章建筑，恢复生态环境；设立一般旅游区，营造宗教文化氛围，开发宗教文化旅游项目，满足游客谈经论道、烧香拜佛等需要；设立旅游功能区，开办住宿部、素食馆、停车场、购物处等，提供衣食住行等旅游服务。

（五）参与性原则

旅游中的一切学习、参与、体验宗教文化的最终目标是为了"社会化"，脱离了社会目标的宗教旅游活动，最终会还原为一种纯粹的宗教活动。宗教旅游的目标之一是使宗教文化中的"合理内核"内化到旅游者的心灵深处，重回社会生活之后，能够应用这些知识化解生活中的矛盾与危机。而要实现这一目标，旅游者就要高度参与到宗教旅游中来。

在开发方式上，要从观光旅游向体验旅游转变，前者就宗教文化的物质性资源进行静态式的开发，以游客参观陈列式宗教景观、建筑和塑像等为主要方式，由于这种游览形式单调，"白天看庙，晚上睡觉"。

（六）合理性原则

宗教文化旅游不能仅以市场为导向，以经济效益为衡量成功与否的标准，必须同时兼顾社会效益和生态效益，对于宗教文化中不适宜开发的内容必须预留足够的禁忌空间。如果将宗教文化中所有神圣内核统统推向旅游市场的前端，宗教文化在褪去自身神圣色彩的同时，宗教文化旅游必将失去可持续发展的基础。有限度的合理开发，这既是遵循宗教文化发展规则的需要，也是尊重宗教徒感情的需要，同时还是保护宗教神秘感的需要。事实上，合理的限制开发非但不会减弱宗教文化的吸引力，相反，还会因为保留了神秘空间而使宗教旅游资源更具有无穷魅力。

三、宗教旅游开发的主要措施

（一）解放思想，正确认识宗教文化

经过改革开放30多年的发展，宗教是一种特殊的文化形态的理念日渐深入人心，但是由于宗教事务政策性强，问题比较复杂，社会上仍有一些人对宗教存有偏见，一些部门也对宗教文化旅游怀有疑虑。因此，发展宗教文化旅游首先需要解放思想，更新观念，才能扩大视野，大胆开发、利用

宗教文化旅游资源,广泛吸引国内外游客,发挥宗教文化旅游的综合社会效益。

首先,要正确评价宗教文化,分清宗教与封建迷信之间的区别,使全社会都能具有宗教基本常识,积极引导宗教与社会主义社会相适应,挖掘宗教文化与时代发展相适应的价值观、伦理观、生态观,通过旅游这一平台在更大的层面发挥作用。

其次,转变思想,更新观念,促使优秀宗教文化与健康旅游活动充分互动,有机结合。

第三,开阔视野、放眼世界,广泛吸引国内外游客。云南是世界上唯一具足佛教三大部派的地区,作为连接中南半岛的桥头堡和南亚东南亚国际大通道的过渡带,云南宗教圣地如宾川鸡足山等在东南亚享有盛誉。

第四,面对宗教文化旅游的实际,组织专业研究队伍,运用宗教学、旅游学、社会学诸学科的理论知识和研究方法,对云南宗教文化旅游资源进行全面考察,了解不同阶层、年龄、性别、职业游客的旅游偏好,在科学研究、掌握宗教文化旅游发展规律的基础上,积极规划,引导宗教文化旅游与社会主义社会相适应。

（二）理顺关系,协调相关部门利益

目前,云南宗教文化旅游中宗教、旅游、园林、文化等部门多头共管,致使职能不清、责权不明、条块分割、政企不分等现象较为突出。即使由地方政府部门统一协调,设置风景名胜区管理委员会进行管理的较为成熟的景区如鸡足山、巍宝山等,也存在政府部门职能不清、与旅游公司政企不分等弊端。可以说,现有旅游管理体制严重制约了云南宗教文化旅游的发展,建立适应社会主义市场经济体制要求的大旅游管理体制势在必行。尤其是宗教旅游开发最重要的两个部门的旅游局与宗教局,更应该携起手来共谋宗教文化旅游的发展之路。

一方面,宗教局应该依据《宗教事务条例》,妥善管理宗教场所,严格打击借旅游开发之机而大肆修寺建庙的歪风,同时对破损、残缺的合法宗教建筑进行维修,对历史悠久的宗教文物及时进行补救与修复,对文物周围粗制滥造、文化品位低劣的违章建筑进行强制性的拆除或改造。同时监管教职人员的行为,重点打击借旅游开发骗取游客钱财的假和尚、伪道士,对于一些旅游景点"有观无道"的现象予以重点关注,尽快安排道士进驻,不给不法分子以可乘之机。

另一方面,旅游局应该完善旅游基础设施,制定合理的旅游路线,增强景区的可入性、可游性,为游客提供住宿、饮食、交通、购物、娱乐、导游等方面的便捷服务。云南一些拥有丰富宗教文化资源的地区,因为交通、景区基础设施等方面的制约,使宗教文化旅游难以有效展开。在旅游开发的大背景,宗教活动场所同时成为旅游场所,因此旅游局和宗教局必须充分发挥自身职能,在追求旅游场所经济效益的同时兼顾宗教场所的神圣性。此外,旅游局应该积极学习国家宗教政策和专业宗教知识,改变"重旅游、轻宗教"的思想。

我们认为,在宗教文化比较发达,旅游资源比较丰富的地区,宗教文化旅游无疑作为地区旅游业的重点支柱产业。对此,可以尝试设置宗教文化旅游办公室由县政府直接领导,配备既熟悉国家宗教政策,又了解宗教历史文化,既懂得旅游市场业务,又具有管理才能的专业干部,对本地区宗教文化资源进行集中调研,统一制定旅游规划,协调相关职能部门的关系,处理日常事务,促使宗教文化与旅游活动有机结合、良性互动。

(三)加强培训,提高旅游从业人员、宗教人士以及游客的文明素质和专业水平

宗教文化旅游是涉及旅游者、旅游从业人员、宗教人士等多方行为主体的综合性社会文化活动。任何一方在思想观念、行为习惯、文明素质上的缺陷,都将影响宗教文化旅游综合效益的发挥,而任何一方文明素质的提高也将对其他行为主体带来积极的示范效应。

首先,提高游客文明素质,对于宗教文化旅游具有特别重要的意义。绝大多数游客缺少宗教文化常识,触犯宗教禁忌、破坏生态环境等行为时有发生。我们有必要采取多种措施引导游客的宗教旅游行为。比如在销售门票的同时免费发放宣传材料,就宗教文化、宗教礼仪、生态保护等方面内容予以简要介绍;在宗教景区的醒目位置设立宣传告示栏,展示宗教文化的博大内涵;构筑游客与僧人的互动平台,消除游客对宗教文化的偏颇

认识等等。

其次,旅游从业者包括导游、景区经营者、服务者以及旅行社、旅游公司等,其专业水平也亟须提高。大部分导游缺乏宗教文化知识,在讲解中信口开河,触及不到宗教文化的精华,反为宗教神秘文化、甚至是封建迷信张目。宗教旅游场所大多居于深山之中,游客餐饮、住宿、购物等存在诸多不便,散商乘虚而入,在寺观周围高价出售劣质产品,与宗教旅游场所的文化氛围格格不入。有关部门可以聘请专家为导游讲解宗教文化知识,或者适当发动出家僧侣或在家居士参与导游;同时规范景区经营者的商业行为,营造景区浓厚的宗教文化氛围。

第三,部分宗教旅游景区虽然富丽堂皇,但缺乏修养深厚的高僧大德,部分道观至今仍然没有道士入住,有观无道现象比较突出。甚至一些知名寺院宫观的住持,都不能为游客讲经说法、答疑解惑。普通僧道多是小学、初中毕业,具有大专以上学历者少之又少,面对游客的提问时,或东拉西扯、不着边际,或哑口无言、赧然而笑。仅仅依靠殿宇、楼台、塔院等物质文化吸引游客的宗教文化旅游是不完备,也是注定不能持久的。宗教精神文化的发扬,依靠的是修养深厚的大师,而不是富丽堂皇的庙宇。如果缺少高素质的僧团,宗教文化的传承与发展将面临诸多困难,宗教文化旅游也将无从谈起。因此,我们必须在政府有关政策和部门的引导下,通过开办佛学院、保送高等学府深造、组织学经会、举行研讨会等形式提高宗教人士的修养水平,寺院本身也应积极配合,制定严格的学习制度,僧人仅仅掌握唱念敲打的做法事本领是远远不够的。同时,地区性的宗教组织如佛教协会、道教协会等也应该发挥自身连接政府和信众的桥梁纽带作用,与学者一道,对宗教作出符合社会发展、提升旅游文化品位的阐释。

(四)注重宣传,提升云南宗教文化旅游的知名度

宣传是提升云南宗教文化旅游的知名度,形成品牌效应进而形成巨大旅游市场的重要策略。云南宗教文化旅游资源丰富、历史悠久、特色鲜明、品位较高,但是若不能充分宣传营销,同样会造成"寺在深山无人问"的被动局面,一些不具有区位优势的著名宗教风景区如昭通大龙洞、武定狮子山等,尤其如此。

首先是媒体宣传。媒体宣传的范围广、影响大、效果好,是不容忽视的营销途径。我们既可以选择传统媒体如广播、电视、报刊、杂志、广告等,也可以选择新兴媒体如网络、手机等。云南的著名宗教文化景区如宾川鸡足山、巍山县巍宝山、香格里拉松赞林寺等,在区内、省内的知名度尚可,但是在全国其他省份的知名度就差强人意了。如果仅仅依靠历史形成的知名度、美誉度而不思现代发展,云南宗教旅游景区会在相邻省份如四川、广西、贵州、重庆类似景区的竞争下日渐萎缩。有关部门必须设立专项宣传经费,培训促销人员,通过有影响力的媒体如中央电视台、人民日报、百度网等,加大旅游宣传力度。

其次是活动宣传。学术研讨会、宗教节庆活动本身就是良好的宣传手段。如宾川县举办的鸡足山佛教文化论坛、祝圣寺开光大典等活动极大地提高了鸡足山在国内外的知名度,而建水县举行的孔子文化节活动对于拓展建水儒家文化旅游市场功不可没。有条件的地区可以利用宗教节日、祖师生辰、忌日以及其他重要时日,精心策划、组织一些庆典活动、民俗活动,在吸引更多香客、游人的同时起到良好的宣传作用。

第三是场景宣传。我们可以多拍一些宗教景区的录像、画册,制成精美的纪念品、宣传品,以低价、成本价向游客出售或免费赠送,以达到宣传效果。比如可以将门票制成明信片,明信片不会被游客轻易丢弃,既可以收藏,又可以使用,而无论如何处理都可以起宣传作用,成本也不高;相关从业人员如导游、旅游公司员工、甚至景区经营者、服务员也可印制以宗教景区为背景的名片,等等。

第四是纪念品宣传。宗教文化旅游纪念品不仅仅可以创造旅游效益,也是宣传宗教文化旅游的重要媒介。由于重视不够,投入不足,宗教文化旅游纪念品缺乏特色,宗教意义大于文化意义,对于一般消费者缺乏吸引力,既不利于带动旅游经济的发展,也很难起到宣传宗教圣地的效果。我们可以本着生态性、保健性、文化性、便捷性等原则,结合宗教景区特色,别出心裁设计一批旅游纪念品,并将景区信息印制其上,将会起到很好的宣传效果。

（五）强化管理，规范宗教旅游市场

宗教文化旅游因其依托的资源对象，具有特殊性、敏感性等特征，如果引导不当，旅游活动极易转化为宗教活动。当前，宗教旅游者 80% 以上都具有香客身份，出于功利的目的前往宗教圣地烧香拜佛，他们更看重宗教活动场所的神圣性而不是旅游场所的文化性。对于此类游客我们必须加以引导，有针对性的采取宣传、规范等手段引导其动机。在宗教文化旅游中必须坚持高品位开发的方向，严格区分正当宗教活动与封建迷信、非法宗教活动的性质，防止商品化、庸俗化、功利化的侵蚀。一些寺院聘请学过武功的青少年剃光头发搞所谓的少林武功表演；一些地方随意修庙建塔，拼造宗教旅游景点文化；有的在宗教旅游场所修建娱乐城，严重影响景区氛围；有的置宗教传统于不顾，任意向游客乞讨"功德钱"；有的不择手段招徕游客，建造"鬼府冥殿"，大搞封建迷信活动，这些活动既危害了宗教自身的利益，又不利于旅游的长久发展，必须坚决制止。我们必须对宗教旅游动机深入调查研究的基础上，积极引导规范、管理整顿宗教市场，这是关系到云南宗教文化旅游是否健康发展的重要问题。我们应该明确市场定位，瞄准宗教文化的特色与精华，推出诸如宗教生态旅游、宗教休闲旅游、宗教养生旅游等高品位的旅游项目，既要吸引省内游客，又要吸引省外甚至国外游客；既能满足香客正常的宗教需求，又能满足游客合理的文化需要。同时采取有力措施如门票分期制等，解决宗教文化旅游旺季和淡季游客数量相差悬殊等问题。此外还要制定统一的服务标准，规范宗教文化旅游的出行、住宿、饮食、购物以及接待、导游等行为。有条件的地区也可以考虑组建专业的宗教文化旅行社，为游客提供全方位、专业化的服务。

（六）加强合作，推出精品旅游路线

云南宗教文化往往与自然景观和其他人文景观有机结合、相融嵌套在一起。作为云南旅游的有机组成部分，宗教文化旅游应该从云南旅游业的整体格局出发，与民族风情旅游、生态观光旅游等项目紧密配合，树立大宗教、大旅游、大环境的开发理念。政府有关部门必须加强合作；旅游机构不妨与宗教研究机构优势互补，联合开发宗教文化旅游资源；各宗教内部、相邻省区之间也应摈除门户派别之见,创新思维、寻求合作,联合推出高品位的精品宗教文化旅游路线。无论是跨区、跨省、跨宗教甚至跨境,都应突出文化主题,本着整合现有资源、方便游客出行、实现综合效益的原则,集中展现宗教文化的精彩内容。例如我们可以昆明为中心,设计从滇西南到滇西北的佛教文化旅游线,将云南佛教的三大部派汉传佛教、南传佛教、藏传佛教以及独特的大理白族阿吒力教派的文化底蕴展现出来。宗教文化旅游应针对游客的多样性需求,走多样化的发展道路,不仅要体现在旅游产品和项目上,也要体现在旅游市场和路线上。

Is Religion Social Capital in Japan?

Sakurai Yoshihide

Abstract

In recent times, class differentiation in Japan has progressed to the point of discussing how to combat poverty in the lower middle class. Due to the erosion of social support provided by family and kin relationships, as well as the community, individuals must alone face unemployment, disease, and contingent occurrences that often undermine our daily life. For this reason, a generous social-welfare system is needed; however, financially-pressed governments are not expected to be able to bear the increase in such expenditures. Therefore, the Cabinet Office has come up with policy proposals aimed at improving public-private partnerships and social capital in regional areas.

In the wake of welfare-state crises, a number of major industrialized countries undertook neo-liberal reforms. The results, however, were the above-mentioned class differentiation and social strain. Since then, those nations have sought a third way to reduce the tension between classes and ethnic groups through social inclusion policies such as workfare, efforts. to generate employment and social benefits. In so doing, the theory of social capital, a term originally coined by educational reformer / progressive educator L. J. Hanifan in

1916, and more recently developed by James Coleman and Robert Putnam, has been diffused not only in pedagogy, politics, and social development, but also in discussions of crime prevention and public health.

This paper focuses on the role of religious institutions, organizations, and the spirit of cultivating reciprocity, trust, and social networks, which develops social engagement. First, I will review social services and social capital provided by Christianity in the USA and Theravada Buddhism in Thailand. Then, I will extend my argument to the case of Japan, where both religious pluralism and secularism are institutionalized.

Social capital can be easily realized in American Christian congregations and Buddhist temples in Thailand, except for deep southern Thailand. Since both religious institutions function in the public sphere, they cultivate reciprocity and trust in the community as well as the volunteerism needed to establish associations. Furthermore, as they include most members of the community, political persons tend to reach out to churches and/or parachurches. They naturally join grassroots associations that have delegates to national assemblies. Piety is a necessary condition for politicians in both the USA and Thailand.

In contrast to the religious traditions of North America, Europe, or Southeast Asia, the features of syncretism (no public religion) and secularism (separation between religion and politics) in East Asia give rise to different relations between religion and social capital. Here, we must redefine social capital in religion. What sort of social services do various religious institutions provide? How do religious organizations motivate and train their members to practice reciprocity and be trustworthy not only in religious communities but also in public life?

Perhaps the religious minorities in Japan, i. e. Christianity and new religions, provide psychological stability through social bonds; however, their social networks might be blocked within religious communities. Nevertheless, small numbers of pastors, monks, and other religious workers mediate between denominations and the general public, and their social bridging serves to link their own denominations to outside groups.

Last, the survey of religious social capital in Japan reflects the role of religions that restore reciprocity and trust in contemporary society.

1. The "No-Relationship Society" and Social Capital

Over the past couple of years, the Japanese media has often used the expression "no-relationship society" (a society with no human ties between members). This expression reflects the distress in individualized contemporary society, as seen among solitary-living elderly people preparing for their departure from life and single middle-aged and older people feeling anxiety about their future. Since it has been increasingly difficult for people to receive social support from their family, neighbors, or workplace, at any time, anybody's life may take a sudden turn for the worse due to sudden crises such as unemployment or illness. The expression "no relationship" hints at those social uncertainties.

The level of trust toward Japanese society as a community (order, for instance) is high compared to other countries. In contrast, however, the level of trust toward contractual organizations and institutions is not necessarily high (distrust of the government and bureaucracy, for instance). Therefore, no matter how many times a Scandinavian-type high-welfare high-reassurance society (confident in entrusting one's tax burden) is introduced, the likelihood of trusting the government to effectively steer the welfare society is low. On the other hand, neither is their orientation toward individualism, localism, and volunteerism as high as that in the North-American low-welfare, great-gap society (where confidence in private organizations is higher than in the government). The Japanese are still exploring the future ideal society in between those two poles. However, the reality remains that the media helps fuel the anxiety for their future and helps lower trust in the community while at the same time pretending to be in line with public opinion (opinion poll figures).

The background to the current discussions of social capital is this: when exploring social progress in post-global times, the creation, preservation, and further development of social relationships has begun to carry an extremely significant meaning. Thus, long debated in the discussions of social theories and social policies and measures is how we can implement them to foster and preserve social capital. (Putnam, 1994; 2001; Sato, 2002) Some may point out that, realistically, social capital cannot be generated by force since it is historically and culturally shaped, but that is perhaps a little too pessimistic an observation. Why can't we propose a new way of thinking or policy by which to expand trust and reciprocity within a possible range (Inaba, 2004)? However, at this time, let us not start with the argument to create from scratch a completely new alternative theory and practice it, or to establish a spiritual entity. Rather, we can find a new outlook by utilizing existing resources, i. e. reconstructing traditional elements that seem to be on the verge of collapse (by the logic of forming a relation between beliefs and institution).

And this is the place where religion and the concept of social capital can meet. In the past, in terms of religious mentality, religious institutions and religious relationships were crucial to maintain the ethics of reciprocity and mutual trust. At present, although ultimate existence and transcendental ethics have been lost in secular society, however, the social functions of religion are still maintained. Thus, the time is ripe to analyze and explain religion as a reality that can help foster social capital and restore interpersonal relationships, as well as play a useful role in regaining a sense of trust and nurturing reciprocity. In addition, we can also discuss religion as a potential factor.

2. Social Capital and Religion

One can observe that both historically and in contemporary society, religious cultures, relationships, and institutions can help evolve and inculcate the ethics and relationships of reciprocity. However, strictly speaking, that simply means that the norm of reciprocity, in particular, works among those of the same religion. In a community with a plurality of religious types and sects, the functional range of the norm of reciprocity is limited. Thus, where all-inclusive religious cultures (public and civic religions) are available, the norm of reciprocity can possibly be transformed into social ethics. Those discussions have been taking place in the sciences of history and religion. However, when structuring an analytical social theory, the above fact needs to be verified in more direct and observable religious cultures and with individuals and organizations that define the norms of reciprocity and trust.

In this section, while reviewing studies of religious groups and social capital in the United States as well as case studies of regional development by Theravada Buddhist monks in Thailand, I will build a middle-range theory with which to examine the relationship between religion and social capital more directly.

Christian churches in the United States can be divided into a number of denominations. Yet, the attendance rate of congregations of each sect and the participation rate in various activities are considerably higher than those in European nations. The activities of megachurches (in which several thousands of members can attend services) and parachurches (church-based, faith-based organizations that engage in activities of education, welfare, and politics) underscore the fact that Christianity has not been a mere façade of a traditional culture but remains a religion of missionary and social activities.

One characteristic of American Christian churches is that they are mixed yet divided by race (groups of immigrants) or class as in a "salad bowl" and they have grown in correspondence to the social needs of their members. The mainstream Presbyterian church today is significantly older and smaller in membership in contrast to the respectable urban church organizations. On the other hand, many immigrants from Central and South American countries gather in magnificent Catholic cathedrals. Black churches, many of which are Baptist and Pentecostal, are politically very active and have played a significant role in supporting the Civil Rights Movement. Expanding in recent years is the Evangelical Church; many have built megachurches in the suburbs. Korean churches provide Korean-American members with a variety of services including livelihood support for recent immigrants (Choi, 2003). In other words, in the United States, citizens can obtain social capital by belonging to a Christian church and starting reciprocal relationships with other church members or from the sect to which they belong (Smidt, 2003).

Furthermore, American people from certain sects actively attempt to intervene in personal and family matters (as with the issues of abortion and homosexuality) in the name of Christian values while American politicians talk openly about the U. S. position in their diplomatic policy with a sense of Christian mission. This can lead to political-sociological discussions since Christianity plays the role of civil religion (Bellah, 1970). Still, we should confirm that its foundation lies in the role of Christian churches incommunities.

Next, let us examine cases in Thailand. In Thailand, the word development (phathana) has a distinctive political connotation different from both Japanese and English equivalents. Phathana, the slogan for the National Economic and Social Development Plan that General Sarit Thanarat initiated in 1961, was a concept denoting not only economic development but also order and progress in public spheres such as politics, education and sanitation. Sarit, steadfastly preaching that the King, Buddhism, and the Nation compose the three pillars of Thailand, launched the Royal Project, Development by Buddhism, and Development by the Government (conciliation with Communism and nationalism). This politics of developmentalism lasted till around 1990 (Sakurai, 2003).

During this period of development in Thailand, certain Buddhist monks, mobilized by the government, helped regional areas to adopt and internalize the ideology of development; they, often natives of the rural areas themselves, contributed to overcoming underdevelopment and poverty while collaborating with the government and local development NGOs. Thus, the expression "Buddhist monks engaged in development" symbolically evokes the practice of those monks during that period of rural development in Thailand.

The author analyzed the cases of over 100 Buddhist monks engaged in regional community development in "'Development' Monks in Northeast Thailand" (Sakurai, 2008), revealing that it was implemented based on social capital that Buddhist monks, temples, and rural communities had traditionally built. Discussed in the study were 1) cultural resources (the trust of monks, religious protection), 2) historical and political rationality (while following the government policy of social development, those monks maintained their independence and occasionally implemented development projects considered to be critical of the government), and 3) the use of social capital (some monks become information conveyors and mediators through ascetic practices; networks of monks and sangha).

Please refer to the author's books and papers (Sakurai, 2006) for the relationship between Theravada Buddhist temples and rural villages, the moral influence of "development monks" on villagers, and the process by which those did not stay within the realm of regional development based on localism, but would be elaborated upon by NGO activists and Thai social critics and scholars as alternative theories of development and social capital.

3. Religious Cultures and Social Capital in Japan

In Japan, are religious group members actively engaged in the activities of their own local community and civil society? If religion cultivates social capital, we should be able to observe certain facts as to how the activity and experience of religious organizations have inspired political interest, promoted the activities of citizens' groups, and enhanced confidence in social systems and social reciprocity.

To examine these issues, a secondary analysis of extensive

observation data sets was conducted. Using the data from the 4th World Values Survey, I measured whether the respondents' social attributes and the membership in religious groups have influenced their political interest, sense of trust in general, and political action. [1]

Meanwhile, Soka Gakkai (SGI) of the Nichiren Buddhist sect, a new religion in Japan boasting 8.21 million nominal household members, created a political party called Komeito. In the 2010 Upper House election, Komeito received over 7.64 million votes (nine candidates were elected in the electoral districts and proportionally-represented constituencies).

In terms of the number of votes received or vote-gathering capability, the Komeito party shared third place with "Your Party," a new conservative party, following the ruling party, the Democratic Party of Japan (DPJ), and the largest opposition party, the Liberal Democratic Party (LDP), accounting for 13% of the total votes. In general, since religious groups in Japan are well connected with certain political parties and persons, when election time comes, their members turn into vote-getting machines as party-endorsed candidates or personally endorsed candidates; however, only Soka Gakkai has its own political party. Therefore, it is better to separate Soka Gakkai from other religious organizations since being a Soka Gakkai member means being a Komeito supporter and one is expected to possess high political awareness and be highly politically active. Now, analytically, we can read the general political awareness and action of religious groups in Japan. I decided to analyze data by separating the membership of religious groups including Soka Gakkai from the

---

① This data analysis is done by Shigenori Terasawa, Ph. D candidate Hokkaido University who allowed me to refer to his research findings. (Terasawa, 2010)

membership without it.

Specifically, I quantified the following responses to the question items as variables of attitude.

Table 1 Citizens' Attitudes

> + Political Interest: How interested are you in politics?
>
> + General Trust and Confidence: Generally speaking, do you trust people?
>
> + Institutional Confidence: How much confidence do you have in the government, political parties, the Diet (Congress), and public administration?
>
> + Political Action Experience: Have you engaged in any of the following political activities: a petition drive, a boycott of particular products or a corporation, a demonstration, or a strike?

Table 2 A Regression Analysis with Citizens' Attitudes as a Dependent Variable (Figures: Standardized Partial Regression Coefficients)

	Political interest		General trust		Institutional		Political action	
	a	b	a	b	a	b	a	b
Age	.407 *	.393 *	−.003	−.005	.304 *	.288 *	.031 *	.027 *
sex (man=1)	.155 *	.152 *	−.137	−.109	−.010	.004	−.081	−.117
Academic career	.135 *	.117 *	.339 *	.322 *	.052	.041	.117	.083
Household income	.052	.051	.071 *	.070 *	−.004	.000	.041	.053
Spouse (have=1)	−.057	−.055	.242	.291	−.026	−.024	.404	.383
Job (have=1)	−.017	−.018	−.168	−.179	.013	−.011	.113	.054
City size	.019	.026	−.034	−.019	.001	−.002	.085	.092
Buddhism	.038	.042	.142	.008	.036	.036	.262	.198
Judaism—Christianity	−.030	−.024	1.052	.931	.041	.030	−.846	−1.003
Others	−.003	−.012	.648	.701	.029	.019	.029	−.030
No religion	—	—	—	—	—	—	—	—
Frequency of participation	−.211	−.224	.051	.007	−.061	−.059	.031	−.020
Belongingness to religion (yes=1)	.054	.105 *	−.021	.011	.015	.051	.256	.463
Buddhism × Belongingness	.164	.195 *	−.050	−.002	.043	.046	−.032	.020
Judaism—Christianity × Belongingness	.134	.117	−.056	−.012	−.073	−.078	.000	.049
Others × Belongingness	.121	.118	−.046	−.005	.067	.063	−.032	.017
Adj R² / NagelkerkeR²	.197	.202	.048	.047	.088	.088	.113	.110
N	1277	1399	912	960	1146	1200	568	598

(Note) * 5% sig. *1% sig. N number of samples 4th World Values Survey
  a including SGI, b excluding SGI

The findings obtained from this analysis are: there is no relationship between membership in a religious group and political interest, general trust and confidence, institutional confidence, and political activity. Only when Soka Gakkai is included, is there a significant relationship between membership in a religious group and political awareness. By contrast, social position and attributes such as age, gender, education, and income all have a significant relationship with the above attitudes. In all the samples, the percentage of membership in a religious group was not high from the beginning. Thus, it is possible that the effect of religious-group membership was not measured appropriately.

Next, let us briefly examine the social activities of religious organizations in general. From religious organizations listed in The 2007 Religion Almanac published by the Religious Affairs Division, Agency for Cultural Affairs, we sampled 903 groups of inclusive and independent religious corporations under the jurisdiction of prefectures and the Ministry of Education, Culture, Sports, Science and Technology, and then conducted a mail-in survey (recovery rate: 27. 5%) on the social activities of religious groups. Approximately 85% of the groups responded that they conduct social activities. Table 3 shows the variety and characteristics of activities by religious group. [1]

---

[1] This research is ongoing study by the author, who was the supervisor of the research program "Comparative Study of Socially Engaged Religion in the East and West," the granted research of Japan Society for the Promotion of Science from 2007 to 2009.

Table 3 Specific Practical Examples of Social Activities

+ Disaster Relief: dispatching disaster relief volunteers, donations, providing relief supplies.

+ Environmental Conservation: Energy saving, recycling, reforestation.

+ Arts and Culture: art, music, theater arts, historical preservation, lectures, research.

+ Local Community: participation in events including festivals, participation in activities of various + local organizations.

+ International Exchange and Cooperation: overseas aid, development aid, student exchange programs.

+ Social Education: parenting class, Boy Scouts, summer camp.

+ Welfare: nursing care, visiting the elderly or the disabled, soup kitchen or hospital volunteering.

+ Civil Rights: anti-discrimination or human rights movement, residents' movement.

+ Peace: anti-nuclear, antiwar and pro-Constitution movements.

+ Health and Alternative Medicine: health food, natural farming, Eastern medicine, healing.

+ Sports: sports coaching, providing space for athletic activities.

+ Corporate Management: management seminar, corporate ethics lecture, in-house training.

+ Politics: supporting a political party, making election campaign speeches.

Table 4 Most Important Social Activity

	Buddhism		Christianity		New Religion		Total	
Disaster Relief	19	(38.0 %)	3	(3.9 %)	9	(19.6 %)	31	(18.0 %
Local Community	8	(16.0 %)	0	(.0 %)	7	(15.2 %)	15	(8.7 %
Environmental Conservation	8	(16.0 %)	0	(.0 %)	5	(10.9 %)	13	(7.6 %
Arts and Culture	10	(20.0 %)	7	(9.2 %)	4	(8.7 %)	21	(12.2 %
Welfare	1	(2.0 %)	11	(14.5 %)	2	(4.3 %)	14	(8.1 %
Social Education	3	(6.0 %)	16	(21.1 %)	2	(4.3 %)	21	(12.2 %
Civil Rights	0	(.0 %)	8	(10.5 %)	1	(2.2 %)	9	(5.2 %
Peace	1	(2.0 %)	6	(7.9 %)	1	(2.2 %)	8	(4.7 %
International Cooperation	0	(.0 %)	10	(13.2 %)	4	(8.7 %)	14	(8.1 %
Politics	0	(.0 %)	0	(.0 %)	1	(2.2 %)	1	(.6 %
Sports	0	(.0 %)	0	(.0 %)	0	(.0 %)	0	(.0 %
Health and Alternative Medicine	0	(.0 %)	9	(11.8 %)	4	(8.7 %)	13	(7.6 %
Corporate Management	0	(.0 %)	4	(5.3 %)	2	(4.3 %)	6	(3.5 %
Others	0	(.0 %)	2	(2.6 %)	4	(8.7 %)	6	(3.5 %
Numbers of Religions	50		76		46		172	

In traditional Buddhism, common types of social activities are disaster relief (year-end fund-raising drives), conservation of the regional environment (premises such as the grounds of a temple), and the arts and culture (protection of Buddhist culture); in Christianity, they are social education (construction of preschools to higher education schools), welfare (management of medical care and welfare facilities and institutions), and international exchange. In new religions, these activities vary widely including disaster relief.

However, in Japan, the general public is not very aware of the social contributions and activities of religious organizations. The schools, hospitals, and social welfare institutions founded by religious organizations and missions are valued only for their convenience and service the same way other public and private facilities are appreciated. The ideals of their foundation are not recognized by ordinary citizens when they use those facilities. And thus, institutions that strongly promote religious aspects will be avoided.

4. Summary and Issues '

Next, we shall summarize the main points in this paper.

1) The Japanese government cannot continue to finance the ever-increasing cost of social security, so what is urgently needed is a new policy to restore interpersonal ties and reciprocity in order to entrust social services to the private sector. In developed countries in the post-welfare state era, attention has been focused on implementing social inclusion policies and cultivating social capital in hopes of easing the anxiety and tension that are associated with the increasing divides between classes and ethnic groups.

2) When the concept of social capital is employed as a middle-range theory, one is led to the impression that analyses of social process are lacking. Findings of studies of Christian churches in the United States commonly conclude that the participation by a church in its construction facilitates social participation as well, yet the degree of relevance varies depending on inter-denominational differences and the social standing of the church (whether it is the confessional type or the regional culture type). Concerning the relationship between Buddhist monks and regional development in Thailand, although macroscopic analyses of time periods and regional variations may be possible, how Buddhist monks, village temple committees, villagers, and out-of-village organizations and persons have implemented services regarding individual issues and through which affiliation have not necessarily been clarified in a sufficient manner. Thus, both survey research and ethnographic research are needed.

3) Based on World Values Survey results, we analyzed the relationship between membership in a religious organization and

participation in civil society; in particular political action, and relations were observed only in some sects and denominations. Thus, the argument that religion can become social capital is supported only limitedly. However, the survey results of the main religious organizations in Japan revealed diverse social participation by each church, confirming that they provide social services to the general public.

Lastly, there are the issues raised in this study.

In the case of Christian churches in the United States or Buddhist temples in Thailand, it is possible for them to establish their position as an official religion (public religion) and become more or less an integral part of the community. They can also be subject to political mobilization because of the large membership base, community center-like functions of their institutions, and the potential to bring a great many votes. That is why religion has social capital and can facilitate social participation. By contrast, regarding the religious situation and the religion-and-politics relationship in Japan, this argument must be examined from a rather different viewpoint.

In fact, Japanese society was ahead of others in adopting religious pluralism. Shintoism is rooted in the cultural tradition of nature worship as well as mura (village) festival and rituals, while Buddhism is based on ancestor worship. With this spiritual basis, there are a number of religious groups in Japan for individuals to join: Buddhist temples, Shinto shrines, "ko" religious associations, and organizations of foreign religions such as Christianity and Islam, as well as new religions. The sense of secularism in which religious groups and people do not bring their religious beliefs into public spaces is thoroughly practiced in terms of the separation of church and state. Behind the scenes, though, there are strong relationships between religious groups and political persons aiming to get the votes of the groups' members. Still, in contrast to that religious situation, 70% of the citizenry claim to be irreligious in that they have no religious affiliation or commitment, supporting secularism.

That religious cultures and religious organizations possess social capital or engage in social and political activities by utilizing social capital—what does this mean and what does this signify? Perhaps it means that those groups can help maintain the psychological stability of their members and provide social services through a network of social bonds in the case of minority religious cultures and religious institutions. But those are often closed to the general public and other religious groups. On the other hand, there are religious workers who mediate between denominations and work with the general citizenry, and thus their religious action of social bridging serves to link their own denominations with outside groups.

In conclusion, while cautiously observing the traditional and emerging qualities of religious workers and religious activities, researchers who look to examine the relationship between religion and social capital should continue to reflectively ask what can be done to address the issue of fostering interpersonal bonds and restoring reciprocity in contemporary society.

Reference

Bellah, Robert N. , 1970, *Beyond Belief: Essays on Religion in a Post-traditional World*, Harper & Row, NY.

Choi, Gil, 2003, ' The Korean American Church as a Social Service Provider,' Tirrito, Terry and Cascio, Toni eds. , *Religious Organizations in Community Services: A Social Work Perspective*, Springer Publishing Company, NY, pp. 152 – 170.

Inaba, *Keishin*, Altruism in New Religious Movements: The Jesus Army and the Friends of the Western *Buddhist Order in Britain*,

University Education Press, Tokyo.

Putnam, Robert, 1994, *Making Democracy Work: Civic Traditions in Modern Italy*, Princeton University Press, Princeton.

Putnam, Robert, 2000, *Bowing Alone: The Collapse and Revival of American Community*, Simon & Schuster Paperbacks, NY.

Sakurai, Yoshihide, and Somsak Srisontisuk, 2003, *Regional Development in Northeast Thailand and Formation of Thai Civil Society*, Khon Kaen University Press, Khon Kaen.

Sakurai, Yoshihide, 2006, 'Multiple Dimensions of Socially Engaged Buddhism: The Case Study of Northeast and Southern Thailand,' eds. By Ruben L. F. Habito and Keishin Inaba, *The Practice of Altruism: Caring and Religion in Global Perspective*, Cambridge Scholars Press, London.

Sakurai, Yoshihide, 2008, *Tohoku tai no kaihatsuso: Shukyo to shakaikoken* (*Development Monks in Northeast Thailand: Religion and Social Engagement*), Azusa Shupan, Tokyo.

Sato, Hiroshi, 2002, *Enjo to social capital ron no kanousei* (*Possibilities of Assistance and Social Capital*), Institute of Developing Economics, Tokyo.

Smidt, Corwin, 2003, *Religion as Social Capital: Producing the Common Good*, Baylor University Press, TX.

Terasawa, Shigenori, 2010, Oral presentation at 'Religion and Social Capital' session of Annual Meeting of the Japanese Association for Religious Studies, September 5th, 2010, Tokyo University, Tokyo.

Human Dignity

——Image of God: Inseparable?

Pier Cesare Bori

The first Chinese edition of Picơ della Mirandola's *Discourse on Human Dignity*, *Lun rende zunyan*, has been recently published by the Beida University Press. The translation is the result of a course which was held in Beida in March-April, when this translation was produced, used and improved. It was a wonderful experience, and I am grateful to the people who participated or helped to affect it. The work was hard, and some ultimate questions underlying our work had to be put aside, avoiding them even in my introduction to the Chinese edition. One of those questions is the one I pose with the title of this paper.

1. Affirmations about human dignity are frequent and widespread in many cultures and traditions. There is, however, an important difference between the traditional assumptions of human dignity and this idea in modernity. The first article of the Declaration of Human Rights in 1948 says: "All human beings are born free and equal in dignity and rights," adding that "they are endowed with reason and conscience and should act towards one another in a spirit of brotherhood. " In other recent documents, a whole conceptual

constellation is therefore made to surround "dignity", endowing this term with a meaning that differs from the many common traditional affirmations concerning human dignity. In actual fact, the historical path that leads from the modern age to the contemporary conception of dignity is somewhat complex, and Humanism and the Renaissance are only one of the first steps

There is no doubt that the idea of man as an image of God has a great importance in the evolution of modern philosophical anthropology and ethics in the West. It can be argued (Bori, 2008) that in the modern era there has been a turning point in the interpretation of Gen. 1. and 2. In fact, the idea of man, as such, as the representative of God played an essential role in the criticism and crisis of theocracy not only as it was found in the medieval model but also, in some way, as the original theological-political model of all monotheisms. As a consequence, the modern association of "dignity" and "rights" could be enunciated, protected and affirmed precisely through this new reading of Gen.

The interpretation of Genesis 1. 26 – 28 (the creation of man in the image and likeness of Elohim the creator, with dominion on earth) played a significant role in the formulation of Giovanni Pico della Mirandola's idea of man. Pico says of God, the "optimus artifex" after having created mankind, without having been able to provide models or archetypes for him:

> At last the best of makers decreed that the creature to whom he had been unable to give anything wholly his own, should have in common whatever belonged to every other being. He therefore took man, this creature of indeterminate image, set him in the middle of the world and thus spoke to him: "We have given you, Adam, no fixed seat nor features proper to yourself nor endowment peculiar to you alone, in

*order that whatever seat, whatever features, whatever
endowment you may responsibly desire, these same you may
have and possess according to your desire and judgement.
Once defined, the nature of all other beings, is constrained
within the laws prescribed by us. Constrained by no limits,
you may determine it for yourself, according to your own free
will, in whose hand we have placed you. I have placed you
at the world's centre so that you may thence more easily look
around at whatever is in the world. We have made you
neither of heaven nor of earth, neither mortal nor immortal,
so that you may, as the free and extraordinary shaper of
yourself, fashion yourself in the form you will prefer. It will
be in your power to degenerate into the lower forms of life,
which are brutish; you shall have the power, according to
your soul's judgement, to be reborn into the higher orders,
which are divine (www. brown. edu/ Departments/Italian_
Studies/pico).*

The human being as "work of an undefined image", of a God
who dwells in obscurity, means for the youthful Pico not simply a
narrative invention, but a profound religious and philosophical
insight, to which we shall be returning.

2. The strong but individualistic and aristocratic affirmation of
the dignity of man was only the first step. Another step was the
theological debate that took place in Valladolid, Spain, in 1550 –
1551, where the emperor had summoned a commission of jurists and
theologians to deal with the moral problems raised by the conquest of
the West. The Dominican Bartolomé de Las Casas, in reply to
Sepúlveda, spoke out in defence of the Indians for five days.
Sepúlveda was a humanist, and among his many arguments put
forward the humanist (and Aristotelian) case against the

"barbarians". Las Casas, on the other hand, argued that the Indians were not barbarians: they were neither impious, nor illiterate, nor animal-like, nor pagan: they were made in the image of God.

3. Another step was represented by radical Protestantism. The considerations of F. Ruffini, a precursor in the study of the history of religious liberty, concerning the relationship between the Reformation and religious freedom are still valid, and may be applied in general to the theme of human dignity:

> *From the principles whence the Protestant Reformation notoriously derived its impulse, no modern mind, guided by logic alone, could fail to deduce the necessity of proclaiming liberty of conscience and worship at least within the orbit of Christianity; and so true is this that, merely owing to the influence of that necessary correlation, it is customary to date the advent of that form of liberty without further question from the Reformation. But logical correlation does not imply succession of historical facts; and from those principles the Reformers themselves, owing to a variety of historical causes, did not deduce the proclamation of religious liberty (Ruffini 1912, p. 53).*

On the other hand, the principles of the Reformation, on coming into contact with humanist culture, produced a variety of radical reformers who were destined to exercise an influence upon the subsequent history of religious liberty and human dignity: among them appear the jurist Laelius Socinus of Siena, Biandrata, Ochino and others (Cantimori 2002). Another branch of the Reformation, Sebastian Frank, Jacob Boehme, George Fox and the Quakers, along with others, reappraised the mystic aspect of Christianity. In the seventeenth century the image of God had been extremely important for the radical minority of Quakers. Basic to the vision of mankind they put forward was the vision of the return to Paradise of their founder George Fox, and the idea that human life could be restored to its original innocence as from now. Fox's diary describes a vision occurring at the climax of his period of initiation, at the end of the 1640s, in which his founding experiences took place, and which defined the content of his preaching. This had as a consequence also the first affirmations of the equality of sexes. So Margaret Fell:

> *When God created Man in his own Image, in the Image of God he created them, Male and Female*; *and God blessed them, and God said unto them, Be fruitful and multiply*: *And God said, Behold, I have given you of every Herb, &c. Gen. 1. Here God joins them together in his own Image, and makes no such Distinctions and Differences as Men do*; *for though they be weak, he is strong?* (Women's Speaking Justified... < http://www. qhpress. org/texts/fell. html >).

4. Finally John Locke. John Locke's *First Treatise on Government*, published in 1690, is dedicated precisely to the interpretation of Genesis 1. 28. which according to his adversary, Robert Filmer, should be read in the sense that "Adam was the monarch of the whole world", and the primogenitor of every sovereignty. Locke replies with a reading of Genesis as the foundation of an equality that even finds support in private property. It is a criticism, in a "liberal" direction, of the idea of the monarch as the single sovereign and property owner, the heir of the patriarchal right of Adam:

24. In opposition, therefore, to our Author's Doctrine, that "Adam was monarch of the whole world," founded on this Place, I shall show: 1. That by this Grant, I Gen. 28. God gave no

immediate Power to "Adam" over Men, over his Children, over those of his own Species, and so he was not made Ruler, or "Monarch" by this charter. 2. That by this Grant God gave him not "Private Dominion" over the Inferior Creatures, but right in common with all Mankind; so neither was he "Monarch", upon the account of the Property here given him.

Locke's reasoning simply seems to move freely from philosophy to biblical exegesis. Locke does not abandon his scriptural sources, but rather makes use of them in his philosophical discourse as a kind of source for the knowledge of the condition of nature. Thus in his *Letter Concerning Toleration*: "This the Gospel enjoins, this reason directs, and this that natural fellowship we are born into requires of us." The creation of mankind in the image of God and his dominion over nature's creatures is always there to provide support for the arguments, whether they lean towards philosophy or theology, and indeed the borderline between the two disciplines appear to be rather hazier than current classification allows.

5. Thus, the conquest of the idea of human dignity, as conveyed in the Declaration of Human Rights with all human beings are born free and equal in dignity and rights, is the result of a long history that comprises the debate caused by geographical discoveries, a new interpretation of ancient natural rights, the affirmation of freedom of conscience through the struggle of religious minorities asking for freedom and welfare for themselves and for others (Max Weber 1968, 1209), the conquests concerning the dignity of labour, and so on.

The Virginia Declaration of Rights, in 1776: All men are by nature equally free and independent, and have certain inherent rights of which..., the U. S. Declaration of Independence, We hold these truths to be self-evident, that all men are created equal, and are endowed by their Creator with certain unalienable rights, the French

Declaration of the rights of man and citizen, Therefore the National Assembly recognises and proclaims, in the presence and under the auspices of the Supreme Being, the following rights of man and of the citizen: Men are born and remain free and equal in rights, all these documents assume the complex history I have just outlined (for a more extensive comment, cfr. Bori 2008), and even assume in their background the image of God in man, but these formulations become increasingly "secularised" so that the reference to the image, and even to God, disappears. What is lost in historical depth, is gained in the universalistic perspective: the affirmation of human dignity can easily be accepted by other cultural contexts. The idea of human dignity is widespread in different traditions, such as the Chinese, Indian, Buddhist and Muslim traditions, independent of the image of God, and it is easily accepted, thus also opening the way to the juridical protection of the rights that implement dignity (dignity and rights), which is a Western conquest: a Western conquest, but one fully suited to universal reception (Bori 2009). This could be the reply to the question posed by the title.

The noble affirmation of human dignity by the young intellectual Giovanni Pico della Mirandola in 1486 was therefore only one step towards the final result. These developments would not have been possible without the context of the confident openness towards the world and to life that humanism represented, with its characteristic hermeneutic openness that appreciates every possible source of knowledge of the human being as such. I do not doubt that Jacob Burckhardt, in his still admirable book on the Italian Renaissance, is quite right to point to Pico's Oratio as the most important testimonial of this new attitude.

6. Before concluding, we could however ask ourselves whether this model in turn is not above criticism or even obsolete, if we want

to remove, or at least limit, the violence and arrogance implied in what remains a strong idea of identity. Let us consider on the one hand what Gregory Bateson wrote, some 40 years ago:

> *If you put God outside and set him vis-a-vis his creation and if you have the idea that you are created in his image, you will logically and naturally see yourself as outside and against the things around you. And as you arrogate all mind to yourself, you will see the world around you as mindless and therefore not entitled to moral or ethical consideration. The environment will seem to be yours to exploit. Your survival unit will be you and your folks or con-species against the environment of other social units, other races and the brutes and vegetables (Bateson 1972).*

On the other hand, let us consider the evidence of a possible ongoing important change in the cosmological paradigm. A shift in the world view is to leave aside the purely objective physical consideration of things, leading us to consider decisive the role of the conscious observer. In a much-discussed book, *Biocentrism*, Robert Lanza and Bob Berman (2009). go beyond the so-called Participatory Anthropic Principle advocated by the late physicist John Wheeler (1911 – 2009), according to which observers are required to bring the universe into existence, and in the presence of an observer, the "aspects of universe... become forced to resolve into one state, a state that includes a seemingly pre-life earth" (Lanza-Berman 90). They affirm:

> *The behaviour of subatomic particles-indeed all particles and objects-is inextricably linked to the presence of an observer. Without the presence of a conscious observer, they at best exist in an undetermined state of probability waves.*

Without consciousness, "matter" dwells in an undetermined
state of probability. Any universe that could have preceded
consciousness only existed in a probability state. The universe
is fine-tuned for life, which makes perfect sense as life creates
the universe, not the other way around. The "universe" is
simply the complete spatio-temporal logic of the self (Lanza-
Berman 2009, 127).

This world view is surprisingly similar to the humanistic neo-Platonic one, which constitutes Pico's background. There is no room here to dwell on this subject, but its idea is exactly that of a universe in which, from a philosophical point of view, *omnia in omnibus modo suo*, everything is in everything in its own way, according to Pico· della Mirandola, who obviously took this from similar formulas in Plotinus (*ekhei pas panta en autô … pantakhôu panta kai pân kai ekaston pân*:), in Proclus (*panta en pasin oikeiôs en ekastô*) and in Dionysius the Areopagite (*ai pantân en pôsin oikeiôs en ekastô koinôniai*).

This is possible when we intend "being"-beyond the individuality taken as a symbol of all, beyond the abstractions of critical, scientific, or speculative reason-as a given existence, singular and at the same time linked to a whole that includes the subject and, possibly, the Creator of being itself. Here, reality is multiple and unique, and everything is in everything "modo suo", everything is one. This would be the key to the mystic experience, or knowledge, or insight: which ultimately means partaking in the vision of God, that is in the way God sees things (Bori 2010).

8. There have been various interpretations of Pico: an idealistic interpretation, which saw in his work an exaltation of the "kingdom of Man" (G. Gentile, and also E. Cassirer), and an existentialistic interpretation, which put more emphasis on freedom (the existent man

is called to choose his essence, eg. Paul Sartre).

We would now insist on another more traditional, but also newer interpretation, which might be called a spiritual interpretation. Pico does not say that man actually is the centre; nor he does he say that his essence is pure freedom. According to his tradition, resorting to the same Biblical text, he speaks of passing from "image" to "likeness". He says that:

> The Father infused in man, at his birth, every sort of seed and all sprouts of every kind of life. These seeds will grow and bear fruit in each man who sows them. If he cultivates his vegetative seeds, he will become a plant. If he cultivates his sensitive seeds, he will become a brute animal. If he cultivates his rational seeds, he will become a heavenly being. If he cultivates his intellectual seeds, he will be an angel and a son of God. And, if he is not content with the lot assigned to any other creature, he will become a single spirit with God and gather himself into the centre of his own unity. He who was placed above all things will become superior to all things in the solitary darkness of the Father (www. brown. edu/ Departments/Italian_Studies/pico).

This development and growth from the image to the likeness implies a threefold stage: moral transformation, intellectual expansion and union with the Reality which is beyond any name. This spiritual path, according to Pico, can be retraced in the most important traditions (Bori, 2000).

If we assume it to be possible, the biocentric paradigm could open the way to a sort of omnipotence, risking that arrogance of which Bateson spoke. The conception of human dignity in Pico della Mirandola's *Oration* remains interesting; however, suggesting that "he who was placed above all things will become superior to all things", in some way sharing the point of view of God over things, should not consider this attainment as the starting point of the common humàn condition, but as a spiritual conquest that supposes ethical and intellectual improvement, supposes we could say, the full awareness of the deep interconnections which unite the universe in which we are, live and act.

Reference

J. Burckhardt, *The Civilization of the Renaissance in Italy*, transl. S. G. C. Middlemore, 1878 (on line)

F. Ruffini, *Religious Liberty*, transl. J. Parker Heyes, Williams & Norgate, London, Putnam's Sons, New York 1912 (on line)

Ernst Cassirer, *Giovanni Pico della Mirandola*, *A Study in the History of Renaissance Ideas*, in Journal for the History of Ideas 3 (1942), 123 – 144; 318 – 346.

E. Garin, *Italian Humanism: Philosophy and Civil Life in the Renaissance*, trans. Peter Munz. New York: Harper and Row, 1965.

Max Weber, *Economy and Society. An Outline of Interpretative Sociology*, Bedminster Press, New York 1968.

Ch. Trinkaus: *In Our Image and Likeness: Humanity and Divinity in Italian Humanist Thought*, Chicago-London 1970.

G. Bateson, Form, *Substance and Difference*, in *Steps to an Ecology of Mind*, Random House, New York 1972.

G. A. Jònsson, *The Image of God. Genesis* 1 : 26 – 28 *in a Century of Old Testament Research.*: Almqvist & Wiksell International, Stockholm 1988.

P. C. Bori, *Pluralità delle vie. Alle origini del Discorso sulla dignità umana di Pico della Mirandola*, Feltrinelli, Milano 2000.

H. Cancik, "*Dignity of Man*" *in Stoic Anthropology: Some*

Remarks on Cicero, *De officiis* I, 105 – 107, in *The Concept of Human Dignity in Human Rights Discourse*, D. Kretzmer and E. Klein (ed.), Kluwer Law International, The Hague/London/New York, pp. 55 – 85, 2002.

G. Pico della Mirandola, *Discorso sulla dignità dell' uomo*, ed. F. Bausi, Guanda, *Parma* 2003, Chinese edition *Lun rende zunyan*, Beida U. P. , Beijing 2010.

J. R. Middleton, *The Liberating Image*: *The Imago Dei in Genesis* 1:Wipf & Stock Publishers, Grand Rapids 2005.

Des Menschen Wurde – *entdeckt und erfunden im Humanismus der italienischen Renaissance*, ed. R. Gröschner, S. Kirste und O. W. Lembcke, Tubingen 2008.

P. C. Bori, *Humanism and Political Theology from Pico to Locke*, in Annali d'Italianistica 26 (2008), pp. 77 – 95.

Diritti umani e religioni and Per un' etica mondiale delle religioni, in G. Filoramo (ed.), *Le religioni e il mondo moderno*, *IV*: *Nuove tematiche e prospettive*, Einaudi, Turin 2009, pp. 377 – 396 and 405 – 432.

P. C. Bori, *Ad imaginem Dei. Proposals*, *Conjectures*, in *In the Image of God. Foundations and Objections within the Discourses on Human Dignity*, ed. by A. Melloni-R. Saccenti , LIT, Berlino 2010, pp. 39 – 44.

民族性与普世性之间

—— 改革派犹太人的文化认同及其启示

傅有德

所谓文化认同,是指一个民族共同体对蕴含在自己的文化传统中的基本价值的体认,它在文化的意义上回答了一个民族是谁的问题。美国学者亨廷顿认为,"文化认同对于大多数人来说是最有意义的东西"。

文化认同是一个民族共同体的精神纽带,是其生命延续的精神基础,因而具有很强的民族性特征。在单一文化主导的国度里,文化认同一般不成其为问题;由于不同文明的相遇,小到个人,大到一个民族,都不得不面对和自己的传统相异的文明的挑战,这时,文化认同就成为一个大问题了。犹太民族早在圣经时代就曾先后与埃及、亚述、巴比伦、波斯、希腊、罗马诸多文明相遇;从公元70年开始,一直到1948年以色列建国,犹太人散居世界各地,直接面对各个国家或民族的文化。与不同文明的相遇,尤其是散居在异国他乡,使犹太人很早就意识到自己的文化认同问题。当然,由于现代性的冲击,文化认同就成了关系到犹太民族能否自立的大问题。

犹太人的文化认同在于其宗教——犹太教;改革派犹太人的文化认同在于改革派的犹太教,而改革派的犹太教的主旨主要体现在改革派中央拉比会议通过的若干纲领性文件中。从1885年到1999年,美国改革派犹太教中央拉比大会发布过四个具有重大历史意义的文件,即《匹斯堡纲领》(1885),《哥伦布纲领》(1937)、《改革派犹太教:百年回顾与展望》(1976,以下简称《百年回顾》)、和《改革派犹太教原则声明》(1999,以下简称《原则声明》)。本文将通过引征和分析这四大纲领性文件,阐述改革派犹太人的文化认同,弄清改革派是如何处理传统与现代、民族性与普世性的关系问题的。本文还试图表明,改革派犹太人的文化认同观以及他们对待民族性与普世价值的态度和方式,对于当代中国人的精神文明建设是有借鉴意义的。

一、植根于犹太教传统

犹太教改革派对于犹太人的民族认同和文化认同与历史传统的关系有着清醒的认识。1999 年中央拉比会议在匹斯堡通过的《原则声明》明确指出:"纵观我们的历史,我们犹太人一直深深植根于我们自己的传统,即使我们学习了许多与我们相碰撞的文化。"尽管在该声明发布的时候,历史已经到了 20 世纪的最后一年,尽管犹太人在过去的两个世纪里经历了启蒙运动、纳粹大屠杀、以色列建国等一系列重大的历史事件,犹太人仍然坚信他们之为一个族群与其传统之间根深蒂固的联系。对于犹太人而言,是犹太教塑造了犹太人,没有犹太教,就没有犹太这个民族。关于这一点,《原则声明》之外的其他三个文件也都包含了类似的意思。

既然犹太人的文化认同植根于犹太教,那么,在改革派心目中,什么是犹太教?或者说,犹太教中最基本的概念或原则是什么?对于这个问题,《原则声明》做了明确回答:"本原则声明肯定,犹太教的核心信条是:上帝(God)、律法(Torah)和以色列人(Israel)。"该声明表示:上帝,是"真实、唯一"的存在,他通过圣约与犹太人密切联系在一起。他创造世界,按照自己的形象造人,人们敬畏他,崇拜他,以祈祷等方式回应他。律法,"是犹太人生活的基础",是犹太人珍视的"启示真理",上帝通过它展现了对于犹太人和人类的爱。对于律法,犹太人需要终生学习和躬行践履,学习和履行律法的结果是超凡入圣,使凡俗的生活神圣化。以色列人,是"一个渴望成圣的民族,一个因着古老契约被特选的民族,一个万族之中唯一历史地见证上帝临在的民族。"现在的以色列人,是一个"包容的民族",既包括在以色列国的犹太人,也包括散居世界各地的犹太人。

实际上,用"上帝"、"律法"和"以色列人"这三个概念界定犹太教,是犹太教改革派的一贯立场和做法。早在1885年的《匹斯堡纲领》就明确说:"犹太教为人类保存并捍卫了上帝观念,并奉之为宗教的核心真理。"①摩西律法是古代训诫犹太人完成其使命的体系,"今天,我们仍尊之为具有道德约束力的律法。"以色列人,不再是一个独立的民族国家,而"是一个宗教共同体"。1937年通过的《哥伦布纲领》开宗明义谈犹太教的基础,把犹太教的基本原则归纳为八条,上帝、律法和以色列人是其中的三条。该《纲领》说:上帝"是犹太教的心脏",犹太教对宗教的主要贡献就是其上帝观:他是一、活的神,他凭借律法和爱统治世界。"托拉,无论是书面的,还是口头的,都铭记了以色列人不断生成的有关上帝的意识和法律意识。"关于以色列人和犹太教的关系,该文件称:"如果说以色列人是躯体,犹太教则是其灵魂。"1976年在旧金山发布的《百年回顾》也明确列出了上帝、以色列人和托拉三条(一共六条)原则。关于上帝,该文件写道:"无论个人还是社会,仍将生活植根于上帝的真实存在基础上,随时准备接受新的体验和神圣观念。我们视生命为神秘,相信人类由神创造,分享神的永生,虽然还有一种我们称之为死亡的神秘事物存在。"关于以色列人:"犹太人的特别之处在于他们与神有契约,进而可以洞悉人类处境。在我们漫长的历史中,我们的民族怀着救世主般的希望期待人类赎罪,我们的民族和宗教从来都是不可分离的。"关于托拉(律法),该文件说:"托拉源自犹太人与神的关系。"是历代的立法者、先知、历史学家、诗人、拉比"为我们留下的宝贵遗产"。"几个世纪以来,托拉从未停止过创新,当代犹太人也以其创造力为这个传统链条添砖加瓦。"

要而言之,改革派犹太人把自己的文化认同植根于这样的犹太教:以上帝为最高的存在,接受并实践神圣的律法,相信犹太人是与圣约相联系的与众不同的民族或宗教共同体。这就是改革派犹太人的文化认同的基本方面。在我们看来,犹太教是犹太人的宗教,上帝、律法和以色列人作为犹太教的基本原则,体现了犹太教的民族性。

---

① 转引自《近现代犹太宗教运动》,第327页。

二、汲取西方的普世价值

改革派犹太人把自己的文化认同植根于以上帝、律法和犹太人为基本原则的犹太教。但是,应该指出的是,传统犹太教的内容并非是改革派犹太人文化认同的全部。上帝、托拉和以色列人作为犹太教传统的核心原则只是他们的文化认同的一部分,尽管是基础性的一部分。如果以上原则体现的是改革派犹太人文化认同中的民族性因素,那么,就是在上述四大纲领性文件中,我们还可看到一以贯之的普世性内容,即西方启蒙运动以来风靡世界的普世价值:公平、正义、平等、自由、爱人、和平、人权、公民权、女权,等等。《匹斯堡纲领》明确宣称:改革派"以积极投入现时代的伟大任务为己任","以正义和公正为依据,解决由这些问题引致的种种问题。"《百年回顾》也说:"世界正义与和平"是犹太人的追求。《哥伦布纲领》肯定:犹太教在重视人类的血族关系的同时,认可"人类生命和人格的圣洁和价值以及个人追求自由和自由选择职业的权利。人人平等、民族平等、派别和阶级自由是所有人不可剥夺的权利也是所有人不可逃避的责任。"(第 6 条)这四个文件都不同程度地宣称,犹太人不只是聚居在西方国家中的一个民族或宗教共同体,而且认同启蒙思想家以及《人权宣言》、《独立宣言》所阐述的普世价值。也就是说,西方思想家提出的普世价值对于改革派犹太人来说,不仅不是格格不入的,而且已经成为他们的文化认同的重要组成部分。

应该看到,改革派犹太人之接受西方的价值观是有历史原因的。历史告诉我们,犹太教改革既是犹太人"解放"的结果,也是启蒙运动的产物。前者的意思是说,犹太人在法国大革命后成了法兰西共和国的公民,获得了与法兰西民族同等的权利,改变了(至少在官方文件里)原来受压迫、遭歧视,没有任何政治权利的地位。继法国之后,欧洲多数国家也在法律上承认了犹太人的公民地位。这就是犹太历史上所谓的"解放"。后者在这里既指 18 世纪西方的启蒙运动,也指犹太人内部的启蒙运动(Haskalah)对犹太教改革的影响。犹太人的启蒙运动是西方启蒙运动在犹太人共同体内的反应。二者的共同点在于:对中世纪的传统宗教和教会持批判态度,大力提倡平等、自由、博爱、科学、人权等普世的价值,主张与时俱进的进步历史观。犹太启蒙思想家如门德尔松认为,作为现代犹太人,一方面应该融入西方的主流社会,实现自身的现代化;另一方面又要保留犹太教传统,在文化或精神上坚持犹太人的身份。[①]在"解放"和启蒙的双重影响下,传统的犹太教已经无法应对现代价值的挑战,于是,从19世纪初开始,犹太教内部发生了改革运动,改革派随之登上了历史舞台。在这个意义上,我们说犹太教改革是"解放"与启蒙双重作用的后果。在"解放"和启蒙的历史背景下,改革派犹太人把西方文化中的普世价值融入犹太教,可以说是历史的必然。

三、发掘并弘扬犹太传统中的普世因素

我们注意到,改革派犹太人除了接受西方启蒙运动以来的价值观,如人权、公民权、妇女的平等权以外,还努力从发掘、弘扬或改造传统犹太教中的原则或价值,使之普世化为全世界各个民族共有的价值或真理。改革派的做法是,或者把原本属于犹太人或犹太教的内容普世化,使之变为普世的东西;或者把犹太教固有的普世因素弘扬光大,使之完全与西方的普世价值等同起来。前面提及的公平、正义、平等、和平等西方价值是有其犹太教根源的。它们既是西方的,也是犹太的。改革派犹太人把它们发掘、弘扬,使之成为现代犹太教的重要组成部分。如《百年回顾》所说:"蕴含在传统犹太教中的普世主义的伦理一定要成为我们犹太人的责任中明确的部分。"

关于上帝,《圣经》中常说"亚伯拉罕的上帝","以撒的上帝"、"雅各的上帝","以色列人的上帝"。而且,希伯来《圣经》中的上帝表现出对以色列人特别的关爱。例如,上帝和他们立约,赋予他们律法,使之成为"上帝的选民";把他们从埃及的奴役中解救出来,赐给他们"流着奶和蜜"的土地,在他们需要的时候给以佑助;等等。这些通行的犹太教上帝观显然带

---

① 这就是门德尔松在《耶路撒冷》一书中提出的犹太人的双重任务。该思想对后来的犹太教改革产生了积极的影响。

有强烈的犹太性,即民族性色彩。但是,改革派纲领中的上帝已经不仅仅是犹太人的上帝,而是全人类的上帝了。如《匹斯堡纲领》在阐述犹太教的第一个原则时就说:"任何一种宗教都旨在把握无限的上帝",而"犹太人为人类保存并捍卫了上帝观念,并奉之为宗教的核心真理"。

在传统的犹太教中,犹太人期盼弥赛亚的降临,那时,弥赛亚将带领各地的犹太人打败敌人,回归耶路撒冷去建立一个和平正义的王国。显然,这种弥赛亚带有很强的民族性。但是,在《匹斯堡纲领》中,弥赛亚观就完全变成普世主义的了。该文件说:"在精神和智力文化普遍发展的现代,仍有途径通向在人类中建立真理、公正与和平的王国,这也是救世主(弥赛亚)的伟大希望。"这里突出的是:弥赛亚期盼不只属于犹太人,而属于全人类,因为其目标是"在全人类中建立真理、公正与和平的王国"。

犹太教改革之前,一个普遍接受的观点是,托拉是上帝赐给犹太人的律法,因而为犹太人所专有,它也是犹太人之区别于其他民族的重要标志。但是,改革派的犹太人认为,托拉不仅是犹太人的,也是全人类的。如1999年的《原则声明》所言:"我们相信,托拉是上帝对于犹太人和全人类的爱的展现。"

此类例证还可在改革派的文件中发现许多。由此可见,把原来属于犹太人特有的价值普世化,是改革派犹太人确立其文化认同的一个特别值得关注的做法。

《圣经》(创1:26 – 27)说:上帝按照他的形象,照着他的样子造人。这一本来具有普世意义的观点在改革派的文件中得以重申和加强。正如《匹斯堡声明》所说:"我们确信,每个人都是按照上帝的形象创造的,因此每个人都是神圣的。"每个人的神圣性和与此相关的人所固有的尊严和价值,有其《圣经》的根源,也是人类在过去、现在和未来都应普遍享有的。

我们都知道,《圣经》(利19:18)教导古代以色列人"要爱人如己"。这一原本具有普世意义的"博爱"观也在改革派的文件中弘扬光大,因为《匹斯堡纲领》说得很清楚:"我们承认,我们时代博大的仁爱精神是实现我们的使命的同道。"(P.328)

公平、正义、和平在犹太教《圣经》里占有突出重要的地位。《摩西五经》的诸多律法体现的一个基本原则就是公平的判决,人所熟知的"以牙还牙,以眼还眼"的律法便是其中典型的一例。"惟愿公平如大水滚滚,公义如江河滔滔"（摩5:24），先知阿摩斯的呼喊更是家喻户晓的。类似的这些观念在在改革派的四个纲领性文件里被多次提及。例如《匹斯堡纲领》说"以正义和公正为依据"解决现代社会存在的种种社会弊病。《哥伦布纲领》也说："犹太教将其教义应用于经济秩序、工商业和国内外事务以图建立一个公平社会。它旨在消灭人为的悲剧和痛苦、贫困和退化、专制和奴役、社会不公和偏见以及恶意和冲突。它倡导在平等正义基础上促进敌对阶级和谐关系的形成和创造条件使人性大放异彩。"（第7条）关于和平，它说："自先知时代起，犹太教就向世人宣示了追求世界和平的理想。"（第8条）犹太教"主张依靠精神教育、爱和同情追求人类进步。它视正义为一切国家福祉之基础和世界和平之条件。"（第8条）《匹斯堡声明》说得更加充分："我们寻求对话并与其他的信仰者联合起来，希望一起能为我们的世界带来和平、自由和公正。我们有责任去追求公平与公正，并缩小贫富间的差距，反对歧视和压迫，追求和平，欢迎陌生人，以保护地球生物的多样性和自然资源，摆脱自然，经济和精神的奴役。此时此刻，我们再度肯定社会活动和社会公正为改革派信仰和实践的核心性的、先知性的要点。"通过改革派的阐发，犹太教《圣经》中涵有的公平、正义、和平等价值与西方的价值观完全接轨，成为人类普遍认可和接受的东西，使古老的价值承载了现代的精神，从而焕发出新的生命力。

四、兼顾民族性与普世性

以上所述乃是改革派从传统犹太教中保存、发扬的因素，以及从西方文化吸收的内容。除此之外，改革派还对传统做了大量"祛除"的工作。大致说来，改革之初是"破字当头"，许多信条、习俗被当做过时陈腐的内容被"弃若敝屣"，后来则逐渐趋向于传统与民族性的回归，继承了较多的传统犹太教特有的内容，基本实现了民族性与普世性的兼顾与平衡。

由于直接受到"解放"和启蒙运动的影响，1885年的《匹斯堡纲领》凸显了对传统犹太教的批判与祛除，明显表现出对启蒙价值的青睐于靠拢。这一方面表现在他们把上帝视为"任何宗教"都具有的普遍观念和"宗教的核心真理",倡导"全人类的真理、公正与和平",另一方面表现在对于犹太教的某些律法的摈弃。该纲领明确写道:我们"仅仅坚持那些升华和圣洁我们生活的各种仪式。同时抛弃所有那些与现代文明观点和习惯不适应的陈规陋习。"具体说:"那些关于饮食、宗教洁净、服饰的规定,起源于不同的时代,而且受到了与我们的精神状态格格不入的观念的影响。他们不能给现代犹太人提供宗教的神圣性;在我们时代遵守这些规定,与其说进一步推动,不如说妨碍了现代精神的升华。"还有,"我们不信肉体复活,也不信地狱(Gehenna)和天堂(Eden)是永久惩罚和回报的场所,这样的观念在犹太教中没有根基。"对于重建犹太国家和恢复古代的献祭制度,该文件也很明确:"我们既不务求重返巴勒斯坦,也不向往在亚伦子孙的管理下从事献祭崇拜,更不会恢复任何犹太国的律法。"(第 327 – 328 页)在较长的一个时期,改革派不再相信天堂、地狱,不再行"割礼",不再坚持食用"洁净食品"(Koshah food),不再穿着与众不同的服饰,甚至不再于星期六过安息日而改在了星期日。对于多数改革派来说,"美国就是巴勒斯坦,华盛顿就是耶路撒冷。"犹太人没有必要回到巴勒斯坦建立自己的国家。50 年之后,改革派的态度有了转变。关于犹太复国主义,《哥伦布纲领》做了明确地肯定:"我们认为所有犹太人都有职责建立一个犹太家园,使之成为受迫害者提供的避难港和犹太文化、精神生活中心。"(第 5 条)这是改革派向民族性回归的重要一步。宗教生活也得到了强调:"犹太教生活奉献犹太教理想为特征。它主张教徒忠实参加犹太社区生活,并于家庭、犹太教会堂、学校和其他一切可以丰富犹太教生活、促进犹太教福祉的机构中得到体现。犹太教教还要求人们保留安息日、各种节日和宗教节日,保持和发展这些传统、象征和仪式具有启发价值,在礼拜和引导中发掘独特的宗教艺术和音乐形式、使用希伯来语和其他本国事物。"(第 9 条)在 1976 年的《百年回顾》中,我们也看到了明显的回归民族性和宗教性的痕迹。那里说:"神要求我们以民族责任为起点延伸到犹太人生活的方方面面,做到祷私人化礼拜公共化;庆祝生活中的重大事件;参加犹太教会堂和社区和其他促进犹太民族存续、增强犹太民族生存能力的其他活动。"在犹太教仪式中,"犹太人都要遵循犹太教传统的要求,践行个人自觉,以承诺和知识为基础进行选择和创造。"(第 4 条)。

　　如果说 1885 年的《匹斯堡纲领》表现出更多地去犹太人的民族性和个别性和对普世性的追求,那么在以后的《哥伦布纲领》(1937 年)、《百年回顾》(1976 年)和《匹斯堡声明》(1999 年)等几个重要文献中则逐渐表现出民族性、个别性的回归,以及民族性与普世性的兼顾与平衡。正如《百年回顾》中所说的那样:"直到最近,犹太人的责任与全人类的责任才协调一致起来。这两者看上去是彼此对立的。我们不知道有什么简单的办法去解决这种紧张关系。然而,我们必须直面这两者而不放弃其中的任何一项。对人类的普遍关怀如不伴之以对我们独特民族的忠诚,就是自我毁灭;只对我们民族有热情而缺少对人类的热情,是和先知对我们的教导相矛盾的。犹太教要求我们同时负起普世的责任与个别的责任。"(第 6 条)从改革之初以祛除民族性、个别性,推崇普世性为主调的激进解构,到逐渐认识到传统与现代,民族性与普世性之间兼顾与平衡的重要性,并以此对传统进行重构,改革派犹太人用了 100 多年的时间。可以说,这种兼顾与平衡的认识是犹太人历史经验与教训的结晶。

　　至此,我们做出如下小结。改革派犹太人的文化认同在于他们所接受的犹太教。而他们接受的犹太教,从前面的论述可见,一方面植根于传统犹太教,保留了上帝、律法和以色列人三大核心要素,因而坚持了其文化认同中的民族性,即犹太性(Jewishness);另一方面,他们又使改革派的犹太教带有明显的普世主义内容。其普世性内容的获得主要有三个途径。其一是直接吸收西方启蒙运动以来流行的价值观,如自由、平等、博爱、科学、人权、公民权、女权,等等;其二是从传统犹太教中发掘本来就具有普世性的价值,使之发扬光大而成为完全普世的要素,例如公平、正义、和平、爱人,等等;三是改造传统,将其中原来是犹太人特有的即民族性的内容转化、提升为普世的内容,例如将犹太教的上帝观转化、提升为全人类的核心宗教观;把犹太人的律法普遍化为所有人的律法;把犹太人的弥赛亚观普遍化为全人类的弥赛亚观,诸如此类。直言之,改革派犹太人的文化认同包含了三部分内容:传统犹太教的原则,它们保持了改革派犹太人的个别性或民族性;从西方文化中汲取的普世的价值观,以及从犹太教传统中转化、提升而来的普世性因素,它们构成改革派文化认同的普世性方面。这三部分内容构成了现代改革派犹太教的有机整体。在过去的近两个世纪里,它塑造和改变着改革派犹太人(约占犹太人的一半)的文化认同。从方法论上看,改革派犹太教的纲领体现了 Both/and 的特点,兼顾了传统与现代、民族性与普世性两个方面的因素,在它们之间保持了适当的平衡。

五、对当代中国人文化认同的启示

毫无疑问,今天的中国人面临着一个文化重建和确立文化认同的任务。与 19 - 20 世纪的犹太人类似,我们面临着现代性的挑战,有一个在传统与现代之间做出抉择的问题;我们也同时面临普世价值的挑战,有一个在民族性与普世性之间做出抉择的问题。不仅如此,在高度全球化的 21 世纪,我们面临更多样的文化传统,因此更难做出抉择。在过去的一个多世纪里,中国的知识分子在回应现代性与普世性的挑战中形成了不同的思想派别,如全盘西化论,国粹主义,中体西用论,西体中用论,等等。全盘西化论和国粹主义走向了两个极端,对文化会通与融合的大势视而不见,显然是不足取的。至于"西体中用"论,因其否认中国人文化认同的根在于自己的文化传统,主张以"西学"替换"中学",属于"准全盘西化论",在理论和实践上都不可取,所以这里也无需论述。

值得重视的是所谓"中体西用"论,因为此论在理论上影响深远,至今仍有为数不少的支持和拥护者。"中学为体,西学为用"之论存在一个显而易见的问题,这就是"体用相分",即作为"体"的东西基本上是单纯的"中学"。张之洞在 1898 年成文的《劝学篇》阐发了"务本"与"务通"并举的思想。"务本",要求人们持守"三纲五常"等儒家伦理、道德规范,通过传统的纲常名教来实现立身立命。"务通"则是在"务本"的根基上兼采西学,有限度地引进西方先进科学技术,学习西方的近代工业。张之洞的主张在朝廷的推动下风靡全国,张本人因之成为"中体西用"论的"最乐道之者"(梁启超语)。显而易见,张之洞的"中体西用"论没有对于作为"体"的儒家伦理纲常有所触动和改造,这与前述犹太教改革派的做法大不相同,因为犹太教改革派恰好是对于"体",即犹太教自身的改革。正如犹太教是犹太人的文化认同,儒家思想是中国人——至少是相当一部分的中国人的文化认同。如果说在闭关锁国的古代,儒家思想之为中国多数人的文化认同是合理可取的,那么,鸦片战争之后,尤其是在全球化愈演愈烈的今天,仍然坚持《四书》、《五经》里的儒家思想,而不与时俱进地给予解构与重建,就是逆历史潮流而动,甚至可以说是冥顽不化了。犹太教改革派的经验告诉我们,现代中国人需要新的文化认同,塑造和确立新的文化认同的做法是"创造性地转化"传统文化,尤其是儒家思想。在这样做的过程中,首先应该将我们的文化认同植根于过去的传统,即坚持其中原有的符合人性,适应时代的原则,例如仁、义、礼、智、信;二是敞开胸怀接受西方文明和各国文明中的普世价值,如自由、平等、博爱、公正、和平、科学、人的尊严、妇女权利等等,三是发掘与弘扬中国传统中固有的价值,使之转化为具有普世意义的价值,例如温、良、恭、俭、让、宽、敏、惠,诸如此类。通过这样的解构与重建工作,一个植根于中国传统但又是更新改造了的新文化将问世于21世纪的中国,并成为当代中国人的个体或民族的"灵魂"。

"民族国家"与"文明"

张　旭

　　甘阳在《从"民族－国家"到"文明－国家"》一文中所说:"中国在上世纪的中心问题是要建立一个现代'民族－国家'(nation-state),但中国在21世纪的中心问题则是要超越民族国家的逻辑,而自觉地走向重建中国作为一个'文明－国家'(civilization-state)的格局。"①"民族国家"是一个起源于十九世纪西方的基本政治概念,而"国家"的概念起源则要比它早上两三百年。至于"文明－国家"的概念,它却是西方政治思想范畴体系中一个自相矛盾的概念,因为看起来"国家"和"文明"是两个完全不同的范畴,即文明的范畴是和平性的,或者说是,竞争性的,但不具有国家的主权和国家利益上的冲突性和斗争性。"文明－国家"这种用法会引起思想的混乱,这在亨廷顿的"文明的冲突"学说中也表现得特别明显,并由此引发其无穷无尽的论战。此外,不仅在西方政治思想体系内部,"民族国家"与"文明"这对概念被视为一对矛盾性的概念,而且,"民族国家"与"文明"之间的冲突也被用来解释非西方国家在西方国家追求殖民扩张的世界历史进程中所遇到的根本困境,即古老的"文明"与现代的"民族国家"之间的冲突。通过考察"民族国家与文明"之间的现代张力是如何形成的,将有助于反思我们这次"北京论坛"分会的会议主题:"东西方文明的现代处境"。

　　为了理解"民族国家与文明"之间的张力问题的意义,我首先从大家耳

①　甘阳,"从'民族－国家'走向'文明－国家'",《书城》,2004年第2期。

熟能详的亨廷顿的"文明的冲突"学说入手,揭示亨廷顿的"文明的冲突"的学说的实质乃是不言自明地采用了一个"文明－国家"的概念,由此他才可能在社会、国家、国际三个层面上的不同含义将国际政治中的"文明的冲突"、国内政治中的"文化认同"以及现代社会的"文化价值"等三个不同政治领域的问题贯穿在一起,也就是说,"文明的冲突"学说不仅是一种国际政治学说,也是一种政治学说,它还是一种政治哲学。亨廷顿是如何将通常认为是非政治性的"文明"范畴转变成一个可以运用于国际政治、国家政治和社会政治等不同层面的政治范畴的呢? 与其说亨廷顿利用了"文明"概念本身所具有的歧义性,不如说当现代"文明"概念从"民族国家"概念中产生出来之后,就既作为它的构成部分又作为其"反概念"而存在的。通过西方现代早期思想史各种相互冲突的学说的考察和分析,我们或许能解释清楚"文明的冲突"学说未曾言明的概念混乱的起源。在此,我首先在"民族国家与文明"这一问题的表面重建亨廷顿的论证,然后对"民族国家与文明"问题的诞生和发展的思想谱系做一个线索性的暗示,而更深入的分析则只有留待以后的机会。

美国学者亨廷顿(Samuel P. Huntington)在《文明的冲突与世界秩序的重建》一书中提出了苏联解体之后世界秩序的新概念,即"文明的冲突"(The clash of civilizations)学说,以提供一个解释"后冷战时代"世界秩序中各种力量分分合合的解释模式,九一一事件以及之后的世界历史事件似乎印证了这一解释模式的预言能力和解释能力。

20世纪80年代末前苏联解体之后,人类历史上第一次实现多极化的和多元文明的全球政治格局,原来冷战时代以意识形态划分两大不同的阵营(社会主义与资本主义,发达国家与发展中国家,东方与西方)的国际政治模式已经失效,与此同时,按照近二百个独立主权的民族国家的原则并不能充分解释后冷战时代全球性政治冲突集中在宗教和种族的断层线上的现象。围绕意识形态和超级大国进行结盟的方式已经让位于以文化认同(cultural identities)和文明认同(civilization identities),政治界线的重新划分越来越与种族、宗教、传统等文化线(cultural lines)趋于一致,文明间的断层线正在成为全球政治冲突的中心界线。冷战现实主义的思维模式往往会在文化分裂和文明断层的阵线上遭遇失败。亨廷顿以设问的方式断言:

要想说明这些现象,"不是'文明的冲突',又是什么呢?"

　　这一国际政治的"文明范式"(civilizational paradigm)突出了西方自由联盟与非西方文明之间存在着根本性的"文明的冲突",并带有明显的"美国例外论"或"美国中心论"色彩。亨廷顿看起来将"国家利益"之间永恒冲突的观念扩展到文明层面,将"文明"视为某一文明的核心国家的基本国家利益。一个文明的核心国家在"文明的冲突"中捍卫自己的文明,进行保卫文明的战争,就是捍卫国家的根本利益。而捍卫西方文明的重任就落在了美国身上。"文明的冲突"学说并没有假定全球政治冲突的核心从两大"意识形态"的冷战阵营转移到八大"文明"之间的广泛冲突,而是集中于非西方文明中的中国的崛起给美国霸权带来的冲击和威胁,以及伊斯兰世界的原教旨主义运动给美国国家安全带来的潜在的或现实的威胁。因此亨廷顿预言:"未来的危险冲突可能会在西方的傲慢、伊斯兰国家的不宽容和中国的武断的相互作用下发生。"[①]"文明的冲突"学说所传达出来的美国中心主义的国际政治新思维倒没什么模糊之处。它无非是强调美国的"自由主义的帝国主义"、中国的"和平崛起"和伊斯兰世界的"伊斯兰复兴运动"这三者在当前国际政治格局变迁上的紧张关系。即使发生了九一一事件,美国人仍然坚信对美国构成真正威胁的并不是与高技术结合的恐怖主义极端势力或"无赖国家",而是整个伊斯兰世界的伊斯兰复兴运动以及中国的崛起。从修昔底德或霍布斯的"安全困境"理论来看,一个大国的崛起总会引起其他国家寻求遏制或均势的行动,尤其是"崛起的中国",将成为美国的最大竞争者和美国世界霸权最重要的挑战力量。

　　亨廷顿的"文明的冲突"话语不仅是一种美国中心主义的国际政治新范式,而且也是一种分析当今民族国家的政治认同危机的新范式。在"文明的冲突"的世界政治氛围中,冷战意识形态的凝聚力或自由民主政制的价值,已经无法再为民族国家的政治认同提供足够资源。新自由主义经济的全球化以及通讯的全球化并未带来普遍同质的全球秩序,反而前所未有

[①]　Samuel Huntington, *The Clash of Civilizations and the Remaking of World Order*. London: Simon & Schuster Press, 1996. 亨廷顿,《文明的冲突与世界秩序的重建》(以下简称《文明的冲突》),周琪等译,新华出版社,2002 年。第 201 页。

地引发了人们的"文明认同危机",人们比以往的任何时代都更深刻地意识到那些把"我们"区别于"他们"的文化特性、文明因素或历史传统。尤其是在全球化浪潮冲击下的非西方文明,更是要通过本土文化的复兴来伸张自己文明的独特性,建立自身的文化认同与政治认同。那些非西方文明不仅要面对"文明的冲突"的国际政治秩序的压力,而且也要面对国内的"文明的冲突"的压力,也就是无所不在的种族冲突、民族冲突和区域冲突。如果一个非西方国家要避免内部被分裂或撕裂的命运,或者需要诉诸文明认同来解决政治认同的危机,或者需要诉诸政治认同来解决文明认同的危机。非西方文明在向现代民族国家转型时,这种国家内部的"文明的冲突"(自身的传统文明与外来的西方文明的冲突,民族、种族和宗教信仰的冲突)始终是主旋律。如果它不能成功地建构自己的国家认同与文明认同,它极有可能沦为一个"自我撕裂的国家"。可以说,"文明认同"不仅是国家之间结盟或冲突的基本因素,而且也成为国家内部维持政治认同的基本因素。

　　亨廷顿在《变革社会中的政治秩序》(1968)中提出了非西方文明建构现代民族国家的过程中所面临的"政治秩序稳定性"的问题,而在"文明的冲突"的国际政治语境中,这个问题就成了一个国家如何既能维持文明自我更新的张力,同时又不被追求西方式的现代化目标自我撕裂的问题。在《文明的冲突》中亨廷顿分析了最自我撕裂的国家:诞生于奥斯曼帝国废墟之上走凯末尔主义"全盘西化"路线的土耳其。土耳其在欧盟成员、突厥语同盟和伊斯兰复兴这三个文明认同上难以做出明确的取舍,这个大半个世纪摇摆不定的国家一直无所适从。[①]土耳其的例子表明,一个非西方的文明在接受西方现代文明的目标时都不可避免地遭遇到自身内部的"文明的冲突",使得它在从文明转向现代民族国家的过程中经受自我撕裂的文明认同与政治认同的危机。

　　从西方现代民族国家形成的条件和过程来看,欧洲民族国家体系就是拉丁基督教文明与其他文明之间的"文明的冲突"的产物:"文明的冲突的

---

① Samuel Huntington, *The Clash of Civilizations and the Remaking of World Order*. London: Simon & Schuster Press, 1996. 亨廷顿,《文明的冲突与世界秩序的重建》(以下简称《文明的冲突》),周琪等译,新华出版社,2002 年,第 153 – 160 页。

模式提供了一种观察各种文明之间的关系以及这些关系是如何塑造国家
体制的机制。历次十字军战争的失败与拜占庭、伊斯兰中东世界、蒙古、及
伊斯兰奥斯曼帝国诸种文明对欧洲军事边界的逐步渗透相结合,导致欧洲
国家网状结构的内聚性爆裂。并且,这种情形又与正在进行的同伊斯兰奥
斯曼文明之间的战争相互作用,推动了宗教改革运动和宗教战争的发生,
摧毁了拉丁基督教世界。"①当欧洲成功地建立了民族国家体系和世界殖
民体系之后,"世界历史"出现了大分岔,中国开始在与西方的"文明的冲
突"中被纳入以西方文明为核心的世界体系之中。列文森说:"近代中国思
想史的大部分时期,是一个使'天下'成为'国家'的过程。"②

　　在非西方文明迫不得已的痛苦抉择和屈辱承受中,现代化国家建设全
面压抑甚至是摧毁了旧有文明,"文化虚无主义"和"全盘西化论"也一度甚
嚣尘上。然而,一旦当它恢复了自己的力量和意志时,它就会重新肯定自
己旧有的文明理想。亨廷顿揭示了"文明的冲突"的"主奴辩证法":非西方
文明在被西方文明摧毁的恐惧中获得自我保存的生存意识,经过漫长的西
方化的自我教化和重建使自身实力日益增长,直到足以抗衡西方现代文明
时,非西方文明开始得到机会重新伸张自己的文明的目标和模式,而国内
的西方外来文化与本土文化之间的力量对比也开始发生逆转。这就是当
今非西方国家广泛兴起的"本土化运动"和"宗教复兴运动"的实质。在中
国则是儒家文化民族主义的蓬勃兴起。这种"文明的冲突"的主奴辩证法
通常有两个不同的阶段。经历了"第一波现代化"的剧痛,由"第二代本土
化运动"所推动的"第二波现代化",开始颠倒"第一波现代化"过程中文明
力量的对比,"本土化运动"、"宗教复兴运动"或"文化保守主义"广泛兴
起,"文明认同"也从自我分裂、怀疑和苦恼日益转向强有力的自我肯定的
意志。民众在情绪上和利益上更倾向于"政治民族主义",而文化精英则倾
向于推动"文化民族主义"。无论精英,还是民众,对国家、文明传统、本土

---

　　①　维克多·李·伯克,《文明的冲突:战争与欧洲国家体制的形成》,王晋新译,上海三联书
店,2006 年,第 120 页。参见,吉登斯,《现代性的后果》,译林出版社,2000 年,第 152 页。
　　②　列文森,《儒教中国及其现代命运》,郑大华,任菁译,中国社会科学出版社,2000 年,第 87
页。参见,邹谠,《二十世纪中国政治:从宏观历史与微观层面看》,香港:牛津大学出版社,1994 年,
第 206 – 224 页。

文化和本土宗教的自觉意识和认同感开始日渐强烈。他们不再将"第一波现代化"的成功归结为西方化的成就,而是视为民族国家建设和旧有文明传统的凝聚力的结果;与之相反,现代化过程的巨大社会变革所造成的无家可归感、自我殖民的屈辱感、传统价值的沦丧以及道德秩序的失序,则归咎于西方化长久地割裂传统文化纽带的恶果。就此而言,"文明的冲突"学说不仅提供了当代非西方国家的"文明认同危机"的答案,而且也对日益多元化和分裂化的社会的整合提供了出路。

正如韦伯所说,西方现代化历程成功地实现了社会各个体系的分化,尤其是伦理的理性化和宗教信仰的私人化,建构了现代伦理秩序与政治制度之间相互制衡和互动的社会整合模式。而对于非西方文明的现代化转型而言,日益分化的利益政治和意识形态无力承担起整合社会的任务,而各种传统的社会整合机制和理念又早已被弃置。社会分化的程度愈加剧烈,不同社会阶级和阶层之间、不同地区之间、同一地区的不同单位之间的利益的差异、矛盾和冲突就越剧烈。一个社会在政治上越是加速民主化进程,对权威的颠覆性和社会离心化的倾向就越强,陷入社会混乱的可能性就越大。民主化不仅可能成为挑起地区矛盾、民族矛盾、阶级矛盾和文化矛盾的诱因,也可以成为国家和民族分裂的正当化理由。①在日益多元化的现代社会中,只有文明传统和文化价值能取代世俗化的意识形态或爱国主义以及宗教,安顿动荡社会的伦理和人心,并给消费社会意义失落的心灵以精神动力和精神关切,化解民主化的离心倾向,缓和贫富人群日益尖锐的阶级对抗与社会矛盾,加强受到侵蚀和威胁的政权合法性基础,提供跨越阶级、种族、宗教界限的团结纽带和共同情感,成为深入人心的凝聚性力量。一个没有文明认同的国家认同容易远离社会健康状态,仅靠"爱国主义"、"民族主义"、"保守主义"的政治动员难以维系长久稳固的政治认同。尤其是在"文明的冲突"的多元文明的世界秩序中,非西方文明彻底皈依西方文明或融入西方主流社会是不可能的,也是不必要的。且不说西方文明未必会接纳一个非西方文明的核心国家,即使牺牲自身的利益满足西

---

① 亨廷顿等,《民主的危机:就民主国家的统治能力写给三边委员会的报告》,马殿军,黄素娟,邓梅译,求实出版社,1989 年,第 54 页。

方文明的苛刻要求,恐怕也无法让西方人满意。"中学为体、西学为用"的旧原则表达了一个基本的理念,即非西方文明的现代化更多是"工具文化"层面上的西方化,至于古老文明千百年来形成的基本价值观念和情感方式,仍然是我们文明认同和文化归依的根。因此,"21世纪中国人必须树立的第一个新观念就是:中国的'历史文明'是中国'现代国家'的最大资源,而21世纪的中国能开创多大的格局,很大程度上将取决于中国人是否能自觉地把中国的'现代国家'置于中国源远流长的'历史文明'之源头活水中。"①21世纪的中国在其和平崛起之后,压抑一个半世纪之久的文明诉求会逐渐复苏,它不会长久满足于做一个西方式的民族国家,满足于国家的主权和富强的目标,会重新坚忍不拔地追求"文化中国"的文明理念。21世纪中国的"第二波现代化进程"的目标就在于,在政治理念、思想文化和人心人性三个层面上重建文明国家的基本价值体系,追求一个民主化的社会公正的现代社会,一个基于文明的伦理生活方式和文教传统的文明国家。

正是在这一新的世界历史语境中,我们从国际政治秩序、国家的政治认同和社会整合三个不同层面考察了亨廷顿的"文明的冲突"学说。在这三个层面上,"文明"都具有政治的含义,并且由于它是国家的一部分,因而在国际上它的非国家政治的部分则成为国家政治在国际中冲突或结盟的重要因素,其重要性已经完全取代了冷战时代的意识形态的地位。然而,按照通常的理解,文明或文化本身是"非冲突性"的,也就是"非政治性"的,因此,人们纷纷指责亨廷顿将非政治的"文明"的范畴转变政治的范畴。这些激烈的论战的混乱局面都没有试图在现代性的"民族国家与文明"问题上先将"文明"的复杂含义澄清。

亨廷顿未曾言明的"文明"概念指的是基于从自然状态中建立起来的主权国家之上的民族共同体或政治共同体的整体的生活方式。因而,现代世界的"文明"在本质上是基于民族国家的,因而,"文明的冲突"就基于民族国家之间的永恒冲突,这并不因为文明或文化本身的非政治性而有所减损。就文化民族主义作为民族国家的最高可能性而言,"文明"的确具有超越于民族国家的层面,但这一层面不能离开民族国家而独立存在。因此可

① 甘阳,"从'民族－国家'走向'文明－国家'",《书城》,2004年第2期。

以说,各种文明在这一层面上主要是"竞争性"的,但在其最基础的从属于民族国家的层面上基于永恒的"国家间无政府状态"则注定是相互"冲突性"。"文明冲突论"和"文明对话论"争论的要点端在于此。当然,即使就文明层面而论,无论是古典哲学(比如柏拉图的《理想国》373e,亚里士多德的《政治学》1333b8,希罗多德的《历史》,修昔底德的《战争史》),还是现代历史主义和文化哲学,也都有更充分的理由支持"文明的冲突"学说,即"不可能所有的国家都具有同一种文明(Nomos)"。它的另一种表述是:"政治共同体是一个相对封闭的社会,无限开放的世界国家即使不是不可能的,也绝对是不可欲的。"所谓的"全球文明"或"普世文明"的含混观念,不过就是"世界国家"的替代品。

现代"文明"概念诞生于主权国家的观念之中,后来又作为主权国家的"反概念"而存在。这种概念上的含混性是"文明"概念的思想谱系的复杂性决定的,它既包含着古典的内涵,又包含着完全现代的内容。在西方古典世界,希腊的城邦,罗马的帝国,基督教大一统的教会,都有其独特的人性概念、善好政制的观念以及教化的观念,这些观念构成了文艺复兴时期人文主义传统的文明或人文的观念。然而,真正现代的"文明"概念是由霍布斯奠基的。霍布斯第一个提出了"自然状态"的概念,并将"文明状态"与之相对。而文明状态就是摆脱了自然状态的主权国家。主权国家作为"文明状态"的政治形式,硬生生地切断了希腊罗马人文教化传统以及文艺复兴时期的人文主义者的"文明"理念。我们大致可以说,西方古今文明观念的断裂就发生在霍布斯为现代国家进行严密论证的时刻。[1]那些基于城邦之上的希腊教化的理念、基于共和和帝国之上的罗马人文主义的理念以及基于教会之上的基督教的文明理念,甚至是文艺复兴时期的人文主义者的"人文"的观念,在那一"霍布斯的时刻"都被基于主权国家的政治形式作为"文明状态"所取代。由此也开启了现代"民族国家与文明"之间持久的张力和困境。

霍布斯将主权国家与"文明状态"等同起来,因为没有主权国家的"自

---

① Leo Strauss. *Gesammelte Schriften*, Vol. 3: *Hobbes' politische Wissenschaft und zugehörige Schriften-Briefe*, edited by Heinrich Meier. Stuttgart: J. B. Metzler, 2001. S194 – 195.

然状态”就是“人对人是狼”的永久战争状态：“除了凭借自己和发明所提供的，人在没有其他保障情况下生活着，在这种条件下无从发展实业，因而由此获得的成果是不可靠的，因为地球上不存在文明，没有航运，也没有通过海运进口的商品；没有宽敞的楼群；没有移动和搬运沉重物品的工具；没有时间观念；没有艺术；没有通讯；没有社会，更糟糕的是，充满了持续不断的恐惧和暴死的危险；人活得孤独无依，贫困潦倒，污秽不堪，野蛮不化，人命短暂逝去。”①霍布斯将“文明状态”或“和平状态”的第一个产物称为“利维坦”。为什么霍布斯将主权国家的建立视为巨大的“文明”的成就，对此施米特解释说：“古典欧洲国家成功地实现某种完全难以置信的东西：在内部创造了和平，并且在法律概念上排除了敌人。它成功地消除了中世纪地方自卫的法律机制，结束了16、17世纪双方都自认为是正义的教派内战，并在国内创造了安宁、安全与秩序。众所周知，‘安宁、安全与秩序’的格言正是‘治安’的定义。在这种国家内部，实际上，只有‘治安’（Polizei），不再有‘政治’（Politik）；原因在于，宫廷阴谋、派系对抗、反对派斗争、反叛暴动，简言之即‘动乱’，都被看成是政治了。具有伟大意义的政治，崇高的政治，当时仅仅意味着‘国家间政治’。国家间政治的基础是一个主权国家承认其他与之相对的主权国家，承认它们为主权国家，并以此决断相互友好、敌对和中立。”②

“从公民社会到市民社会”，“从政治到治安”，这一过程在16、17世纪欧洲被视为真正的“文明”。在这一转变过程中，洛克为它提供了一个关键的要素，即文明状态应该包括私人财产权的保护，这是所谓“资本主义文明”用法的内涵，即市民社会的文明概念。当卢梭在霍布斯的主权概念之上发展出“人民主权”的概念时，民族作为历史形成的“同质性的人民”，就成为国家主权的真正实体和主体，于是，“民族国家”的观念在卢梭这里成熟了。经过赫尔德的民族主义和历史主义以及黑格尔的“市民社会与伦理国家的二分”，民族主义从此代表了主权国家的最高文明形式，这一观念在

---

① 霍布斯，《利维坦》，黎思复，黎延弼译，商务印书馆，1985年，第95页。

② 施米特，《政治的概念》，“1963年新版前言”，载于《施米特文集》第一卷，上海人民出版社，2004年，第91页。

纳粹德国时期达到前所未有的顶峰。在现代哲学最完备的知识体系中,康德将人类各个领域按照各自的先天原则分化并固定下来,于是,文明或文化一方面在狭义上作为一个相对独立的社会领域而存在(比如"文化"不同于"科学"),另一方面,又在广义上作为社会各个领域的总和而存在(比如,也有"科学的文化")。由此,我们就会看到,一方面,按照康德或新康德主义,文明作为社会各个领域的总和是非政治的,尤其在所谓的"文化"和知识领域中,文明是非政治性的;但是,另一方面,按照黑格尔的《法哲学原理》和《历史哲学》中的思想,文明作为高于市民社会的"伦理国家",不仅是政治性的,而且还具有世界历史的意义。那种认为"文明"概念代表了独立的"价值领域",因而是非政治的新康德主义观念,只是一种韦伯所说的"理想类型",而不是社会实在和历史现实。那些"文明对话论"或"文明和平论"与亨廷顿的"文明的冲突"学说之间的论战,在政治哲学的根本上再现了康德与黑格尔之争。显然,黑格尔对康德的批判在很大程度上会支持亨廷顿的观点。

因此,"民族国家与文明"真正的问题是,"民族国家"与"文明"唇齿相依,从其现代概念诞生之日起,"文明"就基于主权国家而存在,主权国家最低的目标或存在的理由是自我保存,其最高的目标或存在的目的则是追求"文明"。"文明"为民族国家提供其存在的目的,民族国家为"文明"提供生存的空间、民族的基础和国家的保障。在"文明的冲突"的新世界历史的语境中,"民族国家"与"文明"问题对我们来说恐怕是这样一个问题:在我们长达一百五十年对西方现代民族国家目标的追求中,我们是否依然珍视并坚持追求我们自己的"文明"的目标? 在 21 世纪头一个十年过去之后人们还禁不住会进一步追问,西方基督教文明的世俗化形式的自由民主制是否已经耗尽了西方现代性的全部可能性,进而西方文明(无论是希腊的、罗马的、基督教的,还是英国的、德国的、美国的)是否已经不再能为人类提供别的新的文明的可能性?

西学视野下儒学现代转型
应有的几个维度

孙向晨

现代社会有其自身的结构,在经历了几百年的发展之后,在全球范围形成了它的压力;任何一个后发现代化国家在因应现代社会时,其传统价值形态都会与现代社会形成了某种紧张,甚而对社会造成极大的扭曲,产生灾难性的后果。

要建立适应现代社会的价值形态,首先要确立现代社会最基本的价值事实是什么? 笔者以为这个核心的价值事实乃是个体主义。[①]当然这并非笔者一己之妄见,有许多学者对此有过论证,在此就不一一引证了。[②] 笔者着意的是"个体主义"在现代中国曲折而复杂的经历,这从某种角度折射出现代中国的价值进程。事实上,只有当社会生活本身日益以个体为本位,只有当个体结束其自然性的意涵,[③] 在现代的社会、政治、经济、法律各层面都取得其独立地位时,我们才有可能真正理解作为现代性价值形态的个体主义及其积极和消极的作用。也只有在这个基础上,我们才能来理解基

---

① 此处的个体主义,主要是指西方 17 世纪以来发展出来的一种思想,其基本意涵与西方中世纪的社会、政治、经济制度的消解有关,强调个体的自主,以及从严格等级化的社会制度中解放出来的意义。在现代汉语中,individualism,或译为个人主义,但由于在一段时间内,个人主义带有强烈的贬义色彩,无助于我们正确理解 individualism 在现代社会中的客观作用,故译为个体主义。

② 如查尔斯·泰勒的《现代性的隐忧》;安东尼·吉登斯的《现代性的后果》;路易·迪蒙的《论个体主义》;史蒂文·卢克斯的《个人主义》等。

③ 个体的自然性的意涵和政治性的意涵,参见科耶夫《黑格尔导读》,译林出版社,2005 年。

督教因应现代价值形态或者说其现代转型的基本特点，以及儒家思想如果想在现代社会建立其有效的价值形态所应有的变革。

一、个体主义的积极价值

现代性价值的基础性结构就是对个体本位的强调，黑格尔的哲学中，他赋予"个体"以极高的价值，它是普遍性和特殊性相结合的一个"范畴"，它是"自由"的承载者，它是现代世界价值观的体现者。马克思亦深受黑格尔的影响，个体自由也是共产主义实现的先决条件。在古典世界的意义上，人们总是把个人看作整体中的一员，一如个人之于古希腊的城邦；或将人看成宏观秩序中的一个环节，在中世纪，则把人看作是以上帝为中心的基督教共同体中的一员。在中国的传统中，个人则是整个家族中的一员，以家族的荣耀和延续为己任。这里只有整体的自由，只有城邦的自由，只有家族的自由，没有现代个体意义上的自由。在西方，个体意识的逐步觉醒开始于文艺复兴，借助于对古典文献和艺术的复兴，个体逐渐从当时各种外在和内在的束缚中解放出来，中间经过宗教改革，直到十八世纪启蒙运动，基本完成了现代个体主义的内涵，个体逐步取代上帝而成为世界的主人。这中间尤其以霍布斯、洛克以及后来功利主义发展出来的个体主义最为重要，其在现代社会中占据着主流地位，[1]用麦克弗森(Macpherson)的话说，那是一种"占有性的个体主义"。[2]这种个体主义影响极大，奠定了现代社会的价值基础；同时消极因素亦不小，需要不断警醒和防范。现代意义上"个体"的诞生从某种意义上可以说是现代世界与传统社会断裂的一个基本标志。黑格尔是这么看的，按法国哲学家埃利·阿莱维(Elie Halevy)的说法："在整个现代欧洲，事实是，个体已经以他们的自主意识为先决条件的，每个人都在要求得到所有其他人的尊重，认为其他人都是自己的同伴或平等者；在社会上表现为，也许是越来越表现为，产生于构成社

---

① 个体主义具有多种形态，参见 Steven Lukes，*Individualism*，Basil Blackweil，1979。

② C. B. Macpherson，*Political Theory of Possessive Individualism*，Oxford University Press，1962.

会的个体的自觉意志。个体主义学说的出现和成功本身就足以表明,在西方社会,个体主义是一种真正的哲学。个体主义是罗马法和基督教伦理的共同特征。正是个体主义,使得在其他方面大相径庭的卢梭、康德和边沁的哲学之间具有了相似性。"[①] 事实上不仅现代欧洲如此,整个现代世界都是以这种个体的自觉作为先决条件的,这在中国的现代进程中也已经得到了佐证,也就是黑格尔所谓的每个人"自由"的历史目的。

尽管埃利·阿莱维指出,个体是罗马法和基督教伦理的共同特征,但却如黑格尔所言,在罗马法和基督教伦理中,个体呈现的只是它的理念形态,还没有真正形成它当下的现实力量。这种现实力量来自于近代经济上的一种新的形态——即现代的市场经济。这种以个体主义为基础的现代经济在亚当·斯密那里得到了最初的总结,现代经济制度的核心理念——私有财产、劳动、商品交换、市场经济、自由竞争都是以个体为其先决条件的,以至于哈耶克以《个体主义与经济秩序》为题,立场鲜明地以个体主义为基础为现代市场经济张目。显然,那种潜藏在罗马法和基督教伦理中的个体理念,只有在现代经济活动中,才生机勃勃地找到了它真正的载体。[②]

一旦个体的理念在现实中找到了自己的肉身,找到了自己的具体存在,个体立刻在政治上提出了它自己的要求。在政治上,个体主义成为反对君权神授和反对父权制的利器,这大致可以在霍布斯的《利维坦》和洛克的《政府论》中看到。此外,法国大革命和美国独立战争也都是以天赋个体的人权作为口号,来奠定其公民在现代社会的政治权利基础。我们看到从霍布斯到卢梭,从康德到边沁,尽管各自学说的差异很大,但都是以个体主义来阐释政治哲学问题的。他们的一个共同立场就是批判古典政治哲学中不平等的观念,尤其是在柏拉图和亚里士多德的政治哲学那里的"不平等"观念,明确个体之间的平等是现代政治哲学的共同起点,从而明确自由乃是每个人的自由。个体主义的理想只有在现代国家中才可以得到实现,作为"利维坦"的现代国家通过霍布斯式的契约,把公民的普遍性和个别性结合起来。现代国家代表着普遍性,同时又以承认个别性的人为前提。作

---

① 转引自 Steven Lukes, *Individualism*, Basil Blackweil, 1979, pviiii.
② 参见,拙文"基督教与现代性:科耶夫对黑格尔的解读",香港,《道风》2002 年第 17 期。

为公民的个人,他既有自然性,又有政治性,自然性是其个别性,而政治性则带有普遍性。两者的结合在黑格尔眼中就是"个体"的真正实现,公民间的权利得到平等承认,个体的独特性受到尊重,人性得到真正的满足。

二、个体主义的消极后果

个体主义尽管在历史上起到巨大的解放作用,对于确立个体在现代社会的价值,对于确立现代的政治、经济、法律、宗教体系有着很大的贡献。但是在个体主义中,就其基本内涵而言不可避免地包涵着严重的后果,那就是个体主义在道德上有自私的倾向,在价值上有虚无的倾向,在文化上有相对主义的倾向,在群体认同上有趋于消解的倾向。这一切对于现代社会中的道德认同、价值认同、文化认同、民族认同、国家认同,也就是说,对于社会的凝聚力,对于社会的和谐发展,对于社会的发展目标都构成了极大的挑战。

从个体主义的起源上看,在历史上个体主义理论的起源与个体的自我保存倾向密切相连。在霍布斯和洛克那里,个体主义都是以保护自己的生命,保护自己的财产为起点的,近代个体主义的兴起以自我利益为基础,以保全生命和财产为目的,并在此基础上结成社会。卢梭最早对这类个体主义进行了批判,他认为这种个体主义追求的只是幸福的条件,反而把幸福本身给遗忘了。而现代美国哲学家艾伦·布卢姆(Allen Bloom)则直接称这种个体主义是一种"活命的哲学"。[①] 这种"活命哲学"逐渐取代了英雄主义,取代了崇高价值,成为了受人推崇的生活准则。由此这种个体主义包含的某种侵犯性的因素也逐步释放出来,自我利益的追逐则必定导致竞争以及冲突。

从道德领域看,个体主义的一个直接后果就是"道德评价的私人化"倾向。英国哲学家休谟在十八世纪个体主义诞生之初就已经看到,人们赋予个体的诸多价值都是虚妄的,个体最根本的价值标准就是情感的主观好

---

① 布鲁姆:《走向封闭的美国精神》,中国社会科学出版社,1994年。

恶。因此传统道德那种超越个体的道德标准就被转化为个体的喜好问题，还原为情感的偏好问题。道德所依存的共同体，在这里没有丝毫的价值，道德也就不再有共同的标准可言。由此，个体主义在道德问题上采取了去道德主义。这种倾向对于现代社会中任何超出个体范畴的价值目标都是一种消解。

从价值评价上看，个体主义认为，基于对于其他个体的尊重，每一个人都不应该去挑战另一个人的喜好标准。启蒙运动在尊重个人权利，倡导相互尊重、相互宽容的同时，也埋下了价值相对主义的严重后果。因此从道德评价的私人化倾向必然走向价值的相对主义，从而抹杀文化的进步性。价值相对主义强调价值观念的主观性，漠视道德真理，对自我之外的任何重大价值采取漠然置之的态度，对于自我本身则采取了放任主义，人生的全部意义固限于自身。这在西方二十世纪六十年代以后的精神蜕变中表现得最为明显，这种生活态度在中国新一代年轻人中也已经变得非常流行，在生活的价值层面上除了物质化的诱惑外，完全失去了判断的标准和方向。这是非常值得人们警惕的个体主义思潮的恶性后果。

从社群的角度看，除了个体主义带来的放纵感外，个体主义还会进一步导致社群价值的虚无感，过度强调个体会使个体从一切形式的社群中剥离出来，从而削弱社会和集团对个体的控制。由此，个体虽然换来了自由，却失去了安全感，成为现代社会中典型的孤独人和陌生人。这严重动摇了个体对于群体的依赖，以及在群体中寻求安慰的能力。因此，个体主义的一个极大危害在于它对于集体主义、民族认同、社群价值的解构。我们知道，个体主义以个体自由为本位，核心价值是个体权利，无论是集体主义还是民族认同，都是以群体的价值为归属，以集体精神和民族精神为倚靠，因此两者之间不可避免地会有很大的冲突。那么，以个体利益为基础的个体主义如何可能支撑起整个集体、社群和民族的价值观念呢？如何能够形成一个命运共同体呢？因此，任何一种适应现代社会的价值形态，一定要有某种东西可以制衡单纯个体利益的泛滥，一定要在个体主义中找到某种东西来支撑普遍价值，这是现代社会面临的最大挑战。

三、基督教因应现代社会的三个基本维度

面对个体主义在现代社会中的两重性,或者说面对现代价值形态的两重性,我们必须找到一种主流的社会价值体系,它既能肯定个体主义的积极方面,又能抵制个体主义的消极方面。在这方面西方近代的新教改革给人以很大的启发。这一精神转型远远超出了宗教范畴,在社会生活的各个方面起着作用。借助于改革后的基督教,个体主义也不再仅仅是理论的、观念的,它被制度化法律化,深入到社会生活的内部,成为一种生活方式,牢牢地扎根在现代社会中。同时基督教的个体本位、社群认同以及普世价值使它很好地因应了现代社会的特点。

1. 确立个体本位

正如我们在前面已经看到,现代社会在政治、经济、法律、道德等多个层面确立了个体主义,它们对于保障现代社会的顺利运作是非常有效的,这是现代社会和谐运作的一个基础。所以在对待个体主义这个问题上,我们必须首先在制度层面上保障每个人的权利,凸现每一个人的价值,这是社会进步的主要标志之一,这也是社会具有创造力和创新能力的基本保障。否认这一点在政治上无疑是倒退的。在这方面,基督教的改革自觉地做了调整,尽管我们可以从《圣经》中找到个体主义的思想渊源,在《圣经》中早已有在上帝面前人人都是罪人的这种平等观念;耶稣也号召门徒抛开家庭和人际的纠缠跟随他去传布福音,从理念上凸现了个人的价值,可以说基督教已经有了这种消除社会等级以及家族对个人束缚的思想传统。但在中世纪,基督徒必须依靠教会作为他和上帝之间不可缺少的中介者,教会置于个人之上,因此基督教《圣经》中隐含着的个体主义在现实中并没有机会完全实现出来,甚至像霍布斯这些近代思想家都认为基督教在中世纪是罗马帝国的翻版,是一个黑暗王国。自马丁·路德以后,"因信称义"成为基督教的首要教义,个体的称义和拯救不再依靠教会,圣经的理解不再依靠神父的中介,良知判断的自主地位得到了前所未有的确认,拯救成

了个人的追求,信仰成为个体和上帝之间的私人事务。原本等级化、组织化、教条化的宗教被个体化、私人化、信仰化了。关于这一点,特勒尔奇和韦伯都对此做了大量的论证,特勒尔奇说:"个体主义的真正的持久获得,要归功于宗教,而不是世俗的运动,要归功宗教改革,而不是文艺复兴。"① 韦伯的新教伦理更是我们所熟悉的。因此我们看到作为承载着价值体系的基督教,尽管坚持个体本位的要求是出于宗教内部改革的需要,但它同时却非常好地适应现代社会的个体转向。这意味着,在基督教中所承载的价值体系不会因为现代社会的个体主义的冲击而丧失殆尽,反而给现代社会中孤独的个体带来心灵的慰藉。

2. 强调社群认同

诚如我们在前面指出的,个体主义在现代社会的负面影响是毋庸置疑的,托克维尔在观察早期的美国社会时,就已经注意到这个问题了。他说:"个人主义是一种只顾自己而又心安理得的情感,它使每个公民同其同胞大众隔离,同亲属和朋友疏远。……利己主义可使一切美德的幼芽枯死,而个人主义首先会使公德的源泉干涸。但是,久而久之,个人主义也会打击和破坏其他一切美德,最后沦为利己主义。"② 但同样是在美国,托克维尔也发现了抵制个体主义消极后果的有效途径,那就是自由结成的社群,早年是清教的宗教团体,后来是各种公民团体,以及最终是对美利坚合众国的认同。我们知道,宗教从来不是单纯个体的活动,改革后的基督教也不是一个完全个体化的宗教,在基督徒的生活中,一直有着强烈的社群主义传统。在这一点上,基督教的改革也为人们提供了范例。尽管新教徒摆脱了天主教式教会的束缚,经过宗教改革后的教会,神职人员已经失去了在中世纪教会中神父的职权,每一个基督教徒都具有平等地获得拯救的可能性,神职人员不再具有特殊地位。但基督徒的团契生活和教会的社群生活从来没有消失过,反而得到了加强,并形成了新的形态。即它更明确地

---

① Ernst Troeltsch, The Social Teaching of Christian Churches, George Allen & Unwin LTD, 1949, Vol. I, p. 328.

② Alexis de Tocqueville, *Democracy in America*, Alfred A. Knopf Inc. 1976, Vol. II, p. 98.

是在个体主义基础上建构起来的共同体生活。原本作为拯救机构的宗教共同体成了个体自愿结合的团契。这样在确保个体本位的前提下,通过人们自觉自愿地联合起来,在社群中培养归属感,在社群中寻找慰藉,有效地抵制了消极的个体主义泛滥。因此,基督教既为现代性的个体主义提供一种终极基础,避免使自己成为与现代社会相对峙和格格不入的力量;同时又是一种整合个体的社群力量。这为现代社会中的"陌生者"、孤独者提供了精神的和现实的家园。任何一种适应现代社会的价值体系如果想站得住脚则必须提供真正的社群生活。

3.普遍主义的价值追求

个体主义的两重性就在于一方面现代社会是以个体主义作为价值基础的,在经济、政治、法律、宗教等各方面以个体主义作为其延展的基础;另一方面,个体主义由于其内在的自我中心以及孤立主义的倾向,势必对维系整个社会的价值造成冲击。宗教改革在强调拯救的个体性之后,不忘强调社群的重要作用,较好地解决了个体主义两重性的冲突,同时,基督教由于信仰上帝的普世性,因此尽管得救的是个体,其价值观念却是普遍的,被认为应该是整个人类共享的。这在精神层面解决了个体主义的孤立性问题,破解了单纯社群的狭隘性,为人类的发展提供了方向,提供了动力。这就是基督教为人类生活提供的一种超越的维度和普遍主义的价值追求。

就基督徒而言,基督教提供的价值观超越了单纯的民族、文化的因素而具有普遍性,在精神层面为人类提供了一种普遍追求的价值。当然不是基督徒,就不会认同基督教的教义,不会信仰这一切,也不认同它的普世价值。但是,从基督教在现代社会的成功经验来看,它给人的启示是,必须要有某种超越民族、超越社群的普世向度,才能破解某种狭隘性,同时避免相对主义和虚无主义的产生,给社会价值以行动的力量,从而起到凝聚人心的作用。所以,我们要注意到普遍主义的价值追求,是一个意识的形态,而非现实的实现。尽管没有实现出来,但必须有这个维度。这方面基督教又为我们提供了一个成功的范例,美国早年的"公民宗教"也从中借鉴很多。托克维尔在对美国的观察中同样看到了这一方面:"设若一个社会的政治纽带变得松弛,而道德纽带却未得到加强,这个社会怎能不崩溃?假如一个民族不服从上帝,这个民族如何掌握自己的命运?"① 这里托克维尔通过"上帝"这个概念来理解美国建国之初那些价值观念普遍性的基础,他说,"如果没有共同观念,就不会有共同的行动,没有共同的行动,即便人仍然存在,但社会肌体已经不在。因此,一个社会的建立并走向繁荣,有必要通过某些主导观念将所有公民的心智团结一致;而要做到这一点,只有每个人的意见发端于同一个源头,每个人都同意接受某些现成的信仰。"② 从《独立宣言》到美国宪法,美国的立国者们通过赋予这个国家某种普遍性的特质,从而确立其在整个人类历史上的地位:即这是人类的一个"新"世界,这是一个使自由重生的新天新地,由此美国人把立国的信念与他认为的人类普遍信念完全一致起来,从而形成他的气度和眼界。美国的爱国主义在于它强调的不仅仅是美利坚合众国这个单纯的国家,它赋予这个国度以普遍的意义,即这是一个保有人类普遍价值的国度,爱美国于是演变成了捍卫人类的普世价值,这就是美国人的信仰。这确保了美国人具有超越单纯个体主义和民族主义的某种世界观,可以激发出他们超越个体而为普世价值献身的热情。

四、儒家现代转型的三个维度

无论是欧洲进入现代社会时所经历的宗教改革,还是美国立国时期所宣扬和追求的普世价值,我们看到,从这些传统文化共同体中生长出来的价值体系,在因应现代个体主义观念时,都有了某种转型。笔者将其概括为个体本位、社群认同以及普世价值这三个维度。当前中国社会正处于大规模的社会转型时期,应该对这个问题有充分的自觉意识,彻底梳理个体主义的精神脉络,在传统思想中寻找因应现代价值体系的资源,以实现传统价值观的现代转型。面对个体主义的现实,现代社会在应该支持个体权利的地方,不应该有丝毫的犹豫,这是现代文明的基础。另一方面,不能片

---

① Alexis de Tocqueville, *Democracy in America*, Vol. II, p. 8.

② Alexis de Tocqueville, *Democracy in America*, Vol. II, p. 8.

面地理解社会现实与价值体系之间的关系,价值体系对于社会现实并非一味的支持,一味地顺应。当追求个体利益成为社会的主流现实时,价值体系应该对此有所制约,对于个体主义的消极影响不能束手无策,无所约束,而是应该积极建立适合中国人自己的社会价值体系。在这方面,除非从中国人自己生活的传统价值思想中寻找资源外,别无他法。一种大的文明体具有某种整全性,在产生问题的同时往往包含了治愈它的药方,轻易地舍弃是一种妄自菲薄。我们必须看到,社会价值体系事实上不单是一套理论体系,它必须活生生地存在于每一个人的思想意识中,在人类历史上,在各大文明体系中还很少能有完全移植另一套价值体系而获得成功的先例。由此,因应现代个体主义的挑战,并没有现成的道路,每一个社会都应该运用自己的传统文化资源来对付这种挑战。基督教改革是一条路,美国早期的"公民宗教"是一条路,中国的儒家能否担当起这种角色,则还是一个未知数。但无论如何,上文中提到的三个维度却是应该予以重视的。

首先,儒家在进入现代社会后,始终没有经历过像基督教宗教改革这样的现代转型,也没有像美国"公民宗教"这样建立起一套国家的信念体系。我们知道中世纪的天主教更多体现的是一种共同体原则,是整体先于个体的;这与儒家所强调的家族先于个体,在结构上是类似的。但基督教经过宗教改革以后很好地完成了自己的转型,确立了个体本位。而儒家在这方面始终没有明确的转型。现代新儒家的发展,试图在儒家的思想资源中找到某种应和现代价值形态的东西,以牟宗三为例,他在儒家的性心学中,找到了与康德思想相契合的要素。这非常好地体现了儒家思想在现代社会中寻求发展和转型的特点。但是,我们应该看到,在新儒家的思想发展中,关于个体的论述还有很多问题,其一,心性问题立足于良知而没有全面阐述个体权利的捍卫,其二,新儒家的努力充其量只停留在理论层面上,这与作为活生生的基督教的现实改革不可同日而语。个体主义在西方已经有了很长的发展阶段,它的积极因素和消极因素都有了充分的展现,说儒家现在就可以超越个体主义,还言之过早。但儒家必须放下身段,看清现代社会这个现实,从而不仅仅是停留在理论上,而且能够现实地体现出对于个体本位的尊重,并在这个前提下提出超越个体主义的方向。但儒家迟迟未能做到这一点,既有其理论上的障碍,个体本位与亲亲本位在理论上还没有得到疏解;同时这种困难也同中国的现实发展有很大关联。一方面,49 年以后个体主义作为负面的价值在中国的现实中始终没有获得过应有的地位,个体从未在理论上给予明确的论证,在制度上给予明确的保障。这一步在现实中才刚刚开始起步。个体主义在现代社会的存在中不仅作为一个价值事实,而且也作为一种健康的自觉的价值观念存在,这在中国显然还需要一个漫长的过程。另一方面,儒家在现代中国丧失了其现实存在的土壤,科举的终结、私塾的消散、家族的凋零、乡村社会的瓦解,于是,即便儒家在理论形态上处理好了其与现代社会中个体主义的关系,但在现实中却还远没有找到其落实的途径。这是儒家现代转型中最为根本的问题,否则一切都只能流于理论上的空谈,它对于现实始终不具有教化作用。所以,儒家对于个体本位的确立具有双重的尴尬,一是要在理论上梳理清楚其与个体主义的关系;二是要以此重新在现实中找到自己的位置,而这理论与实践的双重任务无疑是儒家现代转型所必须面对的。

其次,在社会－价值层面,应该鼓励基于个体自由的社群观念,从而使人有极大的归属感,使各种道德规范有落实的空间。马克思在批判近代思想时就指出,单纯的个体获得的自由只是抽象的,当那人想要获得真正的自由时,那人只有"在真实的集体条件下,各个个人在自己的联合中并通过这种联合获得自由"。① 此话显然也能得到现代社群主义的认同。从中国文化自身来看,我们也可以找到对社群的独到理解。余英时先生在"从价值系统看中国文化的现代意义"一文中 ②谈到,儒家的道德观必须在人伦秩序之中才得以实现,这既不同于个体主义,也不同于现代群体主义,而是强烈的人伦关系,这也是儒家固有的强调"亲亲"的思想。确实,中国文化非常强调伦常关系,如君臣、父子、夫妇等关系,从中也可以延伸出一种中国式的社群关系,如家族关系、乡里关系等。任何一种现代社会的主流价值体系都不是在与传统的决裂中诞生的,而是很好地整合了传统的资源。作为现代社会排头兵的英国,从来就是一个善于妥协的国家,在其现代化的过程中,最大程度保留了传统的势力和资源,这在英国的习惯法,在英国

---

① 《马克思恩格斯选集》第 1 卷,第 82 页。
② 余英时,《文史传统与文化重建》三联书店,2004 年,第 442 – 492 页。

的君主制,在英国的圣公会中都能看到。这一切并不妨碍英国是近代最早的个体主义学说诞生地。儒家的社群关怀,必须经过某种转化,成为现时代予以认同的价值体系,伦常关系并不一定被排斥在现代社会之外,而应该再次成为现代道德的基础。在强调现代社会个体本位的同时,丝毫不需要拒斥传统的价值观念,这是幼稚的自由主义者们常常看不到的。在现代西方社会中,保守主义对于家庭价值观就非常重视,而这种保守主义并不排斥现代政治以个体权利为基础的建构。现代儒家思想也可以从中获得启示。这就是为什么丹尼尔·贝尔说,他在政治上是自由主义者,但在文化上是保守主义者。从经济基础决定上层建筑的思路来看,这似乎是很矛盾的。经济的自由主义似乎决定了政治上的自由主义和文化上的自由主义;但这是非常要不得的简单化的思想。事实上,社会的稳定态与其说用"决定""被决定"的模式来解说,不如以诸因素互补的结构来界定更为恰当。政治上的自由主义意味着对于个体本位的认可,而文化上的保守主义,这意味着在价值上反对单纯的个体主义和自由主义,而保有传统的价值。在这个意义上儒家和政治自由主义是可以相结合的。无需硬生生地捏造出儒家自由主义;在政治上以个体为本位的自由主义,应该为儒家的价值形态保有存在的空间,而在社会文化和价值等实质性的道德和教化层面上儒家应该扮演更为积极的角色。也就是说,在现代个体主义搭建的政治舞台上,儒家的价值观应该扮演主要角色。尽管舞台上可以有各种角色,但在中国文化这个大环境中儒家仍应该是一个主角,这将充分制约个体主义滋养的各种消极势力。

对儒家的提倡似乎难逃文化保守主义的标签。但这种文化上的保守主义要在现代社会成立,必定需要经过某种现代性的"转型",也就是说,它应该是一种基于自由主义底线之上的保守主义,而不是消除一切异己的保守主义。一种极端的保守主义,由于其反民主的倾向,以及其与其他极端主义,甚至是专制主义之间的暗中联系,很容易为现代社会所唾弃。因此,与其在政治上强调保守主义,不如在文化上强调保守主义;政治上的保守主义非常容易转化成专制主义;儒家要复兴,更多的应该着眼于文化上的复兴,在价值体系层面的复兴,在社会层面而不是政治层面找到儒家复兴的落脚点。所以,本文既强调现代价值形态必须以个体为本位,必须与自由主义共享对于宽容精神的倡导。又倡导对自由主义的限制,强调基于传统价值的社群认同。在这些概念的背后是政治自由主义和文化保守主义的结合。

最后,在近代化的过程中,由于西方强势文化的压迫,以及船坚炮利的入侵,儒家固有的"天下"观念,在近代逐渐被压缩成一个民族国家的概念,这在康有为、梁启超等人的著作中看得尤为分明,这是一个巨大的文化转化,而且是一种被迫的转化,一种宏大的胸怀被迫转化为狭窄的民族意识。虽然这种转化以成为现代世界体系,或者说现代民族国家体系中的一员为使命。但就文化和社会价值体系层面而言,这对于以儒家文化为代表的中国文化的自信心是一次极大的打击。于是后世就有了"中国特色和普遍规律相结合"以及"与国际接轨"之类的说法,这在制度层面固然有其合理性,但是在文化的核心价值层面上则完全处于一种弱势的心态。在不同时代,说法上虽然不同但折射的心态却大抵是相同的,那就是对于自身文化的一种自卑,对于强势文化的认同,所整合出来的无非是较西方世界次一等级的东西,而"中国特色"则常常沦为一种借口。事实上,在现代社会,一种文化只有以人类的命运为己任,以"天下"苍生为己任,这个文化才有自我超越的能力,才有发展的动力。

此外,强调"天下为怀"是为了破解保守主义和社群认同的狭隘性,同时强调文化的动力和眼界。时下关于儒家的"天下"意识如何转化为民族意识的论文已有不少①。而本文意在其"反向转化",也就是将压缩为民族意识的儒家文化重新还原其本来面目,还原其"天下"意识;从外在的原因来看,其主要针对的是基督教的普世性,以及美国所口口声声的"普世价值"。这里要注意的是,强调儒家的"天下"意识并不是要像西方人那样要强力输出价值形态;更多的是着眼于一种文化发展的根本动力,当一种文化只是局限于自身民族的复兴时,它的眼光是局促的,是排外的;目标是有限的,动力是不足的。儒家的文化理论在历史上从来不是一种种族理论,

---

① 比如复旦大学历史系姚大力先生的文章,"'天下兴亡,匹夫有责'的再诠释与中国近代民族国家意识的生成",《世界经济与政治》2006年第10期;北京大学哲学系吴增定先生的文章"从'国家'重返'天下':中国古代天下观的当代意义"《文明的和解——中国和平崛起以后的世界》,人民出版社2005.11。类似的文章还有不少,在此就不具体展开了。

甚至也不是一种民族理论。中国古代的"华夷之辨"更多的是一种文化理论,甚至"中国"这个概念也不是一个地域称谓,更是一种文化称谓。儒家文化要复兴首先就要还原其本来的意识目标。在儒家的复兴中应该恢复传统所固有的"天下"观,适时地提出儒家的天下关怀。所以,对于中国学人而言不仅要有继往圣绝学的担当,更要有为天地立心,为万世开太平的境界。一个国家的"软实力"必须是内在的,必须是活生生的,单纯的爱国精神是有限的,被动的,而且非常容易陷入狭隘的民族主义的陷阱,因此必须把爱国主义、民族精神和人类的命运结合起来,才能真正发展出国家的"软实力",其所激发起来的热情也必将超越狭隘性,而凝聚为社会发展的真实动力。

第三部分

◎ 全球化时代的宗教对话

评多元论和排斥论

赵敦华

在宗教间对话（inter-faith dialogue）有无对话可能性的问题上，现在有三种立场：排斥论（exclusivism），包容论（inclusivism）和多元论（pluralism）。排斥论认为只有一种宗教是真宗教，其余都应被排斥在真宗教之外；排斥论否认不同宗教对话的可能性。包容论亦认为只有一种宗教是真宗教，但同时认为其余宗教是真宗教的部分表现，因此应被包容在真宗教之中；包容论为了发展自己的目的而与其他宗教对话，其代表人物是天主教神学家拉纳（K. Rahner）。宗教多元论则认为各种宗教都以共同的神性为基础，应在此基础上进行求同存异的对话，达到共存的目的。宗教多元论体现了宗教宽容和文化多元的时代精神，它的代表人物众多，如希克（John Hick）、史密斯（Wilfred Cantwell Smith）、孔汉思（Hans Küng）等人的著作被翻译成多种文字，为许多宗教信徒和宗教学学者所接受。

对于宗教对话的规则，早在 1983 年，美国神学家斯威德勒（Leonard Swidler）就公布了"跨宗教、跨意识形态对话的十项准则"（ Journal of Ecumenical Studies，1983）如下：

"第一项准则：跨宗教、跨意识形态对话的首要目的是学习，即，改变和增加对现实的看法和理解，并采取相应的行动。

第二条准则：跨宗教、跨意识形态对话必须做两方面的工作，即在各个宗教或意识形态团体内部，以及在宗教或意识形态团体之间同时进行。

第三条准则：对话的每一个参与者必须是完全真诚的。

第四条准则：在跨宗教、跨意识形态对话中，一方不要用自己的理想与对方的实践相比较，而用自己的理想与对方的理想相比较，用自己的实践与对方的实践相比较。

第五条准则：每一个参与者必须自我界定。比如，犹太人从内部界定犹太人意味着什么，其他人只能从外部描述他像什么。

第六条准则：每一个对话的参与者对不同点不可固执己见。

第七条准则：对话只能在平等者之间进行，用梵二大公会的话说，这是 par cum pari（以平等对平等）。

第八条准则：对话只能在相互信任的基础上进行。

第九条准则：参加跨宗教、跨意识形态对话的人对自己以及自己所属的宗教或意识形态传统至少应有最低限度的自我批评。

第十条准则：每一个参与者最终要试图从内部去体验对方的宗教或意识形态。"

这十条可以说是关于对话的伦理规则。孔汉思和斯威德勒一起，由宗教多元论和普世宗教发展出全球伦理。可以说，全球伦理也是对话的伦理，以上十条也是全球伦理的准则。

排斥论过去孤独寂寥，除巴特（Karl Barth）的教义学有所涉及，并无专门理论著作。但现在，排斥论开始兴起。A. Torrance 在"Religious Studies or Studying Religion：150th Anniversary Celebrations"，Plantinga 在"A Defense of Religious Exclusivism"（见《基督教信念的知识论地位》第 482 – 503 页）反驳了多元论，为排他论进行理论辩护。简单地说，他们的理由是：基督徒有权坚持自身的信念（belief）为真，而把其他信念斥之为假；这是知识论的权利，而不涉及信仰自由的公民权利；真理（大写的真理）观上的排他主义与政治上的宗教宽容无关；进一步说，排斥错误不是不宽容，不是压迫，而是把相信错误的人从错误的压迫下解放出来，是对真理的皈依。

确切地说，A. 托伦斯和普兰廷格所谓的宗教排他主义实际上是"基督教排他主义"。如普兰廷格所说，排他主义的意思是，凡是与基督教的基本信仰不相符合的信念(不管是个人的,还是哲学的)都是错误的。他把基督教的基本信仰界定为两条;(1)世界是一个全能、全知、全善的上帝创造的,这个上帝是有人格的存在,有目的、有计划、有意图,并能够为完成这些目的而行动;(2)人类需要拯救,上帝通过他的圣子的肉身化、生活、牺牲和升天,提供了拯救的唯一道路。无神论否认这两条,基督教以外的其他宗教否认第二条,按照排他主义的观点,它们都是错误的。

A.托伦斯说,排他主义是唯一正确的选择,因为除此以外的立场都是不可能的。在信仰的是非优劣问题上,除了排他主义外,还有多元主义(彼此不相符合的信仰可以作为独立并行的真理而存在)和包容主义(彼此不相符合的信仰服从一个共同的真理)。后两种立场是不可能的,因为任何关于真假是非的判断都是以一定的信念为前提和标准的;按照某种特定的标准去判断,不可能承认与之不相符合的标准所认定的真理,因此多元主义是不可能的;也不可能让自己认定的真理服从于其他标准所认定的真理,包容主义也是不可能的。A.托伦斯引用神学家德·考斯特(D'Costa)的话说:"所有的多元主义,包括所有的包容主义实际上不过是匿名的排他主义",因为他们都不可避免地把自己的标准当作代替其他一切标准的普遍标准。

排他主义的出发点是承认信仰的前提和标准作用,以及信仰的相对性,这些也是多元主义和包容主义的出发点。差别在于,多元主义认为,不同的信仰不可比,无公度,因此不兼容,可各行其是,并行不悖;包容主义认为不同的信仰有公度,可以取长补短,融合为人类共同的真理;排他主义则认为不同的信仰虽没有公度,但这并不妨碍以基督教信仰为判断真理的前提和标准。

普兰廷格为排他主义所作的辩护可分两部分:第一部分以信仰的相对性为由说明:以基督教信仰为真理标准是基督徒正当的"理智的权利",这种权利既没有剥夺其他人不同的道德准则,也没有否定持守其他真理标准的人的"理智的权利"(intellectual right),因此,既不是非道德的,也没有理性的骄傲。至此,普兰廷格的辩护与持"无公度性"说的相对主义并无什么不同;但是,他并未因此而走向相对主义;个中原因在于,他把基督徒的"理智的权利"变成基督徒必须履行的"认知的义务"(epistemic duty),即,必须以基督教信仰作为唯一的真理标准,并以此排斥不相容标准的;这是他后一部分辩护的内容。普兰廷格论辩的关键是把一种相对的权利(相对于其他信仰而言的正当性)转变为一种绝对的义务(能够判断自己信仰为唯一真理、并排斥其他信仰的优越性)。他有没有提出充足的理由作出这样的转变呢?

　　普兰廷格看到,有两种理由:外在的和内在的理由。外在的理由是,作为一个基督徒,一个人不得不这样做,他不得不恪守他的与生俱来的信仰,不得不排斥其他信仰;正如一个伊斯兰教徒也会用同样的态度对待自己的信仰和其他信仰一样。普兰廷格认为完全外在的理由是偶然的、不充分的,他从他的"改革宗的认识论"的立场出发,提出了"合适的功能主义"(proper functionalism)的理由。按照这一理论,如果产生一个信念的认识能力和认识环境是合适的,如果这种认识能力的自然的目的是产生正确的信念,如果这一信念为真的或然性较高,那么这一信念就可被确信为真。这四条标准把真理的主观条件和客观条件概括得很全面,他可以说,不管基督徒还是非基督徒,都要遵守这些真理标准。但是,普兰廷格紧接着做了一个转化,他把加尔文的教义理解为可以取代这些标准的功能。他说,加尔文所说的"神圣的感觉"、"圣灵的内在见证"以及《圣经》揭示的人类的罪和悲惨的状况,都具有满足这些标准的功能,因此都可以视为真理的标准;按照这样的标准,证明基督教的那两条基本信仰为真,其他与之不相容的信仰为假。

　　普兰廷格的做法实际上是用信仰来证明信仰,即用某种特殊的教义所具有的认知的功能,来证明基督教一般的教义。我们可以提出这样一个问题:某种特殊教义的认知功能能够代替普遍的真理标准吗?伊斯兰教徒、佛教徒或无神论者的某些特殊信仰也有证明他们各自的一般教义或学说的功能,按照普兰廷格的逻辑,这些特殊信仰岂不也可以取代真理的普遍标准?其他宗教乃至无神论的一般信仰岂不也能用同样的方式证明为真?要之,普兰廷格是在基督教信仰内部证明信仰的真理性的,他从一开始就把与基督教信仰不相容的信仰排除在证明的过程之外。A. 托伦斯直截了当地宣称:"总之,关于上帝的言谈在对上帝之道的认识中找到自身的最后基础,而通过迎合与重建的方式使圣灵显现出来,这种认识才会发生。"如果基督教神学完全建立在圣道或圣灵的显现的基础上,它当然不需要与外部的话语进行对话和交流,排他主义的真理性也只能在一个封闭的信仰体系中被证明。

普兰廷格至多只是证明了,在任何一个封闭的信仰体系中,排他主义都是正确的。其他宗教和无神论也可以用同样证明方式来排斥基督教信仰。如果排他主义对不同信仰的各方都是真的,宗教对话与交流不仅是不需要的,而且是不可能的。A.托伦斯说,这正是排他主义的目标,因为只有当包容主义不可能时,基督教才能"教育"、"解放"那些基督教以外的人,并最终把他们包容进基督教之中(如果他们接受"教育"和"解放"的话)。

在我看来,排他主义与包容主义是可以相容的,因为两者是针对不同情况说的。在不同意见的对话开始时,对话各方不可避免地持排他主义;即使有人认为对方的意见与自己是一致的,他也是以自己的意见为基础去理解对方的,仍然是"隐性的排他主义";就对话的出发点而言,排他主义是正确的。但是,为了使对话能够有效地进行,并达到积极的成果,对话各方至少要设定,他们的分歧是可以调和的,不同的意见包含着共同的真理;以包容主义为目标的对话的结果很可能是各种意见的融合,不是被融合在一方的意见之中,而是被融合在一种前所未有的新意见之中。因此,就对话的目标与实际所能达到的结果而言,包容主义是正确的。我们应该把对话看作一个过程,一个真理发生和完成的过程;这个过程开始于排他主义,结束于包容主义。正如黑格尔所说,真理是一个过程。我们现在更要记住:真理不是一开始就掌握在某种特殊身份的人的手中的、他人不能染指的圭臬。

Religious Exclusivism in a Globalized World

Miroslav Volf

In 2008, Prime Minister Tony Blair and I started teaching a course at Yale entitled "Faith and Globalization". Our assumption is that religious faiths and globalization are among the most powerful forces shaping the world today. The future of the world will depend greatly on how these two forces, partly colliding and partly reinforcing one another, relate to each other. Throughout the course, at the center of our attention are two great issues: (1) conflicts between faiths as a result of globalization pushing people of different faiths more tightly together and rapidly changing their worlds, and (2) the need to infuse globalization processes with a greater sense of justice and solidarity and direct them more toward the global common good.

The very first session of the course was held on September 11, seven years to the day after the terrorist attack on the World Trade Center and the Pentagon. Our theme was the "Ambivalence of Faiths." We explored how faiths can inspire people to horrendous acts of violence (e. g. terrorism) as well as motivate them to engage in sustained acts of kindness designed to "mend the world" (e. g. Jubilee Year efforts at the Third World debt relief). After my introduction and Mr. Blair's lecture, the discussion ranged broadly, mirroring a spectrum of concerns that a diverse body of students brought to the class. But the very first question posed during that first session stayed with us throughout the entire course.

Yasir Qadhi, a Muslim graduate student, was first to raise his hand. "Certain elements of faith are by definition exclusivist, whether we would like them to be so or not," he said. "For example, large segments of Christianity believe very strongly that unless you accept Jesus Christ as your personal Lord and savior, you are basically excluded from God's grace. That very belief is, of course, anathematical to Muslims. So the question arises: [Since] we are not able to change these fundamental beliefs, how can we make people genuinely love and care about one another when they believe that that person, who is outside their faith tradition, is outside of God's grace?" Mr. Qadhi singled out Christians. Many Muslims display the same exclusivity, a sense that Islam is the true religion, and so do other religious groups as well.

Mr. Qadhi's question was not merely about interpersonal relations, about our ability as private individuals to care for neighbors whom we consider outside God's grace. It was about politics. He was also inquiring about the ability of people who belong to exclusivist faiths to advocate equal treatment of all people in a given state. "How can we be expected to treat someone with whom we think that God is displeased the same [way] as someone with whom God is pleased?" Secular and religiously impartial states mandate just that: equal treatment of all, of those who do what is deemed pleasing to God and of those who do not. But God does not seem to treat all equally. Does loyalty to God then clash with loyalty to the state? If so, religious exclusivism leads straight to political intolerance!

In response, Mr. Blair immediately recognized that the problem of exclusivism is, in my words, the 800-pound gorilla sitting in the space where, pushed by globalization, faith meets faith. It is crucial, he insisted, to find "a way that people could really be comfortable, whilst they believe that they have the truth, with the truth of somebody else." [①] The second time we taught the course, early on the same issue surfaced, and again it stayed with us throughout the course.

Can religious exclusivists, adherents of different religions, live comfortably with one another under the same political roof? What kinds of political arrangements would be necessary for this to happen? Can belief in the one common God support such political arrangements? Or is the belief in one God the major source of religious exclusivism and therefore a cause of unending political strife? These are the key questions with regard to the public role of faith in an interconnected and interdependent world.

Let's start with the last question: Is monotheism by its very nature religiously and politically exclusive?

The True God Against the False Gods

Jan Assmann, an Egyptologist who has written extensively about the historical emergence of monotheism, has argued that the basic monotheist idea is not that there is only one supreme God. Many enlightened polytheists thought the same. It is rather that the one God is the true God and that all other gods are false. Parmenides, the great early Greek philosopher who influenced Plato and with him the whole of Western thought, strictly distinguished between "truth" and "falsehood" in the realm of knowledge. Moses, argues Assmann, was

---

① See http://www.youtube.com/v/qtVTcvIyWdA (accessed April 29, 2010).

the Parmenides of religion. He was the first to make a distinction between truth and falsehood in the realm of religion. As truth is opposed to falsehood, so the one true God is opposed to all other gods (idols) and to all false opinions about the one God (heresies). Monotheism, Assmann argues, is always "theoclasm", an endeavor to destroy all other gods and all alternative opinions about God. [①] Now, that's religious exclusivism!

Historically, monotheism was not just an aggressively exclusivist religious idea. It was also a political vision. One influential version of this vision goes like this: The indivisible power of a single earthly ruler should mirror the indivisible power of the one God. And since God's power extends through the whole cosmos, the power of the earthly ruler, God's representative, should extend to the ends of the earth. According to this view, the belief in the one true God makes the centralized power of a single ruler imperialistic. [②] In sum, monotheists are out to destroy all religious convictions other than their own and subdue all disagreeable peoples! One God—one religion and one rule in the whole world! That's religious exclusivism underwriting political expansionism.

If aggressive exclusivism were in the DNA of monotheism, how could Muslims' and Christians' allegiance to the one God lead to the common good? Indeed, how could they live together without pervasive conflict? With Christianity and Islam, we would have two monotheistic religions, each religiously exclusive and each politically imperialistic. The problem with monotheism would have doubled! Unless Christian

---

① See Jan Assmann, *Moses the Egyptian. The Memory of Egypt in Western Monotheism* (Cambridge: Harvard University Press, 1997); Jan Assmann, *Die Mosaische Unterscheidung, Oder der Preis des Monotheismus* (Muenchen: Carl Hanser Verlag, 2003).

② On this see, for instance, Aziz Al-Azmeh, "Monotheistic Monarchy," *Journal for the Study of Religions and Ideologies*, 10 (Spring 2005), pp. 133 – 149. Similarly, Regina M. Schwartz, *The Curse of Cain: The Violent Legacy of Monotheism* (Chicago: University of Chicago Press, 1997).

and Muslim understandings of God were completely identical (which they are not), how would having a common God help? At best, one group would see the other as heretics, and be implacably opposed to them in the name of the full truth about God and God's ways with humanity. The more each was attached to God, the worse things would get between them.

Defenders of monotheism have some ready responses.

Response No. 1: Monotheism is no worse than polytheism. Polytheistic societies of the ancient world were not known for their peacefulness. When they went to war, their gods marched alongside them. [1] Jumping to today, even though some Hindu thinkers argue that polytheism promotes decentralized "liberal pluralism" whereas monotheism promotes a state-centered society intolerant of all pluralism, [2] it is not clear that in contemporary India, polytheistic Hindus are less aggressive and more pluralistic than monotheistic Muslims or Christians.

Let's assume that this response to the critique of monotheism is persuasive (as I think it is). Even so, it doesn't get us where we need to be; it's a victory in a small skirmish, not in a decisive battle. We need monotheism to be socially beneficial, not merely less detrimental than polytheism! Since our goal is to promote the common good in societies with Muslims and Christians living side by side, we need to show, not that polytheism is as aggressive as monotheism, but that monotheism is not necessarily socially and politically exclusive.

---

① See Jean-Jacques Rousseau, *The Social Contract*, IV. 8. For a contrary argument that polytheism, for all its defects, is more peaceable than monotheism see David Hume, *The Natural History of Religion*, ed. H. E Root (Stanford: Stanford University Press, 1956), pp. 48 – 51.

② See S. Gurumurthy, "Semitic Monotheism: The Root of Intolerance in India" (Madras: Center for Policy Studies). < http://www.bjp.org/history/htvgm-10.html >, accessed on May 4, 2007.

Response No. 2: Monotheism is democratizing. It is true, the defenders of monotheism concede, that monotheism was used to support centralized and top-down forms of rule: one God, one (human) lord, and one religiously unified and expanding empire. [1] But it is also true that in all three monotheist faiths monotheism was used to support decentralized and bottom up forms of rule: no lord but God. [2] When the people of Israel decided to have a king, the response of the prophet Samuel, speaking in God's name, was this: "This is what the LORD, the God of Israel, says: 'I brought Israel up out of Egypt, and I delivered you from the power of Egypt and all the kingdoms that oppressed you.' But you have now rejected your God, who saves you out of all your calamities and distresses. And you have said, 'No, set a king over us'" (1 Samuel 10:18 - 19). God and the king are not aligned; they are alternatives[RJM1].

This argument moves us in the right direction, but it too doesn't get us yet to the goal. For bottom-up, democratic forms of rule are not sufficient by themselves. As social "wars" in any schoolyard make manifest, people can be as tyrannically exclusive as are the rulers. People, too, can prefer to live in religiously and socially homogenous spaces [RJM2]. If Christians and Muslims (along with other religions) are to live under the same roof, it is important for them to affirm political pluralism and not just democracy. The question then is this: Can believers in one true God affirm social arrangements that include people with different religious (and non-religious) perspectives on life on equal terms?

---

[1] See Juergen Moltmann, *The Trinity and the Kingdom. The Doctrine of God*, trans. Margaret Kohl (Minneapolis: Fortress Press, (1993), pp. 192 - 202.

[2] So Kathryn Tanner, *Christ the Key* (Cambridge: Cambridge University Press, 2010), 208 - 209.

Response No. 3: Monotheism is inclusive. Because God is one, the world God created is one as well, the defenders of monotheism rightly insist. It is not divided into hostile regions by competing divine powers, not split into realms of light and darkness by incompatible moral visions. A single unifying truth binds all human beings, and the same demands of justice are equally applicable to all. [1] The correlate of "one God" is "all people". Nothing could be more inclusive than monotheism. [2]

Agreed—in part. The stress on universality is an important, even indispensible contribution which monotheism makes in today's world. Globalization processes are erasing walls that separate diverse communities and are gradually intertwining all into a single interdependent humanity. If we are not to remain mired in conflicts, we need a common set of rules and a common vision of the global common good. [3] While honoring differences, we need to understand humanity as one. This is exactly the consequence of the belief in the one God.

And yet, there is a problem. Though monotheism is inclusive, it is inclusive on its own terms. You are "in" if you embrace the one true God, creator of the world, and if you accept God's commands as binding for all. But you are "out" if you don't. Exclusivism is the obverse of monotheism's inclusivism. Must we then conclude that Muslims and Christians, just because they give allegiance to the one true God partly differently understood, will be unable to live under the same political roof and work together for the common good?

---

[1]   On this, see Hans Zirker, "Monotheismus und Intoleranz," *Mit den Anderen leben*, eds. Konrad Hilpert/Juergen Werbick (Duesseldorff: Patmos, 1995), pp. 95 – 96.

[2]   See Joseph Ratzinger (Benedict XVI), *Introduction to Christianity*, trans. J. R. Foster (San Francisco: Ignatius, 2004 [1969]), p. 136.

[3]   See Chapter XIII.

Religious Exclusivism—Political Pluralism

The decisive question regarding the relation between the allegiance to the one God and the ability of Christians and Muslims to coexist in a single state and pursue the common good is this: Can they be religious exclusivists while embracing pluralism as a political project? Let's first clarify the two crucial terms in this question, "religious exclusivists" and "pluralism as a political project".

Religious exclusivists believe that their religion is the true one. Most of them don't necessarily think that other religions are totally false. Though these religions are not true as ways to salvation, they may contain truth about God and moral life, some more and others less. But religious exclusivists will judge the truth of other religions (and other world-views more generally) by whether other religions conform to exclusivists' own religious beliefs and practices. In contrast, religious pluralists believe that all religions are roughly equally true; they are simply different but equally "efficient" ways of scaling the same mountain.

Some Muslims and Christians are committed religious pluralists. Most of them, however, are religious exclusivists. They are true to the basic monotheistic insight: there is no god but God, and the categories of "true" and "false" apply to religions. Equally importantly, a majority of those Christians and Muslims who are passionate about their faith's social impact are religious exclusivists. That's a problem—if political exclusivism follows in the wake of religious exclusivism. Each group will then want to control the public space, pushing the other out. And if it comprises a sufficiently strong majority, it will insist that all who live in the land embrace its faith, or submit to its rule as second-class citizens, or be forced to leave. These are not merely theoretical options. Christian and Muslim rulers and governments have implemented them in the past and still do in many places today. The sixteenth century Christian principle cuius regio, eius religio—the religion of the ruler is the religion of the people—is one example. [1] The Muslim idea of a dhimmi, according to which a non-Muslim subject of a Muslim ruler enjoy protection but not equal rights, is another.

But is political exclusivism a necessary consequence of religious exclusivism? We know that religious exclusivists cannot be religious pluralists; the two are polar opposites. [2] Can religious exclusivists be political pluralists, however? That's the decisive question. By political pluralism, in its pure form, I mean the view that all religions, though not considered to be equally true by those who embrace them, are equally welcome in a given nation or state. There are two basic conditions of political pluralism:

1. The state does not favor one religion (or overarching interpretation of life) over the others, but is impartial toward them, indeed toward all overarching interpretations of life, whether religious or not.

2. Each religion is allowed to bring its own vision of the good life into the public arena, and do so by drawing on the resources of its own sacred books and traditions.

These are of the "ideal type" conditions of political pluralism. No state embodies them perfectly; they sketch a direction toward

---

[1]   See Chapter XIII.

[2]   On closer inspection, the line demarcating the polar opposites of religious exclusivism and religious pluralism is not as sharp as it is often made to be. Pluralists cannot avoid all exclusivism; some religions, like those involving human sacrifices, for instance, are always out. And exclusivists virtually never insist that others are totally different, totally false; instead, they affirm that other faiths have overlapping elements and shared truth with theirs.

which a properly practiced political pluralism should be aiming. A state like England, for instance, where Christianity is an established religion, may prefer one religion to all others for historical or practical reasons, and yet give full freedom to others and seek to be impartial toward them within these constraints. From my perspective, such a state would count as politically pluralistic. For successful common life of diverse groups within a polity more is needed than pluralistic political institutions, such as absence of prejudice and ability to pursue the common good. I'll address these in subsequent chapters. But pluralistic institutions are essential.

Can religious exclusivists agree to the above two conditions? More specifically, is it possible for Christians and Muslims who embrace exclusive monotheism to agree to these conditions? The answer is a simple "yes," for two reasons, one factual and one theoretical.

It is an uncontested fact that many Christian and Muslim religious exclusivists endorse the impartiality of the state toward all religions and the right of each to engage in public debates. The so-called "Christian Right" in the U. S. is a good example. Those who belong to it are Christian monotheists and undisputed religious exclusivists. They are also committed to bringing their religious convictions to bear upon public life in our country. And yet they grant the same right to religious groups with whom they strenuously disagree (even if they wish that there were no such group in the U. S.). Moreover, when the preferred candidates or causes of the Christian right lose in elections, its members stay engaged with the democratic process. ①

① See Jon Shields, *The Democratic Virtues of the Christian Right* (Princeton: Princeton University Press, 2009).

In addition to many Muslims in the West who embrace liberal political institutions, an example in Islam may be Nahdatul Ulama, the largest Muslim socio-religious organization (with over 40 million members) in the most populous Muslim country in the world (Indonesia, with over 240 million inhabitants). In the words of Peter Berger, it is "avowedly pro-democracy and pro-pluralism, the very opposite of what is commonly viewed as Muslim 'fundamentalism'."
[1] At the same time, Nahdatul Ulama is a religious revival movement, deeply committed to a faith whose central tenet is monotheism.

Are these groups anomalies, at odds with Christians and Muslims who are consistent exclusivists—with those who are political exclusivists and not just religious exclusivists? Is it inconsistent of monotheists to embrace political pluralism rather than insisting on a unitary state in which a single ruler (authoritarian version) or a religiously homogenous people (democratic version) is the sovereign? This takes us to the second and theoretical reason why Christians and Muslims can and should agree to the above two conditions of political pluralism.

Monotheism and Political Pluralism

It is not inconsistent of monotheists to embrace pluralism as a political project. To the contrary! Two essential features of monotheism in fact favor pluralism as a political project. Let me put this bold thesis a bit more precisely: two features of the kind of monotheism that Muslims and Christians arguably share (the belief in

---

[1]   Peter Berger, "The Desecularization of the World: A Global Overview," in *The Desecularization of the World: Resurgent Religion and World Politics*, ed. Peter Berger (Grand Rapids: Eerdmans, 1999), p. 8.

one benevolent God who commands all people to love their neighbors) favor pluralism as a political project.

I will identify and explicate these two features of monotheism as they appear in the Christian faith and will do so from a distinctly Christian perspective. This is in line with the approach I have taken throughout this book. I write as a Christian and offer for Muslim consideration a way of thinking about the relation between the two faiths that is both fully faithful to the Christian faith and, I trust, congenial to Muslims. I see no reason why Muslims, who believe that the command of the one God to love neighbors and act justly toward them transcends the boundaries of Muslim communities, could not follow me on the rarely trodden path I am about to embark upon.

Feature No. 1: The belief in the one true God gave religion an essential ethical dimension. Earlier I have noted that monotheism introduced into the world of religions the distinction between "true" and "false." The result was a form of exclusivism that troubles many today. But monotheism brought something else as well, troubling for some but immensely promising for others. With the distinction between "true" and "false" came also the distinction between "just" and "unjust." In distinction to the polytheism from which it emerged, monotheism made justice, law, and freedom into central themes of religion. Whereas polytheistic religions were primarily cultic, monotheistic religions are fundamentally ethical (though not only ethical!). This feature, no less than the distinction between the true and the false God, was one of monotheism's most revolutionary innovations. ① From now on, to act justly, to show mercy, and to love neighbor is to serve God (Micah 6:8). Ritual observance without moral rectitude is worse than empty; it is a counterfeit religious coin

---

　① Assmann, *Die Mosaische Unterscheidung*, p. 66.

with which a worshiper seeks divine and human approval for behavior that deserves censure (Isaiah 58:3 – 7).

The one God, to whom Christians and Muslims owe exclusive allegiance, commands love of neighbors—to " do to others as you would have them do to you" (Matthew 7:12) and not to do to others what you would not want them do to you. This is the principle of reciprocity, in doing what is good and not doing what is wrong. Since the one God is the God of all people, the principle of reciprocity applies to all. Acting in accordance with this principle is worship of God, a genuinely religious act. [①]

Feature No. 2: Monotheism decoupled religion from the state and from ethnic belonging. This decoupling took place in two stages.

Stage No. 1: Decoupling of Religion from the State. From the start, monotheism was arguably connected with liberation of Abraham's children from slavery in Egypt. It involved founding of an alternative form of social life "in which human beings do not rule over other human beings but come together in freedom to place themselves under the rule of the covenant made with the one God. " [②] God is the only true lord of the people; the ruler of the state does not rule in God's place. Salvation is not identical with political rule; it is a gift to a community from God.

Stage No. 2: Decoupling of Religion from Ethnic Belonging. In Israel, the one God of all peoples remained attached in a special way to Jewish people, the physical descendants of Abraham and Sarah. The Apostle Paul, the great missionary to the Gentiles, severed that link. He sensed an unresolved tension between the universality of the one God and the particularity of a single chosen people. He insisted

---

① See Chapter VI

② Assman, *Die Mosaische*, pp. 67 – 68.

that all human beings, Jews and Gentiles, are included in the people of God, the new Israel, on equal terms, on account of God's utterly gratuitous love rather than in virtue of any natural "characteristic" or "achievement" of their own. ①

The one God of love is related to all people on equal terms and commands them to love! To us today this thought has a ring of trite truism. In reality it is revolutionary. It has profound and far-reaching implications for the relation between religious communities and the state.

Consider these implications, again from a Christian angle. What happens when the Gospel is preached to all nations in accordance with the belief that God, as revealed in Jesus Christ, is the God of all peoples? If the preaching is successful, churches will emerge as new and foreign social bodies in those nations. Nicholas Wolterstorff, a leading Christian philosopher working on political theology and philosophy today, notes a crucial feature of the Christian church:

> *On the one hand, its [the church's] membership included people from other nations; on the other hand, its membership never included all from any nation. The church included more than Slavs and not all Slavs; the church is not Slavic. The church includes more than Americans and not all Americans; the church is not American. And so forth, for all nations, all peoples. The church is not the church of any nation or people. It does not belong to the social identity of any people.* ②

The presence of the church, a body of people giving ultimate allegiance to the one God, introduces religious fissure in the citizenry

----

① See Daniel Boyarin, *A Radical Jew: Paul and Politics of Identity* (Berkeley: University of California Press, 1994). On Boyarin's thesis see Miroslav Volf and Judith Gundry-Volf), "Paul and the Politics of Identity" (a review article of Daniel Boyarin, *A Radical Jew: Paul and the Politics of Identity* [Berkeley: University of California Press, 1994), *Books & Culture* 3 (4 1997), pp. 16 – 18.

② Nicholas Wolterstorff, *The Mighty and the Almighty* (unpublished manuscript), XI, p. 4.

of a state. This religious fissure in turn changes the very character of the state. As Wolterstorff notes, the state can no longer "express the shared religious identity of the people, since there is no such identity". He continues,

> *The coming of the church undermines the political vision of the ancient Greek philosophers, that government is the highest institutional expression of the religio-ethical bonds uniting its citizenry. Wherever the church enters a society, it destroys whatever religio-ethical unity that society may have possessed. Now there is only religious pluralism.* ①

A fissure along religious lines is a direct result of the second feature of monotheism I highlighted—the decoupling of religion from the state and ethnic community. Now add to this second feature of monotheism the first feature—doing justice and loving neighbor understood as a religious duty, a form of worship of God. The result? If we embrace both together, we have excellent reasons to affirm pluralism as a political project!

Since religion is not identical with the state and since doing justice and loving all neighbors is a religious duty, we must affirm the appropriateness of there being more than one religion in a given state as well as the right of each religious group to pursue its own religious vision of good life. It would be unjust and unloving to grant one religious community—our own—freedom to live according to the dictates of the one God while denying the corresponding freedom to others. ②

I can imagine Augustine and those who followed in his trail protesting. Basing his comments on the parable of the Great Dinner to which gests were "compelled to come in" (Luke 14:23), he argued

---

① Nicholas Wolterstorff, *The Mighty and the Almighty* (unpublished manuscript), XI, p. 4.
② Ibid., p. 10.

that the impious and erring ought to be forced to comply with the truth. In *Concerning the Correction of the Donatists*, Augustine wrote:

> "*There is a righteous persecution, which the Church of Christ inflicts upon the impious.* ··· *She persecutes in the spirit of love* ··· *that she may correct* ··· *that she may recall from error.* ··· *Finally, she persecutes her enemies and arrests them, until they become weary in their vain opinions, so that they should make advance in the truth.*" [1]

Love, and therefore coerce, argues Augustine. But the argument disregards that, as Apostle Paul put it, "one believes with the heart" (Romans 10:10). The heart cannot and may not be coerced. Faith is ultimately a matter between God and the heart. Hence all coercion in matters of faith is excluded.

Notice that these are all *religious reasons* to insist that state be impartial toward all religions and that all religious communities be allowed to live according to their own vision of good life and, if they wish so, to contribute to the public debate about the common good; they are a consequence of Christian and Muslim monotheism. A believer in the one God who is a consistent religious exclusivist will be, just for that reason, a political pluralist!

Freedom of Religion and Apostasy

Properly understood, belief in one God who commands love of neighbor requires pluralism as a political project. Such pluralism is inseparable, however, from freedom of religion. Today, after the Catholic Church has followed fellow Protestants and fully embraced

---

① Nicholas Wolterstorff, *The Mighty and the Almighty* (unpublished manuscript), II, p. 11.

freedom of religion at the Second Vatican Council (1962 – 1965) , ①
Muslims and Christians tend to be deeply divided on the issue. Over
the centuries, however, they have thought about it alike. And both
have also thought about it wrongly, because they have missed
important implications of their most basic convictions about God.

On May 30, 2007, Malaysia's highest court ruled that Lina Joy, a
convert to the Christian faith, had lost her long fight to legally become a
Christian, a struggle during which she received multiple death threats.
Even though in her heart and daily practice she is a Christian, before the
law she is and must remain a Muslim—against her stated wish and
determined efforts. She will be unable to marry her non-Muslim fiancée.
The law says that Muslim women can marry only Muslim men. Since she
must remain legally a Muslim, he, a Christian, would have to become
Muslim to marry her, though she is now a practicing Christian!② During
the decision, hundreds of Muslim demonstrators gathered in front of
the federal court building shouting, "God is great." As he gave the
ruling, the Malaysian chief justice also expressed the opinion of the
demonstrators when he said to Lina Joy that she "cannot at her own
whim simply enter or leave her religion". ③

According to a common interpretation of shari'a, Muslims are
forbidden to convert to another religion and converts are considered
apostates. As Shaykh Ali Gomaa, the Grand Mufti of Egypt and one of
the most respected contemporary Muslim religious authorities, has
stated recently, "Islam prohibits a Muslim from changing his religion

---

① Declaration on Religious Freedom *Dignitatis humanae* (http://www. vatican. va/archive/hist_
councils/ii_vatican_council/documents/vat-ii_decl_19651207_dignitatis-humanae_en. html).

② "Once a Muslim, Always a Muslim in Malaysia," *Asia Sentinel*, May 30, 2007, http://www.
asiasentinel. com/index. php? Itemid = 34&id = 515&option = com_content&task = view.

③ "Malaysian Court Refuses to Recognize Woman's Conversion to Christianity," *New York Times*,
May 30, 2007, http://www. nytimes. com/2007/05/30/world/asia/30cnd-malaysia. html? _r = 1&scp =
3&sq = lina% 20joy&st = cse.

and … apostasy is a crime, which must be punished. " [1] Though some suggest that God will mete out the punishment at the Day of Judgment, [2] most authorities believe that the punishment ought to be imposed in this world. The debate is primarily about the proper character of the punishment, whether apostasy is punishable by death or some lesser penalty. Many Muslims agree. The Muslim public opinion overwhelmingly supports the hardest possible line on apostasy laws, [3] and these laws are enforced without mercy even in countries like Malaysia, a model Muslim democracy.

　　Most Christians today consider Islamic laws of apostasy to be

---

[1]　"Top cleric denies 'freedom to choose religion' comment," GulfNews. com, July 24, 2007, http://archive. gulfnews. com/articles/07/07/25/10141696. html. Some saw this as a reversal of a previously stated position on a *Washington Post* website, in which he argued that, as far as human authorities are concerned, Muslims are free to change their religion; they will be accountable to God for their decision at the Day of Judgment, but are not subject to punishment in this life (http://www. abc. net. au/news/stories/2007/07/24/1987362. htm? section = justin, accessed May 8, 2010).

[2]　"The Qur'an contains a provision that says 'he who has embraced Islam and then abandons it will receive punishment in hell after Judgment Day," says M. Cherif Bassiouni, an expert on Islamic law at DePaul University College of Law, and therefore there is no punishment on earth. Quoted in Lionel Beehner, "Religious Conversion and Sharia Law," Council on Foreign Relations, June 8, 2007, http://www. cfr. org/publication/13552/religious_conversion_and_sharia_law. html.

[3]　See John Micklethwait and Adrian Wooldridge, *God is Back: How the Global Revival of Faith is Changing the World* (New York: The Penguin Press, 2009), 293. Most disturbing of all are actual horrifying executions, such as the beheading of a Somali Christian named Mansuur Muhammed by the Islamist Shabab militia in 2008 (See: "Somalia: Christian Aid Worked Beheaded for Converting from Islam," Compass Direct News, October 27, 2008, http://www. compassdirect. org/en/display. php? page = news&lang = en&length = long&idelement = 5661). Condemned for spying for the enemies of the mujahedin and for being a "murtadd" (an apostate), his head was cut off with a knife amidst the cries "God is great." Horrendous brutalities against the apostates widen the chasm between Muslims and Christians to the point that extremists among them think of Islam as a profoundly evil and demonic religion (See examples: "Christian leader condemns Islam: Preacher Franklin Graham calls Islam 'wicked, violent,'" MSNBC Nightly News, http://www. msnbc. com/news/659057. asp; Chuck Baldwin, "Our Politically Correct Theologian-in-Chief," The Covenant News, December 13, 2002, http://covenantnews. com/baldwin02). Most Christians understand, however, that evildoers often don the cloak of religion in hopes of somehow sanctifying their base goals. They also know that in a failed state like Somalia, in which the government does not exert full sovereignty and militias rule over significant swats of territory, life is brutish and short for many, not just for the "apostates."

inhumane. In the light of these laws, the statement in the Qur'an that there is "no compulsion in religion" (Al Baqarah, 2:256), rings hollow. But before condemning Islam as a "wicked" religion, Christians should remember that there is no such statement in the Bible. ① They should also look into the mirror of their own history. From early on, apostasy was considered a serious sin—so serious that during the first Christian centuries many considered it impossible for the apostates to receive forgiveness.

When the Roman Empire became Christian, the religious practice of withholding forgiveness became a civil law. Apostates were "punished by deprivation of all civil rights. They could not give evidence in a court of law, and could neither bequeath nor inherit property. To induce anyone to apostatize was an offence punishable with death." ② In the Middle Ages, both canon and civil law classed apostates with heretics—and the harshest imaginable penalties were imposed on them. In what sense did the church embrace freedom of religion through most of its centuries long history? People were free to embrace faith and enter the church. Once in, they could neither leave it nor deviate from its basic convictions. In either case, they would be leaving the truth. But leaving the truth is wrong, and one can never have the right to do what is wrong.

---

① The declaration on religious freedom of the Second Vatican Council notes this explicitly. "Revelation does not indeed affirm in so many words the right of man to immunity from external coercion in matters religious." The argument of the declaration is based on biblical and theological understanding of the dignity of person, not on explicit biblical text. The revelation, the declaration states, "does, however, disclose the dignity of the human person in its full dimensions. It gives evidence of the respect which Christ showed toward the freedom with which man is to fulfill his duty of belief in the word of God and it gives us lessons in the spirit which disciples of such a Master ought to adopt and continually follow" ("Declaration on Religious Freedom *Dignitatis humanae*, No. 9 [http://www. vatican. va/archive/hist_councils/ii_ vatican_council/documents/vat-ii_decl_19651207_dignitatis-humanae_en. html]).

② "Apostasy," *Catholic Encyclopedia*, http://www. newadvent. org/cathen/01624b. htm (accessed May 8, 2010).

We are back at the connection between religion and truth, which, as Assmann has argued, came about with monotheism—first at the religious level (one God, one truth, one choice) and then at the political level (one God, one earthly rule, one acceptable way of life). But if my argument in this chapter is correct, we are back at a seriously misguided appropriation of that connection. The advocates of the laws against apostasy disregard two truly essential and socially revolutionary features of monotheism: the decoupling of religion and the state, and the tying of religion to loving all neighbors and to doing justice. Apply these features of monotheism to the question of religious freedom, and the partiality of the state toward one religion as well as the laws against apostasy must go.

The central problem of Muslims and Christians throughout their unhappy history with religious freedom was the failure to apply consistently the principle of reciprocity, a basic form of loving neighbors and doing justice. When Christians or Muslims were an overwhelming majority, they felt justified curtailing the full freedom of others to exercise their faith. When they were a minority, however, they demanded for themselves full freedom to exercise their own religion. Each was unwilling to grant to others what they claimed and enforced through the power of the state for themselves—a patently unjust and unloving stance. [1] Similarly,

---

① The question of reciprocity was at the center of the debates about freedom of religion during the Second Vatican Council at which declaration on religious freedom was issued, one of the most innovative documents of that council. Initially, many bishops as well as theologians insisted on the asymmetrical relationship between the Catholic Church and other religious communities, whether Christian churches or other religions. Because it is the "true religion", the Catholic Church felt that it could claim for itself what it was, under the same circumstances, unwilling to grant to others. Within the ranks of the Church, the strongest and most effective resistance against this position came from the then newly established "Secretariat for Promoting Christian Unity", under the leadership of Cardinal Bea. Non-Catholics, the argument went, react negatively to the Church when it fails to act according to the principle of reciprocity (see Pietro Pavan, "Einleiting und Kommentar [Declaratio de libertate religiosa]", *Lexikon fuer Theologie und Kirche* [Herder: Freiburg, 1967], 13, 704 – 5).

both Muslims and Christians engaged in missionary activity and readily accepted converts from other faiths. Yet each group severely punished both their own members who abandoned the true faith and the followers of other faiths who may have led them astray. Again, a glaring case of a lack of reciprocity—more appropriate to armies at war and how they treat defectors and spies than to religious communities committed to worshiping the one and common God who commands love of all human beings.

To be consistent with their convictions about God, Christians and Muslims must embrace two simple principles:

1. All persons and communities have equal right to practice their faith (unless they break widely accepted moral law), privately and publicly, without interference of the state.

2. Every person has the right to embrace another faith and leave his or her own.

When Christians and Muslims deny either of these principles, they can be rightly accused of transgressing against the most basic principles of justice. Even more importantly, when they deny these principles they dishonor the one God who commands them to love all people and do justice.

Identity, Separation, Impartiality

Almost a millennium ago, a medieval pope, Gregory VII (1020 –85) wrote a friendly letter to Al-Nasir, the king of Mauretania. In it he wrote:

> *Almighty God, who desires all men to be saved (1 Timothy 2:4) and none to perish is well pleased to approve in us most of all that besides loving God men love other men,*

and do not do to others anything they do not want to be done unto themselves (cf. Matthew 7:14). We and you must show in a special way to the other nations an example of this charity, for we believe and confess one God, although in different ways, and praise and worship Him daily as the creator of all ages and the ruler of this world. As the apostle says, "He is our peace who has made us both one" (Ephesians 2:14). [1]

In this letter, the Pope's theological starting point and his goal are close to my own: the one God who commands love is the foundation of peace between Muslims and Christians and of their common witness to the world.

Would Pope Gregory VII have agreed that pluralism as a political project follows from these theological convictions? Not very likely. His relations both to earthly rulers and to Muslims suggest otherwise. He saw himself above earthly rulers. He had the emperor of Germany, Henry IV, come to him barefoot amid ice and snow, stripped of his royal robes and clad as penitent, and absolved him from censure only after three days of fasting and waiting in the wintry weather before the closed doors of the citadel in which the pope resided. As to Muslims, his conciliatory letter to king Al-Nasir was only one side of the story, a less prominent one. Pope Gregory VII tried, unsuccessfully, to organize a crusade to free the Eastern Church from the Seljuk Turks. Like many great theologians and church leaders through the centuries, Pope Gregory VII would have bristled at the idea of political pluralism.

Were all these Christians through the centuries who did not think in terms of political pluralism wrong? It is correct to say, I think, that

---

[1] Gregory VII, "Letter to Anzir, King of Mauretania", *The Christian Faith in the Doctrinal Documents of the Catholic Church*, ed. Jacques Dupuis (New York: Alba House, 2001), pp. 418 – 419.

they did not consistently apply the belief in the one God who commands love of neighbor to the relation between church and state. There are many reasons for this failure, including the fact that they lived in the religiously homogenous world of medieval Europe. We live in a different world. Ours is a highly interconnected, interdependent, and religiously mixed world. As a rule, many religions inhabit a common political space. For us, it is crucial to seize the promise of political pluralism contained in Christian and Islamic (and Jewish) monotheism. If we do, the common God of Muslims and Christians will become "our peace," as pope Gregory VII suggested to the Mauritanian ruler. ①

In a religiously pluralistic world, how should the believers in one God understand the relation between religion and the state? I'll sum up the position I am advocating in three simple principles—all three related to one another, and all three grounded in the belief in one God who commands love of neighbor.

Principle No. 1: No identity between religion and state. A state is the state of all its citizens who are, as a rule, divided along religious lines. God's laws, as understood by a particular religious community, are binding for that community. They are its ethical code, and not necessarily the law of the land to be imposed on all citizens. In case of conflict between the communal ethical code and the law of the land, a religious community will feel obliged to "obey God rather than any human authority," as the apostle Peter said when the earliest Christians were prohibited from proclaiming that God raised Jesus from the dead (Acts 5 : 29). Subordinating human authority to God's authority is an inescapable consequence of giving

---

① The pope slightly distorted the original meaning of Ephesians 2, which refers to Christ on the cross as "our peace" rather than to God.

ultimate allegiance to God. The monotheist principle that "there is no god but God" means that God's command is above any human law.

Over the centuries Islam has been associated more with the tendency to identify religion and the state than Christianity has been (though Christianity has exhibited similar tendencies as well). Islamist thinker Sayyid Qutb (1906 – 1966), one of the most influential thinkers of the Muslim Brotherhood, is a modern example. For him, the sovereignty of God requires that the society as a whole be ruled by God's law, the shari'a. [1] But many Muslims disagree, as the example of Fethullah Gulen, a Turkish religious leader with a worldwide following, shows. For him, as for many Muslims throughout the world, the aim of Islam is more spiritual and ethical than political. [2] He affirms the need for religion to influence the culture and the state, but denies the identity of religion and rule.

Principle No. 2: No complete separation between religion and the state. Jesus Christ has, famously, said to the Pharisees: "Give to the emperor the things that are emperors, and to God the things that are God's" (Mark 12:17). Guided by these words of Christ and mindful that Christ was crucified as a political criminal by the Roman power, over the centuries Christians have had an ambivalent relation to political power. When they came to wield power after the conversion of Constantine, theirs was, in a sense "an accidental empire". [3] Fittingly, the idea of complete separation of religion and

---

① See Sayyid Qutb, *Milestones* (Lahore: Kazi Publications, 2007), pp. 87 – 90.

② See on this Paul Heck, *Common Ground: Islam, Christianity, and Religious Pluralism* (Washington D. C.: Georgetown University Press, 2009), pp. 166 – 168. Olivier Roy writes in a similar vein more generally about revivals in Islam: "The contemporary religious revival in Islam is targeting society more than the state and calling to the individual's spiritual needs" (Olivier Roy, *Globalized Islam: The Search for a New Ummah* (New York: Columbia University Press, 2004), p. 3.

③ So Mark Lilla, *The Stillborn God: Religion, Politics, and the Modern West* (New York: Knopf, 2007), p. 40.

state was originally conceived and implemented in the Christian cultural environment during the Enlightenment.

And yet, for believers in the one God who commands love of neighbor, separation of religion and state will not do. For them—Jews, Christians, and Muslims alike—God is the God of all people and therefore the God of all citizens of a state, whether they believe in God or not. The commands of the Master of the Universe are the moral law for all. A religious community will therefore seek to persuade its compatriots of the rightness of its moral vision and to infuse the laws of the land with the values embodied in God's commands. Many Christians today oppose the idea of a secular state—either in the sense of a state being detached from religions by a wall of separation or in the sense of a state advocating a non-religious world-view. They maintain that such a state cannot be fair toward people with robust religious convictions. They reject strict separation of religion and state, and advocate impartiality of state toward all religions. ①

Principle no. 3: Impartiality of the state toward all religions. The only adequate option open to Muslims and Christians as citizens of the same state is to advocate the impartiality of the state toward all religions: no religion is preferred by the state and all religions are impartially supported. This allows Christians and Muslims to be faithful to two fundamental impulses of monotheism simultaneously—to (1) honor the conviction that God is the God of all people and to (2) obey God's command to act justly and practice neighborly love toward all people.

---

① See especially Nicholas Wolterstorff, "The Role of Religion in Decision and Discussion of Political Issues," in Robert Audi and Nicholas Wolterstorff, *Religion in the Public Square: The Place of Religious Convictions in Political Debate* (Lanham: Rowman & Littlefield, 1997), pp. 67 – 120.

The Challenge of Otherness:
Differences and Analogies between Systems
of Multireligious Presence in Europe

Alberto Melloni

Abstract

One of the most important experience made by the Roman Catholic Church in the 20th Century concerns the meaning of "the other". Since the Middle Ages one of the defining point of the *Christianitas* was its difference in comparison to the other which was by definition an enemy. The Muslim, the Jew, and mostly the Heretic were paradigm of an unremedied distance between the sphere of salvation and the sphere of damnation: the role of the law was exactly that of identifying at whatever price the other and expel him from the Christian body.

Modernity challenged this idea from outside: trying to teach and to impose to the Churches a neutral space of citizenship and rights where ecclesiastical laws and condemnations had to be uneffective. The result of this effort of the 19th – 20th Century was very important and what is now called western constitutionalism comes from such a separation between church and state uncer a principle of *laicité*. However these measures where accepted as a "secular" pressure, and in the intransigent Catholicism rejected as an imposition. A similar refusal of a neutral political authority can be found in different religious context, where secularization instead of eradicating religious fundamentalism is feeding it.

The real change came for Roman Catholicism from inside: inside its spiritual experience, inside its historical self-perception, inside its theological framework. Scientific exegesis did show a different Jesus, rooted in Jewish tradition and eschatological Messianism. The misisonary experience of the 10th Century imposed to the Christian agenda—first of all in Anglican and Protestant milieu, later among Catholics—the issue of unity among those who professed the Name of Jesus: the ecumenical movement (since 1948 represented by the World Council of Churches and since 1965 accepted by Vatican II for the Roman Catholic Church) gave to the most obvious "other" available to the common people experience a positive meaning and it made of the "other Christians" brother to be loved and understood. Last but not the least the pontificate of John XXIII gave a new language to the Roman Catholic magisterium: the other in confessional terms, the other in religious terms and mostly the Jews became the subject of a common quest for what unifies instead of a research of the divisional reasons.

Such an impulse was solemnly defined at the II Vatican Council in the declaration *Nostra* ? *tate*: it was planned on a document on Jewish-Christian relations after the Shoah, but it was apparently watered with other religions in order to avoid political conflicts with the Arab countries and the Araba Christians. Nonetheless this choice made of an intrinsecist paradigm (Christianity cannot think itself without Judaism) a universal paradigm of otherness: as a source of what is different and therefore vital to think one's identity.

This experience and this "inner" paradigm is very important in the end of the 20th century when the idea of a clash of civilization, interpreted and vitalized by religious experience, became a way to understand the political instability of the post-cold-war times. Inter-religious dialogue so emerged during the pontificate of John Paul II not as a polite respect of a foreigner, but as a tool to re-establish a proper harmony among differences based on internal resources and not simply relying on external orders which calls for disobedience.

1. Looking over the "divine surprise"

One of the facts that shock an observer of this last decade is that religions are more and more liable to enter the scene of political conflicts, and sometimes they seem able to inform the entire meaning of a conflict: the Irish pattern-where confessional difference has been absorbed within national identity-looks like an old style war. [1] Clash of civilizations and clash of religions come so close that the media are unable to discern the difference between the religious foundations of a conflict, and religious conflict. [2]

Our post-cold war times have given the chance to each and every group and even individuals to wage war: after decades in which only two men were able to start a doomsday conflict, now even kids (as in Zaire) [3] and youths (as in Algeria) can kill—and they can also do this as "believers". [4] War in the name of a faith is not a new creation, but after a century of ideological struggle it looks like a ghost: new catalogues of martyrs and heroes are splitting the victims

---

[1]　G. La Bella, *La questione irlandese* (Roma: 1996).

[2]　S. P. Huntington, *The Clash of Civilizations and the Remaking of World Order* (New York: 1996).

[3]　See J. Skinnader, *Premières réflexions sur la crise du Rwanda*, in J. & P. Desk, *Spiritan congregation* ([Paris]: 1995).

[4]　M. Giro-M. Impagliazzo, *L'Algeria in ostaggio* (Milano: 1996).

into opposing sides.

Literature is hurrying breathlessly run get a convincing explanation of a "divine surprise", [1] which often turns itself into an abyss of horrors, we have seen in the Balkans. [2] To my knowledge the best attempt to explain the phenomenon is the framework offered by a stimulating book of Huntington: he predicts a clash of civilizations, and he describes a cultural (hidden) stereotype which is often used to frame facts. Namely that religious difference is one of the basic, unchanging axes which separates peoples and countries: from this point of view "the world" is only a marketing abstraction; different "worlds" are what does really exist, with a desire for peaceful coexistence and a corresponding inclination to misunderstand each other. Each one of these "worlds" looks to the presence of other worlds within its border as a challenge, a risk or even a real problem. According to Huntington, the revenge of God, turns itself into a struggle between humans. [3] The existence of multireligious cohabitation—as in many European cities—is an uncomfortable reality: both the media and individual consciences are attracted much more easily by the contemplation of difficulties.

In facts problems do exist: and a lack of interpretation is evident in western reflection—either historical, juridical, or political. Current explanations are conflicting and weak. Some authors are tempted by a neo-Victorian view of the international scenario: multireligious coexistence reflects a capacity created by the western

---

[1] A. Riccardi, *Intransigenza e modernità. La chiesa cattolica verso il terzo millennio* (Roma: -Bari 1996).

[2] See P. Mojzes, *Yugoslavian Inferno: Ethnoreligious Warfare in the Balkans* (New York: 1994); H. T. Norris, *Islam in the Balkans. Religion and society between Europe and the Arab World* (Columbia: 1993).

[3] G. Kepel, *La rêvanche de Dieu. Chrétiens, Juifs et Musulmans à la reconquête du monde* (Paris: 1991).

tradition of tolerance. Modern Western tolerance is a quid which other countries, cultures and religions need. If they are unable to accept it by consent, an appropriate dose of violent, though humanitarian interference can teach these savage people the art of tolerance. [1] A different approach thinks that multireligious coexistence cannot be confronted with tolerance in the meaning that tolerance assumed after Peace of Westphalia. [2] The coexistence of religions is and has to be dealt with as a truly new issue. After the death of God, religions have inherited from him an unexpected capacity to shape identity and ethnicity:[3] a perspective which can be faced only through a secularized appeal to a fundamental ethic. Only the search for new patterns—like a world ethic, or a secularized reading of religious sources—can be helpful. [4]

Both these approaches, however, are seriously challenged by the whispering impotence of a tolerance' system in the West and by its capacity to orient other areas through trustworthy leadership. Where a search for religious identity is consistently massive, words differing

---

① G. Mattai-B. Marra, *Dalla guerra all'ingerenza umanitaria, con appendice di documenti* (Torino: 1994). A typical case is that of Afghanistan: the former "freedom fighters" of Reagan's times are now depicted in western literature as the Medieval clerics opposed to women's rights...

② A particular version of this approach is also looking for a theological foundation of the new world order, see J. W. de Gruchy, *Christianity and Democracy: A Theology for a Just World Order* (New York: 1995). On the Weltethos approach see: *"Projekt Weltethos". Beitr? ge aus Philosophie und Theologie. Zum 65. Geburtstag von Hans Küng*, Hrsg. von Bernd Jaspert (Hofgeismar: 1993); A. Auer, *Zur Theologie der Ethik. Das Weltethos im theologischen Diskurs*, Fribourg-Freiburg i. B. -Wien: 1995); *Erkl? rung zum Weltethos. Die Deklaration des Parlamentes der Weltreligionen*, Hrsg. H. Küng-K. J. Kuschel (München-Zürich: 1993); on recent developments ? *kologisches Weltethos im Dialog der Kulturen und Religionen*, hrsg. von Hans Kessler (Darmstadt: 1996).

③ Ethnicity and Nations (Houston: 1979); H. Ditten, *Ethnische Verschiebungen zwischen der Balkanhalbinsel und Kleinasien vom Ende des 6. bis zur zweiten H? lfte des 9. Jahr.* (Berlin: 1993).

④ P. Knitter, *One Earth, Many Religions: Multifaith Dialogue and Global Responsability* (New York: 1995); the deepest approach is that of P. C. Bori, *Un consenso etico fra le culture. Tesi per una lettura secolare delle scritture ebarico-cristiane* (Genova: 1991), with some revisions in *Per un percorso etico tra culture. Testi antichi di tradizione scritta*, a cura di P. C. Bori (Roma:: 1996).

from "fundamentalism" are lacking. [1] The chador, [2] women's rights, polygamy and children reincarnating great masters——do not fit into a system which, even when it matches freedom and rights, is unprepared to manage freedom conflicting with rights. [3] The *impasse* is hidden under a sense of superiority: it does exist, and it calls for comprehension. But what type of comprehension? A comprehension consisting of purely sociological description? An extreme case for constitutional law? A platform for futurist projections?

The assumption of this paper is that history (along with sociology or a juridical approach) can be helpful: in fact the process and the problems of a multireligious society can pose new questions. They can push historical research to revise—as also happens for political equilibrium—stable truths and truisms.

1. The long run questioning two commonplaces

If one looks at the arguments used in debating on the limits and possibilities of multireligious coexistence, one gets that a certain number of historical assumptions are taken for granted, whereas they are inconsistent or under severe revision.

---

[1] A historical perspective on Christian communities in M. Percy, *Words, Wonders and Powers. Understanding Contemporary Christian Fundamentalism and Revivalism* (London: 1996); for Islamic tendencies W. M. Wyatt, *Islamic fundamentalism and modernity*, (London-New York: 1988). See also *The struggle over the past. Fundamentalism in theodern world*, ed. by William M. Shea (Lanham-New York-London: 1993); Th. Meyer, *Fundamentalismus. Aufstand gegen die Moderne* (Reinbek bei Hamburg: 1989).

[2] L. Parisoli, *L'affaire del velo islamico. Il cittadino e i limiti della libertà*, in ? Materiali per una storia della cultura giuridica? 26(1996)/1, 181 – 208.

[3] About the impact of 'ilm? niyya see the PISAI Dossier, Islam et la? cité, in ? Etudes Arabes? 91/92(1996/2 – 1997/1), ed. by Habib C. Moussali; Mohamed-Chérif Ferjani, *Islamisme, la? cité et droits de l'homme. Un siècle de débat sans cesse reporté au sein de la pensée arabe contemporaine* (Paris: 1991).

One of the commonplaces at work in the discussion is the wrong assumption that tolerance (and a parallel doctrine of rights) is a modern tool created by modern western societies to curb the native, violent inclination of established churches. [1] An image of tolerance as the antagonist of a religious *and therefore intolerant* background is often accepted unquestioningly. [2] Such a perspective holds that the ideas of tolerance and human rights were created *ex nihilo* by modern philosophy as a remedy for religious wars and conflicts. In such a perspective Antiquity and the Middle Ages are considered to have been intolerant, because of a conceptual impotence. The Constantinian change becomes irrelevant. [3] From Aristotle, to Roman law up to Thomas Aquinas, ancient philosophy shared a view of "right" as referring to an existing entity. Only an unexpected deviation from the tradition——due to William of Ockham—— allowed for an interpretation of ius as being a subjective characteristic of human beings. Ockham's "aberration"—so to say—would have pioneered tolerance in political thought. [4]

---

[1] See the volumes *Religious Human Rights in Global Perspective. Legal Perspectives*, and its companion book *Religious Human Rights in Global Perspective. Religious Perspectives* J. D. van der Vyver e J. Witte, Jr. , eds. (The Hague: 1996) in particular the introduction of J. V. Dervyver, in *Legal...*, XVII-XXXV; and J. Witte, in *Religious...*, XVII-XXXV.

[2] E. g. *Naissance et affirmation de l'idée de tolérance*, 16ue-18ue siècles: *Actes du 5ue Colloque Jean Boisset*, ed. M. Péronnet (Montpellier: 1989); a different approach B. Plongeron, *De la Réforme aux Lumières: tolérance et liberté: autour d'une fausse idée claire*, in ? Recherches de Science Religieuses? 78(1990), 41 - 72.

[3] P. Brown, *Authority and the sacred. Aspects of the christianisation of the Roman world* (Cambridge-New York-Melbourne: 1995).

[4] From Lachance and Villey, to Jordan and Lecler: L. Lachance, *Le concept de droit selon Aristote et S. Thomas* (Ottawa-Montreal [2]1948; M. Villey, *La formation de la pensée juridique moderne* (Paris: [4]1975) and the 2 volumes of *Philosophie du droit*, (Paris: [3]1982). Less useful, D. Composta, *Il concetto di diritto nell'umanesimo giuridico di Francesco Vitoria o. p.*, in *I diritti dell'uomo e la pace nel pensiero di Francisco de Vitoria e Bartolomé de las Casas*, a cura di C. Soria (Milano: 1988). Also W. K. Jordan, *The Development of Religious Toleration in England*, 4 vol. s, (London: 1932 - 1940) and J. Lecler, *Histoire de la tolérance au siècle de la Réforme*, 2 vol. s (Paris: 1955).

This leitmotif, disseminated throughout the historical literature, was slightly modified by an apologetic neo-Thomist perspective. ① Authors such as Maritain or Finnis, maintained that Thomas Aquinas' concept of right fits perfectly within the framework of a new (and therefore more tolerant) Christendom——but similar changes do not affect the general historical scheme just recalled. ②

Only recently have historians cracked this stereotype. New analysis on Roman antiquity shows the value of a *pax deorum* based on the unknown and unknowable nature of God. ③ There is increasing reflection on the historical meaning of christianizing the Empire: not simply as a change which " perverted " an original purity of the Church, but rather as a move which changed the density of available arguments. ④

In the past twenty years we have become more conscious of differences and changes: the clash between great churches and heretic churches is no longer considered a blatant struggle of classes, but rather as a complex reality, with varying degrees of violence, severity and arguments. ⑤ The transposition of " pagan " violence against religious minorities into Christian intolerance against the pagan has

---

①   See J. Finnis, *Natural law* (Oxford: 1980).

②   See B. Tierney, *Public Expediency and Natural Law: A Fourteenth-Century Discussion on the Origins of Government and Property*, in *Authority and power. Studies on Medieval Law ad Government presented to W. Ullmann*, ed. by B. Tierney and Peter Linehan (Cambridge: 1980), 167 – 182.

③   See M. Sordi, *Tolleranza e intolleranza nel mondo antico*, and P. Zerbi, *Medioevo: tolleranza o intolleranza religiosa*, in M. Sina (ed.), *La tolleranza religiosa. Indagini storiche e riflessioni teologiche* (Milano: 1991).

④   G. Ruggieri, *La storia della tolleranza e dell'intolleranza cristiana come problema teologico*, in "Cristianesimo nella storia" 17 (1996), 463 – 484.

⑤   See B. Tierney, *Origins of Natural Rights Language: Text and Context*, 1150 – 1250, in "History of Political Thought" 10 (1989), 615 – 646; *Religious Rights: An Historical Perspective*, in J. Witte, Jr. , e J. D. van der Vyver, eds. , *Religious Human Rights in Global Perspectives*, J. Witte jr. ed. (The Hague: 1996), 17 – 45, in part. 30; *The Idea of Natural Rights. Studies on Natural Law and Churche Law*. 1150 – 1625, (Atlanta:1997).

been moderated or criticized by various authors, who were able to mix the killing of the *errantes* and the killing of the mistake. [1] The Jewish themselves-the target of a hate subculture-experienced varying degrees of tolerance (in the Christian east as well as in the Christian west) until the end of the 15th century——precisely the time which is usually considered to be *terminus* a quo for a history of tolerance. [2] As for individual and natural rights, Brian Tierney's most recent work has carefully examined the origins of ius and has proved definitively that a subjective comprehension of ius can be traced back to medieval canon lawyers:[3] even if the express definition of a natural religious rights came late in the debate, the conceptual instruments are traditional. I do not know a parallel work on Islamic jurisprudence and the origins of the millet, but Bernard Lewis' study of Jews under Islam has shown, since various decades, that a sophisticated regulation of religious differences can be traced from Quran foundations. [4]

This, of course does not mean that the Christian emperor or the medieval lawyer developed an acceptable degree of coexistence between religious experience. It simply tells us that a simplification can often be an oversimplification. To reaffirm that modern tolerance has medieval roots does not change the pattern of facts, but affects the

---

[1] *L' intolleranza cristiana nei confronti dei pagani*, in "Cristianesimo nella storia" 11(1990), a cura di P. F. Beatrice e F. Paschoud.

[2] In a Jewish perspective, J. Katz, *Exclusiveness and Tolerance: Studies in Jewish-Gentile Relations in Medieval and Modern Times* (Oxford: 1961).

[3] B. Tierney, *The Idea of Natural Rights. Studies on Natural Rights, Natural Law and Church Law* 1150 – 1650 (Atlanta:1997).

[4] B. Lewis, *The Jews of Islam* (Princeton: 1987).

level of interpretation against a "falsified notion" of tolerance. ①
What history is finding out is something else: over the last centuries
western society has incorporated into her own experience and
conscience that it has to be "tolerant": it had, in other words,
developed a "perfect" system to prevent intolerance from a religious
factor, and (even when it is unable to acknowledge basic human
rights to others) this has a pedagogic motivation in order to implement
a better order. Tolerance is a truly modern tool, but it has inherited—
silently—previous arguments and criteria: this is not simply a matter
of change in chronology. It is important because it tells us that *within*
a Christian society, and within Christian tradition—even when a
culture of the enemy was hegemonic—it would have been possible
arguing in terms of rights (or only in terms of tolerance?). *A fortiori*
it should be possible to the Churches to reflect on this subject in a
pluralistic context, not simply from a passive position of institutions
regulated by civil powers, but playing a positive, active role.

Another argument coming in the discussion on the limits and
possibilities of multireligious coexistence is much more a matter of
prejudice, than a historical analysis. It is easy to hear and read that
the contemporary coexistence of religions in the very same political
space is something new. ② Something new, of course, exists, and by
definition one should mistrust the equivalence between long term
perspective and rigid continuity. It is surely wise to underline that in
the past four centuries, definitions of the limits of religions' influence
have been clearer delimitated than in some previous times: but

---

① On 18th Century development see B. Plongeron, *Aux sources d'une notion faussée: les langages théologiques de la tolérance au 18e siècle*, in *Bulletin de la Société de l'Histoire du Protestantisme Fran? ais* 134 (1988) 219 – 238 e J. Delumeau, *La difficile émergence de la tolérance*, in *La Révocation de l'Edit de Nantes*; éd. par R. Zuber et L. Theis (Paris: 1986) 359 – 374.

② *Christlicher Glaube in multireligi? ser Gesellschaft. Erfahrung-Theologische reflexionen-Missionarische Perspektiven*, Hrsg. Anton Peter (1996).

situations of multireligious neighbourhood or coexistence did exist, in the past, along a *limes* which crosses cultures and continents, and within the very body of European Christendom.

When we talk of cohabitation, we should underline a difference between confessional borders and religious differences. Even if Christians, after the 16th century, got used to talking about themselves as "religions", the coexistence is by no means related to their presence (ruled according to the principle of "modern" tolerance). [①] A really multireligious presence did exist, and it worked. Thanks to the Jewish community and economic exchanges with Islamic countries, a *complicatio* took place: it was not because of a tightness of religious obligation that antisemitism became more violent, rather in correspondence with to strengthening of the regime Christendom. This balance of conflict and coexistence, however, has roots which have not been properly explored. Much research is needed to understand the border between Christianity and other religious worlds (one might remember that the encounter between Buddhism and Christianity does not belong to America's contemporary history, but the Middle East of the fourth century; [②] or we would welcome studies on the real impact of repressive manifestoes in European juridical history, which can reveal a harsh hate as well as lack of implementation in repression; and when Christianity and Islam did meet, among Christians there was a theory of voluntary martyrdom, which explains how the 7th Century saw the "challenge" of a new religion [③]).

---

① See *Tolerance and intolerance in the European Reformation*, ed. by O. P. Grell & B. Scribner (Cambridge: 1996).

② Ch. S. Prebish, *Historical dictionary of Buddhism* (Metuchen, NJ: 1993). T. Tweed, *The American encounter with Buddhism* 1844 – 1912. *Victorian Culture and the limits of dissent* (Bloomington and Indianapolis: 1992)

③ On Juan Alvarez and Eulogius of Cordoba see D. Millet-Gérard, *Chrétiens mozarabes et culture islamique des VIIe -IXe siècles* (Paris: 1984).

In Europe's past and in the deepest strata of its history there is also the experience of a meeting which took place far from home. The renegades question, for instance, is very interesting: prisoners of Islamic countries the "renegades" had quitted Christianity for Islam. When some of them had the luck to escape, they posed serious problems to the religious authorities: living witnesses of a possible encounter, they were a heresy for Christendom. [1] Far from the Mediterranean, merchants and travellers found the challenge of cohabitation: the heavenly harmony within Indians' tribes and natives' villages of the new world—as well as the sophisticated culture in Chinese courts—impressed the European observer.

These are only seeds of future research, rather than definitive conclusions. Nonetheless they show that deeper historical knowledge—able to maintain a balance between general trends, particular histories, dormant realities-can be useful. When one goes back to revising the two dominating theses concerning the issue of multireligious relationships in our world—the ideological character of current explanations becomes self-evident. Neither by underlining the tool of tolerance nor the novelty of a "*necessitata*" coexistence of religious difference can one trace the origins of our present uncertainty. If there is a spreading perception of danger, and a threat to western tolerance , this has to be explained by a different background.

If one loses this diachronic depth there will be no understanding, and even the danger of something worse. Only a passive, cynical acceptance of the shoa's effects may conceal the fact that a European

---

[1] B. & L. Bennassar, *Chrétiens d'Allah, L'histoire extraordinaire des rénegats XVIe-XVIIe siècles* (Paris: 1989).

Jewry did exist, though in a condition of discrimination and persecution;[1] and beside this, a Christian presence—affected by colonialist echos—did exist within Islamic society or Buddhist kingdoms. The massive number of immigrants arriving from Islamic countries, and the formation of a considerable non-Christian community of peoples from Africa and Asia, has deeply affected the *degree* of complexity within Europe; but they have not created a multireligious society. And the limits of European tolerance are challenged not only by an identity revenge of competing minorities, but from an internal, genetic limit, which pertains to the realm of the political relation between churches and societies.

2. The juridical background of a missing analysis

The lack of comprehension I have talked about, is mostly a deficit of historical depth, which affects political elites as well as religious leaders. It is expressed through an undefined fear about the future—a fear which is seeking juridical protection. Paradoxically the mistrust for the other is expressed in terms of a threat to (or a violation of) legal order, and the lack of historical perspective are concealed by the demand to respect a confessional history which is a habit of recent privileges. [2] A realistic approach to the juridical instrument and situation *de facto* created or regulated, shows that it is

---

① C. Iancu, *L'émancipation des juifs de Roumanie* (1913 – 1919). *De l'inégalité civique aux droits de minorité: l'originalité d'un combat à partir des guerres balkaniques et jusqu'à la Conférence de paix de Paris* (Montpellier: 1992); E. Benbassa-A. Rodrigue, *Juifs des Balkans. Espaces judéo-ibériques, XIVe-XXe siècles* (Paris: 1993).

② Description in *Religioni e sistemi giuridici. Introduzione al diritto ecclesiastico comparato*, a cura di F. Margiotta Broglio, C. Mirabelli, F. Onida (Bologna: 1997); an classical anticlerical perspective from the ULB in *Pluralisme religieux et la? cité dans l'Union Européenne*, éd. A. Diekers (Bruxelles: 1994).

characterized by a double movement. European legislation shows differences in laws matched by analogous results in practical life. Contradictory evidence of this process is easy to find.

On one side, Europe knows a rich plurality of systems regulating religious difference and the relationship between states and churches. [1] Finland, Sweden, Norway, Denmark and in some ways Great Britain have a constitutional State Church. In a reformed system secularization and control over ecclesiastical affairs seem to match each other with a certain degree of plausibility: only isolated reformers like Kierkegaard criticized such a situation from a "religious" point of view. Even in Sweden, where a constitutional reform will deprive the Lutheran Church of the *status* of ecclesiastical reflex of national identity-that Church will have particular privileges. [2] Even the disestablishment of the relations between the Crown and the Church of England does not imply a systemic change of basic attitudes... [3] Greece—and recently Serbia, Bulgaria and Romania [4]—have a different system discriminating between a national dominating religion, and other cults tolerated to various degrees: like fascist Italy and Spain, the difference between the people's religion and the other beliefs can affect many practical aspects of minoritarian communities' life, but the Greek solution—adhering to the principle of the *European convention on human rights*—seems to be acting as a model for East European countries. A good many of the European countries with a catholic "majority" (sociologically speaking) regulate their ecclesiastical affairs through a constitutional reluctance to commit the

---

[1] See *Stato e chiesa nell' unione europea*, ed. by G. Robbers (Baden-Baden: 1996).

[2] R. Sch? tt, *Stato e chiesa in Svezia*, in *Stato e chiesa nell' unione europea...*, 322 – 324.

[3] See Robbers..., and V. Bogdanor, *The Monarchy and the Constitution*, (Oxford: 1995), 215 – 239.

[4] P. Mojzes, *Religiuos Human Rights in Post Communist Balkan Countries*, in *Religiuos Human Rights in Global Perspective. Legal Perspectives*, cit. , 263 – 284.

State to one confession, and a practical bilateral regulation of the issue. Concordats were stipulated in Germany, Italy, Spain and Portugal, [1] and influenced the entire architecture of the system: even other confessions and religions (either as corporation or federation) have been attracted into an orbit of bilateral relations. A proportion (or disproportion) of forces and the national (or international) character of religions is the exchanging platform for solutions. [2] Some scholars—like Silvio Ferrari—argue that separationist countries—France, Belgium, the Netherlands, Ireland—are defined only *ex opposito*: [3] how can one define a common identity of nations which have written into their constitution the invocation of the Trinity (like Ireland), or the principle of *laicité* (like France)? [4] Usually, these differences—although culturally neglected—are described to extract the core of a European *ius commune*: the primacy of individual consciousness seems to be the really dividing line between Islamic countries and western countries. Arranged in different ways, western laws and constitutions seems to guarantee from a « prohibition of the free exercise » because of cultural superiority (things are more difficult about the statement that no law shall be made « to respect an establishment »). [5]

Apparently the only thing which will never be subscribed to by Europan States is the interchangeability of their system. Ideological

---

①　*A Concordata de* 1940, *Portogual-Santa Sé* (Lisboa: 1993).

②　J. Julg, *L'? glise et les états. Histoire des concordats*, Préface de Jean Chélini (Paris: 1990).

③　J. Martínez Torrón, *Separatismo y cooperación en los Acuerdos del Estado con las minorías religiosas* (Granada: 1994).

④　See J. -M. Mayeur, *Regard d' un historien sur la liberté religieuse et le régimes des culte en droit française*, in « Trasversalités » 62 (1997) 275 – 282, presentation of the volume *Liberté religieus et régimes des cultes en droit français. Texte, pratique administrative, jurisprudence* (Paris: 1996); of the same historian *La question laïque XIXe -XXe siècle* (Paris: 1996).

⑤　*Political Order and the Plural Structure of Society*, ed. J. W. Skillen and R. M. McCartney (Atlanta: 1991).

and national pride will not allow the admission that so different methods produce comparable results. People of different Christian denominations can live in the same way in different countries: actually the condition of an *acknowledged and established* religious minority in England do not seem preferable to that of an Italian one, and *vice versa*. Even where the churches had for a long time asked for a "special" status proportional to the religious identity of the country (like the Catholic church in Italy or the Orthodox church in Greece), practical discrimination does not work any more on an individual basis: the guarantee of freedom— *infra fines*—can be compatible with unequal treatments. [1] One perceptive thesis maintains the principle that there is, indeed, a "constant" at work: where the US has been assuming the issue of equality and imposes limitations on confessions which do not affect the association of people in any other way, Europe has developed a system where freedom is privileged, even if an unequal cooperation with corporate churches can create a difference. [2]

The contradiction of evidence is the outcome of a process: for decades different systems produced different situations, particularly in relation to the proper goal of these solutions. The system of toleration (toleration of a neutral state, or of a confessional kingdom) was built to guarantee peace among conflicting Christianities. Changes on the level of inter-Christian relations did affect the meaning of a system which has performed extraordinarily well as far as expected results are concerned: if it seems evidently inadequate for new needs this takes us back to the questions raised in the beginning.

---

[1] See M. Root, *The Concordat and the Northern European Porvoo Common Statement: Different Paths to the Same Goal*, in *A Commentary on Concordat and Agreement*, ed. J. Enfiss-D. Martensens (Minneapolis: 1994), 138 – 151.

[2] *Diritto e religione in Europa occidentale*, ed. S. Ferrari-I. C. Ibán (Bologna:1987).

3. Learning from changes

No matter about difficulties: is the substance of a tolerant system a universal value, which has only to be sponsored by or imposed on other countries? Does the vacillating stability of this system where great populations' migrations are occurring, mean something more than a simple extension of an actual therapy to a larger population? Can solutions (born into a world where religious difference *meant* Christian confessional pluralism) be adapted to a world where a huge religious market is now populated and confronted by a vocal Islam, a rooted Buddhism, a resurgence of violent Hinduism (not to mention the persistence of a Catholic/Anglican war within the EC itself!)?

In fact, historically speaking, [1] one should focus on something else: namely the impact of the ecumenical movement and its ties with multireligious issues. Contemporary theology usually reflects on the relation between ecumenism and interreligious dialogue in terms of continuity, or development. [2] Sometimes even some guidelines of ecumenical effort (dialogue, the search of points in common, doctrinal statement, convergence) are presented as a model for an interreligious encounter. Maybe this is positively useful: I think nevertheless that the changes that have occurred in the churches'

---

[1] Of course jurists might offer a better inventory of fundamental tools, variable details and developing guidelines. The task of a historian is different, but nonetheless-hopefully-relevant. A sociological description in B. Tibi, *Il fondamentalismo religioso* (Torino: 1997) and E. Pace, *Il regime della verità. Il fondamentalismo religioso contemporaneo* (Bologna:: 1990); see also *Fundamentalism*, « Concilium », 3 (1992); less perceptive *Gli odierni fondamentalismi nelle religioni del Libro*; *Ai quattro angoli del fondamentalismo. Movimenti politico-religiosi nella loro tradizione, epifania, protesta, regressione*, a cura di R. Giammanco (Firenze: 1993).

[2] *Christianity and the world religions. Paths of dialogue with Islam, Hinduism, and Buddhism*, (by) Hans Küng, Josef van Ess, Heinrich von Stietencron, Heinz Bechert (London:1993).

conscience over the last half-century can offer new resources to the issue of a multireligious society.

Ecumenical experience modified the scenario and affected the problem, because it forced us to step up from a reluctant acceptance of tolerant society as a hypothesis to a consideration of freedom as a positive space in which the conscience can experience its proper vocation. Since tolerance was an "outsider" coming in to regulate interconfessional antagonism, a great deal of reflection deriving from patristic writings on the *tolerantia Dei* and His υπομον? was wasted and left aside. If—when—the churches prove themselves able to regulate and overcome their conflict in a perspective of communion, a new path will open up and all the previous solutions will need to be updated. [1]

The very concept of truth should be updated. Tolerance and freedom have been for at least two centuries a big issue for the Christian, particularly the Catholic, as far as they were unable to approach truth without a particular conception of truth, claiming absoluteness for it. [2] The « freedom opposite to the religion's virtue » which Leo XIII condemned in *Libertas* (June 20, 1888), was considered a serious threat to a stable and established equilibrium, [3] but actually it was the declaration of shameful impotence: where the tyranny of truth comes to feed violence, when the State acts as *tertium* between religious differences and adopts rules able to prevent a situation of religious conflict-this means that a deep perversion of Christian purposes did occur. When, on the contrary, truth and its

---

[1] See my *Tolerance and Rights. An Exploration of Medieval Canon Law*, in *Perspectives actuelles sur la tolérance*, sous la dir. de J. Doré (Paris: 1997), 47 – 66.

[2] H. Waldenfels, *Der Absolutheitsanspruch des Christentums*, in « Hochland » 62(1970), 202 – 217.

[3] On Leo XIII's times see also A. Acerbi, *Chiesa e democrazia. Da Leone XIII al Vaticano II* (Milano: 1991), concerning the political issue.

absoluteness finds a path for communion, tolerance ceases to be a civil imposition and it acknowledged as something proper to the Christian experience of freedom.

Civil instruments to regulate the conflict—the principle of *cujus regio*, confessional establishment, separation and concordats—*obviously* become similar as far as effects on confessional differences are concerned. And *obviously* they seem ineffective and unable to regulate a quite different phenomenon like multireligious coexistence. Something effective can only come from a deep reflection on truth: the more Christian theologians are able to grasp within their own religious traditions the dimension of a welcoming truth, to understand the meaning of otherness as a fundamental dimension of truth, to express evangelization in terms of revelation of an Otherness——the more European societies will be delivered from the *aporia* they are living in.[1] Can our situation be described as a secularized culture using a system of moral references based on Christian history, to enforce a superiority complex of mistrust and denigration toward other forms of religious thought?

Such an effort can support the due extension of the idea of freedom. One of the great and painful efforts of the 20th century Catholic theology—and later of doctrinal teaching—has been that of accepting the State's neutral position not simply as hypothesis, but rather as a thesis, coherent with Christian positions and worries concerning freedom of conscience. Churches—and the Catholic

---

[1]　The issue of infra-ecclesiastical defence of human rights rests, in my opinion, on a different basis and it touches on different dynamics. A theological approach in G. Ruggieri in *La verità croocifissa fra Trinità e storia. Per una determinazione del rapporto tra verità e comunione*, in 《 Cristianesimo nella storia 》, 2 (1995), 383 – 406.

Church in particular—did not walk on this path alone. [1] The 1948 *Declaration of the UN*[2] on human rights spelt out a world where human beings were *free* to speak and believe: the legal reflection on "Church and State" had been confronted by the disaster of WW2 and the challenge of Communist regimes underlined a definition of human rights capable of marking the difference between capitalist and socialist societies. Each religious formation understood his place in this system in different and changing way during these years: in the US Baptist Bible Belt, as well as in the Catholic Veneto or Bavaria, a religious majority did exercise a strong pressure to guarantee their privileges not on a basis of "truth", but rather as a defendant of a legal, political majority and its own rights.

Only little groups, or cultured circles reflected on the issue of freedom since the early Fifties without a "tactical" approach: that particular situation shortened the list of those who decided to take the risk of publication (one could recall Catholic Intellectuals or the Catholic Conference for Ecumenical Questions as promoter of meetings and exchanges[3]). Even very prudent positions were suspected, and at the same time the "objects" where not removed by condemnation:

---

[1] On the WCC, see L. Vischer, *La liberté religieuse et le Conseil Œcuménique des Églises*, in « Concilium», 18 (1966), 47 – 55; and N. Koshy, *The Ecumenical Understanding of Religious Liberty: The Contribution of the World Council of Churches*, in « Journal of Church and State », 38 (1996), 137 – 154.

[2] Cfr. UNESCO, *Autour de la nouvelle Déclaration Universelle des Droits de l'homme* (Paris: 1949). A recent reflection in T. C. van Boven, *Religious Liberty in the Context of Human Rights*, « The Ecumenical Review », 37 (1985), 340 – 357; Th. Meron, ed. , *Human Rights in International Law*, Oxford: 1985); and N. Lerner, *Religious Human Rights Under The United Nations*, in *Religious Human Rights in Global Perspective. Legal Perspectives*, cit. , 79 – 134.

[3] *Unité chrétienne et tolérance religieuse* (Paris: 1950); *Tolérance et communauté humaine. Chrétiens dans un monde divisé* (Paris-Tournai: 1952); *L' Église et la liberté* (Paris: 1952).

looking again within the Catholic ghetto, the silencing of John C. Murray[①] did not prevent Pius XII from voicing inquietudes about Feeney's intransigent conception of the Church and State relationship. The double and conflicting 1953 statements—the Ottaviani address on the confessional State, and on the other side Pius XII's address *Ci riesce*—show that traditional positions were ready for a new enforcement or a deep revision, but for sure were untenable as such.[②]

Vatican II and *Pacem in terris* marked the turning point:[③] avoiding the trap of rights as immunities or empowerment, Pietro Pavan (who drafted the encyclical), offered a solid basis to *Gaudium et spes* and to *Dignitatis humanœ*.[④] The assumption of the human beings' dignity as core of the argument, and peace as horizon (*titulus*) of the ecclesiastical intervention—opened up a new way: freedom had not to be a disturbing intruder in the realm of truth, but rather the companion of a church which becomes available to

---

① See J. Komonchak, *The Silencing of John Courtney Murray*, in *Cristianesimo nella storia. Saggi in onore di Giuseppe Alberigo*, a cura di A: Melloni, D. Menozzi, G. Ruggieri, M. Toschi (Bologna: 1996), 657 – 702. See also T. P. Ferguson, *Catholic and American: The Political Theology of John Courtney Murray* (Kansas City: 1993); J. K. Pavlischek, *John Courtney Murray and the dilemma of Religious Toleration* (Kirksville: 1994); D. Gonnet, *La liberté religieuse à Vatican II. La contribution de John Cortney Murray* (Paris: 1994).

② Cfr. A. Riccardi, *Governo e "profezia" nel pontificato di Pio XII*, in *Pio XII*, ed. A. Riccardi himself, a cura dello stesso autore (Roma-Bari: 1984) 31 – 92. Apologetic attotudes in J. B. Hehir, *Religious Activism for Human Rights: a Christian Case Study*, in *Religious Human Rights in Globlal Perspective. Religious Perspectives*, cit., 97 – 119, especially 107 – 109.

③ P. Pavan, *Il momento storico di Giovanni XXIII e della "Pacem in terris": sua incidenza negli atti conciliari e nella vita della chiesa e sua incidenza nella società contemporanea*, in *I diritti fondamentali della persona e la libertà religiosa. Atti del V colloquio giuridico* (8 – 10 marzo: 1984), a cura di F. Biffi. (Roma: 1985), 149 – 154. See also *Jean XXIII devant l' histoire*, éd. G. Alberigo (Paris: 1988).

④ See J. Hamer, *Histoire du texte de la déclaration*, in J. Hamer-Y. Congar, éd., *Vatican II. La liberté religieuse*, Unam Sanctam 60 (Paris: 1967), 53 – 110; T. F. Stransky, *Declaration on Religious Freedom of Vatican Council II. Commentory* (Glen Rock: 1966); P. Pavan, a cura di, *La libertà religiosa. Dichiarazionr conciliare "Dignitatis humanae". Testo conciliare e commento* (Brescia: 1967), 7 – 117.

acknowledge the *mirabilia dei* outside its own borders.

4. Perspectives

To enlarge the idea of freedom does not mean to surrender responsibility-but to move that problem on to the political plane.

Constitutional laws and governmental styles had proved themselves able enough (not always!) to guarantee human rights and religious freedom rights to minorities, even when the pressure of majorities had been strong and politically organized.[1] Different believers can participate in such a process—as Gutierrez said in a fascinating title—« drinking at their own sources ». Differences in the guarantee of religious freedom still affect Europe: so we can also feel the irony of the Holy See's plea against the Patriarch of Moscow, who seems able to get from his Duma, things that the Pope has been asking for a long time from the Italian Parliament...[2] However, when difference becomes irritating, often the problem arises from a deficiency in the religious understanding of its own tradition and life, and not always in religious legislation. It might be thought that those residual deficiencies will act according to the "prophecy" on this century by Gustav Mahler in the famous final D of his last symphony: it can last much more than you expect, but it will end, sooner or later. But precisely our post-cold-war times make us conscious that the accomplishment of secularization and modernization through

---

[1]　J. Witte, Jr., *Christianity and Democracy: Past Contributions and Future Challenges*, « Emory International Law Review », 6 (1992), 55 – 69.

[2]　Something should be probably added on the problem of Uniatism, "the handicapped son of a divorced couple": on the background see B. Korsch, *Religion in the Soviet Uniion*, *A bibliography*: 1980 – 1989 (New York-London: 1992).

democratic rules even on human rights, [1] is part of the problem, not the solution.

Others can look to the ecumenical pattern as a way to clonate a successful method: such an ambiguous position—relevant also in a signal event like the Assisi meeting and its repetition—assumes that interreligious relationship can be based in terms of proximity. The effectiveness of the "undivided church"'s myth, should be reproduced through another temporary myth: an undivided religious anthropology, the link among all those who acknowledge monotheism or spiritual conception of life and death——the mutual acceptance on this basis is much better than conflict, but worse than an awareness of the meaning of differences.

Both the crisis and the success of the ecumenical movement are basic to our understanding of the terms of relationship with other religions, not only because they can suggest models and patterns. The real issue is otherness and the capacity of each religious system to understand on his own theological basis the right, the existence, and the meaning of the other. [2] The point is not a simple theology of rights, [3]

---

[1]　M. E. Marty, *Religious Dimensions of Human Rights*, and W. J. Everett, *Human Rights in the Church*, in *Religious Human Rights in Global Perspectve-Religious...*, 1 – 16, and 121 – 141; H. Bielefeldt, *Zum Ethos der Menschenrechlichen Demokratie. Eine Einführung am Beispiel des Grundgesetzes* (Würzburg: 1991).

[2]　See *L'alterità. Concezioni ed esperienze nel cristianesimo contemporaneo*, a cura di A. Melloni e G. La Bella (Bologna:1995).

[3]　See the special isse of « Concilium » 124 (1979), *The Church and the Rights of Man*; after this H. U. von Balthasar, *Die "Seiligkeiten" und die Menschenrechte*, in « Communio. Internationale katholisches Zeitschrift », 10 (1981), 97 – 106; G. Thils, *Les droits de l'homme et perspectives chrétiennes*, Leuven: 1981; a statement of the ITC came in: 1983, *Les chrétiens d'aujourd'hui devant la dignité et les droits de la personne humanaine. Commission théologique internationale*, 1 – 7 décembre: 1983 (Città del Vaticano: 1985); E. Fuchs-P. A. Astucki, *Au nom de l'autre. Essai sur le fondement des droits de l'homme* (Genève: 1985). Recent studies: J. F. Collange, *Théologie des droits de l'homme* (Paris: 1989); on the reception of Vatican II declaration C. Jarczyk, *La liberté religieuse 20 ans aprés le Concile* (Paris: 1984). A more systematic approach in e W. Kaspar, *The Theological Foundations of Human Rights*, « The Jurist », 50 (1990), 148 – 166.

but a right proper to theology to reflect on a *veritas filia temporis*. [1]

In practice this means that the problem of western law and society is not to sit and wait, proud of his solution of tolerance and its objective results in terms of freedom and equality. It is not enough to wish Islamic nations would find a way to implement a tolerance which will only provoke fundamentalism. Mostly it means something for the churches: now a temptation is coming, namely to appeal first to political powers rather than to other churches, first to parliaments rather than to religions. Signs of a different approach are visible: even with its own ambiguities and uncertainty the "Assisi '86" sets a standard. [2] And therefore the Churches can also be enabled to acknowledge the challenge of a multireligious society as grace and opportunity to serve the universal community of human beings. Three temptations were common in the past and may possibly become operational again in the future:

-a demand by from the State to churches in order to guarantee a civil religion[3]

-a demand by from the Churches to the State on moral issues (a tyranny of values?)[4]

---

[1]   The sentences come from Aul. Gallius,, *Mist. Act.* , *XII*, 11, 7, ed. G. Bernardi-Pierini (Torino: 1992), II, p. 912; it reappears in Bernardus Chart. , *Metol. III*.4, (ed. Walb), p. 136; see F. Saxl, *Veritas filia temporis in Philosophy and History-Ernst Cassirer Festschrift*, ed. R. Klihminsky-N. - J. Poton (New York: 1963), 197 – 222; E. Garin, *Medioevo e Rinascimento* (Roma: 1954), 195ss—— ref. In E. Jeauneau, *Nani sulle spalle dei giganti* (Napoli: 1969).

[2]   See my *La rencontre d' Assise et ses développements dans la dynamique du Concile Vatican II*, in *Le christianisme vis-à-vis les religions*, sous la dir. de J. Doré (Paris: 1997), 99 – 130.

[3]   *The Church' s public role. Retrospect* and prospect, ed. by Dieter T. Hessel (Grand Rapids: 1993). On a theological foundation of human rights see R. Traee, *Faith in Human Rights: Support in Religious Traditions for a Global Struggle* (Washington: 1991), e, più recentemente, H. Cox e A. Sharma, *Positive Resources of Religion for Human Rights*, in *Religion and Human Rights*, J. Kelsay e S. B. Twiss eds. (New York: 1994), 61 – 79.

[4]   C. Schmitt, *Die Tyrannei der* Werte, in *Säkularisation und Utopie, Ebracher Studien. Festschrift für Ernst Forsthoff*, Stuttgart 1967, 37 ff.

-a demand by from public opinion（and/or media）to express in confessional（or religious）terms the uncomfortable search for identity in a society becoming not simply multiconfessional, neither secularized *and* multiconfessional, but rather multireligious as such.①

In the limits of democracy proper to a complex society ruled by media consent, the task to link reconciliation, memory and justice is the challenge for religions. If the believer can—if the believer wants to invest in such a service to the unity of humankind—which is the earthly name of their gods—they will be able not simply to receive a civil benefit from outside,② but to deepen their own faithfulness to their vocation to a superior duty. Possibly this "listening" to the difference can teach and can sound like a voice calling to conversion, speaking the word in different ways, and singing on unknown tunes. What a theologian and passionate fighter of ecumenism like Jean-Marie Tillard wrote, is true: that the Spirit is talking to the Churches through other Churches;③ this is true and is the "sacrament" of a meaning of each and every otherness. This could be a way to discovering what evangelization is, beyond the multiple and sticky caricatures imposed by a colonial culture. The conflict between respect and mission is a post colonial heritage and debt: even for early modern theologians and canonists an "unjust" conquest was to refuse

---

① See L. Swidler, *Human Rights and Religious Liberty from the Past to the Future*, in *Religious Liberty and Human Rights in Nation and Religions*, L. Swidler, ed., （Philadelphia: 1986）, VII-XVI: proceedings of the conference gathered on November: 1985）in Pennsylvania, by the 《 Journal of Ecumenical Studies 》, the Religion Department of Temple University and the Jacob Blaustein Institute for the Advancement of Human Rights, New York.

② This is the position of *Conscience oblige. Entretien avec Claude Geffré*, in C. Sahel（éd.）, *La tolérance. Pour un humanisme hérétique*（Paris: 1993）, 55 – 70.

③ J. -M. R. Tillard, *Conversion, oecumenisme*, in *Cristianesimo nella storia. Saggi in onore di Giuseppe Alberigo...*, 517 – 536.

and condemn. ①The opportunity and the challenge of a multireligious society is to receive the Gospel and to walk, looking for an "elsewhere", where the evangelization can discern God himself working to build unity and to make understanding grow. ②

---

① See J. Muldoon, *The struggle for justice in the conquest of the New World*, in « Monumenta Iuris Canonici », C. 9, 707 – 720 and *Medieval Canon Law and Formation of International Law*, in « Zeitschrfit der Savigny-Stiftung für Rechtsgeschichte », Kan. Ab. 81(1995), 64 – 82.

② *Michel de Certeau ou la différence chrétienne. Actes du colloque "Michel de Certeau et le christianisme"*, éd. par Claude Geffré (Paris: 1991), and the collection M. De Certeau, *Mai senza l'altro* (Bose: 1993). See S. Scatena, *La libertà religiosa*, in the proceedings of the conference on *Derechos humanos* held at the University of Quilmes, Buenos Aires, in November 1997, ed. by A. Migone.

Dialogue Between Civilizations in the Age of Globalization: Can Religion Promote Peace among Civilizations?

Arvind Sharma

I would like to address this issue by adopting four perspectives in succession: a religious perspective, a secular perspective, a civilizational perspective, and a metaphysical perspective. I adopt a religious perspective because some religions have come to be identified with certain civilizations: for instance, Hinduism with India, Confucianism with China, the Eastern Orthodox form of Christianity with Russia, and so on. I also adopt a secular perspective because some civilizations, notable the modern Western, tend to distinguish between a religious realm and a secular realm. I adopt a civilizational approach *per se*, given the popularity of the clash of civilizations thesis, and I adopt a metaphysical approach because it might have significance in common for all civilizations, even as it transcends them.

I start with an event which provides *a counter example* to my thesis, that religion can promote peace among civilizations—namely, the events of September 11, 2001 which highlight the clash between the West as a civilization and Islam as a religion, and raise the question whether peace could be achieved through religion in the context of civilizations. Allow me therefore to dwell on the event for a minute.

The cataclysmic events of September 11, 2001 have produced many results. One of them is a steady flow of books highly critical of not only Islam in particular, but of religion in general. The stream continues unabated. The criticism of religion, indeed of any system of beliefs and practices is not a bad thing in itself, for beliefs and practices must be constantly tested in the cleansing crossfire of criticism. It was not for nothing that Marx famously described the criticism of religion as the beginning of all criticism. Truth after all is said to be like a torch, the more it is shaken the more it shines.

But to be critical is not necessarily to be correct. So while it is true that religion has often been associated with negative developments in the history of humanity, it can also be argued that, in the same way, it is *also* associated with positive developments. Instead of viewing religion as an *evil force*, it is more in keeping with the evidence to view as a *force*, which is capable of being harnessed for both good and evil. Just as fire is a natural force, which is capable of both cooking our food and burning our house down, religion is a force in human affairs, an institutional rather than a natural force but a force nevertheless, which may be capable of being harnessed for either good or evil.

So the question to be answered is: how might one make religion a force for good in the world, or achieve peace *through* religion, rather than in spite of it. The modern mind tends to be somewhat sceptical when it comes to achieving peace through religion, as it is more accustomed to seeing religion as a threat to peace. In what follows I would like to identify four ways in which this view may be re-examined.

1) In 2006 a global congress on World's Religions After September 11 was held in Montréal. It arrived at a conclusion, which, in hindsight, seems such an obvious thing-like Columbus' egg-that religions tend to be a force for human good when they work together, and a negative force when they are opposed to each other. This is one way in which religions can promote peace—by coming together themselves. This can happen along religious lines, like the mutual study of the scriptures of various religions in the light of each other, as Mahatma Gandhi proposed; or along secular lines, like religions joining hands in fighting environmental degradation. The key is that they should be working with each other rather than against each other. A point worth mentioning here, even if it cannot be pursued any further, is that the role of proselytizing needs to be reassessed in the light of this perspective, for when religions try to convert the followers of other religions to their own they are sometimes perceived as a threat by some civilizations; in such cases they cannot be said to be working together, but rather against each other.

2) The second way in which religion can contribute to peace is by helping bridge the religious/secular divide. Tensions between the secular and the religious realms tend to compromise peace, as illustrated by the controversy over the wearing of the scarf by Muslim women in Europe and even elsewhere. This is an example of the negative appositioning of the two realms. But this need not necessarily be so. The two dimensions could be brought in positive contact by aligning them in a particular discourse, such as that of human rights, for example. The religions of the world could come together—in keeping with the point made earlier—to produce, for instance, their own Declaration of Human Rights by the World's Religions, which would embody their ideas regarding human flourishing. Such effort will then also have the effect of helping integrate secular and religious

discourse as it is emerging in all civilizations as a result of globalization. This idea is the legacy of a project called Religion and Human Rights, an independent initiative founded in 1993, which concluded with a dialogue on religion and human rights in May 1994, where such a proposal was first made.

3) Yet another way, a third way, in which religions may be a force for peace is the role they might play in the context of Samuel Huntington's well-known thesis regarding the forthcoming clash of civilizations. Although it might be true that sometimes certain religions may be uniquely associated with certain civilizations, it is equally true that religions sometimes cut across civilizations and may thus also serve as bridges across civilizations. The way Buddhism brought the Indic and Chinese civilizations together, through the interaction of Indian and Chinese monks, for several centuries from the beginning of the Common Era onwards, is well documented. It is not unreasonable to hypothesize, therefore, that religions may also help mitigate the so-called clash of civilizations, just as they might exacerbate it. If there is a clash of civilizations, then it cuts hopefully across religious boundaries. It *could* be argued that it is religions which are considered true or false, and not civilizations, so that religions generate conflicting truth-claims, and thereby create an atmosphere of conflict. It could *also* however be argued that religions aspire for the universal and thus help overcome civilizational boundaries. The actual outcome will depend on how these insights are operationalized.

4) To the religious, secular, and civilizational approaches canvassed in the first, second, and third points one may add a fourth—a philosophical one, which has a bearing on all of them. This perspective may be phrased as follows: does the truth lie with any particular religion, or does it lie *in-between* them? Is it an *indivisible*

treasure, in the sense that only one party can have it and it cannot be divided up and shared with others; or is it an *indivisible treasure*, in the sense of not being capable of being divided into parts, which individual parties may seize, but is something which can be possessed in common? When I am in a garden, where does the truth of the garden lie: With me? Or around me?

Where Can Religions Meet for a Human Good in the Age of Global Pluralism? Reflections on Wilfred Cantwell Smith and Bernard Lonergan's Faith

Chae Young Kim

1. Introduction

In North America[1] and in Asia[2] in general, the contemporary rel-

---

[1]　Before I first came to North America in 1988, I had learned from a school textbook that racial or ethnic population can be pluralistic. I had imagined that, in North America, one could only find three groups: a dominant Caucasian strain which lived with a small Afro-American population which together, in turn, lived with an even smaller Native American ethnic population. However, at the airport as soon as I arrived, I instantly realized that my anticipations were not well grounded. I came to discover that North American society possesses a diversity that is more pluralistic than in other continents and countries (more pluralistic along ethnic, racial, cultural, political, linguistic, and religious lines). Admittedly, I was able to meet many "traditional Americans" but, in every place, I also met many Asians and many Spanish speaking people. At the same time I also began to realize that I could easily buy Asian food and clothes which I had thought were only available in my home country, Korea. Admittedly, it is easier to buy certain things in my native country. However, in most major cities in North America, I was able to find many different ethnic communities and in such a context, I was able to experience their inner life in a manner, which lay outside the experience of the older traditional American communities as they have continued to exist today.

igious pluralistic situation does not exist as an abstract speculative theory. It exists rather as a concrete empirical fact and it has been an established fact for some time now in our social life. In recent years however, some loss of historical memory has been occurring about the religious pluralism that has been traditional for us in East Asia. Hence, for authentic inter-religious encounters, it is best that we recover our memories of the pluralistic religious experience that has existed for us in Asia. In addition, such a recollection should be viewed as an especially urgent requirement. It is an *imperative* given that, in our world today, all persons (irrespective of geographical distances, religions, class, races and other differences) are experiencing a similar religious pluralism within their different local conte-

---

In addition, and as a counter to my initial false imagination, I have come to realize that various religious traditions have existed over time and apparently side by side. One thinks, for instance, about Christianity, Judaism, Buddhism, Hinduism, Islam, Taoism, and many New Religious Movements. Each religious tradition is not composed of one homogeneous denomination but of many different traditions and denominations. Even among family members, I have found that they do not always belong to the same religious tradition or the same denomination. Some are Methodists, some Catholics, some non-religious or anti-religious, and so on. Even married couples, in many cases, do not belong to the same tradition or the same denomination. Several couples that I knew would attend a Christian service twice each Sunday: a Catholic Mass and then, later, a Protestant worship service. Also, among couples, one would find some major differences with regard to different religious traditions. A couple might go to Church in the morning and then, in the afternoon, to a Buddhist temple with their children. The more that I came to understand the North American religious situation, the more I came to realize how complex the situation is.

North America is becoming more pluralistic and this is also true in matters of religion; more so than in any other places in the world. For this reason, I have speculated that North America is the best place for doing effective field work in matters having to do with religion. But, perhaps this is true not only for religion, but for other fields as well. The present religious situation of North America is quite different from what it had once been with respect to the major Abrahamic religious traditions. The contemporary existence of Eastern religious traditions is adding a new component to the religious situation in North America.

② Historically, the religious situation that has existed in East Asia has been quite different from that of North America. In East Asia, in Taoism, Buddhism, Confucianism, and folk religious traditions, one finds a long history of four religious traditions which have co-existed with each other for a long time. With the exception of Judaism and Islam in China, in East Asia, the major Abrahamic religious traditions have emerged as a new modern phenomenon. Christianity especially has been rapidly growing. In fact, Christianity has become a new crucial component within the contemporary East Asian religious situation. At the present moment, I believe that Christianity is the most rapidly growing religion in China.

xts. In the rapidly changing global times we cannot ignore the emerging new reality of concrete religious pluralism in our world. To meet this challenge, we need to find a meeting point from which to work—a meeting point that will lead to deeper understanding, but where can one find this point? How can one encounter it? Where can we meet? These questions for interreligious study and interreligious understanding present themselves as some of the most difficult questions that one can ask. Frankly, I do not think that these questions have been persuasively proposed or responded to either in religious communities or in academic departments. Of course, several grand theories have been proposed—grand theories about religious pluralism and how religions have philosophically or theologically developed. However, much has not been said about these things in relation to human faith as an inner constituent.

In this sense, we need some kind of new comprehensive seed—a set of tools that can be used constructively within our current pluralistic situation as this applies both to religion and the absence of religion: a new set of conceptual tools that can be used to help create a new reality in our world today. I think thus that we can find what we need by revisiting the work of two modern thinkers: Wilfred Cantwell Smith and Bernard Lonergan. We especially need to think about what Smith and Lonergan both say as a fundamental theme when they speak about the human heart as the locus of faith and as an ultimate reference "point".

Here, in this paper, in a comparative study, I would like to look at how both men understood the meaning of faith as a point of departure or as a key for understanding religion. But, in order to do this, I would like to speak about how one could use the thought of both men in a collaborative way in order to move toward a deeper understanding of religion as religion exists today within a pluralistic world community. Then, I will describe their fundamental category of religion in terms of a faith dimension.

2. Mutual Ambiguity and Method

Smith and Lonergan were what I consider to be the best Canadian scholars of religion in the 20th century. These were the ways they practiced their religious tradition: Smith was an ordained pastor in the United Church of Canada and Lonergan was a priest in the Society of Jesus. Smith had been originally trained in Islamic Studies at Princeton and later he taught at McGill University where he established a famous center of Islamic Studies. Then, he moved to Harvard University where most creatively he served as the director of the Center for the Studies of World Religions for many years. Lonergan on the other hand had been trained as a theologian and philosopher. He taught at the Gregorian University, the University of Toronto, Boston College, and the Harvard Divinity School (for a temporary period) in his lifetime. Unlike Smith, Lonergan did not direct any organization. He did not hold an administration post in any academic center or institution.

Academically their works have been influential within religious studies and also, to some extent, within theology. Smith was especially influential in religious studies; Lonergan, in theology and philosophy. Concretely, Smith engaged in the comparative study of world religions as his life's work (a work that began when he had served in his early years as a missionary in India). Lonergan, on the other hand, did not directly engage in comparative religious study. He did not look at the major world religions and he did not engage in inter-religious dialogue. However, their ideas about having a genuine understanding of religion can be used to compliment each other's thoughts in a way which can give new guidance both to the conduct of religious studies and the work of theology.

The more I read their works, the more I have come to realize how deeply similar their thoughts are. In attempting to confirm my suspicions with respect to similarity, I carefully checked Smith's works and indexes and I tried to see if he quoted anything from Lonergan's works. But, unfortunately, I could not find any footnotes or quotations about Lonergan and his works in Smith's works. I have wondered whether he was even aware of Lonergan's thought.

In contrast, Lonergan knew about Smith's works and he quoted his works. In his three lectures, "Lectures on Religious Studies and Theology," he openly mentions Smith's works. [1] In his lecture at the annual meeting of the American Academy of Religion in 1969, he mentions Smith's idea of faith and beliefs more than once. [2] At that meeting, Smith was invited as one of the respondents for Lonergan's paper. There, Smith and Lonergan exchanged questions and answers. The exchange, as it is tersely reported, simply noted that they fundamentally agreed with each other on their views. [3]

Apart from the report that we have, we do not have other sources about Smith's talks with respect to Lonergan's works, and based on the information that we have, we can only assume that he did not have any

---

[1]　Bernard Lonergan, *A Third Collection* edited by Frederick E. Crowe (New York: Paulist Press, 1985), pp. 122 – 23.

[2]　Bernard Lonergan, *Philosophical and Theological Papers* 1965 – 1980 edited by Robert C. Croken and Robert M. Doran (Toronto: University of Toronto Press, 2004), pp. 30 – 32, 42 – 43, 175 – 76.

[3]　*Ibid.*, pp. 47 – 8.

problems with Lonergan's works and thought. By comparing Smith's own thought with Lonergan's, we can then indirectly seek a degree of verification on the agreement that exists between Smith and Lonergan.

Nevertheless, it has to be admitted that some degree of ambiguity exists. Following their encounter at the Annual meeting of the AAR in 1969, each knew of the other's similar position. But, in subsequent publications, none refers to the thought of the other. One would expect that Lonergan and Smith would give more thought to each other's thinking with respect to issues having to do with religion or inter-religious dialogue matters. For his part, Smith makes no footnotes; he does not give any quotations from Lonergan's thought in his works. Similarly in Lonergan, one finds no references to Smith. Apart from his previous essays, he makes no mention of Smith in any of his major works.

In fact, shortly after the 1969 annual lecture, Lonergan published his *magnum opus*: *Method in Theology* in 1971. There he quoted several key leading figures in religious studies: Eliade, F. Heiler, Ernst Bentz, and so on. He used the most important methodological text for religious studies (as this existed in its early period). I refer to *The History of Religions*: *Essays in Methodology* which was edited and published in 1959 by Joseph Kitagawa and Mircea Eliade. In it Smith contributed one of his best essays: " Comparative Religion: Whither——and Why?". However, Lonergan does not mention this essay in his key work. Instead, as a key for having inter-religious dialogue (on the basis of the religious commonalty of world religions), he refers to an essay by F. Heiler: "The History of Religions as a Preparation for the Cooperation of

Religions"① and Rudolf Otto's *The Idea of the Holy*. ②

By going a bit further into Lonergan's analysis as this seems to exist in his *Method in Theology*, what is interesting to note in Lonergan's quotations is the fact that Lonergan largely quotes from the current major phenomenologist of religion as these existed then among scholars of religious studies. Given the phenomenological approach, their main goal was not to attain any knowledge that would be gained through value judgments. Instead, the object was something that was a bit more limited: a deeper understanding of other religious traditions. Hence, the object was to identify common elements as these existed among different religious traditions (Heiler's essay shows this). However, in doing this, in one's religious studies, one tried to avoid questions about truth (questions about the truth of other religious traditions).

However, with respect to Smith's work and as a point that needs to be adverted to, after publishing his aforementioned essay about methodology in connection with religious studies, Smith began to criticize this aspect which is present in the phenomenological approach to the study of religion. He began to discover the limitations of phenomenology with respect to having a deep dialogic understanding of religion. He thought that it would work to maintain a dualistic barrier with respect to the relation between subject and object. Moreover, he thought that one cannot continue to bracket questions about the value judgment in religious studies. In his studies and reflection, Smith discovered a "hidden" parochial theological project which sought to avoid questions about truth in other religious traditions – an

---

① Bernard Lonergan, *Method in Theology* (Toronto: University of Toronto Press, 1971), p. 109.

② *Ibid.* , p. 106.

avoidance that was proposed in the name of a phenomenology of religion. For Smith, it would be better to develop a theological project, a theological study that would be more honest.

In his religious studies, Smith very critically tackled a modern secularist approach to the study of religious matters. He had been contributing toward efforts to build a new solid context for open theological discourse in religious studies (especially in North America and non-Western countries). Hence, in contrast with the earlier phenomenological study of religion as one finds this in Eliade and others, Smith thought that religious studies should collaborate with faculties of theology (whether Abrahamic, Buddhist, or of other traditions). Smith openly pointed to a "theological" implication as this exists with respect to the current religious pluralism of our times and eventually he published his most controversial book – a book that includes the word of "theology" in its title. An early essay clearly reveals his intention with respect to a new notion for religious studies:

The argument may be summarized briefly, in pronominal terms. The traditional form of Western Scholarship in the study of other men's religion was that of an impersonal presentation of an "it". The first great innovation in recent times has been the personalization of the faiths observed, so that one finds a discussion of a "they". Presently the observer becomes personally involved, so that the situation is one of "we" talking about a "they". The next step is a dialogue, where "we" talk to "you". If there is listening and mutuality, this becomes that "we" talk *with* "you". The culmination of this progress is when "we all" are talking *with* each other about "us". ①

To understand why Smith did not quote anything from Lonergan's presentation of things in Method in Theology, one might try to argue that Smith was not aware of the debt that Lonergan owes to Aquinas. Was Smith aware of the fact that Lonergan's commitment to the study of human interiority was deeply related to his discovery of St Thomas Aquinas and the works of Aquinas somewhat late in his life? In thinking then about Smith's lack of interest in Lonergan's thought, I was led to recall a meeting that I had had in India. Shortly before I came to North America in 1988, I met Smith at the Madras Christian College, in India. I had an opportunity to talk with him about many things. Before I parted from him, I asked a question: "whom or what do you think is the most important thinker or book, except for the scripture of world religions, for your thought?" And, surprisingly, he told me about St. Thomas Aquinas and Paul Tillich. Afterwards, I came to realize that Smith quoted St. Thomas Aquinas many times in his works and he dealt with him in a special section in his book, *Faith and Belief* (1979).

After I began to read Lonergan's works, however, I thought that Smith should have paid more attention to Lonergan's works. In rechecking Smith's answers to Lonergan's annual lecture and after also looking at book index references to St Thomas Aquinas, I began to realize that Smith's discovery of Aquinas was not far or too different from the discovery that Lonergan had. Like Lonergan, Smith did not see Aquinas's vast systems or his books as his focal research point. However, what interested him was Aquinas's interiority – an

---

① Wilfred Cantwell Smith, "Comparative Religion: Whither—and Why?" in *The History of Religions: Essays in Methodology* (Chicago: The University of Chicago Press, 1959), p. 33.

interiority which flows in his teaching and books. Of course, Smith did not develop systematically the discovery of Thomas's interiority and how it functioned as the seed of Lonergan's universal method for all human activities. However, Smith realized that Thomas's massive works were not simply doctrinal agglomerations. They expressed Aquinas's authentic interiority process.

In this context thus, Smith noticed that the flowing of this interiority should not be seen as a parochial 'Christian' feature. It did not reveal a parochial Christian feature, but a global authentic human dimension which exists in Aquinas's thought. He thought that, for Aquinas, the primary object or goal is not to become an institutionalized Christian but rather to become a fundamentally authentic human being. In this context of struggle and effort, Aquinas sought to work with the current heretical world views of this day (as this existed in Greek and Islamic philosophy). If Aquinas had had a parochial Christian mind, he perhaps would not have ventured to meet the heretical philosophies as these existed for many people in the 13th century. Hence, Smith seemed to think that this dimension of Aquinas should be retrieved amongst contemporary 'Christian' academics for the sake of active engagement in inter-religious dialogue or beyond. [1]

We shall later see that Smith's and Lonergan's reading of St Thomas Aquinas's thought was not critically different. However, before going further, I think it should be noted that the key reason explaining Smith's lack of the awareness of Lonergan's books is perhaps the fact that Lonergan explicitly uses the word "method".

---

[1]　Wilfred Cantwell Smith, *Towards a World Theology* (Philadelphia: The Westminster Press, 1981), p. 16.

Paradoxically, this word that Smith has severely criticized is one of the key words that Lonergan considers most important. Lonergan includes this word in his title: "Method in Theology." However, for Smith, such a title could not be imagined. Smith sternly thought that method was not a proper word that could be applied to the study of the humanities in general and especially to the world of religion. He thought during his whole life that it was the most problematic word that one could use to try to understand human beings and religion in general.

In addition, this word this tended to incite controversy and argument not only in Smith's approach to religious studies but for other scholars with respect to the question of approach in religious studies. He thought that questions about method or methodology could be assimilated to the natural sciences, but that they could not be applied to the interiority studies which exist within the humanities and religious studies. He observed that the current method or methodology was not too helpful since it worked to obstruct movements that would lead to deeper human understanding. He was very skeptical about there being any proper involvement of questions about method or methodology in religious studies. As a consequence of his views, after contributing one essay in the methodology book that had been edited by Kitagawa and Eliade, he did not publish any later articles in connection with Eliade and his school within religious studies. He did not even contribute a single essay in the vast work that later appeared in the *Encyclopedia of Religion*. He severely criticizes the modern academic obsession for dealing with questions having to do with method or methodology. He sees this interest as a sort of "ideology".

Methods, so far as they are systematized in formal methodologies, not only are, but are calculated to be, separable from the person who employs them. The concept of methodology, and stress on method in education, imply that one knows ahead of time what one wants, and has only to find out how to get it. In principle it is possible to learn techniques without ceasing to be basically the kind of person that one was before, to come out of the learning process at heart as one went into it. If a university teaches only techniques, proffers only methods of ascertaining what one already wishes to know, then of course students should decide what they wish to know, and in effect should employ the experts to satisfy these aspirations. They should use the university for their own purposes. [1]

In contrast Lonergan thought of method as one of the most crucial words in his thought. He thought that whether we liked it or not, in the modern world, scientific method has been influencing modern society as a very powerful controlling factor in human life. It has obsessively dominated all modern academic disciplines. Religious Studies has not been excepted. As a result of this trend, in the name of objectivity, many studies have been forced to apply a rigidly fixed notion of scientific method to how their research is done (a notion of scientific method which is used as a form of external technology). This is done despite what historical cultural conditions exist with respect to a particular object of study and despite the possible relevance of human interiority as a factor that should be attended to in the life and work of a given researcher and despite the impact of interiority as it affects a particular object of study.

In this respect, Lonergan questioned the uncritical acceptance of scientific method within religious studies and within all academic fields in general. He critically pointed out that it is not wise to assume

---

① Smith, "Comparative Religion: Whither—and Why?", p. 33.

that the method of science (as this is commonly understood) should be seen as " the " absolute method that all contemporary academic disciplines should follow. Instead, if one is to avoid some troublesome over-simplifications, it would be best to realize that scientific method is but an expression of interior procedures (interior procedures which indicate how a scientist is involved in asking his or her questions which lead to interpretations, judgments, and decisions). Lonergan thus invites us to ask a more profound question: a question that questions a taboo which enjoins an uncritical acceptance of the method of science on the part of the contemporary academic community. In this sense, Lonergan's critical views about the nature of methods of science, as practiced today, is not too far from Smith's concerns.

I have been indicating elements in a dynamic and dialectical account of subject and horizon, self and world, ego and blik. The account is dynamic: it regards not just diverse states of affairs but the processes that bring them about. The account is dialectical for it speaks both of development and of limitation, of enrichment but also of failure or distortion or stunted growth. Such a dynamic and dialectical account is relevant to a method of religious studies in two ways. For, first, it is relevant to anticipation about object. Just as we live in worlds as we know them, so too other people, distant from us in place or time, in class or culture, live in worlds as they know them. We must not expect them to live in our world. Again, as we are correlative to the world as we know it, so too are they. We must not expect them to be like us. Indeed, as it does not demean our own humanity that we are correlative to the world as we know it, so we must not think them to be less human than ourselves because they are correlative to their world as they know it. ··· ···

But the dynamic and dialectical account is relevant and not only to correct anticipations about the object of religious studies but also to confronting the student of religion with what a natural scientist would call his personal equation. Not only the people under investigation but also the investigators are human beings. ①

As the above long quotation emphasizes, Lonergan's notion of method is not to be identified with an external mechanical tool that is to be forced on persons who engage in religious studies. In contrast to common expectations, Lonergan sought to identify inner operative processes which are embedded not only in a scholar's object of study, but also in the scholar's self. He claimed that a common set of inner operational activities can be identified in human beings as a common set which includes the ways and means of scientific labor and which does not vary as one moves from one discipline to another since this common set of activities exists in a universal way in the structure or order of human knowing. This structure or order is what Lonergan speaks about in the ground breaking study which one finds in his *Insight: A Study of Human Understanding*. In this work, he takes the structure or order of human knowing and he conceptualizes it as a generalized empirical method which can be applied to all human activities where knowing is involved. In this sense, religious studies or theology does not stand apart from the operation of a common universal method whose presence needs to be acknowledged. In his later work, *Method in Theology*, Lonergan articulates what exactly this method is if one tends to the kinds of questions which must be addressed within theology by practitioners of this discipline. As Lonergan summarizes his thesis which can be described as a kind of methodological first principle:

---

① Lonergan, "Method: Trend and Variations," in *Third Collection*, pp. 18 - 9.

A method is a normative pattern of recurrent and related operations yielding cumulative and progressive results. There is a method, then, where there are distinct operations, where each operation is related to the others, where the set of relations forms a pattern, where the pattern is described as the right way of doing the job, where operations in accord with the pattern may be not repetitious, but cumulative and progressive. [1]

If we reflect then about the above quotations which we have cited, we should realize that both Smith and Lonergan share a common concern. Both worry about possible misapplications of "method" within religious studies and theology and both have the same orientation with respect to how religious should be the study of religion and theology. And so, we may conclude that their intellectual concern about questions having to do with "method" in the study of religion does not clash with each other in terms of a higher view that each sought to defend. The only difference refers to the fact that Smith avoided the word "method" in his works while Lonergan frequently used the term, but for the purpose of proposing a different meaning: a meaning which was formed by a different notion of science, a notion of science which was unlike that which belonged to the methodology of the natural sciences.

Admittedly, it can be said that each man had a different emphasis. Yet, at the same time, one can properly speak about a complementarity and a form of collaboration between the two as each man attempted to move in a new direction – a direction which sought to understand how one can attend to the inner depth dimension of religion as a basis for creating a new consciousness within religious

---

[1]   Lonergan, *Method in Theolog*, p. 4.

studies - a consciousness which can lend its support to a new emergent consciousness of religious pluralism in our world today. Smith's concrete comparative studies of human religious history can support Lonergan's subtly articulated analysis of method in theology and religious studies. Smith's own work counters recent secularist approaches to the study of religion. Obversely, Lonergan's understanding of method in religious studies lends itself to supporting Smith's comparative studies. From Smith's comparative studies of human religious history come many concrete examples which correspond to the operations of Lonergan's understanding of method. Their approach to the study of religion, theology, or philosophy invites us to understand the "location" of religion within human life, and the place and role of inter-religious encounter or dialogue in a pluralistic global world.

3. Faith as the Basis of Religion

As with other human things, the phenomenon of religion presents a vast complex which is not easily understood. While many scholars have tried to provide a definition for religion, they have not been too successful. Perhaps it is simply not possible. The world of religion is not only composed of belief systems but it is also composed of very many rituals and organizations. Some religions and denominations emphasize belief systems within their traditions while others attend more to rituals and rites and how they might organize themselves into many different groups. Native American Religions, Folk Religions, and Shamanism cannot be fully understood if their doctrinal systems would be focused. At the same time too, much of Buddhism, Taoism, and Confucianism cannot be understood if no concern is given to things which have a meaning that is not determined solely by ritual considerations. In this sense, as we think about it, the textual or doctrinal approach which we can find among Asian religions (the philosophies which we may find also), none of these are sufficient if we are to understand and know what is going on. And, in the same way, these things can be said about the Abrahamic religious traditions. Given the inherent complexities that exist in all religions, the more we understand their multilayered worlds, the more we will come to understand and know why it is not possible to insist that we work from some kind of rigid definition for religion. Such a definition cannot be adequately formulated.

1) Person and Subject

A fundamental universal simple fact of religion avers that it exists as a "human" construct. All religions have originated and developed through human beings whether they be Abrahamic religions, eastern religions, or folk religions. Without the past, present and future involvement of human beings, no religion can be born, transmitted, developed, and maintained in human history. If they could not elicit the commitment of any of their followers, they would disappear in real life and turn into dead religions (inhabiting some kind of museum). This is true not only with respect to religions but also with respect to all other human activities in this world.

I think that Smith and Lonergan originally developed this point in their works. They both uniquely insisted on the fact that the locus of human involvement which makes religions and which gives life to human things in human history is something which does not come from the sensible external world, but from the interiority of human beings (as a person to Smith and an authentic subject to Lonergan). For them, religion is not possible without the human subject. Surprisingly, they both opted for an understanding of the whole human subject (in opposition to a fragmented understanding of the human subject which exists in our modern day human world). They tackled the problem that the modern human understanding of the human subject does not pay much attention to the inner dimensions of the human subject. As Smith addressed this question in connection with traditional world religions at a meeting of the International Association of the History of Religions (IAHR) in 1965, he said:

….. and I have argued that what has been called the study of religion must be recognized, rather, as the study not primarily of things but of persons. This, I would contend, is always true; and most of all for the study of today, when even such phenomena as there are may be different from the traditionalist ones. I suppose that my entire thesis can be summed up in the affirmation that the study of religion must be fundamentally a study of persons. Comparative religion is the study of man in his religious diversity. Through it, man is striving to become conscious himself in his fragmented relation to transcendence.[1]

As Lonergan also developed a similar understanding of the human subject in connection with the human world in general in the Aquinas Lecture given in 1968:

Existential reflection is at once enlightening and enriching. Not only does it touch us intimately and speak to us convincingly but also it is the natural stating-point for fuller reflection on the subject as

---

① Wilfred Cantwell Smith, 'Traditional Religions and Modern Culture' in *Religious Diversity* edited by Willard G. Oxtoby (New York: Harper and Row Publishers, 1976), p. 76.

incarnate, as image and feeling as well as mind and will, as moved by symbol and story, as intersubjective, as encountering others and becoming "I" to "Thou" to move on to "We" through acquaintance, companionship, collaboration, friendship, love. Then easily we pass into the whole human world founded meaning, a world of language, art, literature, science, philosophy, history, of family and mores, society and education, state and law, economy and technology. [1]

In fact, as we can see, Smith's and Lonergan's concern for the human interior dimension is not a transitory interest. Instead, it is the focal point of their whole works. Smith began to develop that dimension of faith from his studies of Islam in 1957. The major works on the human interior dimension of faith began with the publication of a modern classic, *The Meaning and End of Religion*, in 1962. After this book, for his whole life he continued to focus and speak solely about the interior dimension of the religious person as this exists in the major world religions. He developed this focus in his other major works: *The Faith of Other Men* (1962), *The Questions of Religious Truth* (1967), *Belief and History* (1972), *Faith and Belief* (1979), and *Towards a World Theology* (1981).

Similarly, but more vastly, Lonergan developed the interior dimension of the human subject in his major work, *Insight: A Study of Human Understanding* (1957). Unlike Smith's works, he did not deal with it in relation to religion and problems posed by religious pluralism. He delineated it mainly as an original philosophical enquiry or quest in order to move toward a more subtle form of self-knowledge. He did not speak much about faith in *Insight*. I think it

---

[1] Bernard Lonergan, 'The Subject' in A *Second Collection* edited by William F. J. Ryan and Bernard J. Tyrrell (Toronto: University of Toronto Press, 1974), p. 85.

can be said that he developed this dimension in his later works, in *Method in Theology* (1971), *A Second Collection* (1974), *A Third Collection* (1985), *Philosophical and Theological Papers* 1965 – 1980 (2004) and in others.

2) Faith and Authenticity

Smith and Lonergan both tried to correct an overly abstract understanding of human understanding as this has come down to us in modern culture. To do this, they proposed that the real problem of human understanding should be concretely known and properly identified. Contemporary notions tend to be steeped in what Smith referred to as "impersonalism"[1] and what Lonergan referred to as "conceptualism,"[2] or "classicism."[3]

In his understanding of things, Smith thought that the use of abstracted external names in the study of the major world religions tended to enhance an impersonalist approach which deflected from focusing on what is happening inwardly in religion amongst believers and so, as a result, inter-religious encounters were not encouraged in a way which could join persons with each other. For this reason, in his first major book, Smith critically looked at the historical development of the coined names which have arisen to speak about Christianity, Judaism, Hinduism, Buddhism, Confucianism, Taoism, and the meaning of these respective religions. He found that, with the

---

[1]　Wilfred Cantwell Smith, 'Objectivity and Human Sciences' in *Religious Diversity edited by* Willard G. Oxtoby (New York: Harper and Row Publishers, 1976), pp. 166 – 70.

[2]　Bernard Lonergan, *Insight: A Study of Human Understanding* (Toronto: University of Toronto Press, 1992), p. 717.

[3]　Lonergan, *Method in Theolog*, p. 302.

exception of the name "Islam",[1] the other names were coined in a context that was governed by Western cultural conceptions. He argued that the use of abstract external names tended to make human beings forget or overlook a dynamic faith dimension which exists in all the different religions. For this reason, Smith strongly claimed that he was abandoning the coined reified names that have been commonly employed in the different religions.[2]

Instead, he suggested two usages: cumulative tradition as "the entire mass of overt objective data that constitute the historical deposit, as it were, of the past religious life of the community in question," and faith as, "an inner religious experience or involvement of a particular person."[3] Smith suggests that it is not enough to look at the external parts of religion. More importantly, one should look to what is interior and how this interior part relates to the development of the external traditions. In fact, one cannot understand the faith dimension of a religion unless one also studies external parts because these dimensions are not separated. They are always embedded or closely intertwined. They resemble the relation of a flower to its root. The external things like flowers would be easily visible and the internal things like faith would be invisible and not known if they were not attended to. Thus, the most important thing to keep in mind is the fact that the both parts of religion evolve together

---

[1]   Wilfred Cantwell Smith, *The Meaning and End of Religion: A Revolutionary Approach to the Great Religious Traditions* (New York: Harper and Row Publishers, 1962), p. 60.

[2]   *Ibid.*, p. 153. In religious studies, Smith's suggestion has been so well accepted that today, in many conversations and in many books, one frequently encounters language which speaks about differing faith traditions as in Christian tradition, Jewish tradition, Buddhist tradition Hindu tradition and other traditions. Amongst many academicians, one finds that they are using labels in a manner which is influenced by Smith's concerns. However, in all honesty, I think that it is impossible to drop the names of religions although is more important to attend to the faith dimension which exists in all religions.

[3]   *Ibid.*, p. 156.

through a process of mutual interaction.

Lonergan also found a similar problem within a context that is governed by what he refers to as "conceptualism" or "classicism" in religion and theology. He concluded that this milieu creates false habits. It tends to turn persons toward focusing on the primacy of logical proofs and a normative notion of culture within religious discourse. [1] This dominant modern intellectual habit (functioning as a bias) then eventually encourages people to forget about the fact that, at bottom, a religion or religious life is about a process of committed human conversion. The dominant conceptualism and classicism led to a way of thinking which tended to fall into language games – language games pertaining to the language of religious discourse. To critically articulate this point in his talks about "doctrines" (as Smith had suggested), Lonergan similarly distinguished between the interiority of human personal involvement and the exteriority of religion as this exists in the growth and the accumulation of tradition. [2] Later on, in a lecture about religious experience in terms of its relation to religious studies and theology, he identified human involvement in terms of authenticity; or, more precisely, in terms of "faith".

In brief, it has seemed to me that the notion of authenticity possesses a twofold relevance: it is relevant to the interpretation of recurrent elements in the observable phenomena collected and catalogued by students of religion; it also is relevant to the inner commitment to which Professor Smith has invited our attention. [3]

3) Faith and Being in Love

It should be kept in mind that Smith and Lonergan did not limit

---

[1]　Lonergan, *Method in Theology*, p. 338.

[2]　*Ibid.*, p. 302.

[3]　Lonergan, 'Religious Experience' in *Third Collection*, p. 123.

their discussions about faith to a discussion which only spoke about the anthropological side of things (the human quest from below upwards in a self-transcending process). More fundamentally, they also spoke about a vector which moved from above downwards. In a subtle way, relatively speaking, this point would be more emphasized in the works of Lonergan than in Smith's. Smith also considered this dimension although he did not apparently feel the need to emphasize the value of making a clear distinction between a movement which moved upwards and a movement which moved downwards. For him, faith occurs in the human heart (whether one speaks about a process that moves from below or one that moves from above). However, to see a corresponding match with the kind of analysis which one finds in Lonergan, Smith's point should be clearly pointed out.

For Smith, faith within human history should not be seen as simply a subjective psychological state, an experience, or some kind of life attitude. More accurately, it refers to "personal" dynamic experience which is embedded in an awareness of transcendence – an awareness which senses an intervention of some kind which comes from a transcendent source (as unnamed as this may be). In his works, faith is always embodied in connection with transcendence and it is not possible to separate this state from this transcendent dimension. I think too that Smith had an awareness of transcendence in terms of there being some kind of transcendent initiative – a transcendent initiative that, in the depths of a person's soul, would work to create faith within it. For an explanation of this, one can look at Smith's religious tradition: the influence exerted by Calvinism and what he learned from his studies of Islam and the Islamic way of life which, of believers, demands a total surrender of the human being. Later, in his broad studies of world religious traditions, he would expand this dimension so that it emerges as the key feature of faith within human history.

To use theological language: the two themes, apparently contrasting, of religion as man's quest for God, or alternatively as God's initiative, His seeking of man, through global history. The latter position has been that of the Muslims, of the Bhagavad Gita, of some Buddhist and of most Christian doctrine. It is easier, of course, to aver faith as God's generous gift in an age of faith than, in an era of forlorn confusion, to argue that its absence is simply God's failure to bestow it. Some will perhaps find congenial a formulation that seeks to converge the two themes: for instance, by saying that faith is a response to God's initiative, to His active Self-revelation. In the course of evolution, the emergence of man as distinct from the brutes, man as endowed with the capacity for faith, man as informed by the universe's transcendence: this much can be seen-perhaps poetically-as a divine gift. [1]

Likewise, in Lonergan, we can find discussions about an initiative which comes from God: an initiative which works to create faith within human souls. To speak about this a bit more accurately, it would be more correct to say that Lonergan speaks about this dimension more in his later works when he speaks about faith and how faith exists within human beings as a species of human response. Especially does one find a discussion about this in the chapter on religion in his *Method in Theology*. However, in the discussion given, he gives a dense analysis which refrains from much elaboration. He only wrote four pages that speaks about faith apart from frequent brief

---

[1]　Wilfred Cantwell Smith, *Faith and Belief* (Princeton: Princeton University Press, 1979), p. 140.

references to faith in other parts and pages of *Method in Theology*. [1]
Nevertheless, I would argue that faith is a focal point for Lonergan in
his works. For instance, it can be said that the unlimited desire to
know in *Insight* is not simply a cognitional datum that a good theory of
cognition should refer to since it is, more fundamentally, an opening
toward faith that moves from the bottom in an upward self-transcending
direction and then, when one speaks about the opposite direction
which moves from above downwards, one has a discussion about faith
as is given in *Method in Theology*. Faith here refers to God's
initiative: an initiative which meets with the human unrestricted desire
to understand and know – a desire which, in its own way, is
something which also ultimately comes from God.

Lonergan described faith differently in contrast with common
images of it. Typically, the divine initiative with respect to faith is
seen in terms of a stern and absolute demand for submission and
obedience. However, in Lonergan's exposition, faith refers to
embracing or entering into a state of love that is being generously
bestowed. For him, faith is the knowledge of "God's love flooding our
hearts. "[2] Faith is operating or is operative as a state of being in love
– responding to a love that is implanted through the free gift of entry
into a person's soul (a person's consciousness). Faith is not akin to
a simple cognitive process of reason, since it is akin to a movement
within the heart, a feeling that moves within the heart. Lonergan
speaks about a relation to feeling when he quotes from Pascal who had
spoken about reasons of the heart. [3] However, it should be noted that
this feeling of love is not an easy comfortable feeling, since it is more

---

[1]   Lonergan, *Method in Theology*, pp. 115 – 18.

[2]   Lonergan, 'Religious Experience' in *Third Collection*, p. 115.

[3]   *Ibid.*

a kind of painful, piercing feeling. He speaks of it in a way which suggests a feeling of awe. [①] Prior to the publication of *Method in Theology*, he did not speak about this kind of feeling at all with respect to faith. In his crucial essay on 'faith and beliefs' delivered at the annual meeting of AAR (given in 1969), Lonergan only referred to the love dimension which exists in faith. [②] However, in any future studies of Lonergan's works, I think that this point should be discussed more extensively when attending to Lonergan's understanding of faith.

Although Smith and Lonergan share a common concern in acknowledging a divine initiative in the human experience of religious faith, it should be admitted that they placed a different accent on how the state or condition of this faith is to be understood. Unlike Lonergan, Smith did not speak much about a key role that is played by feeling in faith. Instead, he placed a greater emphasis on the global aspect of faith in human history. [③] He discussed it as a living quality in human life. [④] Through his comparative global studies of human religious faith in history, he was able to note that faith is not limited to a special groups or traditions. It is a universal human quality, although this does not mean that all faiths in every religious tradition are the same. Like the differences which exist with respect to the external aspects of all religious traditions, all faiths differ from each other and they vary within a given religious tradition. Even within the same tradition, different faiths exist as one goes from

---

① *Iibid.*, p. 106, 112 – 13 and 115.

② I presume that his reading of Otto's *The Idea of the Holy* gave him an insight into the meaning of the "awe" feeling which Loneragan speaks about in his *Method in Theology*. Lonergan's "mystery of love and awe" recalls Otto's words which speak about *mysterium*, *fascinans et tremendum*.

③ Smith, *Faith and Belief*, p. 129.

④ Wilfred Cantwell Smith, *Meaning and End of Religion*, p. 189.

person to person and group to group. One wonders at times if the individual differences are so great that one cannot too readily speak about persons who share in the same faith. Faith differs in its intensity, circumstances, feeling, image, breadth and depth and so on. It is not a static, abstract, fixed, unchanged substance. It is always variously flowing. One's present state of faith differs from that of one's childhood. It flows differently every morning, every afternoon, and so on. Hence, faith is not a noun but is more an adjective or verb as in "faith-ing."

My faith is an act that I make, myself, naked before God. Just as there is no such a thing as Christianity (or Islam or Buddhism), I have urged, behind which the Christian (the Muslim, the Buddhist) may shelter, which he may set between himself and the terror and splendor and living concern of God, so there is no generic Christian faith; no 'Buddhist faith', no 'Hindu faith', no 'Jewish faith'. There is only my faith, and yours, and that of my Shinto friend, of my particular Jewish neighbour. We are all persons, clustered in mundane communities, no doubt, and labeled with mundane labels but, so far as transcendence is concerned, encountering it each directly, personally, if at all. In the eyes of God each of us is a person, not a type. [1]

Lonergan also had a similar understanding about the meaning of faith, although focusing on the feeling and the experience of "being in love". Though he did not develop his thought about faith as a dimension in the context of a global history of religion, like Smith, he recognized how faith relates to the values and meanings of human life

---

[1] Wilfred Cantwell Smith, *Meaning and End of Religion*, p. 191.

in both relative and absolute aspects. [①] Varieties can be distinguished. Given the pluralistic aspects of faith, he fully endorsed Smith's view that faith is rooted in God's love. It is universal in relation to any talk about values. With respect to Lonergan's own views, faith appears to be an invisible universal dimension which is present in all human values and meanings. Without it, all the different human values and meaning cannot really emerge—they cannot emerge in whatever order—whether one speaks of society, culture, politics, or religion. In this sense, faith (as a dimension) is a foundational or transcultural aspect or factor which is operative in human history.

Then love would not flow from knowledge, but, on the contrary, knowledge would from love. It is the knowledge that results from God's gift of his love that, I suggest, constitutes the universalist faith proposed by Professor Smith.

By a universalist faith, then, I would understand the transvaluation of values that results from God's gift of his love. Just as the gift of that love, so too the consequent transvaluation of values is, in some sense, constant. It does not presuppose any specific set of historical conditions. [②]

From such a standpoint thus, we can see that, for both Smith and Lonergan, religion is chiefly concerned not with various external expressions (such as one finds in doctrines, rituals, belief systems, social organizations, ritual systems, and so on), but with varying forms of inner human commitment or involvement: faith as prior to, in relation to, behind or before, or beyond the externalities of religious traditions. The externalities invite one to see that faith has been

---

① Lonergan, *Method in Theology*, p. 116.
② Lonergan, 'Faith and Beliefs', in *Philosophical and Theological Papers* 1965 – 1980, pp. 42 – 3.

working within human souls to make or turn religious traditions into living realities (sometimes faithfully or mildly or critically or heretically or foolishly). Thus, to know a religion, it is not enough to focus on external things as such. One must know rather, how human beings are involved in their traditions and, through their involvement, one must attend to what they experience, understand, judge and decide (sometimes properly and sometimes improperly in their lives). Whether in or out of their traditions, different persons express their faith limitlessly in all the different forms or modes present in the arts, philosophy, business, politics, science, theology, religious studies, communication, friendship, and love. The list is unending and is always open to differentiation.

At this point, both Smith and Lonergan emphasize the varieties that one finds in religious traditions, culture, and faith. For both, what is fundamental is the fact that not only religious tradition or culture but faith also changes. It changes because of all the different human involvements that we participate in—all the different human commitments which exist individually, communally, culturally, historically, or cosmically in human life. With respect to these dimensions, the fundamental constant unchanging thing is always the ultimate point that human beings refer to or to which they orient themselves in their lives. Because of this fundamental point, Smith and Lonergan invite us to attend to that point which is seen or which can be seen by a religious human being who attends to the committed involvement or participation of another person in their religious or human secular traditions. Hence, I think that, for both Smith and Lonergan, their ultimate argument is one which takes its stand not on the articulation of a subtle speculative argument but through an analysis of humanity——an analysis which, for Smith, is focused on a global sense of historical faith——that works in all things, and which, for Lonergan, is focused on an unrestricted universal desire to become fully "human".

In this sense, Smith and Lonergan both claimed that faith, ultimately, is not an abnormal strange element in human life, but a fundamentally normal, necessary element. When modern "secularism" attempts to deny or eradicate this point, a false impression is conveyed: an impression which thinks that faith is not normal in human life, although this kind of diagnosis is both strange and abnormal in the context of global human history. Thus, for them, without a restoration of this point of view in human life, no one can expect that authentic human encounters or fruitful inter-religious dialogue will emerge within the emergent pluralism of our world. Contemporary human culture fails in disregarding the principle of transcendence as faith in human life. This situation reduces or turns human beings into fragmented or absurd beings who do not attend to an interior self-transcending reality which exists within human souls (the human spirit). Such a modern fragmented and absurd culture does not seriously engage in questions having to do with the transcendent dimension of human life as faith. I think that such a conclusion naturally follows from both Smith and Lonergan in their thought. One better understands this implication if one looks at how both men responded to the "death of God" movement. To them it is the modern representative case to show the denial of normal human life as the process of faith.

The word "God" is a symbol; but that to which it refers, is a reality. More accurately, that to which those who have used this word have potentially referred (whether consciously or unconsciously) is real. It is a reality about which none of us knows enough to be either dogmatic or scurrilous; yet about which each of us may, through his own symbols and his own faith, know enough to live by—and indeed, to live in a way that is transcendently final. ① As Lonergan speaks about the "death of God" movement:

It is, then, no accident that a theatre of the absurd, a literature of the absurd, and philosophies of the absurd flourish in a culture in which there are theologians to proclaim that God is dead, But that absurdity and that death have their roots in a new neglect of the subject, new truncation, a new immanentism. ②

4) Faith and Inter-Religious Dialogue

For Smith and Lonergan, religious encounters or dialogue are not akin to what happens in a cocktail party or in face to face formal exchanges. The best analogy is by way of a species of colloquy—a colloquy of faith where the locus of meaning is in the telling of biographical narratives—narratives that express meanings which are artistic, ecological, intellectual, hospitable, and friendly. A context which turns into a community is created through stories, feelings, and gestures. Such an approach has yet to be fully attended to in the context of one's own religion and in other religions. It should be developed by a focus that attends to an inner personal faith dimension in a colloquy kind of way. This is a new vast uncultivated field in religious matters and it is very crucial for the development of genuine inter-religious encounters or dialogue between human beings.

Smith and Lonergan both believed that, by working from the perspective of a faith dimension, more opportunities would be given to

---

① Wilfred Cantwell Smith, *Questions of Religious Truth* (New York: Charles Scribner's Sons, 1967), p. 36.

② Lonergan, 'The Subject' in *A Second Collection*, p. 86.

all persons. More opportunities would be given to them to meet other persons so that, as a result, a new human convergence (a convergence creating a community) could begin to emerge to overcome and heal the fragmentation of modern daily life—a healing which cannot occur if persons were to work from a context that is solely determined by traditional deposits as these are given in different cumulative traditions. These things differ too much among themselves for one to find some kind of common form within human traditions which can be religious or non-religious. However, in terms of faith qua faith as an interior human dynamic, one can find more similarities among both religious and non-religious traditions and one can become more sensitively aware of the fact that we do exist anywhere simply as empty mechanical human beings but, in some way, we exist as faith embodied human beings (irrespective of any differences among religious or non-religious traditions). In addition too, as another fact which should be noted, this dimension also gives us the opportunity to "see" each other as mysterious carriers of an ultimate reference "point" or "reality" in our concrete struggle to become truly human as human beings. Smith articulates this point in his *Faith and Belief.*

Faith intellectually is further, the ability now to recognize (what in our preceding section was but postulated) a truth or a reality lying behind and also transcending any given perception or expression, beyond any "belief". [1]

Similarly, Lonergan also pointed to faith as the common ground of all religions. In speaking about belief, faith functions as an ultimate point of reference.

We may note, however, that by distinguishing faith and belief we

---

[1] Smith, *Faith and Belief*, p. 170.

have secured a basis both for ecumenical encounter and for an encounter of all religions with a basis in religious experience. ⋯ ⋯ Beliefs do differ, but behind this difference there is a deeper unity. ①

Smith and Lonergan also both thought that the faith dimension not only functions as an ultimate vertical reference point, but at the same time, it can be argued that faith functions as an ultimate horizontal point of reference in human history. As human beings, we all participate in this ultimate vertical and horizontal reference point through our participating in either a religious or a non-religious tradition and by our also participating in a common human history which belongs to us as human beings. In doing so, we have already been related in very many ways to each other: vertically and also horizontally in our common human history. This aspect of human history thus gives us a deep sense of solidarity as human beings. Because of this solidarity, inter-religious dialogue or encounters cease to be defensive meetings which can occur among human beings. A new, deeper consciousness of things takes over—a consciousness which is transformed by a mutual critical engagement which continually transforms oneself as, by one's participation, one realizes more and more that one belongs to a larger human community in this world (despite what differences might exist).

Smith developed concretely this point when discussing his notion of world community in the context of a global history of humankind. He believed that all human beings (whether as Christians, Buddhists, Jews, Confucians, Muslims, or non-believers, whatever) all participate directly or indirectly in constructing the world community.

---

① Lonergan, *Method in Theology*, p. 119.

Of course, admittedly, they do not wear the same "cloth", They do not participate in the same way. They have all been participating in the world community by wearing different "clothes" which have been nurtured by different traditions——participating in the community not principally through their "clothes" or outer dress but through their "faith-ing": a "faith-ing" which refers to authentic moments within the life of human beings. As Smith writes:

I do not mean that Christians will cease to be Christian, or Muslims Muslim. What I mean is that Christians will participate, as Christians, in the religious history of humankind; Muslims will participate in it as Muslims, Jews as Jews, Hindus as Hindus, Buddhists as Buddhists. I am a Presbyterian; yet the community in which that I participate is not the Presbyterian, but, at this level, the Christian. I participate as a deliberate though modified Calvinist in the Christian community, and the Christian process. In much the same way, I choose to participate as a Christian in the world process is, the one to which I know that I truly belong, is the community, world-wide and history-long, of humankind. [1]

Though, like Smith, Lonergan did not religiously develop the idea of a world community, he does invite us to participate in building our human society into a larger human community in this world. He sketched this possibility when talking about the nature of communications in human society. Especially in relation to inter-religious dialogue, he suggested that a dialectical moment exists in all human beings which encourages them to become true human beings——a dialectical moment which becomes the foundation for thinking about a universal theory of human community. Admittedly,

---

[1]　Smith, *Towards a World Theology*, p. 44.

Lonergan did not fully develop his idea concretely with respect to inter-religious dialogue. I think it can be said, however, that he points to a seminal first principle (a fundamental seed) which can be used to point to a new direction. He suggests this principle by referring to the example of fellow Christians who have engaged in inter-religious dialogue within and beyond the ecumenical level:

···besides the dialectic that is concerned with human subjects as objects, there is the dialectic in which human subjects are concerned *with themselves and with one other.* In that case dialectic becomes dialogue. It is particularly relevant when persons are authentic and know one another to be authentic yet belong to differing traditions and so find themselves in basis disagreement. It may be illustrated by the ecumenical movement among Christians and by the universal movement set forth by R. E. Whitson in his *The Coming Convergence of World Religions,* by Raymond Panikkar's dialectical theology and by William Johnston's Christian monks frequenting Zen monasteries in Japan. [1] (italics mine)

4. Conclusion

In these discussions, I have tried to show comparatively what Smith and Lonergan have to say about faith as a key element or feature in the structure and nature of human consciousness. And, in the work of composing this essay, I have come to realize that both men can be regarded as champions who argued that the locus of our human reality in terms of its quality is found in the authenticity of being in love—a being in love which exists as faith within human hearts.

---

[1]   Lonergan, 'The Ongoing Genesis of Methods', in *A Third Collection,* p. 159.

Smith and Lonergan both adverted to a common, fundamental problem which exists in our modern intellectual world—a problem with fatal consequences for understanding religion in our modern world. At the core of this problem, a misplaced understanding of human understanding exists—a misunderstanding which exists through an impersonalism or a conceptualism which does not attend to the locus of religion as this exists within the human heart and which exists as an ultimate fundamental point of reference. Such a misplaced emphasis eventually leads and has led to a loss of a sense of religion in modern culture—a loss which follows from not attending to what is happening within the interiority of human hearts (and within the interiority of human souls). And so, persons have tried to overcome this loss through external forms of activity as this exists in the various works and labors which they engage in the workaday world.

For this reason thus, as one thinks about it, one can try to argue that, within this context, a person's work commitments have tended to serve as a kind of "grief" process—a grieving which is intellectually active (and not passive) and which serves as a form of rationalization for persons in terms of how they should understand themselves (or, at the same time, not understand themselves), and in terms also about how they should respond to the world within which they live (or, at the same time, not respond to the world within which they live). Through a form of compensation which works as a species of negative reinforcement, one's daily work and the dedication that is given to it displaces the value of encouraging a focus of attention that should be given to asking radical questions about one's self and the kind of being which one has become in one's life. What is happening interiority within a person ceases to be of interest, or it never receives the attention which it properly merits and deserves. Persons become more and more unreflective and so, as a long-term consequence, a general cultural decline begins to set in and establish itself—a general cultural decline which produces its own philosophy in rationalizations which move beyond individuals and the life of special interest groups. For more and more persons, serious problems are to be solved through ready forms of external action. Self-understanding loses the status which it once had if one recalls the centrality which it had once enjoyed in the tradition which stems from the birth and genesis of Greek philosophy. ①

In addition, and by way of application to religious realms of meaning, for both Smith and Lonergan, impersonalism and conceptualist philosophies of mind affect what kind of self-understanding exists within different religions and different denominations. And so, in order to correct this deficiency, Smith critically engaged in attempting to understand all religions as faith within a global perspective. Then, in his own work, Lonergan, for his part, tried to speak about Christian ecumenism and how a possible meeting point for all religions exists in terms of faith as an inner transcultural dimension (as a transformation and way of living which is to be understood within a self-transcending notion of human subjectivity). Their respective positions can be seen to transcend any particularist or sectarian position which, perhaps, can be found in some theologies of faith. In this sense, their open positions recall the same kind of spirit, the same kind of great global vision which can be

① Recall here the Introduction which Lonergan writes for his *Verbum*: *Word and Idea in Aquinas*. The kind of interiority analysis which one finds in Augustine, and which is taken up by Aquinas in his metaphysics of the human soul, requires an amplification and an expansion of meaning which requires a fresh approach: an analysis which identifies and speaks about the activities of human beings who exist as subjects and not just as substances.

found in Aquinas, Ghazzali, Ramanuja, Chu His, and others who were all involved in traditions other than their own and who attempted to create richer theological cultures which could introduce new meanings into a religious matrix of meaning but in a manner that could lead to a deepening of one's faith and religious commitment. [①]

Finally, in concluding, I think it should be said that what both Smith and Lonergan have to say about faith should be complemented by additional, future studies of religious pluralism. Smith's view can be more fully developed by employing Lonergan's subtle discussion about the nature of human authenticity and how it applies in a concrete analysis of modern culture (especially in economics and in the modern sciences). Conversely, Lonergan's views can also be more fully developed and fleshed out by comparative studies of global human faith in relation to the kind of work that Smith did. In dealing with these matters, Lonergan's thought can be applied to this uncultivated area in a way which could expand his authentic thought in a way that would include the study and understanding of other cultures and other traditions. In these ways, the thought of Smith and Lonergan can become more familiar within the global world.

---

① For a sense about what could be meant here in terms of a transposition of meaning, see Lonergan, "Horizons and Transpositions," *Philosophical and Theological Papers* 1965 – 1980, p. 410. By means of what is new in the development of human understanding, one takes something old and one raises it to a greater, higher degree of perfection. As Pope Leo XIII had urged in his encyclical *Aeterni Patris*: *Vetera novis augere et perficere*: augment and perfect the old by what is new." Cf. Matthew Lamb, "Lonergan's Transpositions of Augustine and Aquinas: Exploratory Suggestions," *The Importance of Insight Essays in Honour of Michael Vertin*, eds. John J. Liptay Jr nd David S. Liptay (Toronto: University of Toronto Press, 2007): 4.

The Islamic Republic of Iran and the Western Narrative of the Revolution

Seyed Mohammad Marandi

Initially, the focus of this paper was intended to be on Iran and the Western Narrative of the Revolution. However, subsequent to the keynote speech by Professor Jurgen Moltmann it appeared to me that significant changes were needed, because it seemed clear that he had not live up to his responsibilities and obligations as an academic and thinker. It is no secret that the representation of Iran, Muslims, and Islam is decidedly negative in western countries. However, it is extraordinary to see a "western" academic of such stature repeat in a keynote speech some of the most bizarre Orientalist stereotypes about the beliefs of roughly one-forth of the world's population.

As is well known, Orientalism describes the various schools of thought and methods of investigation through which Europe came to know the East. According to scholars such as Edward Said, it was and still is through this discourse and its construction of knowledge that the West has been able to legitimise and maintain its hold over the supposedly uncivilized 'Other'. A major and repeated feature of Oriental analysis in all its various forms is that it constantly confirms the thesis that the Oriental is primitive, mysterious, exotic and incapable of self-government. However, Orientalism should not be looked upon as just the rationalization of colonial rule. Far more important, it seems, is how it knowingly or unknowingly justifies imperialism and colonialism in advance of their actual manifestation.

In other words, "Orientalism is best viewed in Foucauldian terms as a discourse: a manifestation of power/knowledge".[1] This is because, as Foucault sees it, discourse is a severely bounded area of social knowledge or "heavily policed cognitive systems which control and delimit both the mode and the means of representation in a given society".[2] It is a series of statements, through which the world can be known, as it is not recognized by simply analysing objective data. Its recognition is brought into being through discourse, which is ideologically loaded, but independent of individual will and judgement. According to Said, discourse is the system of thought which dominant powers establish spheres of 'knowledge' and 'truth' and it is through such discursive practices that religions, races, cultures, and classes are represented. Discursive practices are interwoven with social and power relations, while history itself is indivisible from discursive formations.

The idea of representation is usually based upon a notion of being faithful to the original. However, representation is regularly interwoven with many other things besides 'truth'. It is defined not just by inherent common subject matter, but also by a common history, tradition, and universe of discourse that exists within a

---

① Bill Ashcroft and Pal Ahluwalie, *Edward Said: The Paradox of Identity*, London: Routledge, 1999, p. 68.

② Leela Gandhi, *Postcolonial Theory: A Critical Introduction*, Edinburgh: Edinburgh University Press, 1998, p. p. 77.

particular field. [1] Representation is a phenomenon created by writers, intellectuals, artists, commentators, travellers, politicians, as well as others working within similar discursive formations.

This perspective permits critics to consider numerous 'Western' texts from apparently separate intellectual disciplines such as politics, history, linguistics, and literature, among others, as belonging to a single discourse called Orientalism. What brings these texts together is the common culture and ideology intrinsic to the discursive practices through which they produce knowledge about the Orient. These discursive "practices make it difficult for individuals to think outside them – hence they are also seen as exercises of power and control". [2] However, it should be kept in mind that this does not mean that a discourse is either static or cannot admit internal contradictions.

It is often the case that Orientalist modes of thought and representation are actually able to survive contact with the reality on the ground with which it often seems to be at odds with. One reason for this may be that the need for creating an overall consistency in discourse may constantly prevent the realization of objective analysis as well as commitment to 'truth'. The stronger the discourse becomes the longer it lives and the better it is able to bring about consistency within its borders. This is helped through the continued repetition and adaptation of its motifs.

An important aspect of Said's Orientalism is that it explains the methods through which 'the Other' was constructed by the West as its barbaric, irrational, despotic, and inferior opposite or alter ego. It is a type of surrogate and underground version of the West or the

---

[1]   Edward Said, *Orientalism*, Harmondsworth: Penguin, 1985, p. 272 – 73.
[2]   Ania Loomba, *Colonialism/Postcolonialism*, London: Routledge, 1998, p. 39.

'self'.① What may be even more significant is that through its position of domination, the West is even able to tell the 'truth' to non-Western cultures, in this case the Orient, about their past and present condition, as they are capable of representing the Orient more authentically than the Orient can itself. Such a 'truthful' representation not only aids the colonizer or imperialist in justifying their actions, but it also serves to weaken the resistance of 'the Other' as it changes the way in which 'the Other' views itself. Although this discourse is generated in the Occident, its influence is so powerful that it has significant impact on discursive practices in the Orient as well. 'The Other' may come to see himself and his surroundings as inferior or even barbaric. At the very least it can create a major crisis in the consciousness of 'the Other' as it clashes with powerful discursive practices and 'knowledges' about the world. Eurocentricism, as a result, influences, alters, and even helps produce 'Other' cultures.

It is widely believed that the institutionalisation of Europe's 'Other' began in the late eighteenth century and that this is directly linked to the rise of colonialism and imperialism in the nineteenth century. Nonetheless, Europe's knowledge of the Orient was developed through many centuries of discourse. According to Said, who is also believed at times to be entrapped in the same discourse, Orientalists are the heirs to a long tradition of European writing, which was founded by people like Aeschylus and Homer. In *The Persians*, for example, Asia is presented as a land of disaster, loss, and emptiness, and according to Said such literary texts as well as other writings in general play a pivotal role in the creation of 'the

---

① Alexander Lyon Macfie, *Orientalism*, London: Longman, 2002, p. 8.

Other'.

In *Culture and Imperialism* Said points out how the nineteenth-century novel played a critical role in the actual formation and enforcement of Empire. He also stresses the indispensable role that culture plays in the development of imperialism. Modern European states are shown to be justifying imperialism as they imagine themselves as being on a civilizing mission rather than on a mission of plunder. They view their own culture as " the best that has been thought and said". [1]

Therefore, colonial discourse tends to exclude or minimize reference to European exploitation of ' the Other', while repeatedly pointing to the barbaric nature of the subjugated peoples. This process often takes place without the individual colonizing subject even being consciously aware of it. This is what critics see as the Western method of domination.

Through this Eurocentric discourse of superior wisdom and moral neutrality, a relatively monolithic and homogeneous ' Other' encompassing most of the world east and south of Europe, was created. The Orient, in other words, has actually been constructed by the neutralizing of the stereotypes and assumptions of Orientalists. However, what makes Orientalism so relevant and significant are the discriminatory strategies of this discourse both diachronically and synchronically in the contemporary period. In the words of Childs and Williams:

> *Although the centre of Orientalism's power may have shifted from Europe to the United States, its repertoire of images remains remarkably consistent, and its power is*

---

[1]　Matthew Arnold, *Essays in Criticism First Series*, London: Macmillan, 1865, p. 15.

perhaps greater than in the past. That is because, on the one hand, now, more than ever Orientalists are directly linked to the government policy-making and power politics, and on the other, the stereotyped knowledges of Orientalism can gain global and near instantaneous dissemination thanks to the penetration of the mass media [⋯]. [①]

Western assumptions of cultural superiority have roots so deep that even the social reform movements, such as the liberal, the working class, and the feminist movements were all more or less imperialistic. None of these movements ever seriously touched upon the assumptions of imperialist culture. In literary circles today, writers like Carlyle, Dickens, Eyre, Ruskin, and Thackeray, who believed in colonial expansion and show obvious signs of racial prejudice in their works, are all viewed as people of culture whose works are an integral part of the Western cultural heritage. Their views on blacks and other 'peripheral' races are regarded as of lesser importance and forgivable in comparison to their enormous cultural contribution.

Orientalist discourse contains texts which "vary from genre to genre, and from historical period to historical period". [②] Nevertheless, most of these texts contain comparable notions of cultural difference which are stereotyped and negative. In the introduction to *Orientalism*, Said makes his position quite clear:

> *In quite a constant way, Orientalism depends for its strategy on this flexible positional superiority, which puts the Westerner in a whole series of possible relationships with the*

---

① Childs and Williams, *op. cit.*, p. 101.

② Edward Said, *op. cit.*, p. 23.

Orient without ever losing him the relative upperhand. [1]

In other words, while different religions, cultures, and races are not seen as identical, and in some instances they may be presented as actually being quite diverse, they are still deemed similarly inferior. Not only is this Orientalist discourse clearly visible in the western mass media, movies, television programs, official governmental statements, and it also exists in history textbooks as well, as a recent study indicates. [2]

In the eyes of many Iranians, through this Orientalist discourse, their country along with its people, culture, and politics are often little more than caricatured in western society. This is especially significant, because of the sheer power of the western media and its ability to disseminate information at a global level. Interestingly, in a recent lecture at the University of Tehran, the former Iranian ambassador to China said that in a meeting between the Chinese foreign minister and himself, both men pointed out that the source of information for both Iranians and Chinese about one another is largely from western sources and that these representations are largely negative. This is a point that needs to be addressed not only by Iran and China, but by all economically developing countries, all of whom have a responsibility to break this monopoly of representation.

Due to the fact that most of the information about Iran on global television, on the internet, and even in academic material comes from western and specifically American sources, it can be argued that very

---

① *ibid.*, p. 7.

② Connections and Ruptures: America and the Middle East, Proceedings of the Third International Conference Sponsored by The Prince Alwaleed Bin Talal Bin Abdulaziz Alsaud Center for American Studies and Research (CASAR) at the American University of Beirut. Beirut: American University of Beirut (forthcoming May 2011).

few people in western countries know much about the country. People rarely have the opportunity to understand Iranian, regional, or international politics from an Iranian perspective, because they have little or no access to Iranian points of view.

Persian is not a language that even most so called "Iran experts" in western countries, and especially the United States, have a command of and the few Iranians who work in think tanks or who participate in television programs in the United States are decidedly western oriented. In Iran they are often described as orientalized orientals, or in the words of Jalale Ale Ahmad "west struck". Hence, what they often do is to merely reinforce western stereotypes and reaffirm the belief of the backward, despotic, and dangerous Iranian oriental. Some, claiming to have a more generous world view, but whose perspectives are in reality largely Eurocentric, believe that the Iranians wish to be like "us", meaning western, but that the Iranian government or "regime", as they like to call it, prevents them from doing so.

In should be pointed out here that Iranians, unlike many of their western counterparts, have a great deal of access to western society and thought. Similar to many other countries, Iranian schoolchildren begin studying English from the sixth grade, and in many public and private schools they begin even earlier. All universities in Iran have their own English departments, which have BA programs in English language and literature, translation studies, as well as English language teaching. MA and PhD programs in these fields exist in the larger universities and all universities, of course, teach English as a foreign language. Undergraduate and postgraduate degree programs in languages such as French, Spanish, and German also exist in many major Iranian universities.

English language learning is also a major business, especially in large cities like Tehran. For those millions who have satellite TV, there are literally thousands of English channels beamed into the country. There are countless websites in English (French, German, and others for those who understand other European languages) that Iranians can access, and through these websites they can learn about western cultures, societies, and politics from western perspectives. In addition, many western governments fund large numbers of Persian websites, television channels, as well as other means of communication to influence Iranian public opinion.

Hence, Iranians know quite well what is being said about Iran in the "international community" and, of course, the international community in the eyes of many in the west literally means western countries. Iranians often hear about the "international community's" concern about Iran's nuclear program, and as two thirds of the countries of the world, including members of the Non-Aligned Movement (NAM) and the *Organisation of the Islamic Conference* (OIC) have unequivocally supported Iran's nuclear program, one can conclude that they are not considered by western countries to be a significant part of the "international" community.

The US government alone spends an enormous amount of money each year to fund tens of [1]television channels as well as hundreds of websites and organizations to bring about "regime change" in the Islamic Republic of Iran. This is in addition to the activities carried out by foundations and institutions close to the centers of power in Washington as well as secret funding through intelligence organizations. It is extraordinary that there are now far more western-

---

[1]　http://www.usatoday.com/news/politics/2010 - 10 - 12 - campaignmoney12_ST_N.htm

funded Persian language television channels than there are Iranian-funded channels. This is while, ironically, the US president has recently expressed concern about foreign money being used to influence American elections.

Still the United States claims that such activities are in line with its supposed belief that freedom of information brings about a freer and more open society. However, when one sees how foreign news channels like Aljazeera and Press TV have effectively been prevented from being offered by American cable TV companies, we should not be surprised if some questions are raised. More interesting is how Arabic television channels like Al-Manar, which is close to Hezbollah are banned in many EU countries. This is while Hezbollah is a legally recognized Lebanese political party that has elected MPs and is a part of the Lebanese government coalition. However, what is most extraordinary is how in the United States, anyone who facilitates access to Al-Manar TV, as well as a number of other foreign channels, can be heavily fined and even sentenced up to 15 years in prison. Currently, at least two people are serving long sentences in US prisons under similar charges. [①] It is worth remembering that Al-Manar is not even in English.

Iran is demonized in the west for alleged human rights violation and support for terrorism. Support for terrorism mainly means support for Hamas, the political party elected by the Palestinian people, as well as support for Hezbollah. Iran's attempts to help break the barbaric siege of Gaza (where even children are effectively denied adequate amounts of medicine, food, and clean water) apparently

---

① http://www. washingtonpost. com/wp-dyn/content/article/2006/08/24/AR2006082401461. html

runs against western principles regarding human rights, as the siege has the full support of the EU and the US.

Iran is also attacked among other things for its pursuit of its peaceful nuclear program. The word "peaceful" is used intentionally, because contrary to claims made by western governments and the western media, no evidence has ever been provided that Iran's nuclear program has been anything but peaceful. For roughly two years, Iran did more than halt the enrichment of uranium; it effectively halted almost the entire nuclear program and implemented the Additional Protocol. It allowed the IAEA to carry out intrusive inspections, many of which had nothing to do with the nuclear program and looked more like intelligence-gathering operations on behalf of the U. S. government. The fact that the International Atomic Energy Agency, an undemocratic body largely under western influence, has not found any evidence whatsoever to show that Iran's nuclear program has ever been anything but peaceful, and yet still continues to oppose Iran's nuclear program, is another reason why Iranians have little trust in western governments or the western media. The fact that the western-backed Israeli regime, which constantly threatens Iran with air strikes, has a large nuclear arsenal, does not do much to build trust either.

Ironically, these sorts of criticisms are not directed at Israel which is viewed by Iranians and other Muslim nations as a racist state. In recent years, Israel has launched a brutal war on the city of Gaza, as well as on the people of Lebanon, and over the past few decades through numerous wars on neighboring states, the Zionist regime has killed tens of thousands of civilians. The regime is currently holding over 11,000 Palestinian women and children in its prisons, it continues to colonize Palestinian land, torture prisoners, and it carries out targeted killing. Nevertheless, the term terrorism is not used in the west or by Professor Moltmann for these outrageous acts. In fact the word terrorism is not even used for carrying out shock and awe tactics in Gaza, Beirut, or even Baghdad.

Official Iranian policy has also always held that, while Iran will not recognize Israel, due to it being an apartheid state (similar to its South Africa policy during apartheid), it will respect any decision made by the Palestinian people in this regard. From the Iranian perspective, any decision will have to include all Palestinians living both inside the country and outside it; that would include the millions who continue to live in refugee camps. Regarding Palestine and Lebanon, it is a major mistake for western experts to believe that the Islamic Republic of Iran's support for the people of these countries, especially the oppressed people of Palestine, is in any way cynical. If one looks at the pre-Revolution statements of current Iranian leaders, one will see that the issue of Palestine was a central grievance of the opposition to the Shah. This, of course, is in sharp contrast to the extraordinary support the "Chosen People" who are occupying Palestinian homes receive from the "civilized" West.

Professor Moltmann, in his keynote speech, makes a somewhat peculiar reference to Islam and then makes reference to a statement by the Taliban leader, Mullah Omar as if he somehow represents the views of all Muslims. He quotes him as saying "you love life, we love death". Perhaps that is why another keynote speaker in the conference, the former UK Prime Minister Tony Blair enthusiastically stood side by side with George Bush in attacking Iraq. Perhaps he wanted to give Iraqi Muslims what they allegedly love, meaning death. Professor Moltmann fails to point out how respect and love of life among western leaders politicians, and governments, influenced their decision to provide Saddam Hussain with chemical weapons to use against Iranians as well as the people of his own country (I survived two such chemical attacks). When 5 , 000 people were slaughtered within minutes by means of chemical weapons in the Iraqi city of Halabcheh, the western media and most western thinkers and intellectuals were virtually silent, despite their professed " love of life " in the words of Professor Moltmann. Only after Saddam Hussain's invasion of Kuwait did Weapons of Mass Destruction or Halabcheh suddenly become an issue in the western media. Professor Moltmann also fails to say much about Mullah Omar's Afghani Salafi followers and non-Afghani allies meaning Al-Qaida, and how they were heavily supported and funded by US and other western intelligence services in the 1980s and 1990s or to explain that they are still indirectly funded by US allies, such as the pro-Salafi dictatorships in Saudi Arabia and the UAE.

People throughout the region are under pressure, as despotic regimes for the most part allied to the United States try to ensure their own survival. Under such conditions, hostility towards the United States increases and, ironically, extremist ideologies thrive (such as that of the Taliban leader Mullah Omar). Of course, whether these American-backed regimes can actually survive or not is another question. If these regimes do not survive, how will the people in these countries react to US and western past policies of oppression?

Hence, choosing Arab despots as allies—whether in Saudi Arabia, where women are not allowed to drive or, for the most part, cannot even have an independent bank account—can have serious consequences for the United States in the future. The irony of this is not lost upon Iranians who live in a country where 63 percent of the undergraduate student population is female. Indeed, the head of my faculty at the University of Tehran is a woman.

Professor Moltmann probably knows that the resistance toward the United States in the Islamic Republic of Iran does not have its roots in a "love for death"; rather it has its roots in issues such as the 1953 CIA coup in Iran; the US support for the despotic and corrupt Pahlavi regime; the US (and EU) support for terrorist groups in Iran such as the MEK, PJAK, and Jundallah; US support for Saddam Hussain; and sanctions that, contrary to western claims, are intended to make ordinary Iranians suffer.

Indeed, while Professor Moltmann spoke about Obama's honorable dream of nuclear disarmament and his own fear of nuclear proliferation, he forgot to mention that in Obama's recent Nuclear Posture Review, "the United States claims the prerogative to use Nuclear weapons against the Islamic Republic of Iran, even as Iran remains a non-nuclear-weapons state." [1] There is no need to dwell upon any other of Professor Moltmann's comments, except to point out two more things. He ended his lecture on the subject of love and respect for life with a quote from Hegel who has well known views on racial hierarchy. [2] Also, when he spoke of the right to pursue happiness (he reminded the audience that it is included in the US declaration of independence as if it is a western concept) one wonders if non-westerners, Muslims, and particularly Iranians are included in this category?

The revolution in Iran was in fact linked to the right of Iranians to control their destiny and this was linked to their religious faith, their sense of human responsibility, and their belief in the sanctity of

---

[1] http://www.raceforiran.com/is-iran-now-a-nuclear-target-for-the-united-states

[2] A. L. Macfie (ed.), Orientalism: a Reader, New York: NYU Press, 2001, pp. 13-5.

human life. They wished to be independent of American hegemony and they wished to rid themselves of a corrupt and despotic shah who squandered the nation's oil wealth and who had little care for the cultural or religious values of ordinary Iranians, as he and the ruling class largely mimicked western culture. Through the Islamic Revolution, Iranians were fulfilling their right to purse what they believed and continue to believe will bring about happiness for themselves and their society.

This year the North American Studies department at the University of Tehran, which I head, has enrolled its first group of PhD students. All of them are bright young women and one of them happens to be among the international students invited to the Beijing Forum. Hence, as academics we have an obligation to move beyond stereotypes, especially at a time when western governments are becoming more aggressive and increasingly violent.

全球化大潮下中国宗教的宽容与和谐

刘金光

当今世界已经处于全球化大潮的冲击之中,任何国家、民族、政党、社团组织、宗教和个人,无论是否愿意,都摆脱不了这个大潮的冲击。全球化是世界历史发展进程的一个新阶段,它既增加了社会流动和彼此交流的机会,密切了关系,使人们共同分享各自物质文明和精神文明的成果,也增加了不同文化、包括不同宗教之间,不同制度、包括不同意识形态之间的交融、摩擦,甚至冲突。特别是冷战结束后,随着全球化的发展,在国际宗教方面呈现出的特点令人眼花缭乱。一方面宗教原教旨主义发展势头甚猛,另一方面宗教世俗化的趋势发展也很快;一方面由宗教原因或以宗教名义引发的冲突、纷争愈演愈烈,另一方面宗教和平、宽容、和谐的呼声也日趋高涨;一方面全球移民、文化交流在加强,另一方面文化壁垒各自保守的现象也屡见不鲜。

全球化大潮流,搅动泥沙污浊,冲突与和谐、机遇和挑战、开放与保守俱存。如不及早清淤澄清,我们全球大家庭很难心情愉悦地安心享有全球化带给我们的成果。为此,世界各个方面做出了不懈的努力,各种对话、研讨、座谈不断进行。

中国现在有 2300 万穆斯林,2305 万基督教徒,500 多万天主教徒。信仰佛教的信徒数量很多难以统计。中国佛教、道教、伊斯兰教、基督教和天主教等五大主要宗教共有 105,000 个宗教活动场所,约 300,000 名宗教教职人员。全国共有 3,000 个宗教团体,78 所宗教院校。中国宗教界与世界上 80 个国家的宗教组织建立了联系。

那么,中国宗教面对全球化大潮表现出怎样的态势呢?我认为中国宗教是以它惯有的宽容与和谐来直面全球化大潮的挑战。

首先,源远流长、崇尚"和"的中华文明为中国各宗教的宽容与和谐提供了丰腴肥美的生存土壤。中华民族几千年的文明史上,较少有文明之间的互相蔑视、彼此践踏,更多的是互相尊重、彼此欣赏;较少有文明之间的以大欺小、弱肉强食,更多的是有容乃大、海纳百川;较少有文明之间的高低优劣、生存竞争,更多的是相互平等、和合共生;较少有文明之间的孤芳自赏、一枝独秀,更多的是互补共荣、百花齐放。集中到一点,就是"和而不同、美美与共"。中国宗教,不管是本生的还外来的,就是在这样的土壤上滋养生长。久而久之,水乳交融,中国宗教也带有了中国文化的这些特点,同时也参与成就了中国文化的这些特点。面对全球化浪潮的冲击,中国宗教建基于这样的传统,立足于这样的土壤,必然吸收中国文化的优秀成分,把中国文化的宽容与和谐的传统融会于自身,也就是说中国文明深厚的包容性养育了中国宗教的宽容与和谐。中国宗教的宽容与和谐必将有益于世界宗教的宽容与和谐。

其次,中国各宗教在自身的发展过程中形成了各自特色的宽容与和谐特质。中国五大主要宗教,只有道教是本土的,其他均传自外国,但现今都成为中国自己的宗教。从外国传入中国的宗教不断调试自己,吸收并融入中国的文明传统,逐步形成了自己的宽容与和谐特质。佛教自 2000 多年前从印度传入中国,继承了婆罗门教和耆那教的非暴力和不杀生思想,把这一思想变成自己的基本戒律。佛教认为人的行为是由欲望引起的,人的欲望是无止境的,欲望膨胀的结果,就有了贪的行为,掠夺和战争正是贪的表现。所以佛教提倡灭欲,不杀害生灵,众生平等,不允许种姓压迫的存在,这样,社会、国家和人民之间的和平共处才有保障。这些平等慈悲的思想成为中国佛教和平、宽容与和谐的思想的基石。中国道教继承了道家取法自然的和平论,主张人类处理自己和万物的关系,必须取法自然,人类要以天地为准则,维护世界万物生长变化过程的自然本性,不能人为地去破坏自然本性。道教全真派道徒丘处机在 1220 年正月,不顾自己年迈体弱,以

73 岁的高龄,率弟子 18 人,自山东莱州启程北上,爬高山,涉大川,跨戈壁,越荒漠,为结束"十年兵火万民愁"的局面,劝诫成吉思汗止杀,"欲罢干戈致太平"。《老子》和《抱朴子》等经典所提倡的和平思想,在当今时代为世界和平事业贡献着自己的力量。伊斯兰源于阿拉伯文,其字面意义为谦逊、降服、归顺、服从、和平、纯净等意义。中国伊斯兰教保持了伊斯兰教的根本教义,又与中国传统文化相结合,形成了独具特色的中国伊斯兰教文化,主张和平、纯洁。中国穆斯林与中华民族大家庭中的每一个民族都能和睦相处,荣辱与共,谱写了一曲曲维护和平的赞歌。伊斯兰教提倡"中道",主张当行则行,行止有度,绝不过分。伊斯兰教认为,坚持"中道"原则,是达到与社会相和谐的途径。中国基督教和天主教这两大宗教虽然传入中国较晚,但经过"自立革新"运动和反帝爱国运动,实现了独立自主自办教会的目标,成为中国信徒自办的教会事业,他们主张"与天和好、与人修睦、与社会和谐",积极倡导圣经中"和平"、"和好"、"和睦"的理念,与全体中国人民一道和睦相处,共同维护着和平事业。中国五大宗教在继承和发扬各自特质的基础上,都吸取了中国传统文化"和为贵"的思想,贯彻到各自的教义、教规和行为活动中。各宗教之间互相吸纳融通,形成了中国五大宗教的多元共存、和睦相处。中国宗教还与长时期主导中国儒家思想相互融合,比如在中国儒释道三家共处一庙的情况比比皆是。中国宗教独特的宽容与和谐传统,为世界宗教处理相互关系提供了可借鉴之处。

再次,中国宗教传统的宽容与和谐特质在新的历史时期更加发扬光大并为中国社会和谐和世界和谐做出新贡献。近年来,中国宗教界积极探索发挥宗教在促进社会和谐方面积极作用的方法和途径,"五教同光,共致和谐",做出了有益的尝试,并取得了积极的成果。一方面,中国宗教界努力发扬乐善好施、扶危济困、服务社会,关爱人群的优良传统。各宗教积极发挥各自的优势,在解决自养的基础上,力所能及地积极参与扶贫救灾(比如印尼海啸,中国四川汶川大地震、台湾风灾、青海玉树地震、甘肃舟曲泥石流等)、助学助残、生态环保等工作,努力兴办各种社会公益慈善事业。

另一方面,中国宗教界积极挖掘各宗教关于"和"的理念,努力对宗教经典、教义做出适应时代发展、符合社会进步要求的阐释。中国佛教一直致力于"人间佛教"的实践。中国佛教协会与中华宗教文化交流协会分别于2006年4月和2009年3月共同举办了两次世界佛教论坛,提出了"和谐世界,从心开始"等口号,在海内外产生了广泛而深远的影响。近年来,中国基督教积极开展神学思想建设,努力将基督教建设成为伦理型、道德型的宗教,中国基督教出现了新的面貌。20多年来,中国已经印刷了近7000万册圣经。其中为海外教会印刷了900多万册,使得圣经也正在成为"中国制造"。中国政府对圣经的印刷、销售等多个环节实行免税,圣经的定价只有其他同类普通书籍的五分之一。中国基督教协会于2004年赴中国香港地区,2006年赴美国洛杉矶、亚特兰大、纽约,以及2007年赴德国科隆和巴伐利亚,举办了"中国教会圣经事工展",向世界展示了基督教在新中国发展变化的真实情况,目前正在积极筹备明年赴美国华盛顿特区举办"中国圣经事工展"。中国道教有着崇尚和谐,促进和谐的优良传统,2007年4月召开国际《道德经》论坛,提出了"和谐世界,以道相通"的口号。道教正在积极探索"生活道教"。中国伊斯兰教开展的解经工作,富有成效,不断深化,进一步发掘伊斯兰教的优良传统。中国天主教不断加强制度建设,大力推进民主办教。如果没有宽容与和谐的环境,怎么能出现这样的局面呢?目前,中国五大宗教正在争相开展"和谐寺观教堂"的创建活动。同时,中国的基督教与伊斯兰教还探索开展不同信仰间的对话,并在此基础上积极推动世界基督教与伊斯兰教开展高层对话,以促进基督文明与伊斯兰文明的对话、沟通与和睦,为从深层次上解决当今国际社会的危机,促进世界和平,发挥积极的、建设性的作用。此外,中国五大宗教参与了许多世界性的和平交流行动,《中国宗教界和平委员会章程》规定了该委员会的宗旨是加强我国各宗教团体及其信徒维护和参与世界和平事业,发展同世界各宗教和平组织及有关人士的友好往来,共同促进和维护世界和平,并为此而进行了不懈的努力,在世界宗教界赢得了荣誉。同时,中国各宗教还积极参与了如亚欧不同信仰间对话等的国际不同文明对话活动,向当今的国际社会阐述中国宗教宽容与和谐的理念和思想。

最后,中国政府的政策与法律也为中国宗教的宽容与和谐提供了保障。中国政府实行的宗教政策是有史以来最宽容的。无论宗教大与小,强与弱,中国政府都平等对待,毫无偏跛。中国既无国教,亦无占统治地位的宗教。无论是本国土生的宗教,还是外来的"洋教",都在中国享有平等的地位和待遇。事实上,中国各个宗教目前发展最慢,规模最小的反而是土生的道教。中国政府并没有特别优待自己亲生的这个宗教。另外一个宽容就是,无论是信教还是不信教,地位和待遇也是平等的。中国虽然有超过一亿人口信仰不同的宗教,但是与全国总人口相比,信教人口还是少数。为了保护这只占人口十分之一的宗教,中国政府制定了严格的政策和法律,不准歧视和迫害少数信教的人,如有发生,绝对要绳之以法。也就是说,中国公民宗教信仰自由的权利是受到法律保护的。不仅国家的宪法确立"公民有宗教信仰自由的权利、各宗教一律平等、政教分离"的原则,而且2005年最新实行的《宗教事务条例》也是明确以"保障公民信仰自由的权利,维护宗教和睦和社会和谐"为宗旨的。中国共产党虽然不信仰宗教,但是,正因为如此,它对待各宗教才能够秉公执政,不偏不倚。在处理与各宗教关系上,中国政府实行的是不同信仰者"政治上团结合作,信仰上相互尊重"的原则。同时积极支持各宗教努力挖掘和弘扬教义中有利时代进步、健康文明和社会和谐的内容,服务社会,利益人群。在对外关系上,中国政府支持宗教界在独立自主、平等友好、互相尊重的基础上积极开展同各国宗教界的友好交往,广泛参与世界和平、环保、裁军等事业,为建立和谐世界发挥中国宗教界的积极作用。特别是改革开放后,对新的外来宗教依然是宽容的,如五大宗教以外的宗教,随着全球化的发展,越来越多的外国人到中国经商、学习、工作、旅游,甚至居住,中国政府也给予了宽容的政策,信仰自由的保护。

上述四点,既是中国宗教界面对全球化大潮确保宗教宽容与和谐的必经途径,也是中国宗教能够为全球宗教宽容与和谐做出贡献的根本保障。我相信,在全球化时代,中国宗教必将进一步加深与不同国家、不同信仰之间的交流、理解和沟通,增进信任和友谊,坚固交流的桥梁和目标。同时我也相信,中国宗教愿意与世界各国同行共同携手,摒弃偏见,坦诚对话,加强交流,共享经验,为世界宗教的宽容与和谐做出应有的贡献。正如前北京教区主教、全国人大常委会副委员长傅铁山代表中国宗教界所提出的倡议:高扬和平旗帜,维护宗教的纯洁性;提倡宗教宽容与和解,创造和平共处的环境。正视不同文明和宗教信仰的差异,互相尊重,求同存异。这正是中国宗教面对全球化大潮表现出的特有的宽容与和谐特质。

Finding Common Ground in Unity and Reconciliation : A Hindu Perspective

Anantanand Rambachan

The necessity for reconciliation and reaching across religious boundaries presupposes a condition under which relationships, such as those obtaining between individual human beings or human communities are broken and characterized by suffering and hostility or indifference and isolation. Unfortunately, examples of such painful and fractured relationships abound in our contemporary world and in every nation and continent there are relationships requiring healing and wholeness. Why should the attainment of reconciliation be a central concern of religious traditions? What resources do our religious traditions offer that may inspire and motivate us to work for reconciliation? These questions become especially significant in the light of the fact that religion is a factor and a contributory cause in many of the situations of conflict and discord, past and present, active and dormant. We cannot overlook the role of religion in intensifying narrow loyalties, providing a motivation for violence and entrenching divisiveness. Yet religions continue to be a potent source of the visions, values and moral energies which are capable of renewing, transforming and healing human communities. Although we must never underestimate and ignore the destructive potential of religion, our challenge is to discover also and recover the spiritual and ethical insights, often ignored and forgotten, which are essential for the well-being of the world community. One of the unprecedented opportunities of our present context is the possibility of growth and mutual transformation through interreligious dialogue, learning and encounters.

The necessity for reconciliation and reaching across religious boundaries presupposes a condition under which relationships, such as those obtaining between individual human beings or human communities are broken and characterized by suffering and hostility or indifference and isolation. Unfortunately, examples of such painful and fractured relationships abound in our contemporary world and in every nation and continent there are relationships requiring healing and wholeness. Why should the attainment of reconciliation be a central concern of religious traditions? What resources do our religious traditions offer that may inspire and motivate us to work for reconciliation?

These questions become especially significant in the light of the fact that religion is a factor and a contributory cause in many of the situations of conflict and discord, past and present, active and dormant. Among these are the struggles between Muslim Palestinians and Jewish Israelis, Protestants and Catholics in Northern Ireland, and the Muslim North and Christian South in the Sudan. The list can be quite easily extended to include conflicts in Sri Lanka, India, and Pakistan where religion is an important part of the identities of the communities in conflict. The lines of many conflicts are both interreligious as well as intrareligious. Religion, admittedly, is not the sole explanation for any of these conflicts and the religious factor is intermeshed with historical, political, economic, ethnic, racial and cultural dimensions. Yet, we cannot overlook the role of religion in intensifying narrow loyalties, providing a motivation for violence and entrenching divisiveness. We cannot also explain away the relationship between religion and violent conflict by the argument that, in all these instances, religion is being used or misused for the achievement of power in its various forms. It is too simplistic as well to attribute responsibility for conflict and violence to what we may regard as extremist and fundamentalist elements within religious traditions. The relationship between religion and violence is too ancient to be so easily explained. The boundaries of community are not determined only by geo-political factors, but also by theological divides and divisions and the latter are often more resistant to change and transformation than the former. When we reflect on the role of religion as a force for reconciliation, we cannot, sadly, ignore its continuing contribution to human discord and divisiveness.

In spite of the fact that the historical legacy of every world religion is a tarnished one, these religions continue to be a potent source of the visions, values and moral energies which are capable of renewing, transforming and healing human communities. Although we must never underestimate and ignore the destructive potential of religion, our challenge is to discover also and recover the spiritual and ethical insights, often ignored and forgotten, which are essential for the well-being of the world community. We may find encouragement and hope in the fact that those religions have survived which are capable of self-correction, adaptation and change. One of the unprecedented opportunities of our present context is the possibility of growth and mutual transformation through interreligious dialogue, learning and encounters.

My paper is divided into three parts. I will begin with some reflections on the role of religion in fostering conflict through its tendency to represent negatively the worth of those who are considered to be outside the boundaries of its defined community. I then discuss religion as an important source of the visions, values and moral energies capable of healing and reconciling human communities. Finally, I conclude with a few reflctions on the role of religion in a globalized community. My paper is woven with texts and illustrations from Hinduism, since this is the tradition that I know best as a scholar and practitioner. My intuition, however, is that a lot of what I wish to say will be widely applicable to other traditions.

While the role of religion in situations of violence, past and present, is complex and intermeshed with a variety of non-religious factors, religion undeniably contributes to violence by furnishing a view of the other that engenders hostility and creates the conditions that makes violence possible. The significance of this truth may be appreciated by noting the extent to which parties in a conflict often go in alienating the other, emphasizing otherness and in denying any common identity. We find it difficult to destroy the one in whom we see ourselves. "It is difficult", as Mark Juergensmeyer reminds us, "to belittle and kill a person whom one knows and for whom one has no personal antipathy." The denial of the personhood of the other is a predictable and persistent feature of communities in conflict.

Religious traditions that affirm exclusive truth claims often affirm the worth of their own followers in relation to the diminished worth of others and, in so doing, become agents, direct and indirect of violence. Theological exclusivism is too commonly associated with militant attitudes towards people of other religions who are often denigrated and whose traditions must be combated and replaced. The fact is that every religious tradition, at one point or another in its history, has represented others negatively and such descriptions have been the basis for boundary-making, exclusion and violence. There is an urgent need for an ongoing critique of this legacy in all traditions. Notions of mission, salvation, choseness and the relationship between religion and nationality that demeans, excludes and alienates us from others call for re-examination.

If, as already noted, the devaluing of the other is a cause and condition of violence, it is important that religious traditions give renewed emphasis and highlight those teachings and insights that affirm human unity, our shared identity and the unity of all existence. We may begin our exploration of Hindu resources for reconciliation by noting that the will and desire for reconciliation as well as the possibility of its attainment are significantly enhanced when there is a discernment of shared identity with the estranged other.

Looking specifically to the Hindu tradition this vision of shared identity and inclusiveness is articulated in the teaching about the unity of existence in the Ultimate. While this truth is affirmed philosophically in various dialogues of the Upanishads and in numerous other texts, it is also beautifully expressed in suggestive poetic metaphors and similes. One of the most striking occurs in the Bhagavadgita (7 : 7) where God likened the to? the string in a necklace of jewels. While the gems constituting a necklace differ in form and properties, the string that runs through each is one and the same. The string links and unites each gem with the other, however separate they are spatially and different in form and shape. In an analogous way, God is envisioned as the common and unifying reality in all created beings. The Hindu tradition understands God to be the one truth in each one of us, uniting us with each other and with all that exists. The Hindu Advaita (Non-dual) tradition identifies God with the deepest and most profound level of human selfhood (*atman*) that is identical in all beings. Wisdom is a discernment that enables us to see ourselves in all beings and all beings in ourselves. The significance that Hinduism grants to the truth of life's unity may be appreciated from the fact that its discernment is considered to the hallmark of wisdom and liberation. We are invited to recognize the sameness of the divine in ourselves and in all beings. The Bhagavadgita (18:20) commends the knowledge that enables one to see, "one imperishable Being in all beings, undivided in separate beings." A false and inferior way of seeing reality is to regard existing things as isolated, separate and independent of each other and to see in all beings "separate entities of various kinds (18:21)." We are not to deny the uniqueness of individuals, communities and cultures, but affirm the irreducible unity that underlies all. This understanding of life's unity is the justification of its regard for the entire world as a single family (*vasudhaiva kutumbakam*). It is also the source of its core values such as *ahimsa* (non-injury), *daya* (compassion) and *dana* (generosity). Compassion is an integral expression of the vision of life's unity and fundamental interelatedness. The many religious traditions of our world may understand the ground of life's unity in different ways, but it is a crucial shared teaching that is the source of significant common values and obligations. It offers us a space to stand together.

The Hindu understanding of life's unity is all-inclusive. No one can or should be excluded, since the divine, who constitutes the unifying truth, does not exclude anyone and anything. "God," as the Bhagavadgita (13:28), puts it, "abides equally in all beings." This is an antidote to our tendency to deny the personhood, worth and dignity of the other. It is from the perspective of life's unity that we must question exploitative and unjust human relationships, which foster conflict, and divisiveness and it is the same perspective, which urges us to cross boundaries and work for reconciliation. If our world shares a unity, spiritually and biologically, the quality of our relationships should reflect the moral and ethical implications of this truth. Isa Upanishad (6) reminds us that the wise person who beholds all beings in the self and the self in all beings is liberated from hate. iii From the profundity of the Hindu understanding of the nature of life's unity, estrangement from another is estrangement from one's own self and the hate of the other is the hate of one's self. To be in conflict with another is also to be in conflict with one's self. To inflict suffering on another is to violate one's own self.

The Hindu tradition assumes that a person who is truly grasped by the truth of life's unity will find delight in unselfishly striving for the well being of others. Ignorance of life's unity, on the other hand, expresses itself in greed, ego-centeredness, and the infliction of suffering on others through reckless exploitation. This is the reason why the traditions of Hinduism have almost uniformly described the fundamental human problem to be one of ignorance or, in Sanskrit, avidya. Human conflict and suffering are rooted in a fundamental misunderstanding of the unity of existence. Ignorance can be overcome and when it is and when we are awakened to the truth of life's unity, there will be a corresponding transformation in the quality of our relationships.

The view that the human problem at its most fundamental level is one of ignorance and that this ignorance expresses itself in our failure to discern the unity of all existence is central to the development of a Hindu approach to reconciliation and to conflict-resolution. It enables us to see the other, the one with whom we disagree and with who we may be locked in struggle, as a fellow human being who we must not dehumanize or humiliate. This approach was at the heart of the Gandhian philosophy and practice of non-violent resistance (*satyagraha*). Even in the midst of the strongest disagreements, Gandhi never sought to win support for his case by demonizing his opponent. He understood clearly that when a conflict is constructed sharply in terms of *we* and *they*, victory and defeat, the doors to reconciliation and a transformed community are shut. One is left with an enemy, a defeated enemy perhaps, and the next round of the conflict is only postponed. Gandhi included the opponent in the circle of his identity.

In restraining a disciple from a desire for revenge and violence, the saintly Hindu teacher, Ramana Maharishi, asked a provocative question. "If your teeth suddenly bite your tongue, do you knock them out in consequence?" iv Ramana's question implies the truth of life's unity as well as the reality of ignorance. The teeth and tongue are part of the same body and the biting, however, painful, is more in the nature of an error. The consequence is a disposition to understanding and compassion, without which reconciliation is impossible.

Belief in ignorance as the source of suffering disposes one to an attitude of reconciliation and forgiveness since it orients one to look beyond the immediate action to its underlying causes. We are more likely to respond with hate when we believe that those who hurt us have done so because of intentional malevolence. If we see the action as rooted in ignorance and a flawed understanding of reality, our attitude to the other will be compassionate. We are liberated from hate, bitterness and the desire to inflict pain on the other and we are open to reconciliation.

It is clear that the Hindu tradition shares with other world religions an understanding of life's unity that fosters compassionate action in the world and human reconciliation. Our common challenge today is to highlight these core teachings and, more importantly, to simultaneously employ these teachings as the basis of a rigorous religious self-examination, which identifies exploitative and oppressive structures. These are the structures that alienate and estrange human beings from each other and from the n world and which are fundamentally unjust. It is easy to succumb to the temptation of speaking in enticing and platitudinous ways about the need and value for reconciliation while ignoring the challenges of addressing and overcoming these structures which sanction and enable some human beings to inflict suffering on other human beings. Discourse about reconciliation must not become a like a beautiful robe that conceals a diseased body. Reconciliation will always remain an intangible ideal as long as we are unwilling, from insincerity or fear, to unearth and confront the underlying causes of human conflict and divisiveness. The voices of those within and outside our tradition who feel despised, rejected and stripped of dignity must be heard, even in their silence and absence.

Religions need to share a commitment to be less defensive and more self-critical and to hold our traditions accountable to their highest teachings about compassion and caring for others. Very often, the injustices of our traditions are revealed to us only through the eyes and words of others. Their historical experiences and questions help us to change, grow and to be more faithful to the heart of our own traditions.

Although the traditions of Hinduism, I am convinced, offer insights about that can form the basis for relationships of justice, equal worth and dignity for all human beings, privileged and particularistic identities have often been the dominant ones, leading to claims for power and rights denied to others. Hinduism, like other world religions that developed in patriarchal cultures, reflects assumptions about male gender supremacy, which have been oppressive to women. Gender reconciliation, therefore, is one of the important tasks to be pursued by Hindus in collaboration with persons of other religions where this challenge persists. In a similar way the caste system, whatever maybe its historical origins and intentions, has evolved into a religiously legitimized system that values and treats human beings unequally. Its inequities cannot be addressed by offering concessions to those who are disadvantaged and who do not enjoy some of the privileges of the upper castes. The role of religion is to question the legitimacy of such hierarchical social systems that assign differing values to human beings. Our traditions must be united in acknowledging ways in which many persons continue to experience these as oppressive and as negating their dignity and self-worth. We must together proclaim those teachings and those values that promote justice, dignity and the equal worth of human beings.

Spectacular technological developments continue to overcome the barriers of space and distance and to create the conditions for the emergence of a global community and globalization. Science and technology, however, will not provide us with the values that are so critically necessary for the challenges of living in communities of religious and cultural diversity. Religious identities and commitments continue, with ever increasing vigor, to influence people's understanding of themselves, the world and their relationships to each other. Surely, our religions will have to be vital and important sources of the values necessary for guiding our paths in communities of diversity and our traditions cannot do this in isolation from one another.

The major traditions of Hinduism are unanimous in their view that the divine exists equally and identically in all beings. This is the ground of its vision of life's unity and its inspiration for relationships of reconciliation and compassion. When the implications for life in community are enunciated, these are done in terms of a vision of equality and this must be the norm by which we critique social structures and gender relationships. The doctrine of divine equality and the worth of all human beings must inspire and impel us to identify and heal the exploitative and alienating structures of society. Such work is vital and inseparable to the quest for reconciliation.

In his most famous work, Sri Ramacaritamanas the sixteenth century Indian poet, Tulasidasa, employs a striking example to highlight the contrast between righteous and unrighteous persons. He likens the righteous to a sandal tree and the unrighteous to an axe. Even as the axe chops the sandal tree, it returns saturated with the fragrance of the tree. It is the nature of the sandal tree to exude and share its soothing fragrance and this defining quality is not altered by the behavior of the other. The cruelty and injustice of the axe cannot provoke a change in its nature. Like the sandal tree, a righteous person does not become unjust because others are unjust and does not respond with hate towards those who are hate-filled. Goodness in not transformed by the destructive behavior of another.

The urge for reconciliation, nurtured by religious impulses, shares a fundamental similarity with the sandal tree. It is not extinguished by its encounter with hostility and cynicism. It never ceases to share the fragrance of its hope for an inclusive human community where relationships are compassionate and just. Even under the most oppressive conditions, it remains faithful to its vision of a united humanity and gives of itself unselfishly for this end. It is this visionary hope and energy that religions can inspire in the quest for human reconciliation and where they can find meaningful unity.

《法华经》的兼容主义与宗教间的对话①

菅野博史（Hiroshi Kanno）

1. 前　言

　　现在，文明间的对话、特别是构成文明基础的诸宗教间的对话越来越重要。在诸多宗教不得不共存的现代社会，约翰·希克提倡承认诸宗教的平等价值的多元主义。这是为了回避有害无益的宗教间纷争的假说，或许也是可以成为宗教间对话的根据和基础的理论。

　　一方面，约翰·希克认为兼容主义没有完全排除古老的排他主义的独断②，但另一方面，由于约翰·希克的多元主义承认"终极实在"这一中心概念，所以从某种意义上也可以说是一种兼容主义。为便于理解约翰·希克的思想，我们可以举出登山的例子。要登上山顶有许多道路，这许多道路就像诸宗教，而山顶则是诸宗教追求的终极实在。

　　但是，我们知道山不是唯一的，而是有许多山的存在；并且山的优劣也

---

　　① 本文是将笔者以前的两篇论文《〈法华经〉的包容主义与宗教宽容》（何劲松译，《世界宗教研究》增刊，总第 100 期，2004.12，pp. 62 - 70）和《〈法华经〉与宗教间对话》（张文良译，《首届世界佛教论坛文集·论文中文卷 和谐世界从心开始》所收，宗教文化出版社，2006.4，pp. 406 - 417/《佛学研究》总 15 期，2006.12，pp. 65 - 72）合成而修改的。

　　② See John Hick, Problems of Religious Pluralism, London：Macmillan, 1985, p. 33.

不能依据高度这唯一的标准来测定。我们可以说，每座山都有自己的美景，每座山都有自己的独特之处，每座山都有其独特的价值。因此，我认为众山各有胜景的比喻更能贴切地说明宗教多样性的多元主义。从这种观念出发就会产生对宗教间差异的尊重。我个人就是在这个意义上坚持多元主义立场的。

另一方面，在现实中，多元主义的主张也有与信仰者的心情不相契合之点。在我的印象中，对某种宗教抱有强烈信仰的信徒，实际上很难赞同多元主义的立场。我决不认为这样的信徒是不能理解多元主义的蒙昧无知之徒，也不认为他们应该受到批判。毋宁说，或许正是这些信徒们为实现地球伦理、和平和社会正义，已经或者即将通过其不遗余力地努力做着巨大贡献。所以，对于某种宗教的信仰者来说，约翰·希克所说的多元主义的有效性是有商榷余地的。我认为，即使约翰·希克所批判的兼容主义者，只要在某种程度认同尊重人权、保护环境等世俗的价值，就有可能坐到宗教对话的桌子旁。

星川启慈认为，宗教宽容的基础是"对人们认识真理能力局限性的自觉"①。我赞同这一观点。但宗教的历史也表明，正是对诸如开祖所受的神的启示或开祖的觉悟等超越平常人的能力的无条件信奉，才使得某种信仰得以成立。那么，如何解释这种矛盾呢？如果站在极端的排他主义立场上的话，宗教间的对话的确是困难的，但在个人信仰的层面，对宗教的超越性部分的信仰则不妨完全看作是个人的自由。只是在宗教对话中，我们对其他宗教的信仰者表白自己对特定宗教的超越部分的信仰时，有可能难以获得对方的理解。所以我们必须在自己的认识或体验范围内，尽可能用相互能够理解的语言来进行对话和交流。如果能够这样做的话，即使是站在排他主义立场上的人，围绕特定的话题，也可以参加宗教间的对话。

关于人类所面对的环境保护、人口问题、粮食问题等大多数重要问题，主要依靠科学的、或者社会的、政治的方法来解决。但即使找到了解决办法，由于国家利益至上、民族利益至上，以及人类的贪欲作祟，这些办法能

---

① 参见田丸德善、星川启慈、山梨有希子《众神的和解——二一世纪的宗教对话》，东京：春秋社，2000年，第86页。

否被人们所接受,也值得怀疑。考虑到诸宗教在世界人口中占有相当大的比例的现实,以及诸宗教对信徒所具有的一定程度的指导作用,通过宗教间的对话,我们可以期待诸宗教能够共同认识到人类面临的诸多问题以及解决途径,并承担起对各自信徒的教育责任,从而广泛发挥宗教的影响力,促进人类对这些问题的解决。

宗教对话是时代的潮流,但我们不应该只是顺应这一潮流,而应该从各自的宗教传统中发掘出宗教对话的意义和精神。如果不能做到这一点,所谓的对话,就有可能成为迎合新潮的表演,或者为时流所左右的无原则的奉迎。笔者希望通过本文,既能加深《法华经》信仰者对宗教对话问题的理解,也能增强大多数非《法华经》信仰者对《法华经》的理解。众所周知,《法华经》是在印度形成的早期大乘的代表经典,其成立的准确年代尚难断言,但大体上可推断为公元前一世纪到公元后二世纪左右。在中国,《法华经》全本译出的有三种,即西晋竺法护(生年约为 230 年代,78 岁死去)译的《正法华经》十卷(286 年译出),姚秦鸠摩罗什(350－409)译的《妙法莲花经》七卷或八卷(406 年译出),隋朝阇那崛多(523－605) 与達摩笈多(？－619) 合译的《添品妙法莲花经》七卷(601 年译出)。鸠摩罗什译本在东亚佛教圈最为流行,众多注释皆依据此译本。在现代日本社会《法华经》的影响力比较大。因为除了像天台宗与日莲宗那样的佛教传统的宗派,日本最大的新兴宗教的宗派即创价学会、立正佼成会、灵友会都以《法华经》为它们信仰的根本经典。

本文有二节。第一节利用所谓的排他主义、兼容主义、多元主义这一诸宗教关系的框架,考察在宗教宽容问题上《法华经》的基本立场。我认为,《法华经》的基本立场,虽然还有作其他解释的余地,但接近于兼容主义。又,暂且利用排他主义、兼容主义、多元主义这一框架,对于作为《法华经》的中心思想的"一乘"提出三种解释的可能性。从第一节所明确的《法华经》的立场出发,如果参与宗教对话,应该以怎样的态度去参与?《法华经》能够给我们提供什么样的启示?第二节将考察这个问题。

2.《法华经》的兼容主义

本节考察以下的四个条目：(1)《法华经》中的"萨达磨(saddharma)"进行考察；(2)以"统一"为关键词,考察《法华经》的思想特色；(3)《法华经》的兼容主义进行考察；(4)对于"一乘"进行解释。

2.1《法华经》中的"萨达磨"

关于佛陀的根本开悟,原始佛典清楚地使用了悟"法"、尊敬"法"一类的表述。在这种法上冠以"正确"意思的形容词,便是"萨达磨"。《法华经》(Saddharmapu□□arīka-sūtra)将作为佛陀开悟的原点的"萨达磨"当作了经典题目的一部分。这个"萨达磨",竺法护译为"正法",鸠摩罗什译为"妙法"。

那么,《法华经》是怎样把握"萨达磨"的呢?《方便品》的开头这样说道:

> 诸佛智慧甚深无量。其智慧门难解难入。一切声闻、辟支佛所不能知。所以者何,佛曾亲近百千万亿无数诸佛,尽行诸佛无量道法,勇猛精进,名称普闻,成就甚深未曾有法,随宜所说意趣难解。……舍利弗。如来知见,广大深远,无量、无碍、力、无所畏、禅定、解脱、三昧,深入无际,成就一切未曾有法。舍利弗。如来能种种分别,巧说诸法,言辞柔软,悦可众心。舍利弗。取要言之,无量无边未曾有法,佛悉成就。止,舍利弗。不须复说。所以者何,佛所成就第一希有难解之法。唯佛与佛,乃能究尽诸法实相。(T 262.9.5b26 – 5c11)

据此,"诸法"(dharma 的复数形式)也可以说是通过在无数诸佛处经长时间修行而掌握的佛的特性,其具体内容包括四无量心、四无碍辨、十力、四无所畏、四禅、八解脱、三三昧等。词语的说明虽然省略,但这些都类属于佛的能力、智慧、或各种禅定的境地。即"法"不仅是抽象的、客观的真理,而是佛可以通过修行在自身中体得实现的东西,是对上述具体的德目加以说明的佛的智慧、境地。

换言之,《法华经》显示了法的客体性和法的主体性两个方面,前者即作为佛所认识的真理之法,后者即该法在自身中实现构成智慧与慈悲等佛的境界的诸特性。其客体性的法具有普遍性和永远性①。

实际上,《法华经》已指出,不仅现在的释尊,过去佛日月灯明佛、大通智胜佛、威音王佛等都讲说过《法华经》。讲说《法华经》的时间之长和分量有着超乎想象的巨大数字。我想这表明佛能够自由自在地敷衍、讲说《法华经》。那么,诸佛共同讲说的《法华经》究竟是什么呢? 我认为,佛悟出"萨达磨"才成佛,详细讲说这种"萨达磨"的经典正是《法华经》②。至少《法华经》的编纂者是这样想的,所以经典标题的一部分才使用了"萨达磨"。于是,过去、现在、未来所有的佛都将自己悟出的"萨达磨"当作究极的说教共同讲说,其说法的内容即表现为《法华经》③。可以说,《法华经》的普遍性和永久性象征性地得到了显示。

其次,与客体性的法的普遍性并驾齐驱的是任何人都可以在自身中将法主体化、现实化的普遍性。《法华经》用所有众生都能平等成佛这种"一佛乘思想"对此加以说明。从一佛乘的角度来看,《法华经》可以说只是针对菩萨进行教化④。即所有众生都是作为成佛的存在,并被规定为菩萨。在此,将一佛乘思想实践化的常不轻菩萨贯彻着将所有人当作修行菩萨道并在未来成佛的尊贵的存在而给予尊敬的实践。常不轻菩萨的行为表现出以人为最为尊严的思想⑤。也就是说,"萨达磨"的普遍性,从人的主体性来说,是与自身成佛的"自己的尊严"密不可分的。

---

① 释尊开悟的一刹那,心中思考着:"不尊敬他人、不孝顺长辈的生活是无法忍受的"。但是,他下的结论是:因为"见不到只有我都能成为达成〈我确认解脱之自觉〉的人",所以"我毋宁尊重、恭敬我所悟的法理,如果照此生活又将如何呢?"(Sayutta-Nikāya, I, pp. 139 – 140; The Book of the Kindred Sayings, part I, pp. 175 – 176, translated by Mrs. Rhys Davids, P. T. S.)。对于释尊的这一结论,梵天也表示支持,三世诸佛全都表示尊敬萨达磨(saddhamma)。这样,原始经典也再三地指出了法的永远性。

② 应当指出,"萨达磨"作为智慧、慈悲等德性被主体化这一真理,是一种在实践层面上人人都能成佛的思想,即一佛乘思想。

③ 萨达磨是起到使一切众生平等成佛之作用的真理,萨达磨的主体化便带有智慧、慈悲等特性。

④ 参照《法华经》方便品:"诸佛如来但教化菩萨"(T 262.9.7a29)。

⑤ 关于常不轻菩萨,请参照《〈法华经〉中常不轻菩萨的实践及其在中国和日本的接受情况》(《世界宗教研究》增刊,总第 87 期,2002.3)。

2.2 关于《法华经》的统一

首先让我们就诸佛空间的统一加以考察。这是基于见宝塔品的"三变土田"①。简单说来,大乐说菩萨想拜见从大地涌出的多宝塔中的多宝如来,于是释尊答应多宝如来所立的必须从十方世界集合释尊分身佛这一誓愿。所谓分身佛,即佛以神通力创造的佛身之意,在《法华经》中是从释尊的身体化作的佛被派往十方世界,并在各自的世界说法。在此,释尊为集合分身佛,如同所说的"三变土田"那样,将秽土的娑婆世界和其周边的世界净化了三次。

这幕剧的展开,《法华经》说了些什么呢? 大乘佛教认为,除娑婆世界的释尊之外,还有许多佛同时存在,如西方极乐世界有阿弥陀如来,东方净瑠璃世界有药师如来。《法华经》以前的大乘佛教中也有新的佛不断产生,并有与信仰这些新佛相关的说教。

《法华经》虽然认为十方世界存在着许多佛,并将之作为佛教的世界观,但是《法华经》仍然还有别的考虑。这便是重新确立将分散在可以说是散漫的全宇宙中的无数诸佛统一为强有力的佛。《法华经》把统一无数诸佛的任务让娑婆世界的释尊承担起来。如上所述,释尊的分身佛由十方世界集合而来,换一种思路,就可以解释为十方世界无数诸佛全是从释尊身体化作的分身佛。这就是十方诸佛统一于释尊,即诸佛的空间统一吧。见宝塔品的情节不就可以说是诸佛空间统一这一重要思想的戏剧性表现吗?

其次,我们来考察诸佛时间的统一。《法华经》如来寿量品说到释尊的久远成佛(释尊在遥远的过去成佛)。而且,还说到释尊未来的寿命的长远。这样,在过去、未来都具有永恒寿命的释尊能够将原始佛教以来所说的过去佛、未来佛统一于释尊自身。寿量品说道,释尊从久远的过去成佛到遥远的未来,以佛的身份为救度众生而展开各种活动。换言之,释尊起到了过去佛、未来佛的作用。照这种思路,久远释尊的思想便显示了诸佛时间的统一。

这样,当我们意识到《法华经》追求的是诸佛空间的统一、时间的统一,那么,我们就不难发现方便品的一佛乘思想将释尊一生的说教重新统一为

---

① 参照《法华玄义》卷第六上(T 1716.33.751c10)。

一佛乘。这就是第三部分诸教的统一。

在此,我们可以下结论说,《法华经》是一部带有统一诸佛和诸教这一重要特色的经典。

2.3 《法华经》的兼容主义

《法华经》旨在将佛教内部诸佛、诸教统一于《法华经》的教主释尊和《法华经》的一佛乘。以《法华经》为中心将纷然杂呈的佛教统一起来,这在佛教内部可以叫做兼容主义。若考察旨在统一教法的一佛乘思想与兼容主义的关系的话,原来一佛乘思想所说的并不是要将《法华经》以前所说的释尊所有的说教都当做方便而舍弃掉,而是在认识其方便的基础上反过来使所有的说教复活,即苏生。"方便"这一概念具有严格否定《法华经》以外的其他说教和使之再度苏生这两个层面。其证据是《法华经》指出以前被规定为不能成佛的声闻也获得了真正声闻的自觉从而抱有成佛的确信①。这在中国佛教中被称作为"开会",表明《法华经》力图让所有的说教重新苏生。

小时候做游戏时聚沙成塔、描绘佛像、念一声"南无佛",这类例子不胜枚举,无论怎样微小的善行都与成佛联系在一起②。人们常说"小善成佛"③,无论多小的事只要是佛教的善行,都被成佛这一佛教的最大目的所包摄,我想这就是所谓的兼容主义。

五百弟子受记品称,阿罗汉富楼那,其本地是菩萨,为了救度声闻的方便而外显声闻相④。我想这可解释为警告从大乘的立场对声闻作轻率的批判,并暗示将声闻包容于菩萨的可能性,即一种兼容主义。

《法华经》旨在统一佛教,然而不只是强调统一,就像所见到的"开会"那样,要让"多样性"苏生。而统一的中心则是释尊和"萨达磨"。但释尊也是觉知"萨达磨"而成佛的,因此"萨达磨"更为根本。象前节所考察的,我们必须注意到"萨达磨"关系到每一个人,实际上带有作为自身中佛的境界

---

① 参照《法华经》信解品:"我等今者,真是声闻,以佛道声,令一切闻"(T 262.9.18c20－21)。
② 《法华经》方便品列举了这样的小善成佛的实例(T 262.9.8c11－9a27)。
③ 参见《法华文句》卷第六上:"今经明小善成佛。此取缘因为佛种。若不信小善成仏,即断世间佛种也"(T 1718.34.79a24－25)。
④ 参见《法华经》五百弟子受记品:"内秘菩萨行,外现是声闻"(T 262.9.28a17)。

的主体化、现实化。如果在宗派性很强的教条主义中寻求统一的中心,那么"多样性"的尊重就会成为画饼。

《法华经》的兼容主义所关心的原本是将注意力放在佛教内部,就像原始经典所说的"法"的普遍性、永远性那样①,《法华经》的"萨达磨"的普遍性旨在超越佛教的范围。即使对于其他宗教的信仰者,"萨达磨"也决没有差别。即"萨达磨"在任何人身上都可以实现。从这种立场来看,即使所信仰的宗教不同,所有人的尊严都会得到承认。常不轻菩萨的实践就显示了这一点。

但是,对于"萨达磨"的主体化、现实化,如果佛教的特定信仰、修行是不可欠缺的话,那么《法华经》的立场就不是多元主义,而应当说成是兼容主义②。或者,"萨达磨"的主体化、现实化的方法具有扩展到其他宗教或宗教以外的可能性吗?③这是信仰《法华经》的人今后的一大课题。

2.4《法华经》"一乘"思想的三种解释的可能性

《法华经》方便品说明释尊于此世出现的理由和目的。释尊说明:包括释尊在内的三世诸佛,是为了唯一的一件大事而出现于世。这唯一的一件大事就是为众生开、示、悟、入佛之知见④。也就是说,佛为了众生成佛而出现于这个世界。让一切众生成佛,意味着曾视成佛为过高的目标,而将阿罗汉、辟支佛作为最终目标的声闻、缘觉的二乘之人也能成佛。

此"一大事因缘"的部分,是《法华经》中直接表现"一乘"思想的内容,也是《法华经》中最重要的宗教内涵之一。紧接方便品的譬喻品第三中,诸神关于这一内容云:"佛昔于波罗奈初转法轮,今乃复转无上最大法轮"⑤。

---

① 参见注3。

② 《法华经》譬喻品列举了诽谤《法华经》者的严厉、恐怖的罪报(T 262.9.15b22 – 16a7)。类似的情况在普贤菩萨劝发品中也可以见到(T 262.9.62a16 – 23)。本文指出"萨达磨"同"自己的尊严性"联系在一起,如果从宗派性强的教条主义来把握《法华经》的话,列举的这些罪报意味着激烈的排他性。但是,如果把《法华经》理解为讲说"自己尊严"的普遍性的"萨达磨",那么对《法华经》的诽谤则是对"自己尊严"的践踏,罪报的列举就并不意味着排他性,或许还可以解释成能够起到将人们引向对"自己的尊严"的自觉的方向。这也是《法华经》信仰者今后的重大课题。

③ 我想这种情况是相当接近多元主义的立场。

④ 梵本作 tathāgata-jāna-darana(如来的知见)。可以理解为佛的智慧。

⑤ 参见 T 262. 9.12a15 – 17。

此即将波罗奈鹿野苑初转法轮,与《法华经》的"一乘"说法进行对比。释尊受梵天的劝请,为了对先前的修行伙伴、五名出家者说法而去鹿野苑,在那里讲说不苦不乐的中道和四谛八正道,此即第一法轮。与此相对,方便品的"一乘"被定位为第二最高的法轮。

如果说让一切众生都平等成佛是释尊出现的目的的话,就出现了新的问题。即为什么释尊要讲说以阿罗汉和缘觉为最终目标的声闻乘和缘觉乘呢?在此,《法华经》透露了一个秘密,即在《法华经》之前,以声闻、缘觉、菩萨三类修行者为对象所说的三类教法(顺次为四谛、十二因缘、六波罗蜜)及其修行,是方便教。依此达成的理想,也有三种,即阿罗汉、辟支佛和佛。也就是说,声闻和缘觉志向不够远大,开始不能给他们讲可以成佛的道理(佛乘),所以就按照声闻和缘觉的领悟能力,给他们讲声闻乘和缘觉乘等低层次的法,教育他们,让他们成熟。

但是,这一点对声闻和缘觉来说却是秘密,他们都认为教给他们的法都是真实的。在此阶段,在佛的众弟子看来,佛所施之教皆为真实。原本并不存在真实与方便的对比。只是到了《法华经》才指明,存在三乘的说法是方便。因此,声闻乘、缘觉乘只是暂定的、权宜的"假"教,声闻、缘觉也非永久不变的固定的存在,在受到教育、充分成熟以后,他们作为菩萨,最终也会成佛。因为这一教说主张一切人同能成佛,故称佛乘,亦指《法华经》自身。因为只有佛乘是真实的存在,所以又称为一乘。佛乘与一乘结合,也称为一佛乘。此即三乘方便、一乘真实的思想。用中国佛教术语来说,即"开三显一"。

关于如何把握诸宗教的关系,约翰·希克所提倡的排他主义、兼容主义和多元主义,虽然在概括多样化的诸宗教关系方面有笼统简化的缺点①,

---

① 参考西谷幸介《宗教对话与原教旨主义的克服—关于宗教伦理的讨论》(新教出版社,2004),特别是第二章〈排他主义、兼容主义和多元主义的类型论的模糊性〉。西谷幸介认为,作为宗教的类型论,比之希克的假说,乔治·林德贝克的"认知—命题型"、"体验—表达型"、"文化—言语型"的假说,更为有效。请参见 George A. Lindbeck, *The Nature of Doctrine - - Religion and Theology in a Postliberal Age* (Kentucky: Westminster John Knox Press, 1984)。日译请参见乔治·林德贝克的《教理的本质》(田丸德善监修、星川启慈、山梨有希子译,东京:约旦社,2003)。另参考星川启慈〈宗教对话中的"教理"问题〉(星川启慈、山梨有希子编《全球化时代的宗教对话》148 页,东京:大正大学出版会,2004)。

但不可否认其某种程度的有效性。在这里,暂且利用这一框架,考察一乘思想的各种解释的可能性。以下的解释中,第一、第二种解释,是过去的佛教史中实际存在的解释,而第三种解释,即与多元主义相近的解释,则是历史上不曾出现过的解释。

(1)第一种解释,即认为三乘是为一乘而说的,是为一乘做准备的教说。在明确说出一乘教义时,三乘就成为无用的方便之教,可以舍弃。在这种场合,因为只有《法华经》一乘处于超越的高位,而其他一切教说都作为无用之物而被否定,所以可以说是排他主义的立场。

具体而言,《法华经》方便品云,"今我喜无畏,于诸菩萨中,正直舍方便,但说无上道"①,强调舍弃方便。在譬喻品中,围绕应该对什么人讲说《法华经》的问题,可以看出对《法华经》以外的经典,以及对亲近佛教之外的典籍者采取了排他性的态度②。

(2)第二种解释,即如果三乘认为己说为真实的话,就应该受到严厉的批判。但在一乘明确的阶段,如果三乘意识到了己说为方便的话,那么三乘作为趋向一乘的过程的意义就应该得到承认,三乘最终包含于一乘之中。换言之,一佛乘的思想,不单是将《法华经》以前释尊的所有教说作为方便而弃舍(相当于第一种解释),而是在认识到它是一种方便教说的前提下,让所有这些教说"复活"、"苏生"(相当于第二种解释)。"方便"这一概念,可以说既有否定《法华经》之外其他教说的一面,也兼有使之苏醒的一面。这第二种解释,因为主张一乘包摄其他的教说,所以可以说是兼容主

---

① T 262.9.10a18 - 19。但梵本中并没有"舍方便"的明确表现。

② "如人至心,求佛舍利,如是求经,得已顶受。其人不复,志求余经,亦未曾念,外道典籍。如是之人,乃可为说"。(T 262.9.16b1 - 4)。另,安乐行品中,劝戒弟子不可接近外道和梵志等佛教以外的宗教者。即"不亲近诸外道梵志尼揵子等,及造世俗文笔赞咏外书,及路伽耶陀逆路伽耶陀者"(T 262.9.37a19 - 2!)。依笔者的见解,日莲(1222 - 1282)的立场,基本上属于第一种解释,但也包含第二种解释。关于日莲的排他主义理论立场,参考拙论《如来的使者—日莲》(《从法华经思想史学佛教》190 - 206 页,东京:大藏出版,2003)。

义的立场①。

在上面已经指出,根据解释的不同,从《法华经》中可以看到排他主义、兼容主义和多元主义等各种立场。但《法华经》的基本立场是兼容主义,并具体举出了与兼容主义相近的《法华经》的教说。

(3)从超出佛教范畴的普遍真理的角度来解释一乘,这或许接近多元主义的立场②。这时候,主题则成为一乘与多元主义的关系,所以问题不是一乘与三乘的对立,而是一乘与其他宗教之间的关系。的确,一乘可以解释为追求超越国家、民族、性别、文化等所有差别的普遍性真理。但即使说一切众生追求成佛,就像成佛这一佛教特有的概念所表现的那样,这一说法只能被看做是从佛教立场出发的一种兼容主义。

不过,如果我们能够将佛教的最高目标"佛",描述成更具有普遍性的人类优秀品质的所有者的话,会得出什么结论呢?这一立场可能与约翰·希克的多元主义立场相接近。约翰·希克曾将传统宗教中关于"救度"的各种表现,置换为"人类从自我中心到实在中心的生活现实的变革"③,从而表明其拥护多元主义的立场。我最初表达了承认诸宗教的独特价值的立场,从这一基本立场出发,或许就没必要勉强用统一的说法来界定"救度"的思想。

我认为,《法华经》的基本立场,虽然还有作其他解释的余地,但更接近于兼容主义。特别是在印度佛教史中,在承认过去佛教的一定作用的同时,《法华经》力图以新的"一乘"思想,树立宣扬一切众生皆追求成佛的新

---

① 中国天台宗智顗的立场,基本上属于第二种解释,但也有第一种解释的一面。如前面所引"正直舍方便,但说无上道",智顗也在《法华玄义》中作为经证引用此文,以华落莲成之姿,比喻废权立实。智顗的法华经观,与其说是《法华经》至上主义,不如说是圆教至上主义。请参见《智顗与吉藏的法華經观之比較》(北京大学东方学研究院《華林》2,2002.1,pp. 161–169)。

在天台宗的法华经至上主义的形成过程中,湛然发挥了很大作用。从智顗到湛然的历史时期,有主张《华严经》至上的华严宗的成立,有倡导三乘真实、一乘方便的法相宗的成立,还有主张教外别传的禅宗的成立等。或许是为了与这些宗派相抗衡,湛然才开始强调《法华经》至上主义。日莲受到湛然的直接影响。

② 在过去的佛教历史中,还没有从多元主义的立场对"一乘"做出解释的。只有到今天这种诸宗教不得不谋求共存的全球化时代,人类才面对这一课题。但在中国,从唐末以降,主张儒教、佛教、道教三教一致的思想逐渐流行,在日本的江户时代,主张神道、儒教、佛教三教一致的倾向也很强。这也是历史事实。

③ 参见 John Hick, *Problems of Religious Pluralism* (London: Macmillan, 1985), p. 32。

佛教。从《法华经》的这一立场出发,如果参与宗教对话,应该以怎样的态度去参与呢?《法华经》能够给我们提供什么样的指针呢?

3.《法华经》与宗教间的对话——四安乐行与"如来衣座室"

《法华经》这样的佛教经典的故事,是由佛与弟子的对话构成的。因为是佛与弟子的关系,所以在佛教的觉悟和修行的水平上,就不能说是对等的。对话的基本条件是站在完全对等立场上的个人与个人之间的对话,但佛与弟子的对话不是这样的对话。由此看来,我们只能说难于直接从《法华经》中发现宗教对话的指针。虽然如此,从广义上讲,我们可以从《法华经》中学取对话的精神。以下举出《法华经》安乐行品中所说的四安乐行、法师品中所说的"如来衣座室",就这一问题做一考察。

四安乐行讲的是在释尊灭后的恶世弘通《法华经》的注意事项,但其中的内容,对我们现在进行宗教对话,也有参考之处①。

四安乐行的名称,既没有出现在《法华经》中,《法华经》的注释者对此的称呼也有所不同。依据智顗、灌顶的《法华文句》的说法,即身、口、意、誓愿四安乐行②。

在《法华经》安乐行品的开头,文殊菩萨问释尊:"菩萨摩诃萨于后恶世,云何能说是经"③。释尊回答:"若菩萨摩诃萨于后恶世欲说是经,当安住四法"④,并顺次说明了四法的内容。此四法即四安乐行。

第一身安乐行,有行处与亲近处。行处是与菩萨相应的行动范围,亲近处是交际范围。关于行处,《法华经》云:"若菩萨摩诃萨住忍辱地,柔和善顺,而不卒暴,心亦不惊,又复于法无所行,而观诸法如实相,亦不行不分

---

① 日莲认为安乐行品与劝持品的修行是只能二者取其一的,日莲生活的日本和镰仓时代(末法时代)这一特定的时空背景,使得日莲选择了劝持品。但笔者认为,在当今世界这一新的时代条件下,应该重新审视安乐行品中所说内容的价值。

② 参见《法华文句》卷第八下:"天台师云,止观慈悲导三业及誓愿。……是名身业安乐行。余口意誓愿亦如是"(T 1718.34.119a19 – 27)。关于其他注释家,特别是慧思的四安乐行,参见拙论《慧思〈法华经安乐行义〉的研究(2)》(《东洋哲学研究所纪要》20,pp. 53 – 81,2004.12)。

③ T 262.9.37a10。

④ T 262.9.37a11 – 12。

别,是名菩萨摩诃萨行处"①。关于亲近处,分为两类,第一亲近处是对具体的交际范围的限定②,以及不得不交际的场合应注意的事项;第二的亲近处是对存在的空性的彻底认识。

第二口安乐行,主要是关于言语要注意的事项。《法华经》云:"不乐说人及经典过,亦不轻慢诸余法师。不说他人好恶长短。于声闻人亦不称名说其过恶,亦不称名赞叹其美。又亦不生怨嫌之心。善修如是安乐心,故诸有听者,不逆其意。有所难问,不以小乘法答,但以大乘而为解说,令得一切种智"③。

第三意安乐行,是关于心的活动应注意的事项。《法华经》云:"无怀嫉妒谄诳之心。亦勿轻骂学佛道者,求其长短。若比丘比丘尼优婆塞优婆夷、求声闻者、求辟支佛者、求菩萨道者,无得恼之,令其疑悔。语其人言,'汝等去道甚远,终不能得一切种智。所以者何,汝是放逸之人,于道懈怠故'。又亦不应戏论诸法,有所诤竞。当于一切众生起大悲想,于诸如来起慈父想,于诸菩萨起大师想,于十方诸大菩萨,常应深心恭敬礼拜。于一切众生平等说法。以顺法故,不多不少。乃至,深爱法者,亦不为多说"④。

第四誓愿安乐行,即受持《法华经》的人应该"于在家出家人中生大慈心,于非菩萨人中生大悲心。应作是念:'如是之人,则为大失。如来方便随宜说法,不闻不知不觉,不问不信不解。其人虽不问不信不解是经,我得阿耨多罗三藐三菩提时,堕在何地,以神通力智慧力引之,令得住是法中'"⑤。即强调生伟大的慈悲心,誓愿以《法华经》救度众生。

如果从《法华经》的立场参加宗教对话,在推进宗教对话的心态方面,从《法华经》的四安乐行中,可以学到以下三点:

第一,坚持大乘佛教的基本认识,即对空的认识。此即不能够把自己

---

① T 262.9.37a14—17。

② 在对交际范围的这一限制中,可以看出不许接近求声闻者等排他性的态度(T 262.9.37a25—26)。而且,还举出不能接近的职业,表现出对特定职业的歧视,似乎与倡导一切众生皆趋向佛的《法华经》的立场不相一致。不过任何经典都不能完全摆脱时代思潮的局限。实际上,在这一点上,其他的古代宗教圣典也是同样的。

③ T 262.9.38a1—7。

④ T 262.9.38b3—14。

⑤ T 262.9.38c5—11。

的宗教与其他的宗教看做是完全无变化的、固定的存在,而应该看成是变化、流动的存在。重要的是,我们对通过对话而产生的自我变革持开放的态度。从佛教来看,对他者采取友善的、温和的态度是基于对空的认识。

第二,在宗教对话中,应该对其他宗教表示敬意,而不能够随便批判他者、挑起教义的论争。如果不如此,大家连坐到同一张对话桌前都困难。

第三,宗教间的对话的目的,在于通过诸宗教的合作,努力解决全球性的诸多问题,对话者最需要的精神,就是为全人类谋求和平和幸福的誓愿和慈悲。

如此看来,安乐行品所说的注意事项,与《法华经》法师品所说的"如来衣座室"也是相通的①。法师品云,在如来入灭以后,在为四众弟子(比丘、比丘尼、优婆塞、优婆夷,即出家的男女与在家的男女)说《法华经》的时候,必须入如来室、穿如来衣、坐如来座。所谓如来室,即对一切众生的慈悲心;所谓如来衣,即柔和忍辱心;所谓如来座,即一切法空②。

在大乘佛教中,对空的认识基于正确的智慧。因为智慧与慈悲是佛所具备的两大特征,所以以成佛为目标的菩萨,自然也要追求智慧和慈悲。而且,在现实的社会中的菩萨的活动,会遇到各种各样的困难,所以忍辱心也受到重视。当然,此忍辱心的基础,也不外是智慧和慈悲。菩萨的修行纲目六波罗蜜中包含忍辱波罗蜜,是周知的事实。

4. 小 结

如前所述,我个人的基本立场是承认诸宗教的独自价值。考虑到宗教

---

① 我在本文中提出的四安乐行、"如来衣座室",本来都是讲弘通《法华经》的心态的。但这些对我们以怎样的心态进行宗教对话,也提供了启示。宗教对话当然不是布教的场合,而是为了解决全球性的问题,诸宗教相互合作的场所。但,在问题解决方面,能多大程度上贡献出自己的智慧、能注入多大的能量,各宗教之间的良性竞争、相互切磋,也是必要的。各宗教都有必要认真考虑,如何向对方学习,如何深化自己的宗教。

② "若有善男子善女人,如来灭后,欲为四众说是《法华经》者,云何应说。是善男子善女人入如来室、著如来衣、坐如来座。尔乃应为四众广说斯经。如来室者,一切众生中大慈悲心是。如来衣者,柔和忍辱心是。如来座者,一切法空是"(T 262.9.31c21 - 27)。

间对话的重要性,即使是兼容主义者或排他主义者,为了消除对其他宗教的误解、促进宗教间的相互理解,也完全没必要把他们排除在宗教对话之外。只有通过这样的对话,才有可能在解决全球性问题时相互合作,而且通过对话有可能开发自他宗教的潜在可能性,从而带来各自宗教教义的深化。我们没必要害怕自己宗教的某种改变,毋宁说,我们可以期待这样的改变为宗教多样化的新生开辟了道路。

为解决全球性问题这一现代社会的紧迫课题,需要促进诸宗教间的对话。这与《法华经》所倡导的救度众生的菩萨的誓愿与慈悲有着密切关系。在实际的交流过程中,对空的认识与忍辱的精神,必定会做出一定贡献。谈到在宗教对话中"忍辱"的贡献,也许读者们会感到有些奇怪。不过对于在长期的历史发展中,相互没有交流、或者曾经存在严重对立的诸宗教来说,在大家坐下来对话时,忍耐心在消除彼此的误解、增进彼此理解方面是多么重要。多国间的许多国际会议的实例,就说明了这一点。从佛教来看,这种忍耐心的背后,如果没有智慧和慈悲,就不可能是真正的忍耐心。

最后,我想《法华经》所倡导的"尊重赞叹人类的差异和多样性"的宗旨,可以用药草喻品的"三草二木的譬喻"①来说明。譬喻的内容很简洁:满天的云雨普润大地,各种植物(三草二木)随其种类的不同,各自得以生长。三草二木,即小、中、上的药草,与小、大的树木。其中,小药草譬喻人天,中药草譬喻声闻、缘觉,上药草、小树、大树分别譬喻三阶段的菩萨②。这一譬喻所显示的雄浑景象,即千千万万的植物平等接受甘霖雨露,得到充足的水分,在大地上茁壮成长。这不正象征着人类在尊重差异和多样性的基础上,同在一个地球上和谐共生的道理吗?

---

① "三草二木"的譬喻,是《法华经》的七个代表性的譬喻之一。但只有这个譬喻是基于大雨这一印度的自然现象而成立,与为了切合《法华经》的教义而人为创作出的其他六个譬喻不同。所以看起来譬喻的内容似乎与《法华经》的思想有不相一致之处,这是在解释时需要注意的。这一譬喻的主旨在于:1、佛的说法对谁都是平等的;2、众生是多样的;3、佛不是马上就讲说一切智;4、佛在《法华经》中,最终将使众生达到一切智。譬喻的中心意图,是只有经过许多方便的教说,佛才会讲《法华经》,亦即说明了佛不马上讲说一切智的理由。这一譬喻绝不是肯定声闻、缘觉和菩萨本性上的绝对差别。因为在《法华经》中,佛是最终要让一切众生达到一切智的。在正确理解这一譬喻的原义的基础上,我们可以进一步做本文如下的解释。

② T 262.9.19a25 – 20b19.

"经文辩读"中的信仰和责任

—— 以理雅各关于"以德报怨"的译解为例

杨慧林

西方宗教学界的"经文辩读"（Scriptural Reasoning）源自 1990 年代初期的"文本辩读"（Textual Reasoning）。最初是一群犹太学者秉承柯亨（Hermann Cohen）、马丁·布伯（Martin Buber）、列维纳斯（Emmanuel Levinas）等人的思想，试图从跨文化和比较研究的角度重读基督教的《圣经》和犹太教的《塔木德》，后来又延展到伊斯兰教的《古兰经》。

库舍尔（Karl-Josef Kuschel）在 1993 年出版了《亚伯拉罕：犹太人、基督徒和穆斯林共同的希望象征》一书（Abraham : Sign of Hope for Jews, Christians, and Muslims）；1995 年前后，彼得·奥克斯（Peter Ochs）等人创办了"经文辩读"的学会（The Scriptural Reasoning Society, http://www. scripturalreasoning. org. uk/）和刊物（Journal of Scriptural Reasoning, http:// etext. virginia. edu/journals/ssr/）；大卫·福特（David Ford）则于 2007 年出版了《基督教的智慧》（Christian Wisdom：Desiring God and Learning in Love），其中第八章《一种跨信仰的智慧：犹太人、基督徒与穆斯林之间的经文辩读》（"Inter-Faith Wisdom：Scriptural Reasoning Between Jews, Christians and Muslims"），使"经文辩读"引起了学界的更多关注。

就相互关联、相互重合、却又在不同宗教传统中记载各异的"经文"进行"辩读"，其结果必然落实于"对话"而非"独白"，必然确认"相似的至善可以得到不同显现"(the presence of the similar perfectness might be variously identified)①,必然消解一切自我封闭、自我诠释和"事先的信靠"(Pre-assurance)②。因此从根本上说,"经文辩读"的内在精神趋向于一种"公共性"诉求。这种不同传统之间的相互反省,以及由此重构的自我理解,对于"信仰与责任"的讨论可能尤为重要,或许也正是破除狭隘的"身份"立场、在多元处境中寻求价值共识的必要前提。

"价值共识"的关键,其实并非描述何为"共同的价值",而是要回答"价值共识"如何才成为可能。在不同的文化传统和信仰传统中,相似甚至共同的价值资源并不缺乏,但是"身份政治"(politics of identity)关于"价值"的不同解说,往往使"价值"本身被取代;乃至不同的"信念"愈益狂热,"共同的价值"愈益无从谈起。从这样的意义上说,没有"经文辩读"所启发的"破执","信仰和责任"便未必经得起质疑。

犹太教、基督教和伊斯兰教说到底都属同出一源的"亚伯拉罕传统","经文辩读"或许是题中应有之义。而在中国与西方的文化接触和思想碰撞之间,未必天然的"经文辩读"其实也早已开始。比如缪勒(Max Muller)所编订的《东方圣书》③,以及历代传教士对"中国经典"的翻译和引介。缪勒一向被称为西方的"宗教学之父",传教士的基本使命当然是向中国人传布基督教的信仰;这一特定的理解背景,注定会使他们的翻译活动带有"经文辩读"的基本性质。

中国古代经典被西方传教士译介,是"西学东渐"与"中学西传"的典型互动。比如马礼逊(Robert Morrison)在翻译出版《圣经》的同时,也翻译过《三字经》(The Three-Character Classic)、《大学》(The Great Science)等等。白晋(Joachim Bouvet)对《周易》的译介、卫礼贤(Richard Wilhelm)对"中国心灵"的深入发掘,同样如此。更值得注意的,则是曾在香港生活30年、又

---

① David Ford, "An Inter-Faith Wisdom: Scriptural Reasoning between Jews, Christians and Muslims", see the 8th chapter of his *Christian Wisdom: Desiring God and Learning in Love*, Cambridge: Cambridge University Press, 2007.

② Jacques Derrida, *Acts of Religion*, edited by Gil Anidjar, New York: Routledge, 2002, p. 44.

③ *The Sacred Books of the East*, translated by various Oriental scholars and edited by F. Max Muller, Oxford: Oxford University Press, 1891.

在牛津大学担任汉学教授21年的理雅各(James Legge)。

关于理雅各的翻译个案,《圣经》之"道"与《道德经》之"道"、《圣经》之"虚己"与《道德经》之"虚用"当属一种关联性的概念转换①;"以德报怨"和"以直报怨"的辩难,则体现着理雅各对"以意逆志"的根本理解②。

《论语·宪问》的"以德报怨"是从一个"提问者"引出的:"或曰:以德报怨,何如? 子曰:何以报德? 以直报怨,以德报德。"理雅各如实翻译了这段文字:Someone said, "What do you say concerning the principle that injury should be recompensed with kindness?" The Master said, "With what will you recompense kindness? Recompense injury with justice, and recompense kindness with kindness."在译文之后,理雅各专门列出"不是以善报恶,而是以正义报恶"之题(Good is not to be returned for evil; evil to be met simply with justice.),作了详细的注释。③值得注意的是:理雅各在这里将"以德报怨"置换为"以善报恶"(Good is returned for evil)、将"以直报怨"置换为"以正义报恶"(Evil is returned with justice),却并未照用其译文中的Recompense injury with kindness 和 Recompense injury with justice,从而使《论语·宪问》的命题与基督教《圣经》的善恶之说直接对应。

在基督教《旧约》当中,类似于"以直报怨"或者"以正义报恶"的观念本来是显而易见的,比如"以眼还眼、以牙还牙、以手还手、以脚还脚、以烙还烙、以伤还伤、以打还打"(eye for an eye, tooth for tooth, hand for hand, foot for foot, burn for burn, wound for wound, bruise for bruise),《出埃及记》、《利未记》、《申命记》都有相似的表述(出21:24,利24:20,申19:21)。但是问题在于,《新约》的伦理不再是"一报还一报",甚至还主张"爱你的敌人"(太5:44),这当然会与"以直报怨"构成极大的冲突。

---

① 相关讨论请参阅:杨慧林《怎一个"道"字了得——〈道德经〉之"道"的翻译个案》,《中国文化研究》2009第三期;杨慧林《关于"韬光"的误读及其可能详解》,《读书》2010第七期。

② 理雅各引用《孟子·万章上》的名句,作为《中国经典》英译本的题记:"不以文害辞,不以辞害志;以意逆志,是为得之。"参见 James Legge, *The Chinese Classics*, *with a translation*, *critical and exegetical notes*, *prolegomena*, *and copious indexes*, Taibei: SMC Publishing Inc., 2001.

③ James Legge, *The Chinese Classics*, *with a translation*, *critical and exegetical notes*, *prolegomena*, *and copious indexes*, p. 288.

在理雅各看来:这种"直"从来都令他难以理解①。因此相对于"以直报怨",理雅各明确提示读者:"以德报怨之说见于老子《道德经》第六十三章,此处的提问者可能只是就一种自己以前听到过、也有所认同的说法,求证于孔子。"虽然他认为"从这一章可以看出孔子的伦理远不及基督教的标准,甚至远不及老子",但是他马上又援引了《礼记·表记》,并说明这是将"与老子相同的说法"加给了孔子,即:"子曰,以德报怨"。《礼记·表记》的相关段落如下:

> 子曰:"以德报德,则民有所劝;以怨报怨,则民有所惩。诗曰:'无言不雠,无德不报。'大甲曰:'民非后,无能胥以宁。后非民,无以辟四方。'"子曰:"以德报怨,则宽身之仁也;以怨报德,则刑戮之民也。"

——"以德报德,则对老百姓有所鼓励,以怨报怨,老百姓才会有所收敛。所以《诗经》说:一切都是相互对应的,一切所作所为都会有所回报;《尚书? 太甲》说:民没有王就不能互相安宁,王没有民不能开辟四方。以德报怨是苟求容身之人,以怨报德则是该杀之人。"这段文字是将"以德报德"与"以德报怨"对举、"以怨报怨"与"以怨报德"对举,如果"以德报德"对老百姓有所鼓励,那么"以德报怨"只是"苟求容身";如果"以怨报怨"是使老百姓有所收敛,"以怨报德"则实在该杀了。

理雅各显然了解这层基本的意思,因此他照录了这一解释:"宽身之仁(人)"是通过"以德报怨"而"为自己避祸"(He who returns good for evil is a man who is careful of his person. i. e. will try to avert danger from himself by such a course.)。但是既然如此,又怎么能说《礼记·表记》的"以德报怨"是"与老子相同的说法"呢?

如果细读理雅各的原文,我们会发现他似乎要强调"以德报怨,则宽身之仁(人)"只是"被解释为"(which is explained …)"为自己避祸"。他随后引用的则是清人的《四书翼注》:"按照《四书翼注》的看法,询问'以德报

---

① 比如《论语·子路》的一段故事——叶公语孔子曰:"吾党有直躬者,其父攘羊,而子证之。"孔子曰:"吾党之直者异于是,父为子隐,子为父隐。直在其中矣。"理雅各直截了当地说:"除了中国人,谁都看得出孔子和叶公在这一问题上的观点同样是不完全的。"See James Legge, *The Chinese Classics, with a translation, critical and exegetical notes, prolegomena, and copious indexes*, p. 270.

怨,何如'的提问者,其所谓的'怨'只涉及完全可以报之以'德'的小节,如果针对着君主或者父权的大是大非,放弃'义'的原则恐怕就不行了。而孔夫子本人并没有用任何方式限制他的提问。"其后戛然打住,再无点评。理雅各是要借助《四书翼注》证明孔子的"以直报怨"只是"针对大是大非",而在一般问题上也会同意"以德报怨"吗?

"以直报怨"的观念不仅让理雅各耿耿于怀,就连朱熹《论语集注》的解释也未必不是托辞:"怨有不雠,而德无不报,则又未尝不厚也。此章之言,明白简约,而其指意曲折反复。如造化之简易易知,而微妙无穷,学者所宜详玩也。"至于如何"简易易知"、又如何才能"详玩",《论语集注》语焉不详,这也许正如理雅各明明了解《礼记·表记》的意指,却太想寻求哪怕是间接的通融了。

真正让理雅各心有所得的,倒确实是他在注释中特别提及的《道德经》第63章:"为无为,事无事,味无味,大小多少,报怨以德"。理雅各对这段文字的翻译一气呵成:(It is the way of the Tao) to act without (thinking of) acting; to conduct affairs without (feeling the) trouble of them; to taste without discerning any flavor; to consider what is small as great, and a few as many; and to recompense injury with kindness.① ——大道之行,是不刻意之行;为事,是不经意地为事;品尝而不必辨味;以小为大,以少为多;以善意回报伤害。这一段未加注释,而基督教"以小为大"、"以末为先"的逻辑与之正相对应。②

理雅各始终保持着自己的阅读立场,而并非全然接受儒家的思想以及历代注疏,关于"以德报怨"或者"以直报怨"的辩难,便是一个典型的例证。然而上述译解并非就"孔子的伦理远不及基督教的标准"予以发挥,却是反复依据相关的经典,试图找到一种合理的解释。也许应当说:"经文辩读"不可能仅仅发现"相似的至善",但是其中显现的差异之所以成为"对话"而非"独白",则在于理解"差异"、却不是执著于单一的标准。"价值共识"的最终成全,也许只能借助如此的"辩读"。

―――――――――――

① James Legge, *The Sacred Books of China*, *the Texts of Taoism*, Oxford: Oxford University Press, 1891; New York: Dover Publications, Inc. 1962, p. 106.

② "你们中间谁愿为大,就必做你们的佣人;你们中间谁愿为首,就必做众人的仆人"。(可10:43-45)